THE WATCHERS

'A grand piece of scholarship that also grips and enthrals'
Rupert Christiansen, *Daily Telegraph*, Books of the Year

'Stephen Alford has written a gripping account of these cruel
and dramatic events, proving that the survival of Protestant
England was purchased at a very high price indeed'
Nigel Jones, *Sunday Express*

'An intimate and revealing exploration of the men who did the
Elizabethan security state's dirty work. Leading us into the dark
corners, safe houses and interrogation chambers of this twilight
world, *The Watchers* paints a fascinating picture of the threat
facing Elizabethan England – and its determination to deal
with that threat by any means necessary'
Thomas Penn, author of *Winter King*

'Gripping . . . fascinating . . . Alford brings these men, their
worlds and the unfortunate victims of their espionage vividly
out of the shadows' Dan Jones, *The Times*

'A deep and convincing new study of the Elizabethan security
services . . . it is greatly to the author's credit that he tells
us much that is new about the diverse, and frankly bizarre,
personalities who protected Elizabeth from an assassin's bullet . . .
a detailed, believable and often compelling account'
John Cooper, *Literary Review*

'A compelling collection of small, painful, often pitiful stories,
carefully and insightfully told'
Lucy Wooding, *The Times Literary Supplement*

'A rip-roaring story' *Kirkus Reviews*

'Alford . . . has delved deeply into 16th-century archives to
unearth a history of the dark underside to the Elizabethan
golden age – a page-turning tale of assassination plots, torture,
and espionage' *Publishers Weekly*

ABOUT THE AUTHOR

Stephen Alford is the author of the acclaimed biography *Burghley: William Cecil at the Court of Elizabeth I* and a Fellow of the Royal Historical Society. He taught for fifteen years at Cambridge University, where he was a Senior Lecturer in the Faculty of History and a Fellow of King's College. He is now Professor of Early Modern British History in the University of Leeds.

STEPHEN ALFORD

The Watchers

*A Secret History of the
Reign of Elizabeth I*

PENGUIN BOOKS

PENGUIN BOOKS

Published by the Penguin Group

Penguin Books Ltd, 80 Strand, London WC2R ORL, England

Penguin Group (USA), Inc., 375 Hudson Street, New York, New York 10014, USA

Penguin Group (Canada), 90 Eglinton Avenue East, Suite 700, Toronto, Ontario, Canada M4P 2Y3
(a division of Pearson Penguin Canada Inc.)

Penguin Ireland, 25 St Stephen's Green, Dublin 2, Ireland (a division of Penguin Books Ltd)

Penguin Group (Australia), 707 Collins Street, Melbourne, Victoria 3008, Australia
(a division of Pearson Australia Group Pty Ltd)

Penguin Books India Pvt Ltd, 11 Community Centre, Panchsheel Park,
New Delhi – 110 017, India

Penguin Group (NZ), 67 Apollo Drive, Rosedale, Auckland 0632, New Zealand
(a division of Pearson New Zealand Ltd)

Penguin Books (South Africa) (Pty) Ltd, Block D, Rosebank Office Park, 181 Jan Smuts Avenue,
Parktown North, Guateng, South Africa 2193

Penguin Books Ltd, Registered Offices: 80 Strand, London WC2R ORL, England

www.penguin.com

First published by Allen Lane 2012
Published in Penguin Books 2013
006

Copyright © Stephen Alford, 2012

The moral right of the author has been asserted

Typeset by Jouve (UK), Milton Keynes
Printed in Great Britain by Clays Ltd, St Ives plc

A CIP catalogue record for this book is available from the British Library

978-0-141-04365-4

www.greenpenguin.co.uk

MIX
Paper from
responsible sources
FSC
www.fsc.org   FSC® C018179

Penguin Books is committed to a sustainable
future for our business, our readers and our planet.
This book is made from Forest Stewardship
Council™ certified paper.

For Joyce and David Scott

Here is no place to sit down in, but you must rise as soon as you are set; for we have gnats in our chambers, and worms in our gardens, and spiders and flies in the Palaces of the greatest Kings.

Jeremy Taylor, *The Rule and*
Exercises of Holy Dying (1651)

And the watcher – was he watched? He was haunted for a moment by the vision of an endless distrust.

Graham Greene, *The Confidential Agent* (1939)

Contents

PART THREE

Politics and Money

Illustrations

PLATE SECTION

1. The 'Rainbow' portrait of Elizabeth I (AKG)
2. The union of roses (Bridgeman)
3. The card players (Bridgeman)
4. Tormenting a Protestant on the rack (Cambridge University Library)
5. Sir Francis Walsingham (Getty)
6. Babington with his accomplices (Bridgeman)
7. Popish plots and treasons (British Museum)
8. Parry's assassination attempt (Hulton Archive/Getty)
9. Elizabethan locket (Victoria & Albert Museum)
10. Mary Queen of Scots (Getty)
11. Mary's prayer book and rosary (Getty)
12. A letter in cipher (Getty)
13. Elizabeth I's effigy (National Portrait Gallery)

INTEGRATED LLLUSTRATIONS

p. 51. Henri Léonard Bordier, *Peinture de la Saint-Barthélemy par un artiste contemporain* (Geneva and Paris, 1878). Cambridge University Library, shelf-mark Acton.b.26.189. Reproduced by kind permission of Cambridge University Library.

p. 85. Charles Sledd's dossier, 1580. British Library, Additional MS 48029 f. 128r. Copyright © The British Library Board.

Dates and Calendars

Elizabethans exchanged New Year gifts on 1 January each year, though by long convention the calendar year began in Europe on 25 March, the Annunciation of the Blessed Virgin Mary, or Lady Day. A few writers used 1 January as the first day of a new year, yet this practice was not adopted officially till 1600 in Scotland and 1752 in England. Throughout this book I have adjusted all dates to a calendar year that begins, as ours does, on 1 January.

In February 1582 Pope Gregory XIII ordered the use of a new calendar to replace the Julian calendar. Mathematicians had detected a small error in computing the calendar year and over the centuries this had accumulated to as much as ten days in each year. Pope Gregory's solution was to cut ten days out of 1582, so that 15 October followed immediately upon 4 October. This Gregorian calendar, with its system of 'New Style' dating, came into force in Italy and France at Christmas 1582, and in the Catholic states of the Holy Roman Empire in October 1583. The Protestant Tudor kingdoms of England and Ireland did not adopt the new calendar.

Elizabeth's government asked Doctor John Dee, astronomer and mathematician, to look at the New Style Gregorian calendar. Dee agreed that there had been an error in the old computation, but he thought that eleven days, not ten, should have been taken out of the year. In the end Dee accepted the Gregorian calculation and proposed that ten days should be shaved across May, June, July and August. So Elizabeth's government was minded, in March 1583, to change the calendar in line with continental Europe. But there were some objections: firstly, this adjustment could cause schism in England; secondly, it would offend England's Protestant neighbours on the continent;

and thirdly, it would really matter only to 'but a few, viz. such as have traffic with foreign nations, but to the rest of the realm it will be troublesome'. This meant that England continued to use the Old Style of the Julian calendar with ten days' difference between England and most of the countries of continental Europe for the next 170 years.

Officials of Elizabeth's government at home and abroad used the Old Style Julian calendar. Catholic governments, the Roman Catholic Church, foreign ambassadors at Elizabeth's royal court, and English Catholic exiles and émigrés adopted New Style dating from 1582. In this book I use dates in Old Style, but when New Style was being used, or where it is unclear whether or not a writer was working from the Julian or Gregorian calendars, I give both dates in the notes to each chapter at the end of the book. A good example would be Thomas, Lord Paget's letter to his mother on 12 December 1583 'according to the new accompt', by which Paget meant the Gregorian calendar. This would have been 2 December in England and is shown in the Notes as 2/12 December 1583.

Principal Characters

Elizabeth, Queen of England and Ireland (1533–1603), the daughter of King Henry VIII and Anne Boleyn, who succeeded her sister Queen Mary I to the English throne in 1558.

William Allen (1532–94), founder and rector of the English seminary in Douai (which later moved to Rheims), the moral and spiritual leader of English Catholics in exile in Europe, a formidable pamphleteer and polemicist, and a keen supporter of England's invasion by the Catholic powers of Europe.

Robert Beale (1541–1601), an official of Elizabeth's Privy Council close to Lord Burghley and Sir Francis Walsingham, a determined Protestant, and an experienced investigator of conspiracies and interrogator of state prisoners.

Sir William Cecil, Lord Burghley (1520–98), the first of Queen Elizabeth's secretaries (1558–72) and later her lord treasurer (1572–98); Elizabeth's most influential adviser for forty years, and the mentor of Sir Francis Walsingham.

Sir Robert Cecil (1563–1612), Lord Burghley's son, privy councillor and secretary from 1596, who ran a formidable network of secret agents in the 1590s.

Mary Queen of Scots (1542–87), the daughter of King James V of Scotland and Mary of Guise, great-granddaughter of the Tudor king Henry VII, pretender to Queen Elizabeth's throne; deposed in

Scotland in 1567 and kept in English custody from 1568 until her execution by Elizabeth's government in 1587.

Thomas Morgan (1543–c. 1611), Mary Queen of Scots's chief intelligencer in Paris, whose influence lay behind many of the plots against Queen Elizabeth of the 1580s.

Charles Paget (c. 1546–1612), a Catholic émigré, the son of an influential family in Tudor politics and an inveterate plotter against Elizabeth's government.

William Parry (d. 1585), a spy for Lord Burghley in Italy and France who in 1584 conspired to assassinate Queen Elizabeth.

Robert Persons (1546–1610), Jesuit priest, writer and Catholic propagandist, and a collaborator with William Allen on plans for the invasion of England.

Thomas Phelippes (c. 1556–?1626), Sir Francis Walsingham's trusted right hand in secret matters, a gifted linguist, mathematician and cryptographer, whose fortunes fell severely after Walsingham's death.

Philip II of Spain (1527–98), the husband of Queen Mary of England (d. 1558), politically and militarily the most powerful king in Europe, ferocious in his campaign against Protestant heresy, who sent the Great Armada against England in 1588.

Sir Francis Walsingham (c. 1532–90), diplomat and privy councillor, Queen Elizabeth's secretary (1573–90), possessed of a keen eye for security and secret intelligence; a protégé of Lord Burghley, to whom he wrote in 1568: 'there is less danger in fearing too much than too little'.

A Secret History

Of all the ruling families of England none has been more accomplished at projecting its majesty than the Tudors. As usurpers with a tenuous claim to the English throne they had to be. Seizing the crown from the Yorkist King Richard III in 1485, the first Tudor monarch, Henry VII, based his grab for power on the royal ancestry of his mother's noble family, the Beauforts, and his father's connection by marriage to the Lancastrians Henry V and Henry VI. The first of these fifteenth-century kings was a warrior and a model of chivalry, the second posthumously a saintly worker of miracles. Out of these rich and complicated threads of family and history the Tudor kings (Henry VII, Henry VIII and the boy-king Edward VI) and the Tudor queens (Mary I and Elizabeth I) wove a pattern of power and dynasty that is as vibrant and recognizable today as it was five hundred years ago.

Certainly the Tudors still dazzle. Their magnificent buildings are stunning in scale and grandeur, from the solidity of Hampton Court Palace to the splendid gothic traceries of St George's Chapel in Windsor and King's College Chapel in Cambridge. As remarkable is the Tudors' mausoleum in the Lady Chapel of Westminster Abbey, first intended by Henry VII as a shrine for his saintly Lancastrian forebear Henry VI. In royal propaganda the early Tudors never lost an opportunity: even a badge as simple as the double rose of the rival houses of Lancaster and York, the red and the white united, expressed so clearly and neatly the bringing of peace to a kingdom divided in the fifteenth century by civil war.

Henry VIII, who ruled between 1509 and 1547, continued his father's ambitions in the stone and stained glass of palaces and chapels but also through the printing press and the pulpit. At Henry's court Hans Holbein the Younger, a German painter of spectacular talents, produced masterpieces of minute detail, showing members of the royal family and leading courtiers in portraits that have the immediacy of photographs. More obviously political in purpose was Holbein's great mural for the audience chamber of Whitehall Palace, so powerful a representation of Henry VIII, massive and regal, that it made visitors who saw it tremble.

This Henry was the king who changed English history in a way no other monarch had done before. He set England upon a path strikingly different to most of the countries of Europe. Refused an annulment of his first marriage by the Pope, in 1530 Henry's eyes were opened to new possibilities. He broke away from the Church of Rome. Recognizing the insistent calls of God and history, he proclaimed himself an emperor, magnificent in his power, supreme head of the Church of England on earth next under God. These facts of Henry's kingship were pressed home unceasingly from the pulpits and the printing presses. In a beautiful woodcut on the title page of the official translation of the Bible from Latin to English Henry was shown to be in direct communication with God, with no need for the intercession of priests or popes; the interests of the king in his palace and God in his heaven were identical. This whole edifice of projected authority was inherited eleven years after Henry's death by his daughter Elizabeth, who ruled the kingdoms of England and Ireland between 1558 and 1603. And Queen Elizabeth, as her subjects and enemies alike well knew, was very much King Henry's daughter, unbending, wilful, at times severe, a magisterial presence in government.

The impression of Elizabeth's England is fixed firmly in the popular imagination. It was a glorious Renaissance kingdom distinguished by its self-confidence, its wealth, the imperial exploits of its royal navy and its aggressive determination to succeed. Courtiers sparkled, poets and dramatists wrote, and audacious sea captains harried the Spanish enemy. We have to be impressed by the Elizabethan roll call of brilliance: Sir Francis Drake, Sir Philip Sidney, Sir Walter Ralegh, Edmund Spenser, Sir John Hawkins, Ben Johnson, Christopher Marlowe, William Shakespeare, Gabriel Harvey, Francis Bacon, William Camden. Presiding over her kingdom was a queen who in her last speech to parliament, in 1601, said: 'your sovereign is more careful of your conservation than of herself, and will daily crave of God that they that wish you best may never wish in vain.'

Portraits of Elizabeth are as eloquent an expression of that commanding authority. In the 'Ditchley' portrait of 1592, which hangs today in the National Portrait Gallery in London, Elizabeth has an almost supernatural presence. Standing against a storm-racked sky giving way to sunshine, she wears a bejewelled white dress; her feet are planted firmly upon a map of her kingdom; three times the size of England she towers above Europe; she is dazzling, radiant and serenely powerful. The earlier 'Armada' portrait celebrates the royal navy's famous victory over the great invasion fleet sent by King Philip II of Spain in 1588. Here once again the political statements are insistent. The queen is magnificently dressed, her right hand resting upon a globe of the world. Her imperial crown sits next to her, while framed in the background of the painting are two images, the first of Elizabeth's navy sailing in calm waters, the second of the Spanish fleet being dashed against rocks by a terrible storm. These are only two of many portraits. Their message was always consistent: touched by God, unmovable, majestic, serene, Elizabeth was a queen for whom the motto *Semper Eadem*, 'Always the same', was superbly appropriate.

Or so we may think. Lurking in fact behind these clever and persuasive projections of political stability, empire, self-confidence and national myth is a much more complicated and fascinating story. It is a darker story, too, set against the background of a Europe divided and oppressed by religious conflict, civil war and the ambitions of kings and princes. Its themes are faith, loyalty, treason, martyrdom, espionage and a ferocious contest for dynastic pre-eminence.

Elizabeth's England was in fact anything but stable. There were, after all, few secure foundations for stability. As a family the Tudors held on to power rather precariously. After the death of Henry VIII in 1547, the English royal succession swerved unexpectedly between all three of Henry's children: a boy too young to rule for himself and two women, one a Catholic, the other a Protestant. Between 1530 and Elizabeth's accession as queen in 1558 Tudor England experienced a political, religious and social revolution. Henry VIII broke away from the Catholic Church and destroyed the monasteries, ploughing the money he raised from their suppression into war against France. This was followed in the reign of young Edward VI, between 1547 and 1553, by the final obliteration of Catholic worship in England. After Edward's death his half-sister Queen Mary returned the English Church to Rome and set about suppressing Protestant heresy. For the six years of Edward's reign Protestants had ruled England: a few years later under Mary they fled into exile or were burned at the stake for heresy. These profound changes were punctuated by foreign wars, domestic rebellions, the emergence of corrosive theories of political resistance and for many ordinary men and women economic misery. In 1558 Queen Elizabeth inherited a shocked and shattered nation.

It was no wonder that Elizabeth and her government became so adept at masking these harsh realities. Elizabethan propaganda was not a thing of luxury: it was an essential anaesthetic. Elizabeth found an empty treasury and a country sick of war. Yet still the revolution continued. Against the conservative inclinations of many of her own people and to the anger of Catholic princes and potentates in Europe, she and her ministers built a Protestant Church modelled upon that of her father and younger brother, in which the queen exercised the authority to govern. Catholics throughout Europe found this proposition both incomprehensible – how could a woman place herself at the head of Christ's Church? – and deeply offensive.

One thing that Elizabeth did not do, famously, was to marry. She resisted practically every effort to find her a husband; even when a marriage looked possible, the negotiations were scuppered by political and religious reservations. There was no plausible candidate to succeed her. Without either a legitimate heir or a named successor backed by the political elite, England faced ruin. Upon Elizabeth alone rested Protestant England's survival or catastrophe. That is one of the great underlying themes of this book. True, England survived the dynastic ambitions and military might of King Philip of Spain as well as the claim to Elizabeth's throne of a dangerous pretender, Mary Queen of Scots. One mark of Elizabethan success is that the queen survived to die in her bed in 1603. But it was a near-run thing.

A bullet, a dagger or a dose of poison – or equally a fever or disease – could have changed things for ever. And then how easily the Elizabethan world would have come crashing down. Indeed, how contingent upon the fragile life of one woman is the history we know. So let us, for a few pages, imagine the possibilities.

On a morning late in the summer of 1586 the sound of gunfire was heard in St James's Park, the royal hunting ground between the great palaces of St James's and Whitehall in Westminster. It was a volley of fire quite different in sound to that of the cannon which came weekly from the artillery ranges near the Tower of London. More to the point, the sound was unexpected and thus troubling. Quickly it was clear to the officials and servants who ran out from Whitehall that the queen, who had been travelling near the park in her coach, was badly wounded. She was the victim of assassins who, with some planning and a good deal of luck, had at last taken their chance.

Suspicions of murder plots were common in her reign, yet Elizabeth had always seemed oddly unconcerned by threats to her life; after all, she was a queen touched by God, and she had the assurance of divine protection. Some conspirators had plotted to kill her while she walked in her palace gardens with a few of her ladies and gentlewomen, though even the most desperate assassin was disconcerted by the queen's sense of presence and her aura of power.

Firearms, though less effective than a rapier or dagger to the body, put at least some distance between a killer and his victim. And on that late summer's morning this is how fifteen men, some carrying heavy harquebuses, others armed with lighter pistols, had set about killing the queen. Taking her light escort by surprise, they had fired accurately enough into her coach to wound her. The attackers, all young Catholic gentlemen who saw Elizabeth's death as the only way to prevent their families' financial and social ruin, dispersed, galloping quickly away into the countryside surrounding Westminster and London. They left their queen with bullets lodged in her stomach and shoulder. As hurriedly as they could manage, her servants carried Elizabeth to Whitehall, where she was given over to the care of her physicians and ladies. The royal chaplains began to pray earnestly for her safe delivery. Servants and officials in her private chambers had seen her desperately ill before, with sicknesses, fevers and once even smallpox. She had always made a miraculous recovery; surely she was indeed in God's protection. But this, they knew, was different. Those princes and noblemen who had been shot in Europe's wars of religion had struggled against the loss of blood, infection or crude surgery. Few had survived. Elizabeth was alive, for the time being.

Within an hour of the attack Elizabeth's Privy Council, her board of senior advisers, had gathered in emergency conference. They were powerful and experienced men equal to what they were about to do. They were not particularly surprised by the attack; they had expected something like it for some years. And yet there was a feeling of unreality about their meeting, a sensation of nightmare. They knew that they would soon have to meet the extraordinary challenge of rebellion, insurrection, even a civil war. If the queen died, the result would be catastrophe: she had no successor. Controlling their anxieties around the Council table, Elizabeth's ministers were quietly gripped by fear.

But things had to be done, instructions to be sent out, resolutions to be made. They ordered watches to be put on every road and highway out of London and Westminster. There was some hope that the queen's attackers could be captured. Then they prepared their orders. Mary Queen of Scots, Elizabeth's cousin and a dangerous claimant to the Tudor throne, though already in English custody was to be put under even heavier guard and restraint. Any attack on the queen, the councillors agreed, would certainly be coordinated with an effort to free Mary by force. For years English Catholics in exile and foreign Catholic princes had planned for such a mission. The queen's secretary gave a report to the Council on the activities and movements of prominent Catholics, Catholic priests and suspected conspirators in London. The Council ordered London's prisons to be made secure and all Catholic prisoners to be held in close confinement. They instructed the mayor and aldermen of the city to raid the lodgings of everyone under the observation of the secretary and his informants. None of this, they knew, would be easy in a city crammed with people, where the slightest provocation could spark disorder and panic.

As they had done many times before, the Council prepared England for war. In the 'Narrow Sea' of the English Channel Elizabeth's small navy was put on alert. Military orders were sent to the governor of the large garrison at Berwick-upon-Tweed on England's border with Scotland. If the King of Scots tried to take advantage of political instability in England then at least Berwick, whose defences could resist a heavy artillery assault, would hold. Orders went out also to York, to the Welsh border country and to Ireland. Rebellions almost always began in the outlying parts of England where, as the Council well knew, many of the queen's subjects had never fully reconciled themselves to Elizabeth's Church, sympathizing with the imprisoned Queen of Scots. Ireland had been in a state of rebel insurgency for years. Even London in these new and dangerous circumstances was unpredictable, and so the Council sent out instructions for mustering the city's militia. As a precaution the Tower of London was made ready to house the royal court, its lieutenant alerted to the need for vigilance and defence.

While the clerks went off to prepare the Council's letters for their lordships' signatures, Elizabeth's advisers turned their thoughts to the solemn business of hunting down those responsible for the murderous assault upon the queen. They were sure that the attackers worked on behalf of greater powers, probably Spain or perhaps France, certainly the Queen of Scots. That, simply, was the evidence gathered over years of discovering and frustrating plots. They had a law to deal with this kind of emergency, the Act for the Queen's Surety, passed by parliament only the previous year, which gave the Council and queen the authority to summon a commission to bring the traitors to justice. Every councillor in the chamber had also put his signature and seal to an oath of association in which he had promised to hunt down and to kill anyone who tried to murder the queen or threaten her kingdom on behalf of a pretended successor. Once again, those who sat around the Council table thought of the pernicious influence of Mary Queen of Scots. They deliberated, sending for the queen's attorney-general and solicitor-general. For the moment they held off summoning foreign ambassadors to court. How and when they did this would depend upon the queen's health in the coming hours. Soon enough, however, they would have to act.

News and rumour of the attack on the queen's coach, spreading quickly through Westminster, soon reached the crowded streets and narrow alleyways of London. There was anxiety, even a little panic. Some shopkeepers closed their shops, and prudent householders ordered their servants to bar gates and lock doors. Young apprentices looking for excitement and probably also trouble congregated in small groups along the thoroughfares near St Paul's Cathedral. Crowds quickly gathered in the two most important meeting places of London, the churchyard of the great gothic cathedral at the heart of the city, and a little further east at the Royal Exchange, the bourse where English and foreign merchants and businessmen met to make deals and enjoy themselves at the taverns near by. Some Londoners said that the queen had escaped without harm; others reported that she was already dead. There were mutterings about Catholic traitors and a rumour of Spanish agents. Sensible foreigners in London – religious refugees from France and the Low Countries, Germans, a few Italians – felt it was wise to stay away from the crowds. The mood of the city was only excited by the groups of aldermen and parish constables moving slowly through the lodging houses and taverns looking for potentially dangerous Catholics.

London was quiet but tense overnight. A few bonfires burned, the crowds at St Paul's and the Royal Exchange had been reluctant to go to their homes and lodging houses. The night watch dealt with a few minor scuffles. Still there was no proper news.

Whitehall Palace was barred to all outsiders. Councillors met in small groups for urgent conversations; their household servants worked through the night to prepare for the likely removal of the court across London to the Tower. Hidden behind the doors of her privy chamber, Elizabeth was mortally sick, in a deep fever, unable even to talk to her secretary. In the presence of her ladies, chaplains and most intimate advisers, she died very early in the morning.

Not even the most experienced ministers had known anything like this. The memories of some of them went back to the coup staged on behalf of Lady Jane Grey in 1553, the effort by the Protestant government of Edward VI to deprive Catholic Mary of her right to the throne. At least then they had had a monarch, however inadequate she had been, to proclaim to the people.

Where did authority now lie? England was a monarchy without a monarch. As the lawyers' maxim had it, when the king died, the law died: government ceased, to be taken up the instant the breath was out of the monarch's body by his or her successor. But there was no successor, nor was an acceptable one likely to be found any time soon.

This was more than a constitutional knot of technicalities. Facing the prospect of riot, rebellion, civil war and invasion, government could not be allowed merely to crumble away.

Visibly shocked, the councillors gathered themselves in the Council chamber at Whitehall to plan what to do next. They would style themselves as the Council of State, to rule and govern temporarily till a monarch could be found. They would call parliament, a complicated thing to do without the queen's personal authority. More urgently they would move government to the security of the Tower of London. They would send, too, for Mary Queen of Scots to be brought under heavy guard to London to be tried for her treasons by Commission. On Mary they prepared to take drastic action. The instructions to the Scottish queen's jailer would be plain: if Mary or members of her household resisted in any way, or if an attempt were made by armed force to free her from custody, she was to be killed under the terms of the association. The Council of State indemnified Mary's jailer against prosecution for a necessary act of state in a time of emergency.

By instinct the councillors wanted to keep Elizabeth's death a secret for as long as they could. Before announcing it publicly they would move to the Tower. As they, their servants and palace staff went through London, armed and vigilant, they noticed the first signs of panic on the streets: disbelief and anger at the sight of Elizabeth's courtiers removing to the Tower, the bells of a hundred parish churches ringing slowly and deliberately, and crowds gathering, some Londoners arming themselves as best as they could.

An hour after the gate of the Tower had been closed and barred, city officials read the government's proclamation on the streets of the city. The Council of State explained the heinous circumstances of Elizabeth's murder, the existence of a treasonous conspiracy, the resolution of loyal subjects to hunt down the queen's assassins, and the overriding need to protect England's religion, Church and national boundaries.

The first reports of trouble on the streets arrived at the Tower at midday. There was a swirl of news: constables and city officials overmatched by the crowds; Catholic gentry and noble families already raising their tenants to fight; foreign ambassadors, using the disorder on the streets as an excuse not to present themselves to the Council of State at the Tower, urgently dispatching their servants to Dover with news of Elizabeth's death. Locked away in the Tower, the new rulers of England wondered for how long they could suppress the violence that was bound to come before – in days, weeks or months? – the King of Spain's troops fought their way to London.

Within a week Mary Queen of Scots was brought to the Tower. She was tried by a hastily convened commission and executed in the precincts of the fortress. For Europe's Catholics only Philip of Spain, whose ancestry went back to the house of Lancaster, presented a credible claim to the English throne. Even though Mary's son, Protestant King James VI of Scotland, tried to advance his blood claim as Elizabeth's nearest living royal kinsman, he was no match for Spanish power. Indeed, even if Mary had survived to become Queen of England, her kingdom would still have been a Spanish protectorate and satellite. Even France, divided by a war of royal succession, could not compete with the European dominance of King Philip.

That power was clear when the invasion came. Winds, tides and luck favoured Spain; ferrying troops from the Low Countries, the Spanish fleet was little troubled by Elizabeth's navy. The English militias crumbled in skirmishes with troops seasoned and hardened by Spain's long war in the Low Countries of the Netherlands. Supported by German mercenaries, they had marched through Kent to London. Many Englishmen, poorly trained and armed, had defected to the invaders. The far peripheries of England, north and west, were in disorder. Though many loyal English Catholics, horrified by the prospect of foreign domination, fought the invading army, the old Catholic nobility and gentry had seen their chance; for too long they had been fined and imprisoned by Elizabeth's government. Supporting the Spaniards and in hope of positions at the English Habsburg court, they had acquiesced in the inevitable assault on London. It was a city with only ruined ancient walls and it fell within a week. With the fires still burning, the Council of State at last surrendered, isolated and embattled in the Tower of London. It remained for the King of Spain and the Pope to decide how to try the criminal clique of heretics for their crimes.

And so it was that parliament dismantled Elizabeth's religious laws. England was reconciled to Rome; the painful schism was once again healed. Heretics were tried and burned, the shops and printing houses of London's booksellers raided for suspect works. Officials suppressed heretical books: Protestant theology, the dozens of pamphlets printed by Elizabeth's government to justify its actions, Protestant translations of the Bible and John Foxe's *Acts and monuments*, the 'Book of Martyrs', which had celebrated Protestant heroism in the face of Catholic persecution.

And what would the modern history books say about this violent episode in English history? Probably that the regime of Elizabeth I had for many years survived on borrowed time, lamed by a self-destructive policy of crushing religious dissent and incapable of resisting the military might of Catholic Europe. The Elizabethan story would be a peculiar one: a strange aberration in English history when, against prevailing patterns of royal dynasty and religion in Europe, England struggled alone as an isolated pariah state for nearly thirty years. The epithets 'glory' or 'golden age' could never be used of the Elizabethan experiment. They were more properly reserved for the magnificent Christian heroism of King Philip of Spain, the ruler of Habsburg England, in saving Christendom.

It was exactly this scenario – or a close variation of it – that haunted the political deliberations and imaginations of Elizabeth's advisers for nearly half a century. To imagine so catastrophic an end to Elizabethan rule was neither fanciful nor far-fetched. Every feature of it was etched into the government's emergency plans. The queen's ministers recognized this nightmare. Indeed only by doing so did they steel themselves for the great battle they believed was necessary to avoid it. The weapons they used were espionage, relentless interrogation, surveillance, the suppression of dissent, robust treason law, torture and propaganda. This book explains why, how and with what consequences an often ruthless campaign was conducted.

Yet the heightened vigilance of Queen Elizabeth's advisers was in fact potentially corrosive of the security they craved. It is a cruel but perhaps a common historical paradox. The more obsessively a state watches, the greater the dangers it perceives. Suspicions of enemies at home and abroad become more extreme, even self-fulfilling. Balance and perspective are lost. Indeed such a state is likely as a consequence to misconceive or misunderstand the scale of any real threat it faces. Seismic political change – in the form of wars, invasions, coups, popular uprisings – has happened throughout history right under the noses of those who should have seen it coming but did not: those who were paid to watch, and who sometimes built great bureaucratic systems to do so. Such bureaucracies, especially in the twentieth century, very often became self-justifying, cumbersome and sclerotic, strangely distanced from the world around them. In those rare cases where states have managed to destroy their opponents by repression, they have often destroyed also the foundations of a healthy and vital body politic, and been consumed by a destructive institutional paranoia. Rational behaviour has little to do with any of this. Reason, after all, so rarely governs politics. This is particularly the case for governments nervously fingering the hair trigger of emergency.

A danger to any state is the powerful and often circular logic of conspiracy. It is pronounced when fear translates into a sense or feeling of national vulnerability, something very dangerous when it is institutionalized by any government that possesses the coercive means to make its will felt. This is especially true of countries where a narrow or isolated governing elite puts its own political survival before everything else, and where the instruments of the modern state can be used to subdue opposition at home or even abroad. These elites tend to see as identical their self-interest as a governing group and the welfare of the public body. They invest in propaganda. They promote a fear or hatred of outsiders. They feel beset by their enemies. We see regimes like this governing today. All of this may have been true of Elizabethan England – readers of this book will be able to judge that for themselves. Certainly the Elizabethan state was busily fashioning the tools of modern government in conditions of war and emergency in Reformation Europe.

There is no simple way to explain how all this happens. Conspiracy theorists will have their own view; historians, however, have to attend more prosaically to evidence. True, there have always been (and surely there always will be) politicians who pursue their own private interests at the expense of public ones. In Elizabeth's reign the charge of 'Machiavel' was thrown at powerful men in government by enemies who themselves were just as disingenuous and unscrupulous. Some of

Elizabeth's advisers had read the works of Niccolò Machiavelli, others had not, but it hardly matters. Political historians sometimes have to cut through a formidable thicket of self-justifying obfuscation and insinuation to make sense of politics and political actors. At the court of Elizabeth in the 1590s, for example, panics over plots and conspiracies against the queen, stimulated and even manufactured for very cynical reasons, became a form of political currency to buy favour and reputation and to damage court rivals. It would be difficult to describe this as anything other than corrosive and distasteful politics.

More interesting and subtle, however, is when an overwhelming fear of danger becomes part of one's routine mental landscape, shaping the contours of the mind in powerful and sometimes disturbing ways. This is the attitude of the witchhunt, but it is more potent still in politics and government when tangible enemies – with plots and plans, objectives and opportunities – really do exist. Here, it is easy to see danger everywhere. This was the mindset of many of Queen Elizabeth's advisers, intelligent, able and sometimes gifted men. Yet still they were caught up in a terrible accumulation of fear and anxiety. This had some roots in reality. But it also assumed a grim logic of its own: survival at all costs, even to the extent of subverting the will of the queen they sought to serve. At times Elizabeth's ministers acted upon their own authority. The first of the two most stunning examples of this 'monarchical republican' (the phrase is the late Patrick Collinson's) tendency in Elizabethan politics came in 1587, when the Privy Council dispatched the death warrant of Mary Queen of Scots; and the second in 1601, when Elizabeth's secretary secretly negotiated a mechanism for the smooth accession of a foreign king to the English throne in the event of her death. The talent of the English and then British state to preserve and protect itself has its origins in Tudor politics.

But the story I tell is much more than the sum even of these two exciting political moments. War, surveillance, espionage, religious faith, politics and torture are all themes of this book. Only the most determined conspiracy theorist could believe that Elizabeth's ministers were driven by solely selfish motives. As well as fighting their own internal political battles, they sought the good of the state (as they saw it) and the protection of queen and religion. Some of their fears were real. Elizabeth might indeed have been killed: the world they had built might have come crashing down around them. We know that Elizabeth survived; we have to set that knowledge aside, engaging imaginatively with the past. And yet still, for all the uncertainty and unpredictability facing Elizabeth's England, it seems plain that the queen's ministers hypnotized themselves with fear. For those readers who want to learn from history, there may indeed be a lesson here in the nature of the fearsome potential of government and state, of the mystifying dynamics of politics and of the power of perception balanced against a reality. It is not a pretty story – but certainly it is a fascinating one.

Espionage was a thriving trade in the sixteenth century. In war-torn Europe spies did a healthy business of selling news and intelligence mostly for money, sometimes out of religious conviction, but often for both.

Certainly the men and women who rubbed shoulders with one another on the densely crowded streets of Elizabethan London knew what a spy was. If they read books, or had books read to them, so much the better. The translator and teacher John Florio, whose work was well known to Shakespeare, wrote in 1598 of 'a spy, an espial, a scout, a prier, an eavesdropper', and of the spy's business 'to espy, to peer, to pry, to watch or scout with diligence, to ask or enquire for'. In the Geneva Bible, the most popular Protestant English translation of Christian scripture in the sixteenth century, Elizabethans found in the Old Testament (Numbers 13:1–2) a telling verse: 'And the Lord spake unto Moses, saying, Send thou men out to search the land of Canaan which I give unto the children of Israel.' These chiefs of the tribes were, said the Geneva translators, 'The spies': the two words were printed in large letters at the head of the page. So it was plain to Elizabethans that a spy belonged to one of the oldest trades in the world. He was a watcher, a reporter, a listener. He sought out, for advantage and for service. They called his trade spiery, leaving it to their heirs and successors of the eighteenth century to use the French word espionage.

Elizabethans spied for all kinds of reasons, sometimes to put food on a family's table or to buy a new suit of clothes. It was simply a job and not often a very glamorous one. They played the game of patronage, hoping that in return for information their political masters would pay their expenses and find them bits and pieces of preferment. Given the urgency of England's situation in Europe, the queen's secretary, who ran her government, needed eyes and ears throughout the kingdom and beyond. The secret trade grew to meet a political need.

There were few rules and no vetting of volunteers, and so if some spies and informants were brilliantly effective, others were derelict as well as dangerous, spying out of greed or spite or for private revenge. Others wanted adventure, a chance to play a dangerous secret game: they thrived on the excitement. Visceral hatred of the enemy was another motive. Most 'espials' and 'intelligencers' (to Elizabethans the two words meant much the same thing) wrote at some time of their patriotic calling: they spied for God, queen and country. Religious identity was critical. In a book by one Protestant theologian, *An harborowe for faithfull and trewe subjectes* (1559), his printer added by way of emphasis three significant words in the margin of the text: 'God is English'. So it was easy enough to fuse into one the interests of kingdom, government and heaven. Elizabeth's England was often likened by Protestants to Israel of the Old Testament, suggesting that Elizabethans were a people special to God. This important and very powerful sense of self-identity was given its most compelling expression in the 'Book of Martyrs', John Foxe's *Acts and monuments* (1563–83), which told the many stories of the persecuted but in the end triumphant Protestant faithful.

Persecution is a powerful theme of this book: the persecution of Protestants in Europe by Catholic kings and princes, and likewise the persecution of English Catholics by Elizabeth's government. Both sides claimed truth and justice in a bitter religious and theological contest that fractured sixteenth-century Europe. This was strongly reflected in the balance of international politics and military power. Or rather it was an imbalance, for Elizabeth's Protestant kingdom was small, isolated diplomatically and, except for the fact that it was surrounded by sea, practically defenceless against a serious military assault.

To the Catholic powers, especially to Spain, England was a rogue state. Using the common metaphor of the human body, they thought that England's disease of heresy should be cut away to restore the health of Christendom. To many English Catholic exiles and émigrés, the rule of the queen and the government of her ministers was a blasphemy. The émigrés looked instead to the Pope and the Church of Rome for leadership and spiritual guidance. In their eyes, Tudor England's heresy had deep roots in Henry VIII's schism with Rome in the 1530s and his marriage to Queen Elizabeth's mother, Anne Boleyn. As the child of this unsanctioned and offensive marriage, Elizabeth Tudor was for most Europeans a bastard as well as a heretic, and thus her rule was tainted and illegitimate.

As early in Elizabeth's reign as the 1570s some exiles pressed the Pope and the King of Spain for a crusade against England and the forcible removal from power of Elizabeth and her government. English émigrés wrote plans for invasion and worked with foreign powers to topple Elizabeth's government. That they were never successful does not mean that the plans never existed – they most certainly did. Many were wildly implausible, concocted by men whose organizational ability was lamentable. Some, however, were truly threatening. All were dangerous because, put into practice or not, they reflected the imagination of, and potential for, treason.

This book shows how the Elizabethan state, in which loyalty to the queen and the Church of England were bound together as one, fought for its survival politically and morally. Elizabethan writers naturally claimed that providence favoured the queen and her country. The account by John Foxe in the 'Book of Martyrs' of Elizabeth's miraculous preservation from harm in Queen Mary's reign was taken up by all the major English historians and chroniclers of the later sixteenth century. But if we want properly to understand the mindset of Elizabeth's enemies, we have to imagine that there was an opposing narrative to the nationally self-congratulatory one we are used to.

And there was a *very* different narrative, one that sparked with anger and resentment. The English Catholic exiles in Louvain, Antwerp, Rome, Rheims, Rouen and Madrid wrote passionate books about Elizabeth's government of atheists suppressing God's Church as cruelly as the Romans had persecuted the first Christians. The queen was, in this view, a wicked apostate bastard tyrant. The Catholic émigrés planned England's rescue from heresy and damnation, by invasion if necessary, in a cause worth their martyrdom. Elizabeth's government, defending what it saw to be God's true Church of England and their queen chosen by heaven, used every means to defend itself. It is no wonder that throughout these years so vicious a secret war was fought in the shadows.

The war was conducted in England by Elizabeth's government. The motor of government was the queen's secretary, the cool organizing intelligence at the centre of things, the spider who knew every thread of the Elizabethan web.

The secretary met the queen in daily audience. He was always on call. He supervised Elizabeth's correspondence, worked as the point of contact between the queen and her Council, briefed her ambassadors, negotiated with foreign embassies and drafted royal proclamations. He moved with his staff from one royal palace to the next and between his house in London or Westminster and his estate in the country. Information was at his fingertips: his notebooks were packed with items of government business to complete. He was an expert who knew every feature and detail of the Tudor kingdoms from maps and plans and great compilations on the topics of which he needed to be a master: on Church and religion, military matters, foreign affairs and diplomacy, English trade and the queen's enemies both within and outside the kingdom. The most skilled secretaries were practised courtiers who knew that it was wise before a royal audience to know Elizabeth's mood and who understood that when she had to perform the dull business of signing documents it was a good idea to divert her with entertaining and accomplished conversation. A secretary had to be able to steer through often choppy political waters, navigating Elizabeth's notoriously variable changes of mind and direction and the robust and sometimes fractious views of her advisers. It was an exhausting job; even the most gifted of the queen's secretaries complained of the anxiety and physical and mental strain of it. The often febrile intensity of the secretary's work sounds as a sharp recurring note throughout this book.

The royal secretariat produced mounds of documents. There must have been paper everywhere: in the clerks' rooms, in the bound volumes and other archives carried by the Privy Council from palace to palace, as well as hundreds of documents littering the secretary's private chambers at court and those of his houses in London and the country. His clerks were men he trusted, middle-ranking officials whose fierce Protestantism was beyond question, bound to the governing elite by ties of background, education and sometimes even marriage. They worked furiously at administration. While some of the most important and useful government documents were put into reference books, many of the dozens of letters and reports that arrived every day for the secretary were opened, given a short summary by one of his clerks, neatly refolded and put into a filing index. This is how the secret reports and other papers upon which this book is built – very many hundreds of them – were archived and used in the sixteenth century.

The secretary kept the most sensitive documents to himself, though he generally allowed his most trusted staff (often his own private secretaries) to work with them. At the time of Sir Francis Walsingham's death in 1590 there existed 'The book of secret intelligences'. This no longer survives, but from other papers we know that it would have held the names of agents, the aliases and the alphabets (or keys) to the codes and ciphers they used, and the money they were paid. These highly secret papers were locked away in the secretary's secure cabinets.

As the sixteenth century wore on, secret communication became much more sophisticated than it had been even thirty years before – a sure mark of how busy were Europe's spies. Simple codes, in which a symbol stood for a name or a topic in letters written in plain prose, were replaced by complicated ciphers. In these, characters stood for letters of the alphabet and false characters (called 'nulls') were inserted to fool anyone who tried to break the cipher. Even using an alphabet, it was a painstaking business to unpick a fully enciphered letter; one of the conspirators in this book found it so tedious, in fact, that he asked a friend to help him do it. To break an unknown cipher took mathematical skill, great patience and a deep understanding of Latin and all the major European languages, with their differing frequencies of letters and words. In the secretary's office secret ciphers were kept in a special cabinet, organized by drawers marked only with a letter of the alphabet, to which the secretary held the key.

By the 1580s, the most plot-ridden decade of Elizabeth's reign, the secretary had working for him a small team of secretive men. One was an expert breaker of code and cipher who also kept equipment for secret writing. Another was a skilled forger of documents and of the seals used to secure packets of letters. The secretary's archives make plain another fact. Elizabeth's government was able to intercept dozens of letters passing between England's enemies on the roads of mainland Europe, obtained from couriers or postal officials in towns and cities. In the interests of God, queen and country theft and bribery became necessary instruments of the state.

It would be wonderful to have the papers of the secretary and his staff just as they were left at the end of Elizabeth's reign. Instead we have to make do with tantalizing fragments, scattered pieces of a great documentary puzzle that keep historians on their toes. A stunning exception is the surviving archive of manuscripts belonging to Robert Beale, a clerk of Elizabeth's Privy Council. Beale was a powerful character, a plainly spoken man of passionate Protestantism and high intelligence, an experienced bureaucrat and a master of government business. Over his long career, Beale collected the kinds of papers he and his colleagues needed to use every day, organized by themes and topics. Though rebound in the seventeenth century, Beale's volumes in the British Library in London allow us to understand an Elizabethan archive, to touch it and feel it: the stiff pale animal hide spines and covers, the leather ties to keep the books closed, the indexes for speedy reference, and Beale's explanatory notes in what, after the frenetic scrawl of Sir Francis Walsingham or the impossibly compressed minute writing of Walsingham's most secret servant, Thomas Phelippes, is one of the vilest hands of sixteenth-century England – uncompromising and bluntly effective, like, indeed, the man himself.

Unfortunately Beale's papers are exceptional. Time, damp and hungry rodents quickly set to work on the piles of old government papers that lay in heaps in the Tower of London for centuries. Most of what survives today was preserved for us by the enterprising Victorians who, with their rigorous and tidy methods, went through the chaos of papers they found in government and family archives and gave them order. They dated the manuscripts, sorted them into topical categories and bound them into large volumes. They published selected summaries and notes of their contents in austere calendars printed by Her Majesty's Stationery Office. It was a magnificent, even imperial, achievement that brought the fine texture of Elizabethan history to the Victorian libraries of London's private clubs, the public schools and universities, and the country houses of the landed gentry and nobility.

So in fact for many years the work of Elizabeth's secretary and his staff and the world they knew has been viewed through the lens of the Victorian imagination: efficient, measured, self-assured, correct. One of the joys and challenges of writing this book has been to start from scratch, to put the story together piece by piece from the Elizabethan archives, to go deeper and further than the printed histories have ever allowed us to, to look and examine with fresh eyes. What we find is an intense and anxious time in English history, one about as far removed from the comfortable certainties of Victorian professional London as it is possible to imagine. Turning the pages of letters and papers written nearly five hundred years ago is an extraordinary privilege; it is difficult to imagine being able to get closer to the sources than to see the precise moment an Elizabethan spy, rushing to finish his report in Paris, dipped his pen in ink or signed a false name. These are the kinds of sources, some of the most interesting and intriguing of the sixteenth century, stripped to essentials and read afresh, which we can use to understand the secret history of the reign of Queen Elizabeth, to discover what for so long has been hidden.

Here in this book you will find a world shaded in tones of grey rather than drawn clearly in white and black. It may seem at first to be a very different world from our own, yet there is also about it a strange familiarity, and I have often wondered how much the behaviour of human beings has really changed in nearly half a millennium. Elizabethans had hopes and fears, passionate beliefs and long anxieties, points of common reference and understanding, as well as deep hatreds. Many were divided people who lived in fractured countries, trying to find ways to survive, to reconcile belief, action and conscience. Some of the Elizabethans you will read about here acted according to deeply held principles; others sold what they had for money. Many survived while others went to the gallows. Most were caught up in events over which they had no control. Nothing could be more different than the conventional story of Elizabeth's reign, the glamour of court, the heroic quest for a national destiny of peace, stability and empire. This book explores a darker and more disturbing world.

PART ONE

Spying Out the Land

I

Ten Days in November

The Spanish ambassador came to St James's Palace in Westminster on 9 November 1558, a Wednesday, in time for dinner. Briefed by his master, his sacred Catholic royal majesty Philip, King of Spain and Jerusalem as well as King of England, the ambassador had set out from Arras on the 5th. After a brisk sea crossing to Dover he and his party set off for London with no time to waste. Their speed marked the urgency of the mission, which was a special and difficult one. King Philip's wife, Queen Mary of England, the daughter of King Henry VIII and Queen Catherine of Aragon, was dying. At issue were the English royal succession and the Tudor inheritance. Just as important to Philip was the now uncertain future of England's relations with Spain and the other countries of Catholic Europe.

The king's emissary was Gómez Suárez de Figueroa, Count of Feria. He was thirty-eight years old, the captain of Philip's guard, a close royal adviser and a man who used plain words. He said he was unsuited to the intricacies of diplomacy, knowing that he lacked the suaveness of a professional ambassador. But Philip trusted Feria. It was impossible for the king himself to travel to Westminster to visit his wife, for he was busy with the funeral obsequies of his father, the Holy Roman Emperor Charles V, and absorbed by peace negotiations with France. Philip had to know what was happening at Mary's royal court, and Feria was to be his king's eyes and ears in England, a task Philip knew the count would perform without a career diplomat's evasions and circumlocutions.

As Feria drew up at St James's in the cold of an English November, he must have wondered about the likely success of his mission. How sick was Queen Mary? What were the fears and preoccupations of her advisers? What, above all, were the intentions of Mary's half-sister Princess Elizabeth, the daughter of Henry VIII and the detested Anne Boleyn? Elizabeth was twenty-five years old and already deeply experienced in the ways of court politics. Four years before Feria's embassy, in 1554, she had been implicated in an unsuccessful coup against Mary's government. As a result Elizabeth had been sent to the Tower of London and was later held for a time under house arrest in Oxfordshire. Feria himself had met Elizabeth only once before, when he had been in England in 1554 and 1555 on Philip's grand visit to Mary's court. She was then, he remembered, pleasant and welcoming, though that of course was in her interest: she had been a princess under suspicion. Now, in November 1558, the remarkable fact was that the young woman known as the Lady Elizabeth's grace was queen in waiting.

When Feria and his party arrived at St James's he and the Portuguese physician travelling with him, Doctor Luis Núñez, went straight to see Mary. Throughout her reign her health had been poor, and, though court physicians did not know the precise nature of her disease (it may have been ovarian cancer), it was obvious to Núñez and even to Feria that she was mortally sick. Mary was conscious enough that Wednesday afternoon to recognize the count. She was pleased at his embassy. But when Feria produced a letter for Mary from her husband she was not able to read it for herself. It can hardly have been a cheering audience.

Feria knew that he had not a moment to lose; he felt sure that Mary would soon be dead. That same afternoon he met her Privy Council of advisers and officials. They were polite and proper in receiving so distinguished an ambassador but they were hardly effusive in welcoming him. 'They have received me well,' he wrote in a dispatch to Philip, 'but somewhat as they would a man who came to them with bulls [edicts or commandments] from a dead pope.' There was a tangible feeling at St James's that Mary's government, like the influence of Spain in the politics of England, was near to its end.

On Feria's mind were two topics of critical importance. The first was the progress of Philip's negotiations with the King of France for peace. England and Spain had fought together against France, and for England one profound consequence, earlier in the year, had been the military failure of losing to the enemy the town of Calais, ruled by England for two centuries and the Tudor crown's last toehold on mainland Europe. The psychological effects of this bitter defeat were enormous, and it rocked the Anglo-Spanish dynastic alliance. Mary's advisers blamed Spain for the loss of Calais, while the Spaniards put the disaster down to English military incompetence. Feria's meeting with the Privy Council must have crackled with the powerful energies of anger, grievance and uncertainty. What Mary's councillors feared was that King Philip would make a treaty with France without first agreeing the return to England of Calais by the French. In his meeting with the Council at St James's, Feria was probably as emollient as he could be. Yet Calais was never given back to the Tudor crown, and the suspicion of a Spanish sell-out over the town soured relations between England and Philip for decades to come.

Anglo-Spanish peace with France was of course a subject of immense importance and complexity. But the most pressing business of all at St James's Palace on 9 November 1558 was the English royal succession. The question was this: what would happen to the crown when Mary died? She was childless, and her lawful successor was her half-sister Elizabeth, whom Mary detested. It was reported that, in a vicious swipe at Elizabeth's legitimacy, Mary said that she looked like Mark Smeaton, one of Anne Boleyn's alleged lovers: Elizabeth, in other words, was not even Henry VIII's daughter. This was the charge of a double bastardy, for Queen Anne, after usurping the place of Mary's mother Catherine of Aragon as the king's wife, had gone to the executioner's block for the treason of incestuous adultery.

For Mary and her supporters – and for politically minded English Catholics more generally – Elizabeth, as Anne Boleyn's daughter, personified and symbolized the heresy and schism of Henry VIII's divorce in 1533 and England's break with the Church of Rome. So Mary had fought with all her power to keep Elizabeth off the throne, though significantly she had not changed the law of the royal succession, instead putting her faith in the sure hope and expectation that she would have a child to succeed her. By 1558 that hope was gone.

With a certain irony, it was the dead hand of their father that settled the matter for Mary and Elizabeth in October and November 1558. The key to everything was the Act of Succession of 1544. This statute is one of the most important documents in the history of sixteenth-century Europe, for it gave the force of law to those clauses of Henry VIII's last will and testament that set out with great care exactly how the Tudor royal succession would proceed in practically every possible circumstance. In 1546, shortly before he died, Henry determined that if Mary died as queen without a legitimate heir, his youngest daughter Elizabeth would succeed her. In 1558 Mary's privy councillors, knowing that she was very seriously ill, urgently petitioned her to accept Elizabeth's claim to the throne. Mary did this on 28 October, only days before Feria's arrival at St James's, by adding a codicil to her will. Queen Mary left the 'government, order and rule' of the kingdom to her 'next heir and successor, according to the laws and statutes of this realm'. She recognized that her 'dear lord and husband' Philip could no longer play any part in the government of England. Elizabeth's actual name was nowhere mentioned. The distasteful thing was done by the time Feria was in Westminster. Facing an obvious fact, the count told Mary's Privy Council that their king supported Elizabeth's succession.

Of course there was really no choice: barring a remarkable upset, Elizabeth would be queen. Henry VIII's law of succession stood. Parliament and the Privy Council were bound by the dead hand of Mary's father. Mary's advisers knew they were yesterday's men. Some of them were plainly afraid of Elizabeth's revenge for her time in prison. What Feria saw with his own eyes was a government crumbling away. He was quite as impotent, the emissary of the most powerful king in Europe who came to Westminster with grand words but could actually change nothing. Feria spoke to Mary's men for his king – and *their* king too, yet a foreigner – who was trying to manage political change it was entirely beyond even his power to control. Philip was King of England by marriage only, and his own English ancestry, which went back to the house of Lancaster, was much too weak to make him a plausible claimant in his own right. For the time being Philip and Mary were still by the grace of God King and Queen of England, France, Naples, Jerusalem and Ireland, Defenders of the Faith, Princes of Spain and Sicily, Archdukes of Austria, Dukes of Milan, Burgundy and Brabant, Counts of Habsburg, Flanders and Tyrol. Theirs was a grand and impressive royal style that extended far beyond Westminster. It was the manifesto of European Catholic monarchy. But nothing lasts for ever.

The Count of Feria met Elizabeth Tudor, the young woman he knew in his bones would soon be queen, on Thursday, 10 November 1558, the day following his arrival at St James's Palace. She was at Brocket Hall in Hertfordshire, twenty-five miles north of London, very near to her own estate of Hatfield. She had been at the hall since at least 28 October, the day she wrote to one of her supporters as 'Your very loving friend Elizabeth'. In Hertfordshire she was surrounded by her ladies and gentlewomen. But for some time Elizabeth had also been recruiting a shadow government of mainly Protestant advisers – a fact to which Feria, deeply suspicious of those men he called heretics, was very alert.

Feria arrived at Brocket Hall in time for the midday meal of dinner with the future queen and her intimate servants. Like Mary's Council, Elizabeth received him politely but without, as Feria could see, very much joy. The young woman he met that day must have been relieved beyond measure. The anxieties of Mary's reign were lifting, though she did not know how easy her accession was likely to be. The fact that she was now so near to inheriting the throne of the Tudor kingdoms of England and Ireland was stunning, for her rule was never written in the stars. In fact, when Henry VIII wrote his will in 1546 it was wildly improbable that his younger daughter would ever be queen. But Edward VI, at fifteen years old, died in 1553, and after only five and a half years as queen Mary too was dying; both were childless. To Elizabeth it was an act of divine providence that the remote prospect she had of becoming queen was now practically a certainty. Feria saw the facts as they were. With diplomatic correctness he spoke to Princess Elizabeth at one point of Queen Mary's recovery. But if he had had any hope of that, he would not have said to Elizabeth what he did that day, or have been so interested in her reactions and responses.

After a relaxed and lively dinner Elizabeth and Feria spoke privately, though he told her, to make an important point, that he preferred the whole kingdom to hear what he had to say. Always guarded in her words, the princess made sure that the two or three ladies who attended her spoke only English. Feria and Elizabeth probably talked in Italian, though whatever language they used allowed them to have a long discussion. For a woman skilled in hiding her emotions, Elizabeth spoke to Feria with at times startling frankness. On behalf of Philip the count tried to befriend Elizabeth. Sharp and, young as she was, well practised in the arts and dangers of court politics, Elizabeth Tudor knew precisely what Feria was up to.

The count gave Elizabeth a letter from Philip of Spain which the king had written with own hand as a mark of his friendship to the princess. Feria guided Elizabeth through each point Philip made in the letter, just as he had been instructed to do by his master in Arras. The princess was polite. She said she was grateful to Philip for his letter, and that he could be assured she would maintain the good relations that had long existed between Spain and England. Elizabeth told Feria that when she had gone to prison in Mary's reign Philip had helped to secure her freedom. She felt it was not dishonourable to admit that she had once been a prisoner: she believed that the dishonour belonged to those who had put her there; she had been innocent after all. Feria told Elizabeth that she should always consider the king her true brother.

Elizabeth talked much more openly to Feria than he expected her to. He noted one thing above all others: she was very clever. Less flatteringly he said she was also very vain. In a later report to Philip the count wrote that he thought her well schooled in the ways of Henry VIII. This was a warning as much as a compliment. Feria saw that Elizabeth would take as her advisers men suspected of heresy, that is, men who professed the Protestant faith; the count had been told that all the women around the princess certainly were heretics. He was troubled about the future of Catholic England. In what must have been a delicate exchange, Feria told Elizabeth that everyone expected her to be a good Catholic princess. If she abandoned the faith, he said, both God and man would abandon her.

It was obvious to Feria that Elizabeth was very angry indeed at the way she had been treated in Mary's reign: suspected of complicity with rebels, sent to the great fortress and prison of the Tower of London, interrogated and later put under house arrest. To Feria she spoke strong words against senior men in Mary's government. He tried to calm Elizabeth's anger and said that for her own good and for the kingdom's she should not desire revenge against anyone. She replied that all she wanted to do was to make those councillors admit that they had wronged her, and then she would pardon them. More worrying for Feria and Philip was Elizabeth's belief that she owed her imminent succession to the ordinary English people and not to the nobility, and certainly not to her brother the King of Spain. Feria saw that she had great confidence in her popularity, and also that she was determined to be governed by no one.

Feria explained to Elizabeth that Philip had ordered all those Englishmen whose pensions he paid to serve her when the need arose. She wanted to know who these pensioners were. She answered Feria sharply: he was taken aback and, though he pretended not to catch it, her meaning was clear to him: she wanted to be able to decide whether it was right for her subjects to take money from the King of Spain. Already she was jealous of her sovereignty and proud of her independence. Not surprisingly Feria talked to Elizabeth, as he had spoken to Mary's Council the afternoon before, of the peace negotiations with France. Elizabeth, too, was stung by the humiliation of losing Calais; after all, the Tudor monarchs styled themselves as Kings and Queens of France, remembering the heroic conquests of their Lancastrian ancestor King Henry V in the fifteenth century. How different it all looked over a hundred years later. Elizabeth told Feria frankly that if the English commissioners at the peace conference about to meet in Brussels made an agreement without Calais she would have them beheaded.

The conversation moved to the subject of her marriage. Elizabeth told Feria that Philip had tried very hard to encourage Mary to arrange a marriage for her to Emmanuel Philibert, Duke of Savoy, and at Brocket Hall that afternoon she smiled at the memory of it. Feria replied that Philip had only ever tried to persuade Mary to accept Elizabeth as her sister and successor. The king had never dreamed of concluding anything without her consent. Elizabeth said in reply, and none too subtly, that Mary had lost the affection of her people because she had married a foreigner. Feria replied lamely that Philip had been well loved in England.

As Feria left Brocket Hall, he told Elizabeth that he would see her again soon, whether Mary lived or died. If the queen should die he wanted to know what the princess wished him to do. He was minded to visit her. She told him not to do that, but rather to wait till she sent instructions. The English, Elizabeth said with a dash of malicious irony, were resentful of her own partiality for foreigners. That, Feria agreed, was true enough.

Feria tried to make sense of what he had seen and heard so far in his embassy to England. It seemed to the count that King Philip had no influence at all. If Elizabeth had been married off to a safe foreign prince, the situation might have been different. But as matters stood in November 1558 it was plain to Feria that she would marry whomever she pleased, with who knew what dynastic consequences. She would be able to put herself beyond the control of either the Spanish or French ruling families, the Habsburgs or the Valois. Feria was sure that Elizabeth saw herself as the next Queen of England. She believed that she would succeed Mary even if Mary and Philip opposed her succession, which, given Mary's unhappy acquiescence to succession law and the message of Feria's embassy, seemed unlikely. 'God alone knows,' Feria wrote, 'how it pains me to see what is happening here.' He felt wretched and asked Philip to send to London an ambassador better able to cope with business of such sensitivity and complexity. The only thing that improved his mood was the nervous manner of poor humble Doctor Núñez. 'He is my salvation,' Feria wrote, 'for I find myself having to put up with such annoyances and I am so frequently snubbed here, that it consoles me whenever I see him enter my presence so meek and fearful of what might happen to him.'

Feria believed that there were two things Princess Elizabeth seemed disposed to do as queen. The first was to conclude a peace with France. The second was to maintain good relations with both Spain and France. Feria had noted the names of men he thought likely to have influence in the new government. He suspected many close to Elizabeth to be Protestants. Of one piece of intelligence Feria was certain: it was that Elizabeth's secretary, the man who would run the government machine and be her right hand, was Sir William Cecil, thirty-eight years old, educated at Cambridge University and formerly secretary to King Edward VI. Of Cecil, whom he did not know, Feria wrote:

'éste dizen que es hombre entendido y virtuoso pero erege'. He was an able and virtuous man but a heretic.

On Monday, 14 November, four days after visiting Elizabeth at Brocket Hall, Feria wrote to King Philip. He was blunt. There was no hope for Mary's life; indeed with the passing of each hour he expected news of her death. He wrote his diplomatic dispatch with a grim resignation. The night before he set to work on it, on the evening of the 13th, Mary, the queen who had returned her Tudor kingdoms so decisively to the universal Catholic Church after the schism and heresy of Henry VIII and Edward VI, received the sacrament of extreme unction, anointed with holy oil in her last illness. 'Today she is better,' Feria wrote to Philip on the 14th, 'although there is little hope of her life.'

Feria worked hard on his dispatch to Philip, putting some of its more sensitive passages into cipher. He must have been glad to finish it, for he felt oppressed by his embassy, vital as it was. Snubbed at the court of a dying queen, dispirited and beset by business so complicated he felt overwhelmed by it, Gómez Suárez de Figueroa, Count of Feria was surely relieved to hand the sealed packet to the courier. The dispatch rider had it by two o'clock and rode off with it to Dover.

On Thursday, 17 November 1558 Sir William Cecil was the busiest man in England, hard at work putting Elizabeth's government together and winding up the affairs of the old court. He wrote paper after paper, long complicated lists of items of business to get through for a peaceful and smooth succession. Queen Mary had died at six o'clock that morning. Sir William, with the anticipation of a skilled royal servant and politician, was already at Hatfield with Queen Elizabeth. While noblemen and gentlemen came to seek audience with Elizabeth at her court, still Sir William Cecil continued to write. There was little relief, but he was quite equal to it. For three years he had been secretary to King Edward VI, and for three years before that he had served in the household of the most powerful man in England, young Edward VI's protector and governor, Edward Seymour, Earl of Hertford and Duke of Somerset, Henry VIII's brother-in-law. In Mary's reign Cecil had cultivated good relations with important men at court. But he had also been careful to stay as close as he sensibly could to

Princess Elizabeth, a young woman under suspicion, acting officially as the surveyor of her lands and estates. He had known Elizabeth for many years; and in the early spring of 1558 they had met on a visit she made to Westminster when very probably they had spoken about the office Cecil would soon have in Elizabeth's government.

On 17 November the Count of Feria was still in London. Three days earlier he had written his dispatch to King Philip. In fact it was only a week since he and Elizabeth had talked at Brocket Hall. But now with Mary's death at St James's Palace power had shifted absolutely, and God's anointed resided for the time being in Hertfordshire: the queen was dead, long live the queen. Sir William Cecil set out the business of the new reign, including the dispatch of special messengers informing the Pope and the powers of the Empire, Spain, Denmark and Venice of Elizabeth's accession. It seemed unlikely that the Count of Feria would be called to Hatfield for an audience with the young queen: she had made that as plain as was polite a week before.

The proclamation of the accession of Elizabeth, 'by the grace of God Queen of England, France, and Ireland, defender of the faith, etc.', was read out in Westminster and London within hours of Mary's death. Cecil must have worked on it with remarkable speed; very likely he had the text ready for when it was needed. At the great cross at Cheapside in the city of London officials, accompanied by heralds and trumpets, made the proclamation between eleven o'clock and noon. On the following day Sir William wrote, with his usual brisk economy, 'done, to Jugge', by whom he meant Richard Jugge, the newly appointed royal printer, busy in his workshop near St Paul's Cathedral in London. Five hundred copies of the proclamation came off Jugge's press at the very modest cost to the new government of twenty-two shillings and sixpence. Within weeks, every corner of England, Wales and Ireland would know that Elizabeth was queen.

Cecil and many of Elizabeth's other close advisers were veterans of the debacle of 1553, when in defiance of the law Princess Mary and Princess Elizabeth had been put aside from the royal succession in favour of a young married Protestant kinswoman, Lady Jane Grey, chosen by Edward VI in his last fatal illness. That effort had failed. Shutting itself away in the Tower, Jane's Privy Council had never imagined that Mary would gather an army to march on London. But she did, and the Council – paralysed by both Mary's resolution and the knowledge that every adviser to the pretender queen had committed treason by disregarding Henry VIII's succession law – collapsed. So the circumstances of Elizabeth's accession were nothing like those of 1553. But still the new government must have been at least a little nervous. The first proclamation was specially composed to sound both dignified and authoritative, to set out the plain facts of Mary's death and Elizabeth's accession, as well as to emphasize the need for peace and order. The new queen made a public formal record of her 'great grief' at the death of her 'dearest sister of noble memory'. Mary had chosen to 'dispose and bestow' the crown upon Elizabeth as her only rightful heir by blood and lawful succession. Subjects were discharged of all their old bonds and obligations, now owing obedience only to Elizabeth; she promised in return 'no less love and care towards their preservation'. Few words were wasted: from beginning to end the proclamation would have taken a public official a little short of three minutes to read out loud. Richard Jugge's single printed sheet ended with words that must have been shouted by men and women who could only imagine what the future held for Elizabeth, her people and the kingdom: 'God save the Queen.'

Where in this great whirl of activity was Elizabeth herself? Strangely, she is the one person hidden from easy view: perhaps already she was cloaked by the powerful mystique of Tudor monarchy. Little was recorded of her in those first hours and days of rule. But some of her words have survived, to Sir William Cecil as her secretary, as well as to those noblemen who had come to her at Hatfield. To Cecil she spoke of her trust and his faithfulness to her and to 'the state', a phrase that would take on a concrete meaning in the coming forty years. To her lords she spoke of a natural sorrow for Mary, and of her amazement at what she called the burden of her office. She understood this royal burden to be God's will.

Like the Count of Feria in conversation with Elizabeth at Brocket Hall a few days before she became queen, we begin to make sense of her. Feria noted her intelligence, and her vanity too. She seemed to be independent, even wilful. Feria thought that she would refuse to be ruled by anyone. She had smiled at the thought of being married off for the sake of international political convenience; she had laughed when she wanted to and was plain, even sharp, when she had to be; she was able to leave matters unspoken. Now she was queen, Elizabeth drew her authority, not from her father or the law, but directly from God. She was God's representative on earth; her power was blessed by heaven; she was a woman touched by the divine.

Throughout her life the fact of Elizabeth's royalty had always a sharp edge to it. As a girl she had been thrown aside as a bastard when her brother Prince Edward was born, inserted once again into the English royal succession a few years later (though still by law illegitimate) and in Mary's reign imprisoned. There is a suspicion that at least one of Queen Mary's close advisers had counselled Elizabeth's assassination, a notion that, given contemporary thinking on the elimination of dynastic rivals, is not far-fetched. As Elizabeth once said: 'I know what it is to be a subject, what to be a sovereign, what to have good neighbours, and sometime meet evil willers. I have found treason in trust.' She was not sentimental, but instead resolute in defending the boundaries of her royal authority. If divine providence had seen fit to hand her the crown, then it was her duty, and that of her advisers and servants, to keep it firmly in place upon her head. She had to be kept alive whatever the cost, protected against her enemies: her kingdom and people, as well as the will of God, depended upon it. That, shown in the work of spies and informants and the government's policy of security against those it perceived to be its bitter enemies, is one of the major themes of this book.

Queen Elizabeth shared her royal office with no one else. She was counselled, yet kept her own counsel. When she spoke, often reluctantly and in times of political urgency, it was with the weariness of action, of someone forced just a little into the open. In some ways the character of Elizabeth has about it a spy's elusive quality; she was practised at self-protection. Often she was in the shadows: in the privacy of her private chambers or walking in her gardens, briefed by her advisers, acting through her ministers, or even watched by potential assassins. She was more often offstage than on it but present nevertheless as the source of her officials' power, the object of their efforts at fighting the enemy.

Two competing forces produced within Elizabeth a fascinating tension. As a ruler she spoke insistently about her authority. But as a woman in a world of politics dominated by men she had to build a protective barrier between herself and those who wished her to follow policies she did not want to pursue. She was incisive, sharp and clever; she was also deliberately vague and imprecise; and she used in political life the great weapon of delay. Elizabeth was a controlled paradox, skilled rhetorically at using many fine words to say almost nothing at all, to dizzy and confuse her hearers. Even at her simplest she keeps us on our toes. It is recorded that in Mary's reign Elizabeth scratched into a window at Woodstock, where she was being held under house arrest, the lines

> Much suspected by me,
> Nothing proved can be.
>> *Quod* [said] Elizabeth the prisoner

Ten years later, as queen, she wrote for a courtier:

> No crooked leg, no blearèd eye,
> No part deformèd out of kind,
> Nor yet so ugly half can be
> As is the inward, suspicious mind.

Elizabeth refused to be held to one position, for she was aware like no one else around her of the curious vulnerability of God's anointed.

So here were the first hours of Elizabeth's reign and the beginning of the long fight for the integrity and survival of the Elizabethan state. But nothing was yet certain. To the Count of Feria, Elizabeth was clever, vain and minded to do as suited herself. She had no obligations to the powers and principalities of Europe and no obvious commitments, other than the return to Tudor rule of the town of Calais and the vague promise of friendship with Philip of Spain. The first never happened, the second quickly dissolved away. The young queen was possibly a heretic; certainly some of her courtiers and councillors were. So much was unknown. Philip could only begin to make his political and diplomatic calculations. He, like everyone else, would have to wait for Elizabeth and her advisers properly to reveal themselves.

But Elizabethans faced their own struggles. So far as anyone knew in November 1558 Elizabeth's reign was no more permanent than her brother's or her sister's. Elizabeth trusted in God's providence, but she came to the throne after a bitter and disastrous war and in a time of severe economic strain and virulent sickness. The only useful thing to come of the widespread fever of 1558 was its efficiency in killing off some prominent members of Mary's government who could have caused Elizabeth serious political inconvenience. If Elizabeth and her advisers wanted to break once more with the Church of Rome, as Henry VIII had done a quarter of a century earlier, they faced a fierce political and legal struggle. In the reign of Edward VI the English people had worshipped according to Protestant prayer books. They would soon do so again. International peace was about to return to Europe. But what kind of peace would it be, and how far could the new English government trust Spain, France and the papacy?

Elizabeth and her advisers knew that they would have to fight for England's security. The survival of the Tudor monarchy could not be assumed. Quite apart from the fact that it depended only upon the life of one woman – a fragile thing in the sixteenth century – there were at least two other significant factors. The first was Spain. True, his sacred Catholic royal majesty King Philip at first gave friendly guidance to Elizabeth. He even reluctantly offered her marriage; she politely but firmly declined it. But Philip, who at the age of thirty-one already prided himself upon his tactical acuity, would always put the interests of Spain first.

The second factor was the most important of the two. Elizabeth was not in 1558 the only plausible candidate to the English throne. She had a blood kinswoman, the daughter of King James V of Scotland and Mary of Guise of France, and the wife of the French dauphin, Francis, of the royal house of Valois. This young woman's uncles of the house of Guise were some of the most powerful men in Europe. Through her paternal grandmother, Margaret Tudor, she was the great-granddaughter of King Henry VII of England. By his last will and testament, confirmed by an act of parliament, Henry VIII had ignored the claim to the English throne of Mary's family, the Stuarts of Scotland. But no one could dispute the fact that she had Tudor blood.

So Mary Stuart, a Catholic, was a credible royal counter-claimant to a Protestant and, in Catholic eyes, an illegitimate daughter of Henry VIII. Significantly, Henry's Succession Act of 1544 had confirmed Elizabeth's place in the royal succession but it did not restore to her the legitimacy of birth that had been stripped away when Prince Edward was born. That was only done by Elizabeth's first parliament in 1559. Her enemies quickly grasped the point: she was a bastard. Predictably, Elizabeth's advisers were outraged to discover within months of her accession that the dinnerware of Mary and Francis of France was stamped with the royal arms of England. Very tall with hazel eyes, auburn hair and a fair complexion, the great-niece of Henry VIII, kinswoman of Elizabeth Tudor, and dauphine of France, Mary Stuart was in November 1558 a month away from her eighteenth birthday. Before everything else she was *Regina Scotorum*, Queen of Scots rather than Queen of Scotland, using the traditional style of the rulers of Scotland from the twelfth century. But she wanted to be Queen of England too.

This was the broad landscape of Elizabeth's reign. Its contours were formed by the balance of military power in Europe, the clash of religious faiths and the collisions of royal dynasty. Elizabeth, a queen blessed by God's providence who wanted to follow her own path, faced the seemingly immovable object of Spanish power and the fact of Mary Stuart's claim to her throne. No one in 1558, least of all Elizabeth and her advisers, knew how these forces would act upon the politics of Elizabeth's reign, or indeed how long her reign would – or even could – survive.

2

The Lion's Mouth

Elizabethan England was defined by its Protestant faith. It stood resolutely – to many offensively – apart from most of the kingdoms and states of Europe. Between the years 1559 and 1603 the Queen's subjects worshipped with an English book of common prayer and an English Bible. Elizabeth, whose royal arms could often be seen displayed in England's churches, had the care of the souls as well as the bodies of her people. She was God's lieutenant on earth, his deputy and vicegerent, his handmaiden, the giver of his justice. Anyone who professed to be a loyal subject obeyed Elizabeth's proclamations and the laws made by her parliaments, but they also believed in their conscience that she possessed the spiritual authority that for Catholics could be exercised only by a pope. The laws of England allowed for no other interpretation of the powers of heaven and earth.

Elizabethan Protestants commonly called their faith the 'true' religion. Reinterpreting centuries of Christian history, English theologians believed that the English polity, which fused together the authority of a spiritual and a temporal ruler, was the best possible form of Christian monarchy. No other kingdom in Christendom, they believed, was so well established in law and justice. In the early months of the new reign Elizabeth's government proceeded very carefully, keeping to the letter of Mary's laws. England remained for the time being a Catholic country. But within six months of the queen's accession, after difficult and fractious debates in the House of Lords and the House of Commons, parliament in Westminster passed an Act of Supremacy and an Act of Uniformity.

The first of these laws stated that the queen was unequivocally 'the only supreme governor of this realm ... as well in all spiritual or ecclesiastical things or causes as temporal', setting out the words of an oath of supremacy to be sworn by any man holding office in Church and State. The Uniformity statute established in law the Elizabethan book of common prayer and protected it from any kind of public criticism or ridicule. Parliament recognized and defended Elizabeth's historical right as an English monarch to govern her Church solely and without question, and anyone who dissented from this position publicly could be prosecuted. The parliamentary settlement of 1559 was a revolution in Church and State. Elizabeth's supremacy was also a powerful international statement of the independence of Tudor England and Ireland. As her father had done in the 1530s, Elizabeth Tudor dismissed the Pope's authority. To English Protestants, Elizabeth had once again freed their country from the shackles of papal tyranny. But in the eyes of Catholic Europe, struggling to know what to do about Elizabeth, England was a dangerous and infectious pariah of Christendom.

The new settlement of Protestant religion in England was profoundly shocking to a generation of Elizabethans. Nor was it for Elizabeth's Church and government an easy settlement to enforce: a popularly Protestant England was never inevitable. For English Catholics the royal supremacy was at best a conscientious difficulty, but to many it was a monstrous heresy that turned the authority of the Pope and centuries of Church tradition upside down. After the years of division in the reigns of Henry VIII and his son Edward VI, Catholics found in Mary's rule the reconciliation of painful schism, the English Church once again returned to the universal Catholic Church. Defined by the burnings of Protestants, Mary's Catholic reformation offered to Europe a model for the suppression of pernicious Protestant heresy. But Mary's Catholic reformation was torn to pieces by Elizabeth's government. Catholic churchmen in parliament in 1559 fought the new religious settlement as best they could. They hated the new doctrine, preached from the pulpits by Protestant theologians recently returned home from foreign exile. The Abbot of Westminster called these hated exiles the 'preachers and scaffold players of this new religion'. The Archbishop of York, who was soon enough replaced, was staggered by the bizarre notion that a woman could be head of Christ's Church.

When the new laws came into force, in the early summer of 1559,

English Catholics faced the choice either to reconcile themselves to Elizabeth's Church in ways that were not yet clear to them or to go into exile. Most remained loyal subjects who balanced their consciences and civil obligations as well as they could. Some resisted. Many young students and teachers of Oxford and Cambridge chose exile, leaving England to study in the Catholic universities of continental Europe; Louvain was a popular choice and later Rheims. As one spy wrote in 1571, 'divers fugitives are thought to lurk in Louvain as students and scholars there'. Some of these committed and clever young men began to fight the heresy of their homeland with their pens. Heavy works of Latin theology showed what they believed to be the nonsense of Protestant belief. Shorter works of polemic, combative pamphlets written in sharp vernacular English, attacked the government of Elizabeth's ministers. Many of these works were smuggled into England in great numbers, annoying and harrying the English authorities and keeping government spies and informants very busy indeed.

Later émigrés, forced into foreign exile in the Low Countries of modern-day Belgium and the Netherlands by an uprising against Elizabeth in the north of England in 1569, threw their energies into the rescue of their country by war and invasion. Their numbers were somewhere between fifty and seventy; but given that these fugitives and outlaws were of the English nobility and gentry they carried immense weight in a society acutely conscious of the importance of rank and social hierarchy. By 1579 one spy's catalogue of the English Catholic émigré community in France and Italy – priests, students, merchants and other travellers, some paid modest pensions by the Pope – put their number at just short of three hundred. How many Catholics there were in England the government could only guess at, but Elizabeth's bishops and advisers knew that few of the justices of the peace charged with enforcing the statutes on religion were enthusiastic supporters of those laws. The government perceived many potential enemies of the queen both within and without the kingdom.

Most Catholics decided to live in England as peaceably as they could in good conscience; others decided publicly and politically to fight for their country's recovery. But whatever an individual chose to do, one fact was plain. Elizabethan England was a confessional state in which religious beliefs and political loyalties were impossible to separate from each another in any straightforward way. The government held that a truly loyal subject worshipped as the law expected him or her to do in the Church of England. Anyone who resisted the English prayer book risked severe punishment. In the later years of Elizabeth's reign Catholic 'recusants' – a word derived from the Latin *recusans*, a refuser – were fined huge amounts of money and regularly imprisoned for refusing to attend church services. Members of the grandest gentry and noble families in England were held under suspicion by the authorities and were sometimes under active surveillance. The power of the state was turned upon the private and now illegal activities of some of Elizabeth's most important subjects. Some men and women were prosecuted for sheltering Catholic priests who came secretly into England from the 1570s. In these conditions, spies and informants thrived. Throwing everything into very sharp relief was the severity and extent of Tudor treason law. Like Henry VIII and his ministers, Elizabeth and her government believed that determined resisters of royal authority were most probably traitors. The suspicion and even the scope of treason deepened and broadened in the Elizabethan years as the battleground of religion and politics became for many a more dangerous and desperate place.

So what were the Catholic powers of Europe to do about Elizabeth? In quieter times, kingdoms like France and especially Spain may have wanted to leave her alone, balancing the realities of diplomacy and politics against the imperatives of religion. But that was never likely after 1558 because of a complicated interplay of three forces at work in Europe in the later sixteenth century. The first was the religious division caused by the Reformation and the regular outbreaks of violence between Protestants and Catholics. The second was Spanish military power and the global ambitions of King Philip of Spain. The third was Mary Queen of Scots and her claim to the Tudor crown. What is more, Elizabeth's government quickly began to pursue a surprisingly active policy of military support for fellow Protestants abroad, and to do so in a way that seemed calculated to annoy the great powers of Catholic Europe. Though in fact against the queen's instincts, her advisers pressed hard to support Protestant opponents of French regency government in Scotland in 1560. Two years later English troops crossed the English Channel to support Protestant Huguenots in the first of the unrelenting religious wars and disturbances that consumed France in the later sixteenth century. The first intervention was a great success, securing an Anglophile Protestant government for Scotland that could help to protect England's vulnerable northern border. It was possible because the Queen of Scots was in France. But the death in 1560 of Mary's husband, by then Francis II of France, meant that she returned to her homeland in 1561, so causing enormous complications for Elizabeth's government: the Queen of Scots, a blood kinswoman of Elizabeth, was once again in Scotland, with an eye to the Tudor royal succession. Whether she was an active conspirator herself – and on this point historians have disagreed profoundly over the centuries – Mary Stuart was at the very least a focus of what for Elizabeth was plainly treason against the Tudor crown.

When the Count of Feria spoke to Elizabeth a few days before her accession as queen, he feared for the future of Catholic England and told King Philip so plainly. With Elizabeth Philip played a careful diplomatic hand. As the most powerful Catholic king in Europe, he found the heresy of Elizabeth and her government deeply offensive. As the ruler of a global power whose resources were stretched to their limits by years of war in western Europe against France and in the eastern Mediterranean against the Ottoman empire he could not, however, afford financially and militarily to fight England. As late as 1568, Philip hoped that Elizabeth might be brought to her senses. It was a hope against experience. Very early on cracks began to show in Anglo-Spanish relations. Elizabeth's ambassador in Spain was an outspoken Protestant who made offensive remarks about the Catholic faith and called the Pope 'a canting little monk'; not surprisingly, he found himself expelled from Philip's court. In 1568 Elizabeth's government detained Spanish treasure ships that had been forced by pirates into the safety of an English port. The bullion was taken ashore, causing the Spanish ambassador in England to protest that the queen had confiscated it. The treasure ships were helping to fund Philip's tough military campaign led by the Duke of Alba in the Spanish-ruled Netherlands. This campaign alone, conducted against Dutch Protestants, caused Elizabeth's government profound disquiet. Quite apart from the persecution of men and women of the same faith, what if Alba were directed to take his troops across the English Channel? Sir William Cecil, Elizabeth's secretary, wrote in a policy paper in 1569 that England was 'most offensive both to the King of Spain and the French King for sundry considerations and specially for succouring of the persecuted': by this time, many Protestant refugees fleeing from war in France and the Low Countries were settling in towns and cities in southern England. Elizabeth's kingdoms seemed to stand alone against its enemies. Considering the international politics of the moment, Cecil employed a surgical metaphor: the queen was a patient being operated upon by the King of Spain and the Pope, who used Mary Queen of Scots as their scalpel.

Over the years of the 1560s Philip of Spain's patience wore thin. But for all of the problems that existed between England and Spain by 1570 – diplomatic spats, English support for those Spain called rebels and an increasingly frosty trade war between the two kingdoms – Philip held back from isolating Elizabeth completely. Pope Pius V was, however, less forgiving of Elizabeth Tudor's errors and not as patient as Philip was in playing a long international political game. In February 1570, by publishing a bull called *Regnans in excelsis* ('He that rules in the heavens above', the opening words of the bull), Pius excommunicated Elizabeth from the Catholic Church and faith. She was, he said, merely the pretended Queen of England who had usurped 'monster-like' the spiritual authority of the Pope. With her kingdom in miserable ruin, Elizabeth was a heretic and a favourer of heretics, now cut off from the unity of the body of Christ. More significantly for Catholics, in an action that made their obedience to the queen very difficult to prove beyond doubt, Pius freed Elizabeth's subjects from loyalty, duty, fidelity and obedience to the Tudor crown.

When Pius V's bull was nailed to the gates of the Bishop of London's palace near St Paul's Cathedral in London, in one of the most public precincts of the city, Elizabeth's government responded robustly. In 1571 parliament passed a Treasons Act and a law to prohibit and punish the bringing into England of bulls and other instruments from Rome. To deny Elizabeth's right to the throne, to claim that anyone else should be king or queen, to call Elizabeth a heretic, schismatic, tyrant, infidel or usurper: all, whether expressed on paper or spoken out loud, were, if proved by a court of law, offences of treason. So, too, was the reconciliation of any English subject to the Church of Rome by means of a papal bull or document. Loyalty to the English Church and the English state became impossible to disentangle one from the other. Both sides – the Pope in *Regnans in excelsis*, Elizabeth's government in treason law – had marked out the lines of the long battle ahead.

To Elizabeth's advisers Pius V's bull was hardly unexpected: they were used to what they called the malice of Rome. But what made it especially sinister was the fact that *Regnans in excelsis* was published within weeks of the suppression of the Northern Rising, the first major rebellion of Elizabeth's reign. Late in 1569 two English Catholic noblemen of the border country with Scotland, Thomas Percy, seventh Earl of Northumberland, and Charles Nevill, sixth Earl of Westmorland, raised their tenants against the government. Militarily it was an insubstantial rising that was soon put down by a royal army. But its significance lay in the rebels' aims. After only a few years of disintegrating personal rule in Scotland, in 1568 Mary had sought sanctuary in England and found herself an unwanted guest put under restraint. One of the rebels' objects was to free Mary Queen of Scots from this English captivity. The rebellion in the north was also a Catholic rising, marked by the symbolism of a mass celebrated in Durham Cathedral.

The earls of Northumberland and Westmorland failed. Both men forfeited their titles and lands. Westmorland and his wife, the sister of the fourth Duke of Norfolk, escaped to the Netherlands from Scotland. Northumberland, also an escapee to Scotland, was eventually handed over to the English government, which executed him in 1572. To Elizabeth's advisers the message of the Northern Rising was as clear as the government's judicial response was savage. Responding to a military assault against the queen's rule, it determined that those rebels who had been captured should be hanged by martial law, their bodies left to rot on the gibbets as a warning to the men and women of the north. Church bells that had rung to raise rebellion would be pulled down. Those fifty or so rebels who were able to escape abroad with their families were fugitives and outlaws, marked for the rest of their lives.

To Elizabeth's government there were obvious connections between the military ambitions of Philip of Spain, Pope Pius V's excommunication of the queen, the objectives of Mary Queen of Scots and her supporters, the fact of open rebellion in England and the known plot-tings of English Catholic nobility. They were shown in exact detail by the discovery in 1571 of a conspiracy against Elizabeth in favour of the Queen of Scots funded by the Pope and encouraged by the Span-ish ambassador at Elizabeth's court. The principal conspirator was Roberto di Ridolfi, a merchant of Florence who had lived in London for a number of years.

The story of the plot begins in 1569, the year Ridolfi, on the face of it a respectable businessman, was caught bringing money into England from the Pope. For a time, in December of that year, he was held under house arrest by the Elizabethan authorities. They dis-covered that Ridolfi's bills of foreign exchange were for the Bishop of Ross, Mary's ambassador at Elizabeth's court, and for Thomas Howard, fourth Duke of Norfolk. This was clearly suspicious, but nothing certain was proved either way. Only in 1571 did all the ele-ments of Ridolfi's plot come properly to light. Because of the arrest at Dover of a courier working for the Bishop of Ross, Elizabeth's government discovered that Ridolfi had been working as a contact between the Spanish government and English Catholic noblemen sympathetic to the cause of the Queen of Scots. Chief among them was the Duke of Norfolk, who had plotted to free and then marry Mary and to encourage a Spanish invasion of England. In unmasking Norfolk as a traitor to Elizabeth, the Ridolfi Plot struck a blow to the heart of the Elizabethan state. The duke's beheading in 1572 was the price Elizabeth had to pay for resisting pressure from her Privy Coun-cil and a very angry parliament to execute the Queen of Scots herself.

One of the profoundest problems facing Elizabeth's advisers was that of Mary's asylum in England. For nearly nineteen years, between 1568 and her execution in 1587, she was Elizabeth's guest both unin-vited and unwanted. She was believed by the English government to be complicit in the murder of her second husband, Henry, Lord Darnley, in 1567. She was obviously hostile to Elizabeth and wanted her kinswoman's crown; she plotted with foreign powers in Europe on behalf of her own royal claim to England. Elizabeth, nervous of killing a fellow monarch even by justice, refused to put Mary on trial for her life. Equally, it would have been madness for Elizabeth to send her back to Scotland: the consequences for England's security, and for a friendly Protestant government in Scotland, were unthinkable. To return her to France was much too dangerous a prospect. At least in England she could be held at Elizabeth's pleasure. So Mary was isolated, moved between houses and castles in the midland counties of Warwickshire, Derbyshire and Staffordshire, her movements and household controlled as much as possible by the English government. But Elizabeth's ministers could not cut her off from Europe completely, much as they tried – from Spain and King Philip's ambassadors in London, from her Guise kinsmen in France or from Rome. It was known that secret letters passed between Mary, her secretaries and her friends at home and abroad. Eager English Catholic gentlemen volunteered to act as her couriers.

To English eyes it was clear as daylight (though of course concealed in shadow and secrecy) that the Queen of Scots was determined by hook or by crook to get for herself the Tudor crown. They believed that she sat at the centre of a web of European Catholic conspiracy. This toxic fear of Mary provoked in 1585 the Act for the Queen's Surety, one of the most extraordinary and menacing laws ever passed by an English parliament. This statute set out how any action against Elizabeth 'by or for' a pretender to the English crown would be tried by a special commission of privy councillors and lords of parliament. Anyone found guilty of such a conspiracy against the queen – and also the pretender with whose knowledge or assent the conspiracy was planned – could on being found guilty by the commission be hunted down and 'pursued to death'. The statute, in other words, sanctioned vengeance against Mary by private subjects authorized to do so by an act of parliament. True, her name did not appear in the act, but nevertheless the statute was clearly and obviously aimed squarely at the Queen of Scots. Indeed it was the very law that took her to the executioner's block at Fotheringhay Castle two years later.

The Act for the Queen's Surety spoke of 'sundry wicked plots and means ... devised and laid ... to the great endangering of her highness' most royal person'. This was the greatest anxiety of the Elizabethan political establishment. The preamble of the act spoke with painful eloquence to their fears, which were real. This is not to deny that Elizabeth's advisers could be ruthless and cynical; often they were. But from the beginning they saw how precarious England's position was, and they believed the dangers. To discover a plot like Ridolfi's confirmed a suspicion or exposed a danger previously unforeseen. Evidence became tangled up with suspicions, suspicions in turn influenced the reading of future evidence: it was a familiar pattern of thinking for Elizabethan politicians. Treason was cumulative, a self-sustaining and self-nurturing fear, incident building upon incident over many years, a great pattern of conspiracy. And the queen's advisers were absolutely right to believe the truth of plots and conspiracies and plans for invasion and assassination, for those conspiracies and plans certainly existed. What Elizabeth's councillors tended to do, however, was to overestimate their enemies' intelligence, cunning and organization. But the fear was there, and it was painted in the vivid colours of divine providence. Elizabethans believed they were engaged in a great war for truth against lies, light against darkness, Christ against Antichrist, Protestant against Catholic. The ravaged countries of sixteenth-century Europe bore the scars of that terrible struggle.

It was, however, too easy in this Reformation world of absolutes, of the high politics of monarchs and states, to lose the human scale of things. Some men and women in Elizabeth's reign were born to play the martyr. Many others were not, like Charles Bailly, the young courier and servant of the Bishop of Ross whose capture led to the unravelling of the Ridolfi Plot in 1571. Bailly was interrogated and threatened with torture by Elizabeth's government. After two years in the Tower of London he was released and banished from England, leaving a record of his imprisonment in the Beauchamp Tower. The inscriptions of others were all around him, for one of the few unofficial privileges of a state prisoner was to make a mark on the walls, to carve a name, a symbol, a statement of faith, of hope and expectation, even a declaration of innocence. Bailly carved his inscription in the recess of the northernmost window in his cell, from which he had a view of the executioner's scaffold on Tower Hill:

> Wise men ought circumspectly to see what they do; to examine before they speak; to prove before they take in hand; to beware whose company they use; and above all things, to [consider] whom they trust.

He added a line in Italian, 'Gli sospiri ne sono testimoni veri dell'angoscia mia': 'My sighs are true witnesses to my sorrow.' Poor

Charles Bailly reminds us of the human cost of the long secret war fought by Elizabeth's servants for peace, security and religion.

In late October 1572 Elizabethans earnestly prayed for their deliverance from the queen's enemies and the work of the Devil. Elizabeth instructed parsons and curates to encourage as many people as they could exhort to come to church on Sundays, on holy days, on Wednesdays and on Fridays to say special prayers. From the pulpits ministers told the people to behave themselves reverently and to go down on their knees to pray to a merciful God for his protection from the plagues and punishments racking Christendom. In return for repentance they asked for defence against their enemies. And they did so seeking to make sense of the most shocking act of religious violence in sixteenth-century Europe. The people of England knew all too well what had happened in Paris and other towns and cities in France a few months earlier, on the feast of Saint Bartholomew and in the weeks following, when thousands of Protestant men and women were murdered by their Catholic neighbours. There was, in the view of Elizabeth's advisers, no more atrocious practical demonstration of Catholic evil.

Even Elizabethans used to a life that was harsh and often violent were horrified by the massacre in Paris. It was provoked in late August 1572 by the assassination of Admiral Gaspard de Coligny, one of the leaders of France's Protestant, or Huguenot, community. The French religious civil wars of the 1560s had come to an uneasy peace, but bitter resentments continued to fester, with short nasty bursts of violence breaking out on the streets of Paris. Coligny was first of all shot and only wounded; but taking advantage of the moment, the leading Catholic noblemen in Paris met their king, Charles IX, the son of Catherine de' Medici, to plan with great care the killing of leading Protestants in the city. On Saturday, 23 August, they drew up a list of names of those who would be murdered. Just before dawn on the following day Admiral Coligny was killed in his bed. Henry, Duke of Guise, who led the killing party, was present when Coligny's corpse was thrown from the window of his house into the street below. Duke Henry was a first cousin of Mary Queen of Scots, and the eldest of the three Guise

A Protestant commemoration of the massacre in Paris in August 1572, by François Dubois.

brothers; they were members of one of the most powerful political dynasties in Europe; and they were uncompromisingly Catholic.

Coligny's corpse was mutilated by a mob. Quickly the violence spread throughout Paris. At least two thousand men, women and children were killed, though the number may have been nearer to six thousand; nearly six hundred houses were pillaged. Hundreds of Protestants were marched to the Pont aux Meuniers, executed, and thrown into the River Seine. One heavily pregnant woman was stabbed in the stomach by a business rival of her husband's. The murderer and his accomplices then ransacked their victims' house. At three o'clock on Sunday, 24 August the aldermen of Paris went to the king at the Louvre Palace to tell him that the city was beyond their control. Charles IX, who had sanctioned the killing of Coligny and other Protestants supposedly to prevent another civil war between Catholics and Huguenots in France, appears to have suffered a nervous breakdown. The violence was copied in other towns in France. But the horror of what had happened in the houses and on the streets of Paris between 22 and 24 August 1572 was felt far beyond the borders of Charles IX's kingdom.

Queen Elizabeth's advisers heard of the massacre in early September. Even men used to, as they saw it, the duplicity and cruelty of Catholic princes were revolted by the killings. Lord Burghley, Elizabeth's lord treasurer, wrote: 'I see the Devil is suffered by Almighty God for our sins to be strong in following the persecution of Christ's members.' Robert Dudley, Earl of Leicester, another councillor and courtier very close to the queen, called the massacre a 'lamentable tragedy'. All true Christians, he said, looked for revenge at God's hands. God had punished them with the 'just scourge of correction, by the sufferance of his people thus to be martyred, but our sins do deserve this and more'. Only Protestants' vigilance and repentance would deprive the Devil of final victory. This was a war imagined in cosmic terms, Antichrist and Devil on one side, Christ and God on the other. The queen's ministers sought to understand the ways of providence. But they also looked to practicalities. As soon as the massacre was known at court the Privy Council met in emergency session, the coasts of England were prepared for an invasion and Elizabeth's navy was ordered to put to sea.

The man upon whom Burghley and his fellow councillors relied for information from France was Elizabeth's ambassador at the court of Charles IX. He was a gentleman of Kent and London, about forty years old, whose name was Francis Walsingham. Walsingham left no account of what he saw in Paris that August weekend; like many other eyewitnesses he may have found it too painful to recall the massacre. His house as ambassador was in the Faubourg-Saint-Germain, on the right bank of the Seine near the great Gothic cathedral of Notre-Dame de Paris. With Walsingham were his wife and young daughter as well as Philip Sidney, an eighteen-year-old English gentleman who would one day be Walsingham's son-in-law as well as a distinguished poet. Walsingham surely recognized the danger of the first failed effort at assassinating Admiral Coligny. He may even have heard, coming from the direction of the Louvre, a signal for the killings: in the small hours of the morning of Sunday, 24 August, shortly before the murder of Coligny, the bells of the church of Saint-Germain-l'Auxerrois rang out.

Walsingham offered sanctuary for foreigners in peril of their lives. The mob knew this, for it even attacked Walsingham's house. Elizabeth's ambassador was unlikely to have been reassured by the guard King Charles sent to protect him. For weeks after the violence

Walsingham always left his residence in the company of bodyguards, and he was taunted and insulted as he went through the streets of Paris. He sent reports to Elizabeth and her advisers within days of the massacre. He met King Charles and his mother Catherine de' Medici on 1 September. Francis Walsingham, the ambassador of a supposedly heretic queen, negotiated the audience with extraordinary coolness and composure. Charles IX spoke of a plot by Coligny and other Huguenot leaders to kill the royal family. Walsingham, we can be sure, would have taken his own view.

Sir Francis Walsingham went on after his Paris embassy to have a distinguished political career and to build a powerful reputation for his gifts as an organizer of spies and informants. His face is probably one of the most familiar of the Elizabethan court. His portrait in the National Portrait Gallery in London has been attributed to John de Critz the Elder, the son of Dutch Protestant immigrants settled in London, and an artist who received the benefits of Walsingham's patronage. The portrait shows Sir Francis in about 1585, more than a decade after the massacre in Paris. The ambassador of forty was by now the queen's secretary in his early fifties. We see a half-length picture, Walsingham standing just a little to the left, though he looks directly at us with grey eyes. His brown hair is cropped short, his clipped beard streaked with grey, his moustache fashionably brushed up. He wears a black skullcap and a large white ruff around his neck. Over a black doublet, slashed to show its lining, he wears a black surcoat trimmed with fur. Hanging from a black ribbon is a cameo of Queen Elizabeth set in gold. The impression John de Critz leaves us with is of power and control, a man of authority modestly but richly dressed, the austere loyal servant of Elizabeth.

De Critz's Walsingham of the middle 1580s was no longer a young ambassador. But in Paris he had seen for himself the murders of thousands of his fellow Protestants. Walsingham's embassy in Paris was formative. He had encountered at first hand the work of the Devil; he knew how to make his way through the perilous labyrinth of the Valois court; he understood something of Mary Stuart's kinsmen the Guise. Sixteen months after the massacre of Saint Bartholomew, Elizabeth appointed Walsingham as her secretary, the man who sat at the heart of the machine of the Elizabethan state. One of the secretary's tasks was to secure information for Elizabeth and her Privy Council. To do this he sent out spies. Sir Francis Walsingham, always conscious of the enemy at the gates of both Elizabeth's kingdom and God's, was a practised hand in clandestine affairs. Like other men of authority in her government, he would always do what he saw was necessary to defend the queen and the true religion. As a passionately committed Protestant, Walsingham knew the dangers as well as the attitude of mind needed to face them. As a young man, even before his embassy in Paris, he coined an aphorism: 'there is less danger in fearing too much than too little'. For Walsingham, a life in politics confirmed the principle he so neatly expressed.

As they went about their daily lives, ordinary Elizabethans knew something of the dangers threatening their queen and faith. They heard for themselves the words of royal proclamations and of the laws passed by parliament. They talked in the market squares of towns and cities and in shops and taverns, went to church to pray for aid and protection, read or had read to them books and pamphlets and ballads that tried to comprehend a world in which God made the force of his will clearly felt, scourging and punishing his people with the victories of their enemies. They saw public executions for sedition and treason and heard from the pulpits the sermons of Elizabethan clergy and the recantations of Catholic priests who asked for forgiveness. Loyal subjects behaved themselves. Others read controversial books and pamphlets smuggled into England from abroad, causing them perhaps to question the authority of Elizabeth and her government. More dangerous still, some families even sheltered Catholic priests working secretly and illegally in English towns and cities and in the houses of the wealthy gentry and nobility. Many of Elizabeth's subjects knew of the spies and informants who thrived in these shadowy corners of religious faith and political loyalty.

Countries across the 'Narrow Sea' of the English Channel were at war. The Catholics and Huguenots of France killed one another often, as in Paris in 1572, acting out the rituals of worship, cleansing and purifying the stench of Protestant heresy or smashing the Catholic idols of false religion. The formidable war machine of King Philip of Spain rumbled through the Spanish Netherlands, crushing Protestant resistance in a long and hard campaign to which English troops would be sent in 1585. English Catholic exiles and émigrés who were either banished from England or found it impossible in conscience to stay at home lived, taught and plotted in France, Italy, Spain and the Low Countries. Some returned secretly to England, successful in evading the watchful eyes and ears of the authorities. From the later 1570s priests taught and trained in Rome and France entered Elizabeth's kingdoms to minister to English Catholics. Many were captured and sent to prison and the gallows. Both sides fought for the truth as they understood and believed it.

These were not years of peace and stability, a golden age of Elizabeth: they were instead some of the most difficult and troubling in the history of Europe. Any Elizabethan who knew something of the world understood very well the significance and meaning of the prayers of public repentance published by the queen's printer in October 1572. In the safety of the parish church he or she prayed to God that the horror of what had happened in Paris would not be repeated in the crowded alleyways of London or on the streets of other towns and cities in the kingdom: neighbour against neighbour, private hatreds turning to murder, corpses thrown into the River Thames. In the rich Elizabethan English of this specially printed book of common prayer, priest and people said:

> Hearken to the voice of our prayers, our king and our God: for unto thee do we make our complaint.
>
> O Lord, the counsel of the wicked conspireth against us: and our enemies are daily in hand to swallow us up.
>
> They gape upon us with their mouths: as it were ramping and roaring lions.
>
> But thou O Lord art our defender: thou art our health and our salvation.
>
> We do put our trust in thee O God: save us from all them that persecute us, and deliver us.
>
> O take the matter into thy hand, thy people commit themselves unto thee: for thou art their helper in their distress.
>
> Save us from the lions' mouths, and from the horns of the unicorns: lest they devour us, and tear us in pieces, while there is none to help.

3

English Roman Lives

It was in these dangerous and uncertain times, driven on by the thrill of a great adventure, that two young Englishmen arrived at the port of Boulogne in the summer of 1578. They were quickly caught up in one of the spasms of religious war in northern France. They saw 'cruel and heavy spectacles' of killing and came close to danger themselves, robbed by soldiers and stripped down to their shirts. They sought safety in Amiens, where an English Catholic priest called Father Woodward gave them help. The two young men then went to Paris and there played a little at espionage, handing over the letters of English Catholics they had met to Elizabeth's ambassador at the French court, Sir Amias Paulet. From Paris they moved to Lyons. In Milan, where they arrived on Christmas Eve, they lodged in the palace of Cardinal Charles Borromeo. From Milan they went to Bologna, Florence and Siena, and then finally to Rome, where they enrolled in the English seminary to study grammar. One of the young men, Thomas Nowell, signed the register of the seminary using his real name. His friend used a false one, writing the Latinized 'Antonius Auleus'. In English he probably called himself Anthony Hawley, though in fact his name was Anthony Munday.

Munday, eighteen years old and a restless soul, was a budding writer and young adventurer who fell into spying by accident. On his travels he grasped an opportunity, quickly realizing that he was able to tell the extraordinary tale of how he had seen and heard for himself the wicked conspiracies of Queen Elizabeth's Catholic enemies. When Munday returned at last from Rome to London he sold his story, writing pamphlets and short books in lively and vigorous English. He wrote for Londoners like himself – those perhaps in trade or business, young lawyers, civic officials or merchants' apprentices, browsing the shops of booksellers and stationers near St Paul's Cathedral – and in learning his craft as a popular writer he showed that he had a showman's touch for dramatic timing. In London he also gave public evidence against young priests who had been his friends in Rome. The priests, like Munday himself, had by then come back to England. Unlike Munday, they were captured by the authorities, imprisoned and tried for treason. Munday, confronting his former friends with the evidence of their conspiracies, helped to see them to the gallows. All of this happened within the space of two years, between February 1579, when Nowell and Munday arrived in Rome, and the priests' trials in November 1581. What began for Anthony Munday as the adventure of an impetuous young man became a deadly serious career as an unofficial agent of Elizabeth's government.

He was the son of Jane and Christopher Munday, who on 13 October 1560 had him baptized at St Gregory-by-St Paul's, a church built tight against the south-west transept of London's great Gothic cathedral. Near by was the hall of the Stationers' Company, the trade body of Elizabethan printers and booksellers, whose shops were clustered around the cathedral's churchyard. Here stood the great Paul's Cross, an octagonal pulpit with a lead roof, where Londoners came to hear public sermons and recantations of religious error. The pulpit was at the heart of the busy city.

Elizabethan London was a crowded, suffocating, jostling world of pleasure, business and life. The old city was bounded by its ancient walls and gates as far east as the Tower of London and as far west as Bridewell Palace on the River Thames. Beyond Fleet Street and the Temple Bar one entered Westminster and the world of law and politics, dominated by the grand houses of the nobility and the law courts of Westminster Hall but above all by the royal palace of Whitehall. South of the Thames from London Bridge was Southwark, with its bear gardens, inns and taverns, theatres and brothels, Bankside and the Paris Garden. London Bridge was built high with shops and houses; from it were displayed on poles the severed heads of traitors. An armada of small boats carried passengers up and down the river between wharves and landing steps that led to an intricate warren of alleyways and streets. Taking a boat on the Thames for a few pennies was the easiest way to move quickly through a congested and chaotic city.

The streets of London and Westminster were jammed with people and traffic. The population had risen from forty or fifty thousand in 1500 to about two hundred thousand nearly a century later. The city was a dense and chronically overcrowded tangle of town houses and squalid tenements, shops, churches, official buildings, prisons, trade halls, streets and alleyways. It was a city of immense contrasts, exciting as well as dangerous. Great wealth rubbed shoulders with terrible poverty. The city was ridden with disease. Plague, a frequent visitor, killed thousands of Elizabethan Londoners. And everywhere there was a confusion of people, the very rich and the destitute, natives of the city, travellers from other parts of the kingdom, refugees from foreign wars: nobility and gentry, well-to-do merchants, household servants, city officials, constables and law officers, vagrants, pickpockets, nightwalkers and prostitutes. All of these men and women lived, worked, traded, ate, drank and begged in the same crowded streets.

So Anthony Munday, born amongst people and noise, was very much a city boy. And from Anthony's earliest years, in and around Paul's Cross churchyard, his was a world of books. Christopher Munday was a bookseller, and his son's life was influenced from childhood by ink, paper and the printing press. Anthony was an orphan by 1571, a fact which helps to explain why he was later free to wander the cities of Europe. It is likely that he was educated by a Huguenot called Claude de Sainleins (or Claudius Hollyband), a schoolmaster who taught three languages Anthony was keen to learn: Latin, French and Italian.

In August 1576, when he was fifteen, Munday 'put himself apprentice' to the printer John Allde. Already Munday was an aspiring writer. In 1577 he composed a 'Defence of poverty' and wrote a ballad called 'Munday's dream' in August 1578. Soon after that he set out on his journey to Rome. He was bound to Allde for eight years, but he stayed for only two. Outwardly there were no bad feelings on the part of his master, for later Allde gave a testimonial that as his apprentice Munday 'did his duty in all respects, as much as I could desire, without fraud, covin [treachery] or deceit'. On Munday's return from Rome in

1579 Allde was to print *The Mirrour of Mutabilitie*, the first time Munday wrote of his travels abroad.

Munday had the itch for adventure. For seventeen years he had lived in the shadow of St Paul's Cathedral, hearing foreign languages and voices and reading books about other places. In that small area of London lived men and women born in Flanders, France and Germany. In fact there were more than seven thousand of these 'strangers' in the city and its suburbs, many in search of work, others Protestant refugees from war and persecution. Anthony Munday knew that there was a wide world beyond the packed streets of the city. He wanted to travel further than John Allde's printing-house at the Long Shop adjoining St Mildred's church in the Poultry, on the corner of Scalding Alley, east of St Paul's. He was bored and he wanted adventure. He said so in his dedicatory introduction to *The Mirrour of Mutabilitie*:

> But at that time being very desirous to attain to some understanding in the languages, considering in time to come: I might reap thereby some commodity, since as yet my web of youthful time was not fully woven, and my wild oats required to be furrowed in a foreign ground, to satisfy the trifling toys [idle or foolish fancies] that daily more and more frequented my busied brain: yielded myself to God and good fortune, taking on the habit of a traveller.

And so in the second half of 1578 Anthony Munday set off on his journey. He knew that he wanted to be a writer. Probably he had no idea that he would also become a spy.

The story Munday told of his experiences in Rome came out in tantalizing instalments between 1579 and 1582. He had a gift for keeping the readers of his pamphlets guessing. Each part of the tale was a fresh story of derring-do. He called his account his 'English Roman life'. In it he revealed the secrets of the English College in Rome, where about forty young men were being trained to return to England as priests of the Catholic faith. Munday knew that his Elizabethan readers would be horrified by what they read. Rome, as Munday described it, was a place of sin and danger; it was the heart of the enemy's camp. Remembering back to what he and his friend Thomas Nowell had thought when they first arrived in the city, Munday wrote: 'we might well judge Rome to be Hell itself'.

The two young men had made that arrival at dusk on Sunday, 1 February 1579, lodging overnight at an *osteria* in the city. The following day they went to find the English College, 'a house both large and fair' on the Via Monserrato near the Castel Sante Angelo. As soon as they entered the college, students bustled round them, asking about the latest news from England. A man walked by, carrying dozens of wax candles, gifts from the Pope and blessed by him at high mass that day. It was Candlemas, the commemoration of the purification of the Blessed Virgin Mary and the presentation of Christ in the Temple. The candles, they were told, were signs of the Pope's favour.

The two young travellers were welcomed as pilgrims with eight days' free lodging. They delivered letters from Paris to the rector of the college, Maurice Clenock (or Morys Clynnog), a Welshman in his early fifties, a graduate of the University of Oxford and a dabbler in plans for the Catholic invasion of England and Wales. Young Nowell and Munday must have been exhausted. The truth hiding behind Munday's easy heroic narrative was hinted at by Robert Persons, a priest whom they would soon meet in the college. Persons wrote privately of two youths at first turned away from the seminary but eventually admitted because they 'were like to perish in the streets for want'.

Munday, however tired he was, had to think on his feet. It was the cost of hiding his true identity. The surname he was using, Hawley, was that of an English gentleman. Anthony was pretending to be his son. The scholars of the seminary, fresh from dinner, took Nowell to one side. But Munday was asked by a priest to walk with him in the garden. The priest, who knew young Master Hawley's supposed father, asked why he was in Rome. He was not impressed by Munday's answer. 'Trust me sir,' Munday said, 'only for the desire I had to see it, that when I came home again, I might say, once in my life I have been at Rome.'

As a gifted writer Munday had a great ear for dialogue. He also knew what his London readers wanted to hear, the horrors and conspiracies of Rome given a voice. So it is no surprise that in the college's garden the priest denounced the heresy of 'that proud usurping

Jezebel', Queen Elizabeth, likening her to the queen of Israel whose body (so the Old Testament tells us) was devoured by dogs: 'I hope ere long the dogs shall tear her flesh, and those that be her props and upholders.' Out of his pocket the priest drew a piece of paper containing the names of Elizabeth's privy councillors. He called the paper 'a bead-roll', a list of people to be specially prayed for. This was sharp irony. These heretics, he said, would soon be held to account for their crimes. They did not know 'what is providing for them, and I hope shall not know, till it fall upon them'.

Munday gave the priest to whom he spoke in the garden sinister anonymity. With the name of Robert Persons, however, he was much freer, for by the time Munday wrote up his story for the London printing presses Persons, educated at Oxford and ordained a priest of the Society of Jesus – a Jesuit – in July 1578, was one of the most able adversaries of Elizabeth's rule and a wanted man in England. He was about thirty-two years old when Munday met him, able, confident, even charismatic. Munday captured something of his character. He described how Persons had often sat on a chair in the middle of the student body, 'when he would open unto us, in what miserable and lamentable estate our country of England stood'. Persons even prayed 'for that gracious and thrice-blessed queen' – Mary Queen of Scots, Elizabeth's rival, 'now held down by that Jezebel's oppression'.

Munday made it clear that the English College was poisoned by treason. When he fell seriously ill, his fellow students came to sit by his bedside and made what Munday called 'horrible speeches' against their prince and country. One of the scholars even said to Anthony: 'You may be happy, if God take you out of this world here: then shall you never see the bloody ruin of your own country.' Once he had recovered from his sickness, Munday went out one day to the place of Saint Peter's martyrdom with two other scholars. As usual they talked about England. One of them said: 'While two or three persons be alive, we may stand in doubt of our matter in England.' 'Who be they?' Munday asked. Out of delicacy to his readers he gave initials only, but they were three of Elizabeth's leading advisers, of whom two were Lord Burghley, the queen's lord treasurer, and Sir Francis Walsingham, her secretary. 'Oh,' Munday's companion continued, 'had I the hearts of these in my purse, and their heads in the Pope's

Holiness' hands: I would not doubt but ere long, we should all merrily journey homeward.'

Yet Anthony Munday found companionship in Rome as well as treason. Luke Kirby, a priest born in Yorkshire, visited Munday when he was sick, and they became friends. Kirby was about thirty-one years old and a former student of Louvain. We know, thanks to another English spy in Rome, that he had brown hair and a short beard, that his teeth were slightly crooked, and that he spoke with a mild stammer. Munday made other friends too and enjoyed for the first time in his life the rhythm of life in a community of students. Here Munday's gift for writing great narrative was at its best, his ear for dialogue, his nose for scandal. He turned upon the English College those weapons he possessed: a sharp eye, a quick intelligence and a lively pen.

There is an easy descriptive quality to Munday's account of the daily lives of the college's students in their 'house both large and fair'. Four or six scholars shared a chamber, and each scholar had a bed made up of two small trestles with four or five boards and a quilted mattress. The porter rang a bell first thing in the morning, at which the students turned up their beds. A second bell marked prayers, and the scholars spent half an hour on their knees in private devotion. A third bell was the signal for silent study, each scholar reading at his desk. After this the students went from their chambers to the refectory for a breakfast of one glass of wine and a quarter of a manchet loaf, a bread of the best quality. Teaching followed for most of the morning, with the scholars walking in pairs to their lectures at the Collegium Romanum – the Roman College – which had been founded, like the Society of Jesus, by Ignatius Loyola. Some went to lectures in divinity, others to physic, logic or rhetoric. The students had time before their midday meal in the English College to walk in its gardens.

Dinner in the refectory was announced by the porter's bell. The custom, Munday wrote, was for two students to take it in turns to serve everyone at the table, helped by the butler, the porter and a poor Jesuit. Small dishes for each scholar were set out on a round table, and every boy and man helped himself, ready prepared with his trencher, knife, fork and spoon, a manchet loaf covered by a white napkin, a glass and a pot of wine standing near by. The food was very fine indeed, beginning with *antipasto* of meat, Spanish anchovies or syrup of stewed prunes and raisins. The second course was a mess of pottage. Munday, a young man with a ready appetite, enjoyed what he ate but barely knew what was in the pottage, 'made of divers things, whose proper names I do not remember: but methought they were both good and wholesome'. Boiled and then roasted meats followed. To finish there were cheese, figs, almonds and raisins, perhaps a lemon and sugar, a pomegranate, 'or some such sweet gear [stuff, substance]: for they know that Englishmen loveth sweetmeats'. This was indeed very fine dining.

While the scholars ate their main meal of the day, they listened to the reading of a chapter of the Latin Vulgate Bible and then, according to Munday though contested by his Catholic opponents, from their special book of martyrs that recorded the lives of some Tudor Englishmen executed for high treason. One of the martyrs, Munday said, was John Felton, the young Catholic hanged in 1570 for pinning to the gate of the Bishop of London's palace the bull of excommunication against Elizabeth. Munday was saying, not very subtly, that the English College in Rome trained priests whose object was to destroy Queen Elizabeth and her Protestant kingdoms.

Excellent food and edifying verses were followed by an hour of recreation and then, once again marked by the ringing of the porter's bell, private study mulling over the morning's lecture. Scholars went off to the Roman College for another hour of teaching in the afternoon before returning to the English College for a further glass of wine and a quarter of manchet. After this they would withdraw to their chambers, to be called later to scholarly disputations. There was time before supper for more recreation. Munday described how after supper in winter the Jesuits gathered the scholars round a great fire to say terrible things about Elizabeth, her privy councillors and bishops. The students went back to their chambers when the bell rang, and the porter came to light the lamps by which they laid out their beds ready for the night, studying for a little while at their desks. Another bell marked the time for prayer, and priests would begin the Latin litany, the scholars giving the responses. At last they all went to bed.

This was the steady rhythm of the community's life in Rome. It would have been familiar to any student who had studied in a college in Cambridge or Oxford, something Munday, of course, had not. He was a city boy, an orphan, self-sufficient, clever and enterprising, and he did not take well to the discipline of an institution with strict rules for behaviour. Punishments were very much part of the life of a young scholar in the sixteenth century, and Munday relished describing them graphically, knowing full well that his Elizabethan readers saw the Jesuits in particular as the shock troops of the Catholic Antichrist, hardened by strict discipline. Munday made everything he could of their zeal. He knew all the small punishments for minor offences: a scholar not turning up his bed in the morning, or not going down on his knees for prayer, or failing to hear mass before lectures, or forgetting to put his wooden peg in its place to signify whether he was in or out of the college. Munday was punished for all of these offences, 'albeit it were with an ill will'. He had done penance by reading to fellow scholars in the refectory; he had been on his knees in the hall; he had even had to stand with his mess of pottage on the floor before him, scooping up each spoonful. There were also private penances. Munday described how scholars would whip themselves in the refectory, their identity disguised by a pointed hood with eye holes and wearing a special canvas cape that showed a naked back; he had seen the blood trickle to the ground. A Jesuit instructed him in this kind of whipping, which was done with cords of wire. Munday's readers may have remembered a book printed a few years before, an account of the terrors of the holy inquisition, in which the inquisitors wore the same pointed hoods Munday saw in the English College. Here the propaganda value of his writings for Elizabeth's government was tangible. The enemy appeared real and terrifying.

Anthony Munday had an eighteen-year-old's delight in a trencher piled with good food and a scholar's wariness of physical punishment. He possessed all the paradoxes of a Tudor spy. He embraced an institution but kicked against its discipline. He made good friends but later betrayed them to the Elizabethan authorities. He was ambiguous about his faith. Why, after all, had he wanted to study in a Catholic seminary so far from home? Always elusive, at best he told only half a story but he did so with great style.

And Munday thoroughly enjoyed himself in Rome, thriving on the dangerous glamour of the city at a time of carnival: 'the noise and hurly-burly', the horses and coaches, the courtesans displaying themselves at their windows, the disguises, and even murder committed behind those masks. Munday the Londoner, used as he was to the packed streets around St Paul's Cathedral, said he was amazed by the goings on around him. He wrote to surprise his readers. He related how the Jews of Rome raced naked for over a mile to the city's ancient capitol. He described what he called the Pope's 'cursing' on Maundy Thursday, when Pope Gregory, holding a great painted holy candle, was carried in his chair to the gallery over St Peter's basilica, with cardinals singing 'the Pope's general malediction' in mockery of a blessing, cursing Queen Elizabeth, who was, they said, worse than even the cruellest tyrant in the world. That same night Munday saw wicked people gather themselves into the company of the Holy Ghost, the company of charity and the company of death. They walked with crucifixes before them, carrying torches and whipping themselves. Munday described for Protestant Elizabethans a chilling scene of evil.

To Munday, Rome was a city corrupted by the unholy greed of the Catholic Church. He visited the seven chief basilicas and churches of the city, walking a circuit long used by pilgrims. In the churches he met those who came on pilgrimage to the rotten bones of saints. He discovered at the root of everything money and greed, lazy worthless friars and men and women stunned by the fake holiness of supposed relics. This was what Munday expected of the Catholic Church of Antichrist, 'the eldest child of Hell'. The first basilica he described was St Peter's, where Munday saw a great rock made of brass upon which, so Catholics said, Jesus spoke to Saint Peter and pronounced Peter to be the rock upon which Christ would build his Church. Everywhere Anthony found venerated bones and objects. In St Peter's were the remains of the apostles Peter and Paul, the spear that was thrust into Christ's side at his crucifixion, and the handkerchief used to wipe Jesus' face on the way to the place of his execution at Golgotha. He discovered in the church of St John Lateran what were claimed to be pieces of the true cross along with a single bloodied nail, as well as the first shirt made for Jesus by his mother Mary, a glass vial of Christ's blood, and a piece of his coat with his blood still fresh upon it.

At Santa Maria Maggiore Munday saw some of the thirty pence received by Judas when he betrayed Jesus. Munday found three or four more pieces of Judas' silver in Santa Croce. Everywhere Munday saw worthless relics of idolatry and superstition, so much a part of the false religion of Rome Protestant Elizabethans held in contempt.

Munday was in Rome at an important and difficult time for the city's English community. For months the seminary had been riven by a factional tussle between the scholars from England and their Welsh rector Maurice Clenock. Their argument reached a crisis in the spring of 1579. Expelled by Clenock, the English scholars appealed to the Pope, who met them on Ash Wednesday, 4 March. As the result of the audience, Pope Gregory XIII reinstated the students and dismissed Clenock from office. Munday gave an eyewitness account of the meeting. It is a compelling piece of writing. With tears trickling down his white beard, Gregory had said:

> O you Englishmen, to whom my love is such as I can no way utter, con-
> sidering that for me you have left your prince, which was your duty,
> and come so far to me, which is more than I deserve, yet as I am your
> refuge when persecution dealeth straitly with you in your country by
> reason of the heretical religion there used, so I will be your bulwark to
> defend you, your guide to protect you, your Father to nourish you,
> and your friend with my heart-blood to do you any profit.

'Behold,' Munday continued, 'what deceits the Devil hath to accomplish his desire: tears, smooth speeches, liberality [generosity], and a thousand means to make a man careless of God, disobedient to his prince, and more, to violate utterly the faith of a subject.'

So Anthony Munday came face to face with Antichrist, and even kissed his foot. But who was Munday on that day in Rome? Was he the young tearaway scholar, the orphan traveller on a great adventure, the spy, or merely a shy young man awed by the majesty of Pope Gregory? That identity Munday never revealed: it was probably the greatest secret of his months in Rome.

Anthony Munday's 'English Roman life' belongs as much to literature as it does to history. Though in some senses a work of the imagination, it is a powerful account of the visit by a young man to the camp of Queen Elizabeth's most determined enemies. Munday's story says something of the ever-shifting points of his personality and of his acute intelligence. He was at various times a brave traveller on an adventure and a scared boy driven to the English College by near starvation. He was the hero of his own story, the enterprising clever scholar who uncovered the secrets of the Catholic enemy. Above all he was a gifted writer who told a story he knew would both thrill and terrify his fellow Elizabethans. Between the years 1579 and 1582, when London was gripped by news of the trials and executions of priests he had known in Rome, Munday's bestselling account revealed the face of treason and conspiracy. He helped to fix in the Elizabethan mind's eye a lurid and frightening image of a trans-European plot against Elizabeth, revealing the terrible resolution of the queen's enemies.

A sure mark of Anthony Munday's success as a spy turned writer was the enemy's robust response to his charges of conspiracy and treason. Pained by the perversions of Munday's revelations of life in Rome, first set out in *The Mirrour of Mutabilitie* (1579), Doctor William Allen, the inspirational leader of English Catholics in exile, wrote in 1581 to defend the two English seminaries in Rome and in Rheims. With great power, Allen set out his cause to save English souls, defending from the unjust laws made against them Elizabeth's 'Catholic and loyal subjects'. He explained that the mission's purpose was to send priests secretly into England, for which they were trained in the English College. In sparkling prose he wrote:

> This is the way, by which we hope to win our nation to God again. We put not our trust in princes or practices [schemes, stratagems, plots] abroad, nor in arms or forces at home. This is our fight, and for this war, the Society of Jesus and our seminaries were instituted, to this ... our priests and students are trained.

So carefully and finely crafted, these are words to remember in the following chapters.

William Allen knew better than to use Anthony Munday's name, for he did not want to dignify with recognition Munday's supposed revelations. Instead Doctor Allen denounced certain young fellows and fugitives who, after running away from their masters, had dabbled in forgery and theft. They had joined others of ill disposition 'that sometimes thrust themselves secretly into such companies living together as we do'. These fellows who reported on others out of malice and for money Allen called spies and intelligencers. When he wrote of 'false brethren', he had Anthony Munday very much in mind. The great Doctor Allen named Munday's true profession: the young Londoner, the traveller and writer and in the end the betrayer, was before everything else a spy.

Anthony Munday was supremely sure of himself. Making use of his secret identity, he had seen what to Elizabethans was the truth of Rome. He heard treason with his own ears. He was a young man and could not match the subtle dignity of Doctor Allen's prose. He wrote instead with fire and passion, publishing in 1581 a defiant manifesto in verse:

> O Rome, the room, where all outrage is wrought,
> > The See of sin, the beast with sevenfold head:
> The shop wherein all shame is sold and bought,
> > The cup whence poison through the world is spread.
>
> . . .
>
> Let Pope, let Turk [infidel or heathen], let Satan rage their fill:
> > God keepeth us, if we do keep his will.

Within a decade of the horror of the massacre in Paris, Munday's great success was to show once again the terrible dangers facing Elizabeth. 'Our Roman enemies', as Munday called them in 1581, driven on by implacable faith, were at the gates of Elizabeth's kingdom. Soon enough they would bring the battle to England.

4

'Judas his parts'

On 9 July 1579 Anthony Munday was at Douai in the Low Countries, on the way home to London, fame, notoriety and modest fortune. Only four days before, on the first Sunday of the month, a fellow Englishman arrived in the city Munday had left weeks earlier. This other traveller's name, probably, was Charles Sledd.

We know practically nothing of Sledd's life. The facts are few. He spent the months between July 1579 and February 1580 in Rome, returning to England by way of France in May 1580. In London he became an energetic, even a ferocious, pursuer of Catholic priests living secretly in the city. Sledd may not have been his real name; for a time, in Paris, he probably borrowed the identity of one Rowland Russell. He was clever, literate and used to travelling. There is evidence to suggest that he may have been a merchant's apprentice in London in the early 1570s. He was probably in 1579 still a young man (somewhere in his middle twenties) and employable as a household servant, one of the best covers for the work of an Elizabethan spy. Certainly he had a sharp eye for detail and a keen memory for conversations and faces.

Sledd wrote a long narrative of his months in Rome, an extraordinary record of the Catholic Englishmen of the city, their dinners, their meetings and their conspiracies. Whereas Anthony Munday sold the story of his 'English Roman life' from the shops of London's printers and booksellers, Sledd's narrative, to which he gave the very Elizabethan title of 'A general discourse of the Pope's Holiness' devices', was a secret document read only at the highest levels of Elizabeth's government. Later it was used as evidence in one of the most important treason trials of the reign.

And so Charles Sledd the spy is a mystery. He was a careful chronicler, watching and recording. He was also a man who volunteered to hunt down his country's enemies, fired by passion and probably by hatred too. He betrayed others completely and deliberately. He lived and travelled with men he later arrested on the streets of London, and gave evidence against them in a public trial. What were his motivations? The fact was that the silent observer in Rome, listening and noting, came to possess in London a terrible energy. For Catholics Sledd was the great betrayer, employed in Rome as a lowly servant, later giving false witness against men of God. To William Allen, Sledd was as much a hypocrite and a liar as Anthony Munday had been. Both men had pretended to be Catholics to serve their own ends. Sledd, indeed, had taken the holy sacrament while spying on his master, playing (in Allen's words) 'these Judas his parts'.

When Sledd arrived in Rome on Sunday, 5 July 1579 he went to stay at the house of an Englishman called Salamon Aldred. Aldred, a Londoner, was a hosier by trade, and his wife's family had given them the very substantial sum of three hundred crowns to be able to live in Rome. Sledd's stay with Aldred was only temporary, for he wanted to take advantage of the eight days of free hospitality at the English College for English pilgrims to Rome. The condition, not surprisingly, was that he should be a good Catholic. From the beginning, Sledd was under scrutiny. When at last he went along to the English College he was questioned about his faith 'very inquisitively'.

The Englishmen of Rome were on the look out for spies. Sledd was alerted to this by an old acquaintance called Robert Barret, a runaway apprentice now in Rome, whom Sledd had known in London. Barret warned him to be careful of what he said: the suspicion was that Sledd was a spy. Barret also revealed to Sledd that there was a conspiracy afoot. Barret was the servant of a former Welsh bishop, Thomas Goldwell, one of the grandest of the Catholic exiles in Rome. Goldwell, he claimed, was involved in a plot by the Pope and the King of Spain against Elizabeth's England. Sledd, too, would hear all about it if he stayed on in Rome. Barret advised Sledd to go to confession at St Peter's, something he later did. It very probably saved him from prison. Briefed by Barret, and now knowing something of what was happening in the city, Sledd later wrote that he was able to behave like any other Catholic in Rome.

Sledd was given a tour of the scholars' rooms in the English College by none other than Luke Kirby, the young priest born in Yorkshire who had befriended Anthony Munday. Like Munday, Sledd was impressed by what he saw: three or four young men to each bedchamber, and these rooms 'very finely decked and every man his bed appointed alone'. Afterwards Kirby and Sledd went to the room of a gentleman called John Pascall – Pascall was one of the most important Catholic Englishmen in Rome – where they were joined by three other priests. Sledd, still not yet trusted as a reliable Catholic, was questioned closely.

On Monday, 13 July Sledd's eight days of hospitality as a pilgrim expired. It was time for him to go to confession: either that or he was in danger of showing himself 'to be of a contrary opinion than I had professed to be' – that is, not the good Catholic he had claimed. He chose confession. The English Jesuit who gave Sledd absolution also gave him a certificate written in Latin, the 'outward show and manifest token' that he was a Catholic. Sledd was free at last to move about Rome in safety; he was no longer under suspicion. A day later he went back to Salamon Aldred's house. Sledd had loaned money to Aldred in London about two years before, and so the two men came to the arrangement that Aldred would give Sledd board and lodging as a way of settling the debt.

Sledd now kept his eyes and ears open. He began also to use his pen, keeping a journal with short entries for each day. By now it was August 1579, the month Pope Gregory XIII visited the English College, giving it the fantastic patronage of a yearly pension of 3,000 crowns and a charter of statutes. The greatest news of all, however, was the Pope's summoning to Rome of Doctor William Allen and the new exciting phase of Allen's mission to rescue England from heresy. Doctor Allen was expected in Rome any day. His presence would dominate Sledd's narrative in the months to come.

In fact Rome was buzzing with the anticipation of England's freedom from the tyranny of the heretics in Elizabeth's government. Sledd reported his candid conversations with Catholic Englishmen in the city concerning the invasion of England and Ireland. They were excited at the Pope's support for a military expedition of Spanish troops led by an Irish adventurer called Sir James Fitzmaurice and an English priest, Nicholas Sander, to the south-west coast of Ireland. Fitzmaurice, Sander and their men set sail in June 1579, so it was no wonder that the prospects for their mission, for which there was huge optimism, were avidly discussed by English Catholics in Rome. In late August Salamon Aldred gave what Sledd called a 'solemn dinner' at which the guests talked about the Fitzmaurice expedition, as well as the prospects for Queen Elizabeth's proposed union with the Duke of Anjou, one of the most controversial of her marriage negotiations. Was it possible, they wondered, that the queen could really marry a French Catholic, the son of Catherine de' Medici? After Aldred's dinner Luke Kirby and another priest invited Sledd to join them both in the English College 'and by that means to make me priest for to serve my country shortly'.

Most exciting of all, however, was the arrival in Rome of William Allen. This happened three days after Aldred's dinner. It happened to be the same day that Sledd found work in the household of Nicholas Morton, a graduate of Cambridge and a Catholic churchman. Sledd was in the best possible position to be able to act as an eyewitness of truly historic events.

It would be hard to overestimate the authority and moral standing of William Allen in 1579. He was the great hope of English Catholics in exile. He was their guide, organizer and moral compass. To the government of Queen Elizabeth, however, he was probably the most determined and dangerous enemy England possessed other than Mary Queen of Scots: certainly he was the cleverest, the most intellectually assured and the most committed.

Born in Lancashire in 1532 and educated at Oxford University, where he became a fellow of Oriel College and principal of St Mary Hall, Allen had left England soon after the Protestant Church settlement had become law in 1559, travelling and teaching for a time in the Low Countries. He returned home for a time to recover from a serious illness. It was not an easy convalescence: Allen saw at first hand the compromises in their faith that Catholic men and women were making even in a part of England as resistant to Protestantism as Lancashire. The experience shaped him profoundly. Leaving England for good in 1565, Allen went to Antwerp. Three years later he founded a seminary to train priests in the town of Douai in the Low Countries which had moved, by the time Allen was in Rome in 1579, to Rheims in France.

Allen was without doubt the spiritual leader of the mission to lead Elizabeth's England away from heresy back to the Catholic faith. He was passionate, single-minded and determined. At Douai and then at Rheims he trained and drilled the storm-troops of the mission, the young priests who were sent to England to begin the essential work of saving souls. He also became an astute politician, involved from the early 1570s in efforts to persuade the Pope and the King of Spain to mount an invasion of England. Allen was a brilliant polemicist and one of the best English prose stylists of the sixteenth century; he wrote stingingly effective attacks on what he saw as a vicious persecution of the true faithful. What Charles Sledd sensed in August 1579, instinctively and correctly, was the nervous hopeful excitement of a reinvigorated mission to send priests to work secretly in England. Above all, the English community in Rome anticipated the strength and single-mindedness of Doctor Allen's commitment to save his country from Protestantism.

Not surprisingly, September and October 1579 were months of busyness and preparation in Rome. William Allen made his dispositions for the English mission, taking ten men – priests and important laymen – for an audience with Pope Gregory. Afterwards Allen had a private conference with the Pope. With him was John Pascall, Allen's right hand in organizing the mission, his guide, his company during meals, his closest adviser. What Allen wanted to secure was the Pope's blessing and material support for sending priests secretly to England.

Eight days later, with Sledd in attendance upon his master Nicholas Morton and watching and listening carefully, Allen spoke to the guests he had invited to dine with him in the English College. Eighteen men were there. Sledd knew all of them by sight and a few more intimately, and later in his journal he recorded their names and physical descriptions. Two of the diners were Robert Persons, the young Jesuit priest whom Anthony Munday had known in the English College, and

William Allen's confidant John Pascall. But at the centre of everything and everyone was Doctor Allen himself, whose purpose that day was to rally the troops of the faith, to look to the recovery of England. In Allen – in his energy and political savvy, in his intellectual assurance – lay the future hope of their homeland's freedom.

Sledd remembered even the smallest physical features of the man who stood before them, in his late forties, tall and slim, with a reddish beard. The spy noted the wrinkles in his face, the small mole over his right eye, the way his long fingernails rose up at their tips. He absorbed every detail. Most importantly of all, Sledd remembered Doctor Allen's words.

Allen told them all how he had come to Rome at Pope Gregory's commandment and how generous Gregory had been in supporting the English seminaries in Rome and Rheims. Like the Englishmen in Rome, the Pope wanted to see their homeland restored to the Catholic faith. Allen 'thundered out in speech' the expedition to Ireland of Nicholas Sander, James Fitzmaurice and five hundred Spanish troops. The force they led to the Tudor kingdom of Ireland was a promise of the full invasion to come. Allen said that the Pope and other Catholic princes were prepared to do even more than this. And then he spoke of the English mission, the rescue of the kingdom from Protestant heresy, with Gregory's support and encouragement. Allen's speech must have been an extraordinary and moving one, revealing his persuasive power to inspire and to motivate. Six priests were recruited for the mission there and then. They were told to get themselves ready to leave for England by the end of the month.

Allen lost no time. Full of missionary zeal, he and John Pascall went to the Pope to tell him of the six priests and to ask Gregory for money to support the enterprise. They were given three hundred crowns. The priests, Sledd wrote, 'vaunted and boasted not a little in the city how they would hazard their lives for their country's sake'. Blessed by the Pope, the six men set off from Rome for England on the feast day of Saint Simon and Saint Jude, Wednesday, 28 October. Many more would eventually follow them. The new phase of the mission had begun.

In late November Nicholas Morton hosted a dinner for William Allen, John Pascall and other important Englishmen staying and living in

Rome. The dinner was a lively one, and politics was on everyone's minds. Sledd remembered that Doctor Allen was 'marvellous pleasant and he gave to rehearse what news he had heard out of England and Ireland of late'. Pascall was thrilled by the intelligence that he, Luke Kirby and others had heard, by letters smuggled from England, of the successes of Fitzmaurice's Spanish troops in Ireland. Pascall went even further: he was in 'good hope and would joy at his heart to see the Spaniards lords of England', till which time the land was in misery. Pascall wanted to have Queen Elizabeth 'shaked off her estate, which he hoped would not be long before the matter were put in execution'. Allen said that even more priests would be sent to England. His enthusiasm was growing all the time. The new recruits would leave Rome in the coming spring of 1580.

Many months later, William Allen heard about Sledd's account of this dinner. He was outraged, dismissing Sledd as a menial servant and calling him a liar. There was venom in Allen's response:

> As for Sledd's invention of conspiracy made in Doctor Morton's house, was it not very like that he should be made acquainted with the matter, being and living there as a poor knave ... begging of everybody, and known of nobody, and therefore trusted and used no farther of his master but in servile things.

But as William Allen surely knew, the best spies were often humble men. A servant, perhaps unseen and certainly often unacknowledged by his betters, was able to hear and see things other men could not. We can imagine the young Sledd obediently attending on his master's table with very sharp ears to hear.

After dinner on Sunday, 29 November Nicholas Morton met a priest, a chaplain to Cardinal Darrogone. The matter was a confidential one, but Sledd was listening and watching. He wrote that the two men had a scroll of paper upon which was written the names of leading English Catholic émigrés, soldiers and rebels. Sledd suspected here a great conspiracy, for according to his account Morton and the priest spoke of secret signatories and of three copies of a document, one to be kept by the Pope, the second sent to Spain and the third directed either to William Allen or to Sir Francis Englefield, one of the leading exiles in the Low Countries. According to Sledd, the documents recorded the agreements made by the Pope and King Philip of Spain to restore England to the Catholic faith. What Sledd had discovered, it seems, was a master plan for invasion and conquest.

Sledd's time in Rome was coming to an end, for he too was about to be sent back towards England in the company of Doctor Allen's missionary priests. This time Allen himself was travelling with the party back to Rheims. With him was his brother Gabriel, who spoke in a strong Lancashire accent, and whom Sledd clearly did not like: he called Gabriel Allen a clownish man. Sledd described the travellers with his usual precision. Humphrey Ely, who wore a short brown beard, was in his late thirties. Henry Orton, a lawyer, was about thirty years old and an excellent French speaker. Robert Johnson, a priest, was perhaps forty. He was slim, with an untrimmed flaxen yellow beard, a face full of wrinkles and two teeth missing from the right-hand side of his upper jaw. He spoke Italian fluently.

The Allen brothers and the priests bound for England, along with the quietly efficient Charles Sledd, set out on their long hard journey out of Italy after mass on the feast day of Saint Matthew, Thursday, 25 February 1580. They were in a lively mood. Sledd wrote that before supper on that first day Humphrey Ely spoke hard defamatory words against Elizabeth, 'Mistress Bess, Queen of England'. They would 'set her out for another Jezebel'. Elizabeth's tyranny would soon be at an end. Spirits were high.

Sledd and Robert Johnson moved ahead of the others. They left the main party at Siena on 28 February and arrived in Bologna on Friday, 4 March, where they were entertained by the Cardinal of Bologna and lodged in his palace. He gave them a private audience; they kissed his right hand; he gave them both a blessing 'stretching right two of his forefingers'. The cardinal asked them if they were travelling to England. Johnson answered for them both. Yes, he said, they were sent to England by the Pope to reconcile Queen Elizabeth and her people to the Catholic faith: it was His Holiness's pleasure to send priests to England secretly to persuade Catholics to resist her: Gregory was minded to deprive Elizabeth of her princely dignities, by either conspiring her death or supporting open rebellion and an invasion. Johnson told the cardinal that the missionary priests were messengers sent to prepare the ways and means. After all, Elizabeth was excommunicated already. The cardinal replied that he knew of the Pope's intentions 'for all such business as he meant secretly and openly to be be executed'. He wished for their happy success in converting queen and people. If repentance did not come quickly, he said, there would be great bloodshed.

On that Friday evening Sledd and Johnson enjoyed the cardinal's hospitality. They ate supper and had breakfast next morning. When they were about to leave on Saturday, William Allen and his companions arrived at the cardinal's palace. Allen once again instructed Johnson and Sledd to move ahead of the main party, directing them from Bologna to Milan to deliver letters. They were to wait for him in Turin.

The two men, priest and watcher, arrived in Milan on 11 March. They went to the Cardinal of Milan, at whose palace they met nine men and boys, some of them Englishmen, travelling to Rome. Sledd talked to one of the boys, a Londoner of about fifteen whose father had sent him to William Allen's seminary in Rheims, 'requesting them to send him to Rome if they pleased, to the college'. Sledd and Johnson went in the opposite direction, heading for home. Johnson was passionate in his mission: 'he cared not for any in England,' Sledd wrote, 'and they should well understand and also know in England that he would not creep in at a window, for he would go in at the broad door.'

By now William Allen was using Sledd as a courier to carry his letters. It was a task Sledd, like other Elizabethan spies, took to easily. He delivered Allen's letter in Milan and received one in return, and he was able to intercept two packets directed from Rheims. Four days later, on Tuesday, 15 March, Sledd and Johnson caught up with Allen and the others at Turin. Allen replied to the letter Sledd had brought him from Milan and Sledd took it to the Jesuit college in Turin to be posted.

With Sledd working as William Allen's messenger he and Johnson now fell behind the main party. It took the two companions exactly a week to travel from Turin to Chambéry in Savoy, not a surprise given the perilous journey over the Alps in late March. They would have gone over Mont-Cenis, the usual way for travellers on the post road to Lyons. They arrived in Chambéry on 22 March. There they were told that Allen and his companions had set out that day for Lyons, going by the most direct road west. This, they were advised, was a dangerous way to take; a Huguenot rebellion had broken out; they should go to Lyons by way of Lake Geneva, a much longer journey.

Johnson and Sledd ignored the warnings about the dangers of the direct road to Lyons. They arrived in the city only three days after leaving Chambéry, on Lady Day, Friday, 25 March. But they were still behind the main party. The rector of the Jesuit college in Lyons told them that Allen and his companions had set off only that morning for Rheims. He asked Johnson and Sledd to remain in Lyons for the rest of the day. He wanted them to continue their journey with a fellow countryman, a Jesuit novice of about thirty whose name was Thomas Cottam. Sledd described Cottam as a lean and slender man with red hair, a thin beard and a very freckled face. There was a wart or mole on his right cheek about an inch from his mouth.

Seven days after leaving Lyons the three men – Sledd, Johnson and Cottam – arrived in Troyes. After a hard journey of many hundreds of miles Robert Johnson and Charles Sledd were about to part company. Johnson and Thomas Cottam would go to Rheims. Sledd would travel to Paris. The three men set out in their different directions on Monday, 4 April 1580.

It was in the city of Paris that Sledd began in earnest his career as a spy for Elizabeth's government.

When Sledd arrived in Paris on Wednesday, 6 April 1580 he went straight to see Elizabeth's ambassador at the French court, Sir Henry Cobham. Cobham was a man in his early forties, the younger brother of a baron and by 1580 a diplomat of long experience. He would have been used to Englishmen like Sledd, without either invitation or credentials, turning up on his doorstep, just as he was alert to the activities of English Catholics in Paris. Perhaps Cobham was interested in Sledd's information: perhaps he was not. Probably it was a risk for Sledd to reveal himself to the ambassador: he was a pretty suspicious character. For both men it was bound to be a delicate encounter.

Put simply, Sledd's purpose was to betray the priests of William Allen's mission. He had the names of those who had already gone to England. He told Sir Henry that others would follow, some about to cross the English Channel, some shortly to set out from Rome. Sledd also possessed the physical descriptions of twenty of William Allen's recruits, 'their stature, favour and apparel'. He gave Cobham 'an inkling of their pretences' – a suspicion of their conspiracy.

Sledd came again to Sir Henry the next day, Thursday, 7 April. This time he brought letters of English Catholics, showing how useful he could be in intercepting packets of correspondence, trying to prove to Cobham his loyalty to the queen. Sledd picked up from Englishmen in Paris the news that three of the most important Elizabethan outlaws and exiles in Europe would arrive in the city soon. They were Sir Francis Englefield, Sir Thomas Copley and the northern rebel the Earl of Westmorland.

Sledd visited Sir Henry Cobham probably every day for a week. By now he had gathered up the letters of other Catholics, opening them in front of Sir Henry and reading them out loud. If Sledd hoped to impress Cobham with the news of a great conspiracy he was disappointed: they were simply letters of greeting between friends. But Sledd, after a week of trying to earn Sir Henry's trust, got his reward. Cobham told Sledd he wanted him to travel to England with some of Allen's priests. He gave the busy spy five French crowns and a Spanish pistolet to bear the charges of a journey to Rheims, as well as a private seal that Sledd could show to Sir Francis Walsingham, Elizabeth's secretary, as a secret token from the ambassador. Keen to protect himself, Sledd asked for a letter in Cobham's hand, or at least Sir Henry's signature on the papers he had written. He received neither; Sir Henry was wary. Yet Cobham wrote to the queen to inform her that he had been visited by a man lately come from Rome in the company of some priests. He said he would send the man's name by separate letter to Walsingham. And so he did, but Sledd was supremely protective of his own identity. The name he used was that of one of the men he had met in the rooms of an English Catholic in Paris. Cobham wrote to Walsingham: 'I send herewith the advertisement of Rowland Russell, written with his own hand. He is upon his return to England to render further testimony of his good meaning.'

Sledd went, as Sir Henry had directed him, to Rheims, carrying with him letters for William Allen from Paris. He arrived on Sunday, 17 April 1580. Allen asked him to dine in the seminary. After dinner he was invited to hear the sermon of an English priest called John Hart. He found Hart a little before three o'clock preparing to speak. All the English scholars gathered to hear a powerful and uncompromising cry in the battle to save English souls.

The theme of Hart's sermon was suffering for the faith and he began with the passions of Christ. To suffer pain, he said, was to merit salvation all the more. The Pope had appointed men to go into England to expel heresy from that kingdom. Hart said he would rather die than tolerate the heresies of Queen Elizabeth and her advisers. The Pope had excommunicated Elizabeth; the Tudor crown really belonged to Mary Queen of Scots, and for this reason, in support of the Catholic cause, the King of Spain would soon invade England. Those English men and women who could show they were Catholics would be safe: those who could not 'shall be searched and sifted out as the good corn is from the chaff and be put to the fire and sword'. The queen and her councillors would 'have such reward, as obstinate heretics ought to have, by the laws of God'. Hart ended his sermon by urging the congregation to stand firm in their faith. If they should die they died as martyrs. Every drop of their blood shed in the faith would raise ten Catholics.

That Sunday evening Sledd wrote to Sir Henry Cobham with a full report of what he had seen and heard. He wrote at length of John Hart. He had discovered that Hart was one of the priests closest to William Allen, often in his company and 'of his counsel', in good credit with the spiritual leader of English Catholics in exile.

By 20 April Sledd felt he 'could do no good' in Rheims and so he set out on the journey west to Paris. He arrived in the city two days later and that same evening went again to see Cobham. The following day Sledd asked Cobham to sign his papers. Sir Henry refused and Sledd left, knowing that he had outstayed Cobham's welcome, 'not minding to come to his honour any more after that'.

Sledd's work was done in Paris. He had given Sir Henry Cobham the names and descriptions of William Allen's priests. He had met Allen in Rheims and heard John Hart's sermon on England's rescue from Protestant heresy. Although Cobham refused to sign Sledd's papers – a sensible precaution for the ambassador – Sledd at least had a token he could show to Sir Francis Walsingham at Elizabeth's court.

There was now no place for Sledd the spy to go but to London.

5

Paris and London

There were two English spies in Paris in April and May 1580, the clever and elusive Charles Sledd, playing the part of a useful and humble courier of letters, and a man whose social pretensions were a good deal grander. His name was William Parry and for a number of years he had travelled in Italy and France. When Sir Henry Cobham dismissed Sledd and directed him to London, Master Parry was also using the queen's ambassador at the French court to send secret intelligence to Lord Burghley in England.

At the beginning Parry was a volunteer, writing in May 1577 to offer his service to Burghley. He was, he said, a traveller 'somewhat wearied with a long journey', and on those travels he had visited both Rome and Siena. He felt he could be useful to the lord treasurer. His letter to Burghley was an example of fine penmanship, for Parry wished to impress the most powerful man in Elizabeth's government with the elegance of his handwriting. Parry would have been relieved if he had been able to read the words Burghley's secretary used to endorse the packet: 'Master William Parry to my lord'. William Parry was a gentleman – a master, a man of 'worship', of land and status – and he strained every fibre of himself to prove it.

But that was not the whole of Parry's story and situation. He was a Welshman, born in Flintshire, but when is not quite certain. His early years are obscure, though he claimed a long gentlemanly lineage. He had problems with money. The modest marriage he made for land, to the widowed daughter of a Welsh knight, was not enough to meet his costs and so Parry sought employment and patronage. He was not too proud to borrow money at interest, nor was he shy about sending letters to Lord Burghley.

Parry sent a report to Burghley a week after Sledd's dismissal by Sir Henry Cobham. It was 1 May 1580. Parry had a confidence about him that day; he felt bold in the usefulness of his service, and he stressed his loyalty in the queen's cause against her Catholic enemies in Paris. 'My lord,' he wrote,

> the name and title of a true subject have been always so dear unto me, that I cannot but hold him and his religion for suspected that practiseth anything against Her Majesty, whose government and fortune have been no less comfortable to all good men at home, than strange and fearful to her enemies abroad.

Parry had opened up two ways of communicating with the lord treasurer from Paris. The first was by the ordinary post, carried by couriers across the English Channel, sending perfectly innocent letters to show anyone who might intercept them that there was nothing suspicious in his writing to Burghley. But he felt the 'best assured' way was to communicate by a second means. Parry was by now taking his confidential letters to Sir Henry Cobham to go in the ambassador's post, as he had done a week before. He was, he wrote with confidence, in credit with the best men of England and Scotland in Paris and Rome, 'by the hope conceived of my readiness and ability to serve them'. Exaggerated self-belief was a familiar mark of Parry's mercurial personality, writing of the English Catholics: 'I doubt not within few months to be well able to discover their deepest practices.' There was, of course, a price, though a reasonable one: a few trifling gifts for his new friends, 'rather of pleasure than price', to be sent to him from London. Parry, always conscious of his address, used to the Lord Treasurer of England plainer words than courtesy expected, and he knew it: 'As I said before, so I say again; if I be less ceremonious than I should be in writing unto you, I trust you will pardon me, who had rather serve you in deeds, than please you in words.' He would send the books Burghley requested from Paris – Burghley was a great bibliophile – but only those that should in his opinion 'be very necessary for divers respects'. He gave his letter a special mark and told Burghley that following letters would bear the same mark also.

And so on the first day of a new month in the spring of 1580

William Parry, confidently in charge, was feeling very happy indeed in the business of his spiery.

Of Sledd's whereabouts on the day William Parry wrote his letter to Lord Burghley it is impossible to say. Certainly he was somewhere in or near Paris. Did Parry know him? It seems somehow doubtful that Parry, dazzled by the brightness of his own talents and his high social contacts, would notice a man as menial as Charles Sledd. But if by some chance he did, then he may have known that Sledd, the trusted courier of the émigré Catholics, was once again off on his travels.

Sledd left Paris for the large provincial city of Rouen on 5 May and stayed there till Ascension Day, Thursday, the 12th. He was at the port of Dieppe on the 13th, where, blessed by the luck of favourable winds, he joined a ship straight away to sail for England. He had been very busy in Paris and Rheims and was even now in Rouen, noting the names and recording the conversations of English exiles and collecting or copying their letters. And so the poor servant of Nicholas Morton in Rome, the trusted courier for William Allen, the companion of Catholic priests, the English ambassador's informant and above all the spy, was at last ready to meet Sir Francis Walsingham.

Sledd's ship took a day to cross the English Channel, arriving in the bustling port of Rye on the evening of 15 May. Resting overnight, he set out for London the next day. He arrived in the city on Tuesday morning. He was now able to direct his energies quite differently: the watcher would become the pursuer. On the afternoon of the 17th he went to Elizabeth's court. He spoke first to one of Sir Francis Walsingham's private secretaries, Francis Mylles, and then he met Walsingham; we have to imagine the exchange of the secret token of Sir Henry Cobham's seal. It was a short meeting but to the point: Sledd wrote that 'he showed to his honour such business as I then thought meet'. Either at Walsingham's request or on his own initiative, Sledd began to write a long dossier of intelligence from the notes he had brought with him from Rome.

On the Tuesday Sledd had come to London, a priest and three nuns arrived also, helped and guided by a Catholic gentleman. Two days after his first interview with Walsingham, Sledd asked Richard Young, a Middlesex magistrate who became one of the keenest official pursuers of Catholic priests in London, for his help in arresting them. The law was plain enough. Anyone in England foolish enough to communicate on paper or by speech the belief that Elizabeth Tudor should not be queen, or that anyone else should be King or Queen of England, was, if convicted, guilty of high treason. Exactly the same was true of any of the queen's subjects who called her a heretic, a schismatic, a tyrant, an infidel or a usurper of the crown. If a priest sent by William Allen secretly to England avoided all talk of politics but in his pastoral work absolved anyone from obedience to the queen or reconciled them to what the law called the 'usurped authority of the See of Rome' by means of a papal bull or document, he was likewise guilty of treason. The obvious loophole in this act – that a priest who reconciled or absolved any of Elizabeth's subjects without using a bull or instrument from Rome might escape the law – was closed by a new statute in 1581. Four years after that it was made high treason for any Catholic priest – in the government's view, a stirrer of rebellion and sedition – to be in England. Yet even when Charles Sledd set to work hunting priests on the streets of London in 1580, his quarry, if captured, were certain to forfeit their liberty by being thrown into one of London's jails; they might be banished from England or they might be hanged. With the information he possessed, and now with official backing, Sledd was a dangerous man to be walking the streets of London and Westminster.

Sledd met Walsingham again on Thursday, 26 May. In a longer interview than the first, he presented Sir Francis with a paper he called 'the intelligence of the affairs of Englishmen in Rome, and other places'. He also brought to their meeting a long bulletin of foreign news and letters (or copies of letters) written by Catholic émigrés in Rome, Rheims, Milan, Paris and Rouen. As well as working with Justice Young to find priests hidden in London, he had been busy writing and preparing for the meeting. Sir Henry Cobham in Paris had sent on some of Sledd's information a few weeks earlier, but now the time had come for Sledd to reveal everything personally to Sir Francis.

Sledd's surviving dossier is an extraordinary compilation of facts. In a first part he set out the names of nearly three hundred English and Welsh Catholics abroad and the pensions they received from the Pope, as well as the physical descriptions of the priests he knew. The

Charles Sledd's dossier, with Edmund Campion's name inserted, and the identity of an informant on Campion's fellow Jesuit Robert Persons inked out.

second part was his diary of meetings, dinners, conversations and events in Rome and on his journey through Italy and France back to England. It is likely that he wrote it up in London from the notes he had kept abroad. The paper he used was French, made, as the watermarks show, by two different manufacturers. It was the kind of paper that Sledd could have bought for himself in London or have been given by one of Walsingham's staff. Sledd gave his dossier, at which he must have worked doggedly, a grand title. It runs on like the beginning of an essay:

A general discourse of the Pope's Holiness' devices invented and devised first by his English branches, enemies to this Her Majesty's royal estate, concluded and agreed on by his college of cardinals, with the aid of other princes adjoining to His Holiness, which doth pretend the disturbance of the Queen's Majesty and not without murders and many slanderous speeches, divided into several books.

The purpose of this title (which is typically Elizabethan in its ponderous style) was to impress upon Walsingham and his inner circle the significance of the intelligence Sledd had gathered and set out so carefully. One of Walsingham's staff, a clerk of the Privy Council called Robert Beale, gave it a simple abbreviated title, pointing to its significance for the government: 'Priests and seminaries beyond the seas'.

It was obvious that Sledd had produced the most complete reference work then available on Queen Elizabeth's enemies. He surely knew how important his dossier was. The English Catholic exiles of Bologna, Cambrai, Douai, Florence, Lyons, Milan, Naples, Padua, Rheims, Rouen and Venice, but above all Rome and Paris, were stripped bare. Working for months as the trusted courier of Catholic laymen and priests, he knew the names of the émigrés, something of their families, situations and circumstances and often what they looked like. He had a record of treasonous words spoken against Elizabeth and her government. Now his discourse was in the hands of Sir Francis Walsingham and his men, and Sledd had official support in making his investigations in London and Westminster. No wonder that for English Catholics Sledd quickly became one of the most hated and feared priest-hunters in England.

William Parry, still in Paris in June 1580, had nothing like Charles Sledd's fire and passion or Anthony Munday's talent for the printing press. He was a gentleman, discovering information about the English Catholic exiles of the city in his own leisured way, a spy who enjoyed dinners in the company of very important men. On 4 June 1580 he wrote to Burghley. The high prose style and the elegant penmanship were very much Parry's; so too was the seal, the small signet of a lion rampant he pressed into the dark-red wax.

Parry had information on the progress of the former Bishop of St Asaph in Wales, Thomas Goldwell, who had at last arrived in Rheims from Rome. Elderly and claiming ill health, he was a reluctant traveller, hardly filled with the missionary spirit to return to his homeland. Parry believed that Goldwell would either go back to Rome or stay in Rheims in the hope of better fortune.

William Parry's information was certainly useful. It corroborated

Sledd's intelligence and it helped Elizabeth's government to prepare for the coming of William Allen's missionary priests. But Parry was too keen to dabble in gossip and he was easily bored. He needed a serious project to keep himself busy. So when Charles Nevill, sixth Earl of Westmorland – the outlawed rebel who had raised an army against the queen in 1569 – arrived in Paris in the last week of June, Parry took it upon himself to reconcile Westmorland to Elizabeth. He was not invited to do this: indeed only William Parry, the gentleman spy who dined with the English exiles and dangerous foreign ambassadors and then wrote elegantly self-confident letters to Lord Burghley, had the nerve to set about the negotiations with such style and abandon. He sought to impress Burghley with his skills and subtlety. It was, as Parry's story will show very clearly, a dangerous game for him to play.

Anthony Munday, Charles Sledd, William Parry: three Elizabethan spies, three very different men. Each in his own way was elusive, well practised at keeping his own secrets hidden. Each left behind evidence of his activities in Rome and Paris: Munday his books and pamphlets, Sledd his intensely written dossier, and Parry his over-courteous letters to Lord Burghley. These documents say something about their personalities. Munday was the reluctant scholar, used to flouting authority. He was a skilled writer with a gift for telling exciting tales. He knew his audience and he could both enthral and horrify them with the secrets of his 'English Roman life'.

Sledd appears to have been a quiet and unassuming man, trusted as a responsible servant. That is precisely what made him so very dangerous. More than this, he was a plausible spy. His command of detail was devastating. No one could honestly hope to fabricate every detail of his extraordinary dossier and be able to fool Sir Francis Walsingham. This helps to explain why Catholic exiles as important as William Allen turned upon Sledd such venomous hatred. He was Judas; he betrayed absolutely. And yet did he betray for money? There is no obvious evidence that he became a wealthy man by writing his dossier or by hunting down priests in London. At best he probably scratched a living by relying on Walsingham's patronage. In fact, for someone so passionately driven in his official work in England, there is a curious absence of obvious motive. He opened his dossier of intelligence by stating that he had at the beginning set out on his travels 'desirous to learn languages and also to see the natural inclinations and dispositions of strange and foreign countries'. Any subject who left England without a passport from the queen said that, just as he also stated (as Sledd did) that he was a good Protestant. It was a very thin story, and it said nothing of why, after months of working as a servant in Rome, he turned so strongly against men he knew very well. Probably only Walsingham, in their interviews, got the full measure of Charles Sledd. Sir Francis was a penetrating student of human nature, especially human frailty.

William Parry's character may be easier to read. Parry, whose sense of his own importance could be overpowering, loved to dine grandly with knights, earls and ambassadors. He was a social climber and something of a snob, captivated by a life he could not afford to pursue without the dubious help of moneylenders. He lived dangerously on credit, hoping no doubt for Lord Burghley's generous patronage but never receiving it. In his life and in his spying he was, as later chapters of this book will show, perilously self-deluding. If ever there was an Elizabethan spy born for self-destruction, it was William Parry.

In the summer of the year 1580 Elizabeth's advisers watched and waited for the invasion of England by the powers of Catholic Europe. After all, the Pope and King Philip of Spain had already sent five hundred troops to Elizabeth's kingdom of Ireland under the command of James Fitzmaurice. When the force arrived at Smerwick in County Kerry, in the far south-west of Ireland, Nicholas Sander proclaimed a just war against the 'she-tyrant' Elizabeth. Fitzmaurice's men fortified an Atlantic promontory and called to Catholic Europe for reinforcements. That support never arrived. In September 1580 they were surrounded by the queen's troops and navy and, in spite of surrendering, all but twenty-three of Fitzmaurice's men were massacred. Sander survived to die more obscurely. Lord Burghley, sensing the work of providence, later wrote that 'wandering the mountains in Ireland without succor, [he] died raving in a frenzy'. Smerwick was utterly symbolic of a war that was fought with fierce hearts and courageous words but with few resources.

This was not the glorious Catholic crusade that Charles Sledd had heard William Allen celebrating in Rome months earlier. But in the summer of 1580 the queen's ministers were neither celebratory nor complacent. Sir Henry Radcliffe of Portsmouth, one of whose men had returned from a reconnaissance of the Spanish coast, sent news to the Privy Council that great naval preparations were being made in Spain. Other reports by travellers suggested military activity in the western Mediterranean. Surely a Spanish fleet was on the way to England.

The truth was, in fact, that in 1580 King Philip of Spain could not commit troops and ships to the invasion of England. He had neither the military resources, which were deployed elsewhere, nor really the inclination to depose Elizabeth. But in the perception of Elizabeth's government the danger was real and imminent. And perception in politics is a powerful thing. Sledd, and before him Anthony Munday, spoke to deep fears in England of political conspiracy in Rome. They showed something of the passion and organizing intelligence of the leading English exiles. Thanks to an intercepted letter, Elizabeth's government knew only too well the words Nicholas Sander had written in 1577 to William Allen: 'The state of Christendom dependeth upon the stout assaulting of England.' It was a sentence used over and over again by Elizabeth's advisers to justify a state of profound emergency.

And it is here, in the anxious days of July 1580, that we can begin to see how the espionage of Charles Sledd and William Parry and Anthony Munday's lively books influenced the most powerful men in England. At the very least they helped to create and sustain a political mood, though in the case of Sledd the evidence is even stronger: his dossier, presented to Sir Francis Walsingham and filed safely away for reference in the royal secretariat, was hugely significant. Munday's revelations of Roman conspiracy may have been gently encouraged by the authorities. It was very easy for Elizabeth's Privy Council to suppress books it found inconvenient and through long-established relationships with London's printers to support certain writers. There was much of what Sledd and Munday had discovered in the royal proclamation published in July to suppress dangerous rumours of an invasion and to reveal to honest subjects 'the traitorous and malicious purposes and solicitations' of rebels living abroad. The proclamation was written by Lord Burghley, who, as ever, paid careful attention to his words, labouring over the text of the proclamation, working to achieve precision. He defended Elizabeth's rule as queen and her resolve to withstand her enemies; on this last point she expected her subjects to do the same. The proclamation speaks to the experience of Sledd, of those quiet observations, of the reports of malicious conspiracy believed by powerful men in Westminster. Joined to rebels and traitors already living in foreign parts were

> others that are fled out of the realm as persons refusing to live here in their natural country, both which of long time have wandered from place to place, and from one prince's court to another, but especially to the city of Rome, and therein have falsely and traitorously sought and practised by all means possible to irritate all estates against Her Majesty and the realm, and therewith as much as in them might lie to move hostility, wherein by God's goodness and special favour to this realm their designs have been hitherto frustrate.

This is what both Anthony Munday and Charles Sledd had perceived in Rome. The strands of their experiences and narratives could be woven together to make a taut cord of treason. To the readers of Munday's books and for those few Sir Francis Walsingham trusted to read Sledd's dossier, any talk by William Allen or his confederates of an innocent holy mission to save souls was nonsense. In their minds Allen and his agents had a single political objective: to destroy Elizabeth's Church, to bring down her government and to push her forcibly from her throne.

This was war. Allen himself, explaining the nature of the mission, wrote of it in those terms, though he meant not a war waged by armies for political control but one fought by priests for English souls. It was clear to Elizabeth's advisers in 1580 that the danger came not only from Spanish troops and sailors or the Pope's money for an invasion, though that danger felt very real. Thanks to the intelligence given by Sledd, the English authorities waited for the priests from Rome and Rheims. They were the agents of foreign powers, conspirators, stirrers of sedition and rebellion. They were traitors. Sledd's dossier undoubtedly helped to catch some of them. Robert Johnson and the lawyer Henry Orton, with whom Sledd had travelled from Rome, were arrested within weeks of returning to England. John Hart, who had preached the incendiary sermon Sledd had heard in Rheims, was picked up as soon as he landed at Dover. He was taken first to the royal court at Nonsuch Palace and then to the grim Marshalsea prison in Southwark. Johnson, Orton and Hart were early casualties of a very dangerous mission.

In June 1580 the Jesuit priests Robert Persons and Edmund Campion waited to cross from France to England. They had followed in the footsteps of Sledd on the roads from Rome. Campion was forty years old, a former scholar of Oxford University and a teacher at William Allen's seminary at Douai. In 1573 he had gone to Rome on foot to become a Jesuit, and then taught philosophy and rhetoric in Moravia and Bohemia before being called by Allen to Rome in 1580 for service in England. Now, preparing to sail across the English Channel, he disguised himself as a jeweller of Dublin. It was an effective cover, for Campion had spent a little time in the city. Persons, whom Anthony Munday had known in the English College, went first, dressed as a captain of soldiers: it was an extrovert gesture worthy of Munday himself. When Campion knew that Persons had crossed safely, Campion followed him.

For Campion it was a close-run thing. He came within a whisker of disaster. The searcher of Dover, the official whose job it was to check incoming ships and their passengers, had special orders to look out for Gabriel Allen, Doctor Allen's brother, who was understood to be travelling home to Cumberland. The mayor of Dover had a description of Allen, surely provided by Charles Sledd: about forty-five years of age, 'of reasonable stature', with a flaxen-coloured beard. At first the mayor believed Campion to be Allen. But then without explanation he set the Dublin jeweller free. He must have been unsure. Sledd's description of Gabriel Allen was after all pretty meagre, or perhaps another ship had arrived carrying other likely suspects. Whatever the reason, at Dover Campion had a very lucky escape. He and

Persons were now free, for the time being, able to disappear into the Catholic underground of London. In its desperate efforts to track them down, Elizabeth's government began to chase shadows.

Neither Munday nor Sledd had ever met Edmund Campion, and it seems very unlikely that Sledd knew what he looked like. Sledd may have heard rumours, of course, though he made no report of ever having talked about Campion in Rheims, Paris or Rouen. True, Campion's significance was not yet clear. He was, like Persons, one of a number of missionary priests whose secret work in England would be immensely dangerous. But Edmund Campion, pursued for many months by the Elizabethan authorities and only captured by chance, would soon become the most powerful symbol of William Allen's war for souls.

6

Hunting Edmund Campion

Robert Persons and Edmund Campion took their own safety very seriously. They moved around England, meeting only occasionally. The risks, as Campion had experienced for himself at Dover, were high. In late June 1580 Campion preached in secret at Smithfield in London. A fortnight later he and Persons met other Catholic priests for a conference in Southwark, south of the Thames at London Bridge, in the shadow of the Marshalsea prison and within sight of the Tower. Under the noses of the authorities, Campion also set out on paper the aims of William Allen's mission as he saw them.

Campion wrote his statement as one of personal intent. 'My charge,' he said, 'is of free cost to preach the Gospel, to minister the Sacraments, to instruct the simple, to reform sinners, to refute errors, and, in brief, to cry alarm spiritual against foul vice and proud ignorance, wherewith my poor countrymen are abused.' He explained that his Jesuit superiors strictly forbade him 'to deal in any respect with matters of state or policy of this realm, as those things that appertain not to my vocation'. The Society of Jesus, he wrote, had made a league (that is, an agreement) to carry any cross that Elizabeth's government chose to lay upon its priests 'and never to despair your recovery, while we have a man left to enjoy your Tyburn, or to be racked with your torments, or to be consumed with your prisons'. 'The expense is reckoned,' he wrote, 'the enterprise is begun; it is of God, it cannot be withstood. So the faith was planted, so it must be restored.'

The letter was beautifully composed, poised and articulate, an elegant statement of belief and mission – so much so, in fact, that it instantly outgrew its original purpose. Campion prepared the letter for Elizabeth's Privy Council, to be sent only in the event of his capture. The fact he left it unsealed meant that very quickly copies of it began to circulate, passing secretly between English Catholics. Campion's defence was, after all, a crafted weapon to be used in an extraordinary propaganda war. By October 1580 Robert Persons and a printer called Stephen Brinkley had set up a secret printing press a few miles out of London. Later, because of the danger of discovery, Brinkley and his assistants had to move it to a house in Oxfordshire. So Persons and Campion were able to speak to English Catholics in books secretly printed, bought and borrowed, while the two Jesuits, with other priests, moved around England to preach, say mass and hear confessions.

John Hart, the passionate preacher Charles Sledd had heard in Rheims and now a prisoner, was moved from the Marshalsea to the Tower of London at Christmas 1580. There he joined Sledd's former companions Robert Johnson, Thomas Cottam, Ralph Sherwin and Henry Orton. Luke Kirby, the friend of Anthony Munday at the English College in Rome, was held in the Tower also. The four priests and Orton had been there since 4 December.

The Elizabethan antiquary John Stow described how the Tower of London was at once 'a citadel, to defend or command the city', a royal palace, a 'prison of estate, for the most dangerous offenders', a royal mint, an armoury, a treasury for the queen's jewels and an archive for the courts of justice at Westminster. A contemporary of Stow's wrote that the judicial purpose of the Tower was 'to discover the nature, disposition, policy, dependency, and practice' of offenders against the queen. The priests and other prisoners were guarded by thirty yeoman warders under the authority of a lieutenant, Sir Owen Hopton, a man of about sixty who had been in post for ten years.

The Tower of London was surrounded by a wide moat fed by the River Thames. Rising high above every other building was the White Tower, built by William the Conqueror in the eleventh century. Great defensive walls ran between the various towers and gates. St Thomas's Tower stood over the water gate to the Thames, near the wharf dividing the moat from the river. In the inner ward between the Beauchamp Tower and the Devereux Tower was the church of St Peter ad Vincula. Near the lieutenant's lodging, which was in the south-east corner of the inner ward, stood the Bell Tower. Close to that was the main gate, from which one crossed the moat to the Middle Tower, on to the Lion Tower, and out to the city of London. Anyone lucky enough to be able to leave the fortress when the bell rang went from the Lion Tower through the bulwark gate and on to Tower Hill, looking north to the executioner's scaffold and east to Tower Street. Prisoners were often kept in the Beauchamp, Broad Arrow, Salt and Well Towers. Those who could not pay for their own lodging, fuel and candles were supported by the crown. Owen Hopton carefully kept and signed the accounts. Prisoners often carved their names into the stone of the walls. One man, James Typpyng, left an inscription in the Beauchamp Tower: 'Typpyng stand or be well content and bear thy cross for thou art [a] sweet good Catholic but no worse'. Cottam, Hart, Johnson, Orton and Sherwin, kept in close confinement and frequently interrogated, left no marks on the walls of their chambers.

The priests were questioned about their loyalty and allegiance. The official record of what Ralph Sherwin said in his examination on 12 November 1580 is short, even blunt. Did he believe Pope Pius V's bull of excommunication against the queen to be lawful? Sherwin refused to answer the question. Was Queen Elizabeth his lawful sovereign, and should she continue to rule in spite of the Pope? Sherwin would not say. This interrogatory was put to him a second time. Knowing that he risked a charge of high treason for his answer, he prayed not to be asked any question that put him in danger. To Sherwin, in fear of his life, the questions were obvious traps in which he was caught however he answered. To his interrogators, the priest refused to answer plain questions about his loyalty as the queen's subject. They drew their own conclusions.

Not surprisingly, the priests' interrogators returned again and again to Pope Pius V's bull *Regnans in excelsis*, of 1570, by which Pius had denounced Queen Elizabeth as a bastard heretic schismatic and excommunicated her from the Catholic Church. John Hart was questioned about the bull. His interrogators knew that Pope Gregory, who supported the priests' mission to England, had confirmed Pius's bull. They knew, too, that only a few months earlier, in April 1580, Gregory himself had given the 'faculties' of this confirmation to Robert Persons and Edmund Campion in Rome.

Hart told his interrogators that Pius's bull was still lawful. But he explained that Gregory had understood the difficulty faced by English Catholics who were caught between a Pope who commanded them not to obey the queen and their loyalty to Elizabeth. As Hart put it: 'if they obey her, they be in the Pope's curse, and [if] they disobey her, they are in the Queen's danger'. And so Pope Gregory's dispensation allowed Elizabeth's Catholic subjects to obey her without putting their souls in peril. For Catholics this was potentially the untying of a very difficult knot. Significantly, however, Elizabeth's government did not see Pope Gregory's dispensation as any relaxation of *Regnans in excelsis*. In fact they took Gregory's action as proof that Persons and Campion had been charged to enforce Pius's bull against someone whom the Pope believed to be a heretic queen. Whatever they might say about their pastoral work as priests, as agents of the Pope their object (in the view of Elizabeth's government) was a political one.

On 31 December 1580, when he spoke of Pope Gregory's dispensation for English Catholics, John Hart was threatened with torture. Otherwise he, like Ralph Sherwin, may have chosen silence as the best course. Hart was taken to see the rack, the principal instrument of torture in the Tower, a large frame containing three wooden rollers to which the prisoner was bound by his ankles and wrists. The rack's purpose, simply and terribly, was to stretch the human body until it began to tear apart. The middle roller, which had iron teeth at each end, acted as a kind of controlling lock. This meant that the prisoner could be questioned while experiencing a constant amount of pain. It was probably a fairly simple device for even one man to operate. A number of officials, called commissioners, were present when a prisoner was tortured, of whom the lieutenant of the Tower was always one. Sometimes a clerk of the Privy Council would attend, often the man who had brought the torture warrant from the Council to the Tower. Lawyers, with their skills of taking and evaluating evidence, also served as commissioners.

Many Elizabethans would have associated torture with the terrible practices of the Spanish inquisition, or the Catholic persecution of Mary I. John Foxe's great 'Book of Martyrs', *Acts and monuments*, had one woodcut of the racking of a Protestant prisoner in Mary's reign. But the use of torture by Elizabeth's government became common in the 1580s. Some principles of its use were set out in a short pamphlet printed by the royal printer in 1582. The author of this official defence of torture was Thomas Norton, a London lawyer in his early fifties called so often to the Tower to interrogate priests on the rack that his enemies gave him the nickname 'Rackmaster Norton'. Three of Norton's principles were that a prisoner was only ever tortured on the authority of a warrant signed by at least six members of the Privy Council; that no one was tortured for his faith or conscience; and that only a guilty man was ever put to torment. Norton's Catholic enemies hardly believed him. William Allen recounted the supposed exchange between Norton and John Hart in the racking chamber:

> And when Master Hart was taken from the rack, the commissioners talking with him after a familiar manner: Norton asked him, saying, 'Tell truly, Hart, what is the meaning of the coming in of so many

The title page of Thomas Norton's public defence of torture, 1583.

priests into England?' Who answered, 'To convert the land again to her first Christian faith and religion, by preaching and peaceable persuasion, after the manner that it was first planted.' To which Norton said: 'In my conscience, Hart, I think thou sayest truth.'

Allen's words suggest something of the sharpness and seriousness of the ideological clash between Elizabeth's government and its Catholic enemies.

For Elizabeth's government priests like John Hart were agents of a foreign power whose object was to remove a lawful monarch from her throne. They were traitors, and their torture was a necessary act of state. Thomas Norton wrote that no man 'was tormented for matter of religion, nor asked what he believed of any point of religion, *but only to understand of particular practices for setting up their religion by treason or force against the Queen*'. The words in emphasis are critical: the full force of the law was being used against the *means* by which the Catholic faith was going to be brought back to England – by sedition, rebellion and invasion – and not against the faith itself. Catholic writers like Doctor Allen responded that this was simply a lie: theirs was a pastoral mission to save the souls of English Catholics in the face of vicious persecution, with the hope of turning England away from heresy and schism. Catholics likened Elizabeth's government to the authorities of ancient Rome who had persecuted early Christians, calling the queen's ministers 'atheists' and 'politiques'.

By early 1581 Edmund Campion's brilliant and articulate defence of his mission was being read and passed around by people sympathetic to the Catholic cause. The authorities called it 'Campion's brag'. It was a formidably persuasive, even an incendiary, piece of writing. One case reported to the justices of Southampton, and by them in turn to the Council, illustrates how influential it was. One William Pittes was alleged to have said that 'great cruelty was used at this present by imprisoning of good men, whom he termed Catholics, affirming the prisons to be full of them in every place'. He thought Elizabeth 'was deceived, and erred from the true faith'. His daily prayer was to bring her to the Catholic faith. Pittes asked a man called Lichepoole whether he had seen a copy 'of a challenge made by one Campion'.

Lichepoole had not, so Pittes 'immediately pulled out of his purse the copy of the said challenge, and read it unto the said Lichepoole, promising him a copy of the same'. The copy was made and delivered as Pittes had promised. This was the power of Edmund Campion's pen: he was proving a skilled and elusive general in the long war for hearts and minds, and a formidable enemy to Elizabeth and her government.

So dangerous, in fact, was 'Campion's brag' that it had to be answered officially. Here Elizabeth's government ran the obvious danger of making Campion's letter even more widely known and read than it was already, but this was a risk the authorities were willing to take. One pamphlet was by William Charke, a combative Protestant controversialist, and it came off the press of Christopher Barker, the queen's printer, on 17 December 1580. Charke wrote of Campion's 'insolent vaunts against the truth, joined with words pretending great humility'. Another attack came a month later from an Oxford theologian called Meredith Hanmer. He too exposed Campion's deceit, 'where one thing is said in word, and the contrary found in practice and deed'. Campion, he wrote, had set the mother against her own son, the son to take armour against his father, the subject against the prince: 'He hath deposed kings and emperors, he translated [altered] empires, he treads upon princes' necks, he takes sceptres and crowns from kings' heads, and trampleth them under foot.'

The fierceness of the attacks by Charke and Hanmer shows that Campion had the power to make his words felt, even if he himself could not be found. And all the time the temperature of the debate was rising. On 10 January 1581 a royal proclamation ordered the return of all English students from foreign seminaries and the arrest of all Jesuits in England. The intent and purpose of the seminaries, it said, was to pervert the queen's subjects in matters of religion and 'from the acknowledgement of their natural duties unto Her Majesty'. Young English Catholics had been made 'instruments in some wicked practices tending to the disquiet of this realm . . . yea to the moving of rebellion'. A new law made it high treason for a priest to absolve Elizabeth's subjects from their obedience to the queen and to reconcile them to Rome, even without a bull or other document from the Pope.

Laws like this so well expressed the sense of emergency and danger gripping Elizabeth's ministers. Their consequence was that political loyalty to crown and government became impossible to disentangle from loyal worship in the Church of England. This was why the words of William Pittes concerning the cruelty used against Catholics and his prayer for Elizabeth's conversion to the Catholic faith were overtly political. What Pittes said and did was described by the justices of Southampton as a 'matter of offence against the state' and government. Pittes survived his brush with the authorities. He may even have been the same William Pittes who in 1584 went off to William Allen's seminary in Rheims. Was he inspired by Campion? To Elizabeth's advisers the priests both in London's prisons and at large – and potentially also ordinary Catholics throughout England – presented a clear danger. Disturbingly persuasive, men like Campion were political agents of a dangerous and obviously hostile foreign power.

Not surprisingly, Campion was sought with ever-increasing urgency. He was always moving, always in disguise. He wrote in a letter: 'I am in apparel to myself very ridiculous. I often change it and my name also.' Between Christmas 1580 and Easter 1581 he travelled through Nottinghamshire, Derbyshire, Yorkshire and Lancashire. At the end of March 1581 he delivered a manuscript to Stephen Brinkley's printing press in Oxfordshire. Campion called it *Rationes decem* (*Ten Reasons*) and in it he set out Catholic faith and tradition. On 27 June four hundred copies of this very slim pamphlet were laid out on the benches of St Mary's church in Oxford for the scholars to read on the day they gathered to defend their theses. Done right under the noses of the authorities of his old university, it was an audacious publicity coup for Campion. Elizabeth's government was deeply unsettled. The priests were being pursued with energy and urgency. Eleven days before the scholars of Oxford read Campion's *Ten Reasons*, Robert Persons wrote secretly from London to the rector of the English College in Rome that 'Sledd is on our track more than others, for he has authority from the royal council to break into all men's houses as he will and to search all places, which he does diligently, wherever there is a gleam of hope of booty.'

Some time after Midsummer 1581 Maliverey Catilyn, one of Sir Francis Walsingham's agents, was posing as a good Catholic some-

A Catholic view of Elizabethan persecution by Richard Verstegan, 1592: lay Catholics and a priest are arrested and imprisoned.

where near the Sussex coast. Catilyn's speciality, as the coming years would show, was to go into prisons to spy on inmates, reporting their plots, schemes and conversations. His world was the Catholic underground, where he was well connected and trusted.

Catilyn explained to Walsingham by letter that he had met some bad men, yet one now came to travel with him 'who exceedeth all the rest'. The man, whose name he did not give, 'greatly pitied my case': presumably Catilyn, playing the poor Catholic, had told him a tale of woe. The man was careful, and he had refused to talk to Catilyn in the busy port town of Portsmouth. He was a sailor or the owner of a boat. He had been in France at Christmas, and in March 1581 he had brought back to England a priest called John Adams. Adams, as Catilyn knew, had been arrested at Rye and sent to Walsingham to be examined. The man had a brother (or a brother-in-law) 'on the other side' who called himself Richard Thomas but whose real name was Gyles Whyte, from whom, Catilyn wrote, 'he receiveth letters and books for his friends three or four times every year and they see things are conveyed to another brother that he hath dwelling with a merchant at Billingsgate called Cox'. On his last journey Catilyn's new contact had brought back to England three Agnus Deis, small cakes of wax stamped with the symbol of the lamb of God and blessed by the Pope. One was for the shipmaster's wife, the second was for his mother and the third was for his sister. At Midsummer he had helped another priest to land secretly in England at Stokes Bay near Portsmouth, and given him directions on what course he should take. He also had in his keeping, Catilyn wrote, some jewels belonging to Edmund Campion: Campion, after all, had come into England disguised as a Dublin jeweller.

Maliverey Catilyn apologized to Walsingham for having to end his letter quickly. His new contact was near by. 'He is here with me,' Catilyn wrote, 'and therefore I think your honour would do well to see him.' Catilyn pardoned his scribbling. His companions, he said, 'cry to me for speed', for they wanted to be in London that night, 'and for the avoiding of suspicion I dare not be tedious'.

In early July Edmund Campion and Robert Persons were in Oxfordshire. On Tuesday, 11 July they parted. Campion and a fellow priest set out north for Lancashire. They would then travel to Norfolk. Persons and his man set off towards London, but before long Persons heard Campion galloping after him with a request to go instead to Lyford Grange in Berkshire, the house of Master Francis Yates, a prisoner in Reading jail, who had written to Campion to ask him to visit his family. Persons reluctantly agreed to Campion's detour, but he instructed him to stay at Lyford Grange for no more than a day, or one night and a morning. Campion did just that. The mistake he made was to return to the Grange a day later.

This was on 14 July, a Friday, the same day that two royal officials left London. Their names were David Jenkins and George Eliot and they carried a warrant 'to take and apprehend, not any one man, but all priests, Jesuits, and such like seditious persons' that they should meet on their journey. They had decided to ride to Lyford Grange, a known Catholic house, where they thought they might discover priests. They wanted to arrive there at about eight o'clock on the morning of Sunday the 16th.

Jenkins was a pursuivant, a messenger of the queen's chamber. Wearing Her Majesty's livery, pursuivants executed warrants from the queen and her Privy Council. In the 1580s they were busy hunting for priests in London and putting Catholic recusants in prison. At times it was a dangerous job for which some pursuivants found financial compensation in bribery and corruption, either paid for letting people go or seizing the money of those they arrested. With men like Charles Sledd working with the pursuivants, they did not enjoy a high reputation.

The same could be said of George Eliot, Jenkins's companion on their journey to Lyford Grange, who called himself by the grand title of 'yeoman of Her Majesty's chamber'. He had recently recanted his Catholic faith, confessing 'the grievous estate of his life' to one of Elizabeth's most trusted and senior advisers, the Earl of Leicester. Eliot offered evidence of his good will. This was information, for having served in Catholic gentry houses in Essex and Kent, he was able to name names. Eliot did what Sledd had done in Rome, though less comprehensively: he compiled a catalogue of every Catholic gentleman and gentlewoman he knew in eight counties in England.

Eliot did something else which was irresistible in the emergency years of the early 1580s: he revealed the existence of a terrible conspiracy against Elizabeth and her ministers. Eliot told the Earl of Leicester of a plot to murder the queen and her leading councillors. He said that behind it all was a priest called John Payne, trained at Douai and ordained a priest in 1576, whom Eliot had known in Essex. Chief names were those of the Earl of Westmorland, rebel and outlaw, and William Allen. The plan was for fifty armed men, all paid for by the Pope, to assassinate Elizabeth while she was touring her kingdom on progress. Five men would kill the queen, while three groups of four would 'destroy' Leicester, Lord Burghley and Sir Francis Walsingham. Leicester gave the paper to Burghley, who calmly noted in the margin 'Payne to be examined'. Eliot also had information on how Catholic books were being sold secretly by two bookbinders in Paul's Cross churchyard. True or not, Eliot spoke to the anxiety of the moment. London was buzzing with news of books and pamphlets by and against the Jesuits. Eliot was believed, and by the early summer he set to work to infiltrate Catholic families he had not long before served.

Eliot was sure that he and Jenkins would find priests concealed at Lyford Grange. Thomas Cooper, whom Eliot had known in Kent, was Master Yates's cook at Lyford. Through Cooper they could enter the Grange without causing suspicion. Once in the house, they would conduct a search. Their plan was as simple as that. They had no idea that they would find at Francis Yates's house the most wanted man in England.

Jenkins and Eliot arrived at Lyford Grange on Sunday, 16 July at about eight in the morning, just as they planned. They found outside the gates of the house a servant who seemed to Eliot 'to be as it were a scout watcher'. Eliot spoke to the servant, asking after Thomas Cooper, who came out to meet him and Jenkins. Eliot told Cooper a tale. He said that he was travelling into Derbyshire to see friends but had come far out of his way to Lyford because he longed to see him. Cooper invited him to the buttery for a drink. The cook asked Eliot about his friend, Jenkins, 'whether . . . he were within the Church or not, therein meaning whether he were a papist or no'. Eliot answered that Jenkins was not a Catholic, but that he was a very honest man. Leaving Jenkins in the buttery, Cooper took Eliot through the hall, the dining parlour and other rooms to a 'fair large chamber'. There he found three priests, of whom one was Edmund Campion. Also in the room were three Brigitine nuns (not as politically dangerous as priests but still illegal) and thirty-seven other Catholics. Eliot, committing to memory the faces and clothes of members of the congregation, heard Campion say mass. Then Campion sat down in a chair beneath the altar to give a sermon that lasted for nearly an hour, 'the effect of his text being, as I remember, that Christ wept over Jerusalem etc. and so applied the same to this our country of England, for that the Pope his authority and doctrine did not so flourish here as the said Campion desired'.

At the end of Campion's sermon Eliot rushed down to find Jenkins in the buttery. He told Jenkins what he had seen, and they both left the house to summon help. They found it in the person of a local justice of the peace called Master Fettiplace, to whom they showed their commission. Within a quarter of an hour Fettiplace had gathered forty or fifty armed men, who went off with speed to Lyford Grange.

It was at about one o'clock in the afternoon when they knocked at the gates. They were kept waiting for half an hour. At last there appeared Mistress Yates, five gentlemen, one gentlewoman and three nuns. The nuns were now dressed as gentlewomen, but Eliot remembered their faces. The gates were opened, and Eliot, Jenkins and the other men began to search the house, in which they found 'many secret corners', and also in the densely planted orchards and hedges and the ditches of the Grange's moat. The searchers discovered Francis Yates's younger brother hiding in a pigeon house with two companions. But they could not find Campion and the two other priests. It was nearly evening when Eliot realized they needed more help, and so he sent messages to the high sheriff of Berkshire and another local justice of the peace. The sheriff could not be found, but the justice, Master Wiseman, came quickly with ten or twelve of his servants, and the search continued into the night.

Early on Monday morning, the 17th, further help arrived. Christopher Lydcot, a third Berkshire justice, came to Lyford Grange with a large group of his own men. At ten o'clock the priests had still not been found. But the persistence of the searchers paid off, and it was David Jenkins the pursuivant who 'espied a certain secret place which he found to be hollow'. With a metal spike he broke a hole in the wall, 'where then presently he perceived the said priests, lying all close together upon a bed, of purpose there, laid for them, where they had bread, meat, and drink, sufficient to have relieved them, three or four days'. In a loud voice Jenkins called out, 'I have found the traitors.'

Campion and his fellow priests were put under heavy guard. Along with six gentlemen and two husbandmen they were taken from Lyford Grange to Abingdon on Thursday, 20 July, and to Henley upon Thames the following day. At Henley, Eliot, Jenkins, Master Lydcot and Master Wiseman received instructions from the Privy Council to stay at Colnbrook, about twenty miles west of London, on Friday night, the 21st. They entered London on Saturday, processing through the city to the gate of the Tower of London, where Campion and the others were put into the custody of its lieutenant, Sir Owen Hopton. Eyewitnesses told Robert Persons, still secretly in England, that Campion was mounted upon a very tall horse with his hands tied behind his back, and his feet strapped together under the horse's belly. An inscription was put round his head: 'Edmund Campion, the seditious Jesuit'.

There was a rush to the printing press. One printer lost no time at all, going to the Bishop of London and the Stationers' Company for a licence to print a pamphlet called 'Master Campion the seditious Jesuit is welcome to London'. He paid four pence for the licence, which he received on 24 July, by which time Edmund Campion had been in the Tower for barely forty-eight hours. Within days the enterprising Anthony Munday, that young man who had lived in the English College in Rome but knew nothing of Edmund Campion, rushed into print with a breathless (and as it turned out wholly inaccurate) account of Campion's capture, in which Master Jenkins the pursuivant and the sheriff of Berkshire were the heroes. We can imagine eager customers visiting William Wright's shop next to St Mildred's church in the Poultry – 'the middle shop in the row' – to buy Munday's story fresh from the press.

To Catholic writers Campion's story was a heroic tale of martyrdom, sacrifice and persecution. William Allen called it a 'marvellous tragedy . . . containing so many strong and divers acts, of examining, racking, disputing, treacheries, proditions [treasons or treacheries], subornations of false witnesses, and the like'. Allen's mission to save England from heresy and Catholics from their persecutors became the subject of sharp exchanges between Campion's friends and enemies. One of the most energetic of these writers was Anthony Munday, who, after recognizing the mistakes of his first account of Campion's capture, collaborated with George Eliot in writing and publishing the definitive account. Eliot had come to Munday's lodgings in the Barbican and had written and then signed a statement of what had really happened. In these months – between July 1581 and April 1582 – Munday busily answered Doctor Allen's powerful books and pamphlets. Munday, the spy turned writer, relished every encounter with the Catholic enemy.

In fact the characters of Munday and his fellow intelligencers, Charles Sledd and George Eliot, were very much tied up with the story of Edmund Campion's capture. Reputations were at stake; the truth was contested. Both sides in this battle – Allen in Rheims, in London Munday, with Sledd and Eliot forced out of the shadows –

fought to establish the facts as they saw them. Everything they wrote crackled with the powerful electricity of belief and emotion, blurring fact and fiction. There were, for example, two published accounts of what Campion had said to George Eliot in the days of the journey from Lyford Grange to the Tower of London. Eliot's version hinted strongly at a threat to his own life:

> Campion when he first saw me after his apprehension, said unto me, that my service done in the taking of him would be unfortunate to me. And in our journey towards the Tower, he advised me to get me out of England for the safety of my body.

Was it then a coincidence that Eliot had fallen sick at his lodgings in Southwark? The goodwife of the house in which he was staying knew nothing about her lodger till a Catholic widow told her that it was Eliot who had arrested Campion. He wrote that 'the papists take great care for me, but whether it be for my weal or woe ... let the world judge'. Eliot believed that he was a marked man.

Allen's account of what Edmund Campion said and how he behaved was very different to Eliot's recollection. Already he was making Campion a model of Catholic patience and forgiveness in the face of terrible persecution. Allen would have had very little idea of what really passed between Eliot and Campion on the journey from Lyford Grange to London. His words were meant instead as an inspiration for Catholics:

> Eliot said unto him, 'Master Campion, you look cheerfully upon every body but me; I know you are angry with me in your heart for this work.'
>
> 'God forgive thee Eliot', said he, 'for so judging of me: I forgive thee, and in token thereof I drink to thee, yea, and if thou wilt repent and come to confession I will absolve thee: but large penance thou must have.'

7

Out of the Shadows

Three other priests were taken with Edmund Campion from Lyford Grange to the Tower of London. One of them, John Collerton, carved a record of his imprisonment in the wall of the Beauchamp Tower: 'John Colle[r]ton, Pri[e]st, 1581, July 22'. Another, Thomas Ford, a Devonshire man ordained at Brussels in 1573, had been working secretly in England since 1576. William Filby, the third of Campion's companions, had dreamed at Henley upon Thames of his execution. Waking the house with 'a very great cry and noise' in his sleep, he told Justice Lydcot that 'he verily thought one to be ripping down his body and taking out his bowels'. It was for Filby an accurate premonition.

On 26 July Campion was taken to York House in Westminster, the residence of the lord chancellor, where he was examined by a group of privy councillors. Like other priests under questioning he chose silence over confession. Within days, the Council appointed four commissioners to interrogate him thoroughly. They were Sir Owen Hopton and Robert Beale (a clerk of the Privy Council) as well as two lawyers, John Hammond and Thomas Norton (the same Norton who later wrote the government's official defence of torture). The Council's instructions to the commissioners were clear. They were to examine Campion under oath on his loyalty to the queen. To save time and trouble he would be allowed to swear upon a copy of the Catholic Vulgate Bible. If he refused to answer their questions, the commissioners were to put him on the rack.

The examinations began on Tuesday, 1 August. The commissioners went straight to the heart of the matter. Wanting Campion to speak plainly about his loyalty to Elizabeth, they put to him a number of passages from the books of two English Catholic exiles, Richard

Bristow and Nicholas Sander. One of the texts had to do with Pope Pius V's bull of excommunication of 1570, another the so-called Catholic martyrs of the Northern Rising. A third passage, taken from Bristow, suggested that the crown's subjects were not obliged to obey the authority of wicked, apostate and heretical princes. The commissioners wanted to know if Campion believed Queen Elizabeth to be a true and lawful monarch or a 'pretensed queen and deprived'. Campion refused to commit himself to an answer, saying that 'he meddleth neither to nor fro'.

On these questions of loyalty, which in the coming years would be refined and put to other Catholic priests, it was impossible for Campion and his fellow prisoners to answer adequately. Any response to these interrogatories was dangerous. If the priests defended Sander and Bristow they were drawn into matters of politics, practically confessing to treason. If they tried to deflect the questions – common responses were that they did not know the answers, could not tell, or asked not to be pressed – they seemed equally to acknowledge their guilt, using their skills of guile and dissimulation to avoid speaking the truth, or so their interrogators said.

Thus Campion refused to be drawn on questions of loyalty: he would not so easily fall into a charge of high treason. But he began to give the commissioners other information on where he had stayed in England, where he had left his books and which Catholic families had sheltered him. He seems to have revealed the existence of Stephen Brinkley's secret printing press in Oxfordshire, for the press was discovered on 8 August. Brinkley and his four assistants were sent to the Tower. John Payne, the priest alleged by George Eliot to have masterminded the plan for the queen's assassination, was tortured on the rack. The four interrogators in the Tower were busy men. The Privy Council wrote to them on 14 August to thank them for their 'pains', an Elizabethan phrasing that to modern ears is pricked with a bleak irony.

Private confessions were not enough for Elizabeth's government. Any malefactor, from the humblest offender to someone as symbolic as Edmund Campion, had to recant, to be seen to recognize his error and then to repent of it. The most public place of all was the pulpit of Paul's Cross in the shadow of the cathedral, at the heart of London.

Given the restrictions of Campion's close imprisonment in the Tower, his profound opposition to Elizabeth's Church and her government's obvious nervousness at the prospect of any publicity it could not control, such a spectacle was impossible. Instead Campion was taken to St Peter ad Vincula, the parish church of the Tower, where, before his fellow prisoners, he was invited to take part in a formal disputation with theologians of the English Church. On 31 August he faced in rigorous debate the Dean of St Paul's Cathedral and the Dean of Westminster Abbey. The two clergy, recognizing that they had been given time to prepare for a disputation and Campion had not, explained to him that they would question him only upon his 'brag', the letter he had written to the Privy Council.

Strange as it may seem today, this formal scholarly disputation – the kind Campion and his opponents had practised hundreds of times in their university and seminary studies – went hand in glove with Campion's torture on the rack. Both, in very different ways, sought to expose truth and to encourage an admission of error. Indeed, the careful exchange of scholarly points on topics of academic detail had a curious intensity because the debate was held not so far away from the Tower's torture chamber. But this first disputation was not a courteous irrelevance. Anticipating his trial, Campion said that he was being punished for his religious beliefs. He stated that he had been put twice upon the rack, something more terrible to him, he explained, than hanging. Robert Beale, one of Campion's interrogators, pounced on this point. While on the rack had the prisoner been asked about any point of faith? Campion replied that he had not: but he had been asked his whereabouts in England and to divulge the names of his hosts and protectors. Beale's response revealed the danger of Campion's position. This information was required of Campion, Beale said, because priests had reconciled a number of Elizabeth's subjects to the Catholic Church, so withdrawing them from their true allegiance to the queen. This offence, as both men knew, was high treason under a statute of 1581. The government's case against Campion – that in his secret work as a priest he had committed acts of treason – and his defence – that his was a pastoral not a political mission – were clear even in the first disputation.

Elizabeth's advisers were nervous of the publicity caused by three

Richard Verstegan's view of Elizabethan persecution: the rack and other tortures in the Tower of London.

further disputations with Campion in September. News of them leaked out into London. Gossip, especially on a matter as charged and sensitive as the treason of Campion and his fellow priests, was dangerous. Thomas Norton the commissioner, plainly irritated, wrote to Lord Burghley in late September that they had kept a careful written record of each and every objection and response in the debates. Norton felt that the government had been put on the back foot, fighting a swirl of Catholic rumours: 'our cause,' he wrote, 'is not so subject to false reports of his [Campion's] favourers'.

The disputations ended in September, but Campion's torture continued into October. By now the crown's law officers were involved in the interrogations upon the rack, a sure sign that his trial was approaching. There was a cluster of prosecutions in Star Chamber in Westminster Palace of gentlemen who had sheltered and harboured Campion in his secret work throughout England. The record of the trial of six men – one baron, two knights, two gentlemen and a gentlewoman, the elite of Elizabethan society – stated that 'to accomplish his wicked and lewd devices', Edmund Campion had come into the realm and used aliases and disguises 'in a very ruffian-like sort'. They were sent to the Fleet prison to be kept in close confinement 'until they shall conform themselves in obedience and duty towards Her Majesty', each also to be heavily fined.

All of this was preparatory to the main event: the trial of Edmund Campion and other Catholic priests in Westminster Hall in November 1581. Once again, Elizabeth's government was plainly nervous. Campion had to be tried in the correct way, shown publicly to be a traitor, not the victim of religious persecution. This explains why close to the trial the law officers and Privy Council changed their minds about how to indict him. A first indictment stated that Campion 'did traitorously pretend to have power' to absolve Elizabeth's subjects from their obedience to the queen and 'to move the same . . . to promise obedience' to the Pope. The law used here was the one Robert Beale had alluded to in the first of the Campion disputations. To reconcile a subject to Rome by whatever means was high treason by the statute of 1581. But would that suggest, as Campion had argued throughout, that he was on trial for his religious faith, for his pastoral work as a priest? Certainly it might have done – inside the courtroom and outside it, in gossip on the streets of London, in the fierce Catholic pamphlets printed abroad and smuggled into England.

So the indictment was changed. The law officers dispensed entirely with Tudor statutes. They went instead back to the fourteenth century, to a law passed by a parliament of King Edward III in 1352. This act made it treason to compass the king's death, to levy war against him or to adhere to his enemies. But to try Campion under this statute was likewise a risk. True, it had nothing to do with faith, Church or religion. But there would have to be sound and convincing evidence that Campion and the other priests tried with him had indeed plotted abroad. The revised indictment stated that the priests had at various times in Rome, Rheims 'and divers other places in parts beyond the seas' conspired to 'deprive, cast down and disinherit' Elizabeth; 'to bring and put the same Queen to death and final destruction'; to cause a miserable slaughter in England; to set up insurrection and rebellion in the kingdom; and to induce foreigners to make war against the queen. Their crime, simply, was treason.

13

THAT F. CAMPIAN AND THE
REST OF THE PRIESTES AND CATHO-
*liques endited, condemned, and executed, vpon pretence of
treason, and vpon statutes made of old against treasons: vvere neuer yet guiltie of anie such crimes but vniustly made avvay.*

CAP. II.

Itherto we haue made it cleare
that diuers (contrarie to the drift
of this Libel) haue bene cõdem-
ned and put to death ether without al lawe, or els onelie vpon
new lawes by which matter of
religion is made treason. Now it
foloweth and is next to be consi-
dered, whither such other as were accused and appea-
ched of old treasons vppõ a statute made in the dayes
of Edward the third in the 25. yeare of his reigne,
were indeed guiltie of anie such crimes.

The intent of that lawe is to register diuers cases
that were to be deemed treason: in which the first and
cheef is; to conspire or compasse the death of the
Soueraine, or to leuie men of armes against him, and
therof can be by open fact conuinced. Vpon which
special clause father Campian (good man) and his fel-
lowe Priestes and Catholique brethren were, to the
The endi- wonder of the world, arreigned. Namelie endited that
tement of at Rome and Rhemes the last daye of March and
F. Campiã May in the 22. yeare of her maiesties reigne they cõ-
and the
rest. passed the Q. death, the subuersion of the state, and
inuasion of the Realme: feigning (for better coloring
of the collusion) the forsaid places, dayes, and tymes
when this conspiracie should be contriued.

Which forgerie and false accusatiõ, is now so clear-
lie

William Allen's account of Edmund Campion in *A True, Sincere, and Modest Defence of English Catholicques*, 1584.

So how could these charges be proved? Where was the evidence? Out the shadows stepped three men who could offer eyewitness testimony. They were Anthony Munday, once a student of the English College in Rome; Charles Sledd, formerly servant and courier to the priests and exiles; and George Eliot, yeoman of Her Majesty's chamber, who had helped to capture Edmund Campion at Lyford Grange.

William Allen, hardly surprisingly, called the trial of Campion and the other priests of the Tower of London 'The most pitiful practice that ever was heard of to shed innocent blood by the face of justice'. At the same trial Allen was found guilty of high treason in his absence and outlawed. To Elizabeth's government the conviction of Campion and the others was a vindication of its integrity as a kingdom founded upon law. State and Church had to be protected against political enemies. Justice was done. Lord Burghley later wrote bluntly of Campion that he was discovered disguised as a roister (a bully or ruffian) and suffered for his treasons. To counter the image of Campion as a Catholic martyr, Elizabeth's government described him as a crude and common rebel.

The arguments of the trial followed predictable paths. The prosecuting lawyers put to Campion the evidence of Catholic treasons. They set out the efforts of the Pope to remove Elizabeth from her throne. They spoke of rebellion and conspiracy. Campion said he refused to see how these points were relevant to him and the others on trial. 'Let not other men's offences be laid to our charge', was how Anthony Munday remembered Campion's words. The prosecution claimed that the books of Nicholas Sander and Richard Bristow, which had been used by interrogators in the Tower to examine the priests' loyalty to the queen, were set texts in the English seminaries of Rheims and Rome. The men on trial for their lives denied that any such thing was the case. And then Campion deployed the most important and powerful of all the arguments in his defence. His mission, he said, was pastoral and not political. The court could not determine matters of conscience. As priest, he stated, he would never reveal matters of conscience, 'come rack, come rope'.

The crown had to prove its case. And so for the first time in public view the spies and pursuers of priests came face to face with the men they had lived and travelled with and whose loyalty, for reasons of faith or politics or self-interest, they had betrayed. Already their names and reputations were well known to English Catholics: Sledd the priest-hunter, Munday the writer clashing in print with William Allen, Eliot the enemy of Campion. The moment must have been electric. Munday, only two years before this a young scholar in Rome, testified to the conspiracies he had heard talked about in the city. Eliot gave evidence that Robert Johnson, who was on trial with Campion, had fallen into acquaintance with John Payne, the priest who knew of the plot to murder Elizabeth and her senior ministers. In Westminster Hall Johnson denied Eliot's accusation. Luke Kirby, another of the priests on trial, likewise disputed Sledd's evidence that Kirby had attended a treasonable sermon given by William Allen. Kirby, the young Yorkshireman, faced two accusers: the formidable Sledd and Munday, whose friend he had been.

Most devastating of all was the secret dossier Charles Sledd had written for Sir Francis Walsingham, portions of which were read out at the trial. More extraordinary still, there is some evidence that Sledd's file was doctored to fit the circumstances. It takes a keen eye to spot the adjustments: they are small, but their implications are profound. At one point in the manuscript the name of a spy in Paris – a gentleman 'appertaining to Sir Francis Walsingham' – was heavily inked out. There are a couple of other minor alterations. The most significant adjustment of all is easily missed but critical given the fact that Sledd had never set eyes upon Campion till perhaps that very day, or at least after Campion's capture at Lyford Grange. Sledd knew all but one of the men standing in the dock in Westminster Hall: he had served them in Rome and he had walked with them on the long roads through Italy and France to Paris and Rheims. He could describe them, so well in fact that they had been picked up and arrested on the streets of London. He did not know, and certainly had not met in Rome, Edmund Campion. And yet Campion's name was added to Sledd's catalogue of priests who had set out in 1579 and 1580 from Rome to Rheims and England. Just above the name of Robert Persons in the manuscript are the words 'Edmund Campion, priest Jesuit'. His is the only entry without either a concise biography or a physical description.

The truth of all of this has been lost to time. It may be that Sledd, a stickler for detail, added Campion's name to his dossier when he found out about Campion's mission to England. Perhaps it was later added for the sake of completeness. Or it may have been a plain fabrication, by Sledd or by one of Walsingham's men, the purpose of which was to prove Campion's associations with priests in Italy and France Sledd had heard plot treason. The circumstances of the trial, which was a critical and symbolic one for Elizabeth's government, suggest that no effort was spared to bring about success. The priests would always deny the evidence of the spies. It could be said that together Sledd and Munday proved nothing: they merely said the same thing without any firm evidence. And so what were one or two alterations to a document read out in evidence when after all those alterations merely supported the plain facts and truth of what had happened? Campion and his fellow priests were traitors: that had been clear to Elizabeth's government from the beginning. In November and December 1581 there was never any serious doubt that Edmund Campion and his fellow priests would not be found guilty of high treason. That could have been predicted, indeed, from the moment David Jenkins the pursuivant broke through into the priesthole at Lyford Grange.

Predictably the Catholic presses of Rheims savaged the spies for their false witness against the martyr priests. Anthony Munday was 'cogging [cheating, deceiving] Munday', the failed and erring apprentice. Charles Sledd was a lowly servant and betrayer. George Eliot was 'Judas Eliot' or 'Eliot Iscariot'. For the Catholic polemicists, the spies' false testimony and moral bankruptcy put their characters into very sharp relief. Anthony Munday was even at the gallows at Tyburn to see Campion die. The young writer felt a flush of satisfaction at seeing justice done. Answering the pamphlet of a Catholic priest who had

Richard Verstegan's view of Elizabethan persecution: priests are drawn on hurdles to the gallows to be hanged, drawn and quartered.

been there also, Munday stamped on any suggestion of Campion's glorious martyrdom. Campion was smooth, facile, subtle and dangerous. Wickedness, Munday wrote, had been planted in him by the Devil.

On 1 December 1581, a Friday, Campion was tied to a wicker hurdle that was dragged by horses along the roads near St Paul's Cathedral, through Holborn and close to Newgate prison, along Oxford Street and to the place of execution. This was the customary journey from prison to the gallows. At Tyburn he and two other priests, Ralph Sherwin and Alexander Briant, were hanged till each was almost dead and then cut down from the gallows. While each man was still just alive he was cut open and his genitals and bowels, removed by the public hangman, were burned before him. To those who saw it or read about it, this terrible evisceration was the definitive mark of either treason to queen and country or martyrdom for the true faith of Christ. Munday saw it thus:

> Her Majesty to be depriv'd of life,
> > A foreign power to enter in our land:
> Secret rebellion must at home be rife,
> > Seducing priests, receiv'd that charge in hand
> > All this was cloaked with religious show
> > But justice tried, and found it was not so.

A Catholic priest who saw Campion die wrote:

> Religion there was treason to the Queen,
> preaching of penance war against the land,
> priests were such dangerous men as have not been,
> prayers and beads were fight and force of hand,
> cases of conscience bane unto the state,
> so blind is error, so false a witness is hate.

Whatever the truth, it was a grim victory for both sides: for Elizabeth's government security, for Catholic polemicists propaganda.

On the day of Campion's execution John Hart, the priest who had preached on the subject of martyrdom when Charles Sledd was in Rheims, wrote a long letter from the Tower to Sir Francis Walsingham. Hart thanked Walsingham for his special favour and gave the queen's secretary 'such undoubted hope of my life if my conformity shall be agreeable thereunto'. Hart composed and corrected his letter quickly, given fluency by urgency and anxiety. Already convicted of high treason yet so far spared the gallows, Hart wrote for his life.

He made his loyalty to Elizabeth plain from the beginning. He knew from everything that had been said to him in the Tower that 'some great matter' was intended against the realm. He understood that Walsingham knew this also, flattering Sir Francis: 'forasmuch as whiles conspiracies be but yet thought upon, your honour for your singular wisdom doth forecast how to prevent [them] before they take place'. Confirming what Elizabeth's government knew already, Hart wrote that it was William Allen who 'of all others whom I knew beyond the seas must be made privy' to any plot. He offered himself as a spy able to get close to Allen, to know 'the very secrets of his whole heart'.

Hart, who was a member of Allen's circle, offered his service because he possessed the necessary qualifications. He had been close to martyrdom, and nothing (Hart wrote) pleased Allen more than to hear of his scholars' suffering in the Catholic cause. Hart reminded Walsingham that he had been in prison for a whole year. In that time he had been taken to the rack. He was indicted, tried and condemned. Surely his suffering and fortitude would make Doctor Allen trust him. Hart offered his service not to 'pull the neck out of the collar again' – to escape once again with his life – but to serve his prince. He was the first of many priests to offer information on the queen's enemies in return for life and liberty. In Hart's case the result was failure. He remained in the Tower, cheating execution in May 1582 probably by once again offering conformity, only to be banished from England in 1585. He died a year later in Poland. It was a cause of distress to his brother William, a priest in Rome, that John Hart had not died as a martyr with Edmund Campion.

As well as private wrestlings with conscience and loyalty, the execution of Campion and his fellow priests was the talk of London. There was gossip. Words were spoken, probably often in anger, that fell short of treason but were dangerous nevertheless. One Oliver Pluckytt of the parish of St Andrew in Holborn was reported to have said that Campion 'was both discreet and learned, and did say very well [in the disputations], and that he thought in his conscience that he was an honest man'. A neighbour of Pluckytt's asked Pluckytt to confirm whether he had indeed spoken these words about Campion. Pluckytt was happy to say that he had, to which came the reply: 'if you think so well of him that is judged for treason, we do not think well of you.' Pluckytt's words, reported to higher authority, sent him to prison at least for a time.

Campion's execution did not lessen the government's anxiety. Officials intercepted letters, captured and interrogated priests and watched Catholic families closely. Rumours suggested the fact of a political effort to destroy England, as Elizabeth's advisers had believed all along. In these tense months, Sir Francis Walsingham's agents were very busy indeed.

One of the most effective of Walsingham's informants was a man who called himself Barnard. His real name, which he never used, may have been Robert Woodward; we know it only by chance. Often he simply marked papers with a monogram. He may have been a Derbyshire man. He certainly knew the roads between Dieppe and Rome, something that fits with another piece of information from a different source: Charles Sledd, who first met Barnard in 1579 or 1580, said that he was the servant to an English Catholic in Paris called Nicholas Wendon. Indeed Sledd knew Barnard as Robert Wood. So Barnard was, to say the least, an elusive and careful man with keen eyes and ears and a busy pen, not unlike Sledd himself. Barnard's reports were precise; he could write coolly and urgently. He knew the underground community of Catholics very well. Outwardly the honest servant to Catholic families and a courier of letters, he listened carefully to conversations, reported news and gossip and, most significantly of all, read and copied documents passing between seminary priests and Jesuits secretly in England. As Sledd, too, had shown, the best Elizabethan spies were often household servants.

Barnard was supremely effective at what he did. He intercepted for Walsingham one letter that reported the conversion of over two hundred in Staffordshire to the Catholic faith. Barnard knew the priests who were doing this missionary work. He wrote to Walsingham: 'If it may please your honour that I may ... meet with them all, for my acquaintance there is such, as I shall have free access among them all.'

A few weeks later, on 5 January 1582, Barnard noted talk of an invasion force for England to be gathered by King Philip of Spain, funded by the Pope, and commanded by the English rebel the Earl of Westmorland. He reported that Catholics hoped to see Westmorland and the Spanish general Alba in England before Midsummer. The ports and havens had to be watched, for Catholics kept coming in and out of England. They boasted of their success, saying 'a change were at hand'. 'Right honourable,' Barnard wrote to Walsingham, 'the times be dangerous, the people wilful and desirous of change; I fear me there is greater danger at hand than is provided for.' The peril to England's security was very clear. A royal proclamation in April condemned Campion and his fellow traitors. Jesuits and seminary priests were guilty of high treason, it said, and anyone who helped or sheltered them would feel the terrible force of the law.

Elizabeth's government enforced parliament's statutes as rigorously as it could. The press of the queen's printer, Christopher Barker, was busy in 1582 countering the propaganda claims of William Allen in Rheims. Barker printed an official account of the priests' interrogations in the Tower, giving their answers verbatim. Allen responded with a book celebrating 'the glorious martyrdom' of Campion and his fellow priests, using those same interrogations to show their innocence in the face of a ruthless persecution. As more priests went to the gallows for their war against Elizabeth and her kingdom – one in April 1582, seven a month later – Thomas Norton, one of Campion's interrogators, published his robust public defence of its policy against the priests, defending torture as legitimate when it was used 'for the Queen's safety to disclose the manner of the treason'. This defence, too, came off Barker's press, though Norton's name was nowhere mentioned: the pamphlet had the anonymity of high officialdom.

Catholic books presented a huge problem to the government. In the view of Elizabeth's advisers and officials, the books of the English exiles, so effectively smuggled into England from abroad, helped to spread the disease of treason. Thomas Norton wrote: 'You see by these books and such other [how] dangerously [Robert] Persons and the rest still walk abroad.' Persons had left England, it was believed to write on Campion's martyrdom. But the influence of the exiles in Rome and Rheims and the reputations of those priests executed at

Tyburn were enhanced by books read secretly. Little by little, said Thomas Norton, 'a multitude of subjects grow infected'. A priest arrested in London was discovered to have received (and then presumably to have passed on) six copies of a 'traitorous' book on Campion's so-called martyrdom. Forty seditious books were found at the lodgings of a Catholic who lived in Paternoster Row near St Paul's Cathedral. Government informants, justices and officials did their best to seize what they could.

At first the worry was imminent invasion. That fear, however, had steadied a little by the spring of 1582. In the weeks following Campion's execution Barnard expected a rebellion. A few months later he still believed that any danger came from a Catholic uprising in England supported by the forces of the Pope and the King of Spain. But now he sensed little immediate danger. He wrote to Walsingham in late April: for any 'likelihood of rebellion to be this spring or summer attempted, I do not see any hope'. There were only a few priests left in London (we have to suspect that those who had not been captured had gone off into the country), but those who did remain were sheltered by the lawyers of the inns of common law. Like other informants, Barnard gave specific information, to be noted and filed away by Walsingham's office. He knew one especially pernicious Catholic in London called Master Marsh, 'an arrogant papist', who like his sons had spent some time in France. One of those sons now lay at the sign of the White Swan in Holborn, on the corner of Gray's Inn Lane.

Like any good servant, Barnard had trained himself to listen and be silent. For a man who gathered much of what he reported from rumour and gossip, he was well informed. He knew, for example, that after Edmund Campion's execution Robert Persons had left England for Rouen. When Barnard wrote to Walsingham that Persons was now engaged upon a book to defend Campion, he reflected what English Catholics were saying to one another in secret. And that was the usefulness of a man like Barnard. He was able to give Walsingham a feel for the mood of the Catholic underground, leaving Sir Francis and his staff to sort out the likely facts. The value of Barnard, alias Robert Barnard alias Robert Wood alias Robert Woodward, was to report what Catholics were talking about, their hopes, fears and anxieties, and thoughts of the future. His own concerns were more material. In May 1582 he asked Walsingham to have 'some consideration of me towards my apparel, the which is such, as in good faith I am ashamed thereof'. He needed, in other words, a new suit of clothes.

If Barnard was skilled at playing the part of a reliable servant of English Catholics, he was used also to working secretly with other agents. On Wednesday, 9 May he dined in London with Master Wendon, the brother of Barnard's former master Nicholas Wendon. The following day Barnard wrote to Charles Sledd with the details of Catholics' letters and books passing between England, Rouen and Paris. Master Wendon, Barnard informed Sledd, was going to Rome to see his brother, travelling on a passport signed by the French ambassador to Elizabeth's court. Barnard himself had given Wendon a note of the roads from Dieppe to Rome.

Barnard told Sledd that he was not sure when Master Wendon would set out on his journey: 'he is so uncertain of his departure'. But the port was to be Rye. Barnard gave Wendon's description. He would be wearing 'a pair of gascoyne hose black' (wide black breeches), over-breeches of stiff cotton or linen, and a black leather jerkin. Wendon's face was small and lean, 'his beard hath been yellow, but now it is mixed half white'. Barnard thought that few letters would be found upon Wendon but he was not to pass without being searched. Standing back in the shadows Barnard gave his friend Charles Sledd everything he needed to hold and search Master Wendon before he left for France.

Together Sledd and Barnard worked to capture priests and frustrate the secret plans of Catholics travelling between England and France. Or at least that was what Barnard tried to do. In the case of Master Wendon he was thrown only by the simple fact that he could not find Sledd at his lodgings in London. Sledd, an elusive man at the best of times, could be found nowhere. Barnard was mystified. 'I have been divers and sundry times at Master Sledd his lodging but never could meet with him,' he wrote to Walsingham at the end of May. Priests, he said, were slipping through the net, and all because Barnard could never find Charles Sledd at home. 'Right honourable, this is most true,' he told Walsingham. He could not quite believe the strangeness of it all.

PART TWO
Enemies of the State

8

'Sundry wicked plots and means'

In the prosecutions of Edmund Campion and his fellow priests for treason, Queen Elizabeth's government confronted what it perceived to be an overtly political threat to England's security. The scale of the mission to save English souls, which was directed with so much passion and energy by William Allen, speaks for itself. The total number of priests sent into England – 471 are known to have been active in the kingdom over forty years – is a powerful indication of the mission's significance. Each one of those priests was to Elizabeth's government a stirrer of sedition and treason, an agent of political conspiracy, whose purpose was to corrupt the queen's subjects and reconcile them to the Church of Rome. The priests were the Pope's footsoldiers in Rome's war against Elizabeth. Lord Burghley called them 'these seminaries, secret wanderers, and explorators [scouts, spies] in the dark', 'the wicked flock of the seedmen of sedition'.

The response of the Elizabethan authorities was uncompromising. Of the 471 priests, 116 were executed; at least 294 were sent to prison; 17 died in jail; and 91 were eventually banished from England. To William Allen those priests who suffered on the gallows were glorious Catholic martyrs murdered in a vicious persecution. Edmund Campion was the most inspirational and potent martyr of all. As early as May 1582 Allen was distributing fragments of Campion's 'holy rib' as relics.

William Allen was a committed enemy of Queen Elizabeth's government and her Church. He wrote books and pamphlets to counter the arguments of Elizabeth's advisers and clergy and even to maintain the power of popes to depose monarchs who disobeyed God's will. At first in his books he did not criticize Elizabeth directly, though when he did so, just before the Great Armada of 1588, he was ferocious in denouncing a bastard heretic queen. Always there was a single-mindedness about Allen that made him dangerous: his pen and his powers of organization were powerful weapons in a war for religion. 'This is the way, by which we hope to win our nation to God again,' he wrote on behalf of the priests of the English mission in 1581. They did not, he said, put their trust in princes or plots or force of arms.

But here Doctor Allen was disingenuous. From the late 1570s all the way through the following decade, not a day went by when he did not look to the Catholic invasion of his homeland. William Allen would save England from the consuming disease of Protestant heresy by whatever means were necessary, even if what he viewed as a criminal clique of persecuting atheists – Elizabeth's Privy Council – denounced and convicted him as a traitor.

There was someone else, however, who surpassed even Allen's proven ability to threaten the Elizabethan state. While Allen directed the operations of the English mission from mainland Europe – sometimes from Rheims, sometimes from Rome – she was held in custody in England as Queen Elizabeth's unwanted guest. She was celebrated by Catholic exiles to be rightful heir to the Tudor crown. She was Elizabeth's rival and, as Elizabeth herself recognized very clearly, the greatest danger to her throne. She, of course, was Mary Queen of Scots.

Mary Stuart presented Elizabeth's advisers with the most complicated political and dynastic problem of the whole reign. To Catholics like Allen she was queen-in-waiting, by blood a descendant of Elizabeth's grandfather King Henry VII. With no obvious Protestant successor ever endorsed by Elizabeth – she refused to the end of her life to nominate who would succeed her to the English throne – the future of Protestant England was horribly precarious. King Philip of Spain, the Pope and Mary's family the Guise watched and waited; the Queen of Scots was the hope of Catholic Europe. Even after Mary's execution by the English government in 1587, the memory of her cause and the international consequences of her killing continued to shape Elizabethan history in powerful ways. Mary Queen of Scots – whether ruling in Scotland, or a prisoner in England, or a Catholic martyr – cast a very long shadow indeed.

When Mary had landed on the coast of Cumberland in 1568 her monarchy was deeply compromised. She was an escapee from the prison of Lochleven Castle. Deposed by her enemies in Scotland, and strongly suspected by many of having been involved in the murder of her second husband, Henry, Lord Darnley, in 1567, she came to England to beg Elizabeth's family affection in setting her back upon her throne. Under the strong advice of her councillors, Elizabeth refused to meet her cousin. Recognizing the profound difficulty of Mary's case, Elizabeth appointed a tribunal to examine the Casket Letters, the supposed evidence of Mary's complicity in Darnley's death and her adultery with the Earl of Bothwell. The documents were held by Elizabeth's government to be genuine, though this claim has been strongly doubted by historians. Indeed Lord Burghley himself knew they contained some crude forgeries. But if the Casket Letters were shown to be authentic then Mary and her queenship were fatally compromised. The tribunal that met at York and then in Westminster late in 1568 formally recognized the documents' authenticity. This was proof enough for Elizabeth's advisers that the Queen of Scots had been involved in a murder conspiracy against her husband. Though in 1568 not found guilty by a court of justice in England, Mary was sent by Elizabeth to Tutbury Castle in Staffordshire to be held indefinitely under close supervision. The deposed Queen of Scots was forbidden to communicate with any outsider without Elizabeth's knowledge and permission.

On balance it was probably less dangerous to Elizabeth's government to hold Mary safely in England than either to return her to Scotland or to send her to France. But safe custody in secure castles and houses in England was merely the best of the three choices. However she was dealt with, Mary was dangerous. The Ridolfi Plot of 1571 revealed to Elizabeth's advisers precisely how pernicious she was, sitting comfortably at the centre of a web of conspiracy whose four principal threads were money from the Pope, a plan for an invasion of England led by a Spanish general, the liberation of Mary herself and the plottings of powerful English Catholic nobility. The most disturbing revelation of all in 1571 was the treason of Thomas Howard, fourth Duke of Norfolk, a cousin of Elizabeth's through the Howard family of Anne Boleyn. Norfolk was found to be a Ridolfi conspirator. Parliament in 1572 responded robustly, sensitive to the plain if uncomfortable fact that, though ignored by the Act of Succession of 1544, Mary Stuart was Elizabeth's blood successor. What the political establishment of Elizabethan England faced in 1571 and 1572 – as at many moments of political emergency in Elizabeth's long reign – was the appalling prospect of the queen's death with no acceptable royal successor, provoking a foreign invasion and probably also a civil war. After the breaking up of the Ridolfi Plot, parliament pressed for three courses of action. First, cut off the heads of the Queen of Scots and the Duke of Norfolk. Secondly, strip Mary of any pretensions to monarchy. Third, find and establish by parliamentary statute Queen Elizabeth's royal successor: the future could not be left to accident and chance. Significantly, there was very strong support, nourished by the Privy Council, for Mary Stuart's trial and execution. Elizabeth, however, resisted parliament's advice on all but one of the proposed courses of action.

The Duke of Norfolk paid the price of the Ridolfi conspiracy, for in 1572 he went to the executioner's block as a traitor. Terrified of the political consequences at home and abroad of eliminating a blood kinswoman and a fellow monarch, Elizabeth refused to be pressed on Mary by her Lords, Commons and Privy Council. Lawyers in parliament trawled the history of Europe for examples of kings brought to justice by fellow monarchs. The Emperor Henry VII, they found, gave a judgment of death against Robert, King of Naples at Pisa in 1311; Frederick, King of Naples was deposed by King Ferdinand of Aragon in 1501. The lawyers gathered together dozens of legal principles and maxims, many having to do with the fact that the Queen of Scots had been deposed by her own people and was thus no longer a queen. Bishops in the House of Lords quoted texts from the Old Testament to prove Elizabeth's duty to execute Mary. Still Elizabeth was unmoved. Both houses of parliament set to work on a bill to exclude the Queen of Scots from the English succession, seeking to disable Mary's claim to the Tudor crown. The bill, which was turned by Lords and Commons into one 'wherewith the Queen of Scots may be charged' judicially, was quashed by Elizabeth. It was an effort to deal definitively and robustly with the dynastic danger presented to

Elizabeth by Mary; the queen, who was quite aware of what she was doing, merely adjourned parliament before the law could be passed. The best statute that could be used against the Queen of Scots remained the Treasons Act of 1571 and those of its clauses which prohibited any claim upon or usurpation of Elizabeth's title and crown. So far as Elizabeth's advisers were concerned, this was a very flimsy defence against evil.

And that was how in 1572 – the year of Elizabethan crisis, a turning point of decision and direction – those who moved in political circles at the royal court and in the Council saw it. The great massacre of Protestants in Paris in August of that same year, at the feast of Saint Bartholomew, offered further grim evidence of European Catholic conspiracy. The Devil was seen to be at work against the people of God. The events of Bartholomewtide caused Elizabeth's government to re-evaluate the international situation it found itself facing. So it was that Robert Beale, later one of Edmund Campion's interrogators and a man close to both Sir Francis Walsingham and Lord Burghley, was prompted by 'the great murder in Paris and other places in France' to write a discourse, or political paper, for Burghley.

Beale's analysis in 1572 was stark, even terrifying. The killings in France, he believed, reflected the efforts of Catholic princes to destroy Protestantism throughout Europe in a campaign either waged openly in war or by treason and malice in secret. There was a 'detestable conspiracy' to divide the world into a new triumvirate of Spanish, French and papal power. Together Spain and France planned to conquer England. The foundations set down for the coming invasion were the defence of Mary Queen of Scots's title to Elizabeth's throne and Pope Pius V's bull of 1570 denouncing Elizabeth as a schismatic and usurper. The ambitious house of Guise, Mary Stuart's family, manipulated the monarchy of France and sought to confront and destroy Elizabeth probably by poison. Without a sure royal succession after Elizabeth's death, England stood alone and defenceless against evil. Beale remembered the destruction of two leaders of the European Protestant cause, Louis of Bourbon, Prince of Condé, who was killed in battle in 1569, and Admiral Coligny, murdered in Paris in 1572. All European Protestants were in danger. The King of France himself had ordered the killings in Paris. In the Low Countries the forces of the Prince of Orange, leading the Dutch against the Duke of Alba's Spanish army, were weak. Beale wrote:

> It is therefore time and more than time that Her Majesty were thoroughly resolved to take some right course [for] both her own safety and wealth of this realm . . . The French King is become a man or rather an incarnate devil. The Prince of Condé and Admiral be slain. The Spaniard is placed in the Low Countries. The Prince of Orange's forces be like after this to be so weakened as he shall never be able to lift up his head again. We are left destitute of friends on every side, amazed [stunned, overwhelmed] and divided at home: and consider not that where there is any such irresoluteness and security, that estate [state or kingdom] cannot in policy upon any foreign invasion (as is intended against this), continue long.

It was a brutal and cheerless analysis of the international scene.

Beale doubted very much whether English Catholics could ever be trusted by the queen. He wrote in private what Elizabethan officials, sensitive to the charge of orchestrating a religious persecution in England, were always reluctant to say in public. Catholics, Beale said, could never be loyal subjects of Elizabeth. He reasoned thus: it was impossible for those whose religion, founded upon the Pope's authority, believed both the queen's birth and her title to the English throne to be unlawful. What confidence, he asked, 'can be reposed in him, who thinketh in conscience under the damnation of his soul, to owe a more obedience to a higher power'? For an Elizabethan Protestant Beale's logic was unassailable.

Beale had no illusions about the pernicious influence of Mary Queen of Scots. She was the principal cause of the ruin of the kingdoms of Scotland and France and she had 'prettily played the like part' in England. 'All wise men generally throughout Europe cannot sufficiently marvel at Her Majesty's over mild dealing with her, in nourishing in her own bosom so pestiferous a viper.' He suggested a tough course of action to be taken against Mary. To disable the Queen of Scots from the English succession – the policy pushed by Lords and Commons and the Privy Council in parliament but subverted by Elizabeth in 1572 – was merely 'a toy', a trifle and a fantasy. To eliminate

Mary once and for all was the only sure way. Beale's political logic was that the malice of Spain and France, being profound already, could not be 'augmented' by Mary's death. It would be better to be rid of her and take the consequences of her elimination sooner rather than later.

Robert Beale's analysis appealed politically and instinctively to Lord Burghley, Sir Francis Walsingham and other privy councillors. But Elizabeth would not be moved, fearing above all the shattering consequences of stripping away the divine sanction of monarchy by killing the Queen of Scots; and so Mary lived. What followed after 1572 were fifteen years of uneasy and unstable peace between England and the princes and powers of Europe and some very busy plotting on behalf of Mary's cause. It was just as Beale had predicted. For the rest of her life the Queen of Scots and her household were moved between places of safety and seclusion deep in the English midlands, away from London, the coasts and the sensitive borderland with Scotland, under the supervision of custodians and keepers appointed by Elizabeth. Elizabeth's government knew that it had to isolate Mary as best as it could in order to cut off her contacts in England and abroad.

Mary was not cowed by her imprisonment. In fact she seemed to speak and to act with more confidence than her royal cousin of England, forcefully stating her rights even at the most difficult times. In June 1572, when members of the House of Lords and House of Commons were busily looking at the precedents for trying and executing monarchs, Mary wanted to go before parliament to state her own case. While Elizabeth resisted the efforts of her Privy Council and parliament to deal with Mary robustly, the Queen of Scots was just as confidently sure of her blood, parentage and right of next succession to the English crown. Significantly, knowing full well what the implications were, Mary resisted the views of lawyers in the House of Lords by refusing to submit to the legal jurisdiction of her cousin. The Queen of Scots – the unqueened queen, deposed in Scotland, a prisoner in England – always stood proudly upon the dignity of monarchy.

But Mary was above all a realist. She knew that Elizabeth's government wanted to suffocate her influence. She appealed to King Philip of Spain; he was sympathetic to her situation but too busy on the many fronts of Spanish imperial power to devote either time or energy to her cause. With her cousin, Henry, Duke of Guise, she had more success. In fact the young duke became one of her most enthusiastic and active supporters in Europe. In 1578 he talked to King Philip's ambassador, as well as to William Allen, about Mary and her young son, King James VI of Scotland. Mary's situation was always tangled up with greater projects: to free the Queen of Scots without a vision for the rescue of England from Elizabethan tyranny – or indeed to have restored a Catholic England without a royal successor to Elizabeth – never made much sense. The liberation of the Queen of the Scots and the end of Elizabeth's heretical rule belonged together in the minds of Europe's Catholic leaders and English Catholic exiles. And so it was that in the early 1580s the Duke of Guise, with the help of Jesuit priests, began to look to the practical details of a plan to free Mary as well as to save England and Scotland from pernicious heresy.

In 1581 Robert Persons, Edmund Campion's companion and superior in their mission to England, began to think seriously about Catholic prospects of success in Scotland. A Catholic Scotland could offer a safe haven for persecuted English Catholics. Its young king, James VI, had been raised by his mother's enemies and given a thorough classical education and an uncompromisingly Protestant upbringing. In the early years of his rule Scotland was governed through Protestant regents who fought the kingdom's Catholic nobility. But James, by now fifteen years old, was growing in ability and confidence. Might he, English and Scottish Catholics wondered, be persuaded to become a Catholic? James's favourite at court was his cousin Esmé Stuart, first Duke of Lennox, who was perceived to exercise great influence over the king. Here the Duke of Guise, Robert Persons and William Allen saw their best chance of success. Indeed Lennox himself proposed a scheme to restore the Catholic religion in England, Ireland and Scotland, as well as to free the Queen of Scots and to secure the return of Catholic exiles and émigrés to their homelands. Lennox envisaged an invading force of 15,000 foreign troops. He and James would lead Scottish and Spanish troops in Scotland. The Duke of Guise would bring an army across the English Channel from France to land on the south coast of England. The rebel Earl of Westmorland and other English exiles would return to England to raise and arm their tenants. Together, by invasion and rebellion, they would push Elizabeth off the throne and liberate the Queen of Scots.

It was a bold plan to which many – the Duke of Guise especially – gave time, money and resources. But in the end it was hamstrung by changing political circumstances, principally the fall from influence at James's court of the Duke of Lennox and also by the cooling of King Philip of Spain's support for Guise's plan. Nevertheless, the duke's unwavering commitment touched off in England in late 1583 and early 1584 one of the most energetic of the many Elizabethan hunts for conspiracy and conspirators in England. It is known as the Throckmorton Plot, and it is one of the secret threads of the following chapters, involving a young Catholic gentleman called Francis Throckmorton, the Earl of Northumberland, Lord Paget and one of the most elusive of Elizabethans, Lord Henry Howard.

So the Queen of Scots, held against her will in England, had to wait and hope. She depended completely upon her friends. From Paris her supporters and agents tried to send her political and diplomatic intelligence in letters that were brought to her with great difficulty from mainland Europe, smuggled under the noses of Mary's keepers. The couriers who carried these packets were zealous young English Catholic gentlemen. Their secret work greatly interested Sir Francis Walsingham and his spies. After all, what else could these letters contain but evidence of Mary's plottings with Queen Elizabeth's enemies? The truth was discovered in the summer of 1586 in probably the most stunning and controversial of all Elizabethan plots, the conspiracy of Anthony Babington, where we have the chance to follow every twist and turn of Walsingham and his quarry.

To invasion and conspiracies to liberate the Queen of Scots we may add the fear of Queen Elizabeth's assassination. Poison was always a danger; Robert Beale had mentioned it specifically in his frank and worrying analysis of the international scene in 1572. In later sixteenth-century Europe there was something of a fashion for killing important men by firearms. In 1563 the second Duke of Guise, the Queen of Scots's uncle, was shot in the back by a young gentleman assassin using a pistol. The first political killing by firearm in the British Isles was that of the Earl of Moray, a Protestant regent of Scotland (in fact Mary Stuart's half-brother), who was murdered in 1570 by an assassin firing a harquebus, a heavy musket supported on a tripod. The same kind of gun was going to be used to assassinate Lord Burghley in Westminster in 1571 in a plot allegedly commissioned by the Spanish ambassador at Elizabeth's court. The murder plot was revealed to Burghley by one of the would-be assassins, who, instead of finding a reward, went to the gallows. Most shocking of all to Europe's Protestants was the murder, again by pistol, of William of Nassau, Prince of Orange, the leader of Dutch resistance against Spain, in 1584.

Over time, pistols became an assassin's weapon of choice. A pistol, or dag, was much easier to conceal and use than a heavy harquebus, though given the accuracy of firearms in the sixteenth century the killer still had to be very close to his target to be sure of hitting it. In England the law said that a gentleman could keep and carry a pistol if he had the handsome income of at least £100 a year and if the pistol measured 'stock and gun' at least a yard in length. Elizabeth's government was certainly nervous about the use of firearms. In 1579 a royal proclamation on handguns condemned 'the multitude of the evil-disposed who . . . do commonly carry such offensive weapons being in time of peace only meet for thieves, robbers and murderers'. Constables were encouraged to stop anyone carrying a pistol whatever their rank and degree in society. But if thieves carried weapons, then it was sensible for travellers to do the same. It was said that an honest traveller rode out with a case of dags at his saddle-bow – that is, his weapons in plain sight on the arched front part of his horse's saddle.

There were royal assassination scares. The most striking (and in many ways quite the most bizarre) was in October 1583, when a Catholic gentleman of Warwickshire called John Somerville set out from home to kill the queen with his dag. He was quickly arrested for speaking treasonable words against Elizabeth before five witnesses: 'he was in hope to see the Queen's Majesty and he meant to shoot her through with his dag and hoped to see her head to be set upon a pole for that she was a serpent and a viper'. Here was a textbook treason for which the Treasons Act of 1571 was perfected fitted. The officials who investigated Somerville doubted his sanity, believing that his mind had been turned and twisted by the influence of his wife, a priest in disguise and an illegal Catholic book – quite possibly (even probably) a work by William Allen of Rheims. One very sinister fact was that Somerville carried with him on his mission an Agnus Dei, a small wax lamb of God blessed by the Pope, an object of Catholic devotion. Master Somerville got nowhere near the queen – he was arrested in a village in Oxfordshire – but the fact that he was interrogated by Sir Francis Walsingham himself shows just how seriously the government believed the threat to Elizabeth's life to be. Somerville was judged sane enough to stand trial for treason. He was found guilty but hanged himself in his cell in Newgate prison before he could be taken to the gallows.

Elizabeth's advisers knew the queen's killing could quickly bring England to its knees. They saw and felt the horror of the Prince of Orange's assassination in 1584. The terrible, insistent question asked by Elizabeth's Privy Council was this: could the same happen to Elizabeth? They knew already the answer to be a plain yes. A second question then followed on from the first: if Elizabeth were taken away from her people – by an assassin's bullet or even by natural causes – what on earth would happen to England? The queen's ministers felt in their bones that invasion and most probably uprisings and rebellion would follow.

Walsingham and his sources were alert to any suspicion of a murder plot. One such conspiracy came to the attention of the government in 1585 in the form of an anonymous report written upon a single sheet of paper; it had neither date nor signature nor really any clue to the identity of the writer. The official who read and endorsed the paper called it simply 'The speeches of a friar in Dunkirk'. This friar had talked to the English agent about a plot to kill Elizabeth. If, he said, that wicked woman 'were once dispatched and gone' all Christendom would be in peace and quietness. The friar took the agent into his chamber, where he kept a picture of the Prince of Orange's murder. Orange's killer, said the friar, was a native of Burgundy. 'Behold and see well this picture,' the friar had said to Walsingham's informant: 'Look how this Burgundian did kill this prince. In such manner and sort, there will not want such another Burgundian to kill that wicked woman and that before it be long, for the common wealth of all Christendom.'

Elizabeth's advisers were not prepared to sit passively by in the face of threats like this, for in the killing of the queen and in Mary Stuart's claim to the English throne they confronted the nightmare of Protestant England's destruction. They acted in October 1584. At Hampton Court Palace Elizabeth's councillors put their signatures and seals to a document that had been drawn up by Burghley and Walsingham. It was called an Instrument of an Association, a 'bond of one firm and loyal society' whose signatories swore vengeance on anyone who tried to harm the queen. If any attempt were made upon Elizabeth's life, the object of the Association was to bring to justice any pretender to the throne. The Queen's advisers knew that the greatest danger came from Mary Queen of Scots and her supporters, and so to force home a political point they made Mary herself sign the Association: she, too, swore to protect Elizabeth's throne. Given little choice in the matter, the Queen of Scots put her signature to a French translation of the following words:

> we ... do voluntarily and most willingly bind ourselves every one of us to the other jointly and severally in the bond of one firm and loyal society, and do hereby vow and promise before the majesty of Almighty God that ... [we will] pursue as well by force of arms as by all other means of revenge, all manner of persons of what estate soever they shall be, and their abettors, that shall attempt by any act counsel or consent, to anything that shall tend to the harm of Her Majesty's royal person. And we shall never desist from all manner of forcible pursuit against such persons to the uttermost extermination of them, their counsellors, aiders and abettors.

Revenge would be taken against any 'pretended successor' to Elizabeth's throne 'by whom or for whom any such detestable act shall be attempted or committed'. The challenger could be hunted down and executed by the signatories of the Association for a conspiracy engineered on his or her behalf. If that challenger happened to be Mary Queen of Scots herself – either in a conspiracy instigated by her directly or merely upon her behalf by someone else – in subscibing to the Association Mary had pretty much signed her own death warrant.

The Association was a remarkable document which Elizabeth resisted, knowing well enough its implications. But in 1584, unlike in the parliament of 1572, the Privy Council got its way. As extraordinary as the Instrument was the statute parliament passed in 1585 to put the Association into law, the Act for the Queen's Surety, which sought the 'surety and preservation of the Queen's most excellent Majesty'. As Lord Burghley wrote: 'for the Queen's Majesty's safety ... authority may remain after the Queen's Majesty's death to punish and take revenge upon any wicked person that shall attempt to take her life away'.

The language of the statute was, like any Tudor act of parliament, stodgy. Its implications, however, were stunning. In the event of a rebellion, an invasion, an attempt on Elizabeth's life or anything at all 'compassed or imagined, tending to the hurt of Her Majesty's royal person by any person or with the privity of any person that shall or may pretend title to the crown of this realm', a commission of at least twenty-four privy councillors and lords of parliament would sit in judgment on the evidence and pronounce a sentence. This sentence would be put into a royal proclamation by which, under the authority of the statute and with the queen's 'direction in that behalf', all forcible and possible means would be used to hunt down and kill every 'wicked person by whom or by whose means assent or privity' the invasion, rebellion or act against Elizabeth was provoked, as well as 'all their aiders, comforters and abetters'.

Out of this dense language of the law came two startling propositions. The first was that in the event of a national emergency the execution of royal justice would be entrusted to the signatories of the Instrument of Association. Any pretender to Elizabeth's throne – and the likely pretender was Mary Queen of Scots – could be pursued to death for any conspiracy organized in her name. This was licensed revenge, pure and simple. The second proposition was that royal government would continue even after Elizabeth's murder. It was a proposal for interregnum, for a temporary English republic in the name of the continuity of royal government.

To bring her to justice under the act, the commission would have to prove that Mary Queen of Scots had at least 'privity' of any conspiracy: that is, private knowledge of or complicity in it. Elizabeth's government would have to possess material proof that Mary was actively involved in any plot against her cousin or her cousin's kingdoms of England and Ireland. Elizabeth's advisers believed, of course, that Mary was already guilty, however clever she was at hiding her tracks. But what they needed according to the law passed by parliament was the evidence to prove her involvement and complicity in plots against England. That is what drove Sir Francis Walsingham and his men in their investigations in the years after 1585. At last, in the Babington Plot of 1586, they found it: not exactly in Mary's handwriting but, as the following chapters will show, in documents conclusive enough to allow the government to eliminate the Queen of Scots for ever.

The conspiracy of the priests of William Allen's mission; the efforts of Allen and the Duke of Guise to press for an invasion of Scotland and England; the power of the cause of Mary Queen of Scots to inspire Catholics at home and abroad; the fear of Queen Elizabeth's murder; the drastic emergency contingencies of the Instrument of Association and the Act for the Queen's Surety: all of these themes and forces singly and collectively made the years of the 1580s profoundly challenging for Elizabeth and her government. There was a powerful feeling of anxiety and isolation, of imminent catastrophe. Elizabeth's advisers knew that the queen's life, upon which the security and peace of kingdom and religion rested, was a delicate thing. Ministers like Lord Burghley and Sir Francis Walsingham believed that only a passionate and ruthless vigilance could save Protestant England. These were suspicious and dangerous times for the spies and intelligencers of England and Europe.

9

The Secret Lives of William Parry

In June 1580 William Parry, Lord Burghley's gentleman intelligencer, was in Paris, spying on the city's English Catholics. Knowing he could be useful, he sought Burghley's patronage and favour. In his leisured way Parry gathered information without any great finesse, something that troubled Elizabeth's ambassador in Paris, Sir Henry Cobham, who wrote rather uncertainly to Burghley that an Englishman called Master Parry pretended to depend upon his lordship's good favour.

Parry took it upon himself to work as an intermediary between Elizabeth's government and some of the exiles. He spied on the English Catholic nobility and gentry visiting Paris and sought to befriend them. He sent reports to London interceding on their behalf. Sometimes he came close to making deals with them, negotiating favourable terms for their loyalty. There was a purpose to this that Parry, dazzled by his own self-importance, did not recognize. Elizabeth's government was pragmatic about the exiles. They could be won over or they could be divided against themselves, reputations compromised in the eyes of other Catholics by their negotiations with the government. Here Parry – clever, indiscreet and self-absorbed – was the perfect instrument. He was quite serious when he wrote to Burghley on behalf of Sir Thomas Copley, a prominent English Catholic gentleman. Parry praised Copley's family and descent, and noted Copley's satisfaction at Burghley's continued 'goodness and friendly mind towards him'. Copley, Parry wrote, took it 'very grievously that Her Majesty (to whose person and state he always protested so true and so loyal a heart) should by sinister information conceive such mislike of him'. Parry was confident that he had divined Copley's true loyalty: 'In truth, my lord, it seemeth to me that he meaneth good faith and very sincerely and unfainedly to give Her Majesty all the contention he can, and faithfully to serve the same to the uttermost of his ability.'

Sir Thomas Copley was a fairly harmless exile. The Earl of Westmorland, outlaw and rebel, was not. But still Parry wrote on Westmorland's behalf to Burghley. Westmorland, who was twenty-six or twenty-seven when he had taken part in the Northern Rising of 1569, was now ready to fall at Elizabeth's feet, repenting the errors and faults of his youth. Only here in Parry's report to Burghley there was just a shade of uncertainty. He did not know whether 'the reclaiming of desperate men do agree with our state and policy' – this certainly suggests the limit of any instructions Burghley had given to him – but he saw the benefits of it and left the matter to Burghley's 'wisdom and grave consideration'.

Even William Parry may have recognized that these were treacherous waters, but he was unselfconsciously happy to navigate them. He had standing, unofficial yet acknowledged. One mark of his credit in official circles was to receive letters from Burghley. A second was his freedom to send a letter to England with Edward Stafford, Elizabeth's special ambassador to the Duke of Anjou, which Stafford delivered to Burghley at Elizabeth's court. This letter contained a digest of a fortnight's worth of intelligence from Paris in July: the politics of the Pope's cardinals, a book printed in Paris slanderous to Elizabeth, the thinking of William Allen, the Bishop of Ross's standing with the Archbishop of Glasgow (both men were representatives in Paris of the Queen of Scots), and even an account of dinner with the archbishop and two Scottish noblemen. To Lord Burghley Parry was a moderately useful source of information. His cleverness and vanity worked to his advantage – for the time being.

In September 1580 Parry was in London. He would have preferred to speak to Burghley at court but had to settle for a letter. Burghley was too busy to see him. 'Your lordship's small leisure maketh me loath to deliver many things by mouth,' he wrote, 'my letters serving for your better leisure.' He recommended the service of Guido Cavalcanti, an agent of Catherine de' Medici, and enclosed a letter he had come across in Paris. It was the work of 'a busy dealer in English practices', an Italian called Julio Busini.

Parry was pompously self-important in writing to Burghley. He related his many conversations with the French ambassador in London, who, Parry said, talked to him plainly about great and significant things. He boasted about his contacts with Mary Stuart's advisers in Paris: the Archbishop of Glasgow, the Bishop of Ross and, most mysterious of all, Thomas Morgan, Mary's gatherer of secret intelligence. Parry was always alert to Lord Burghley's powerful patronage: he was, he wrote, merely the poor sworn servant of the queen and looked upon Burghley as his best friend, father and lord. Parry was a man rarely given to understatement. But the truth was that Parry the social climber had long lived the kind of life he could not afford to sustain. The easy flatterer was heavily in debt. Soon he would feel the reality of the situation he had made for himself.

The great fall came for Parry in early November 1580. On Wednesday the 2nd he forced his way into a chamber in the Inner Temple in London and confronted Hugh Hare. Hare was both a lawyer and a moneylender who had lent Parry the huge sum of £610, with interest to pay on top. Hare said that Parry broke down the door to his rooms and threatened to kill him. Parry's account was very different. Picking through the depositions of witnesses, he contended the evidence. The broken door and the threat to Hare's life, for example, came from Hare's evidence only, or so Parry maintained. One witness had gone up to Hare's chamber to find 'the nail of the latch of the door thrust out', but he could not say that Parry had done this. The same witness seems to have deposed that Parry had no weapon. Another said in his deposition, according to Parry, that 'no harm had happened if Hare had not threatened to put Parry in a sack'. The threat, then, came from Hare. Carefully and precisely – and no wonder, for his life was at stake – Parry set out in a letter to Lord Burghley the weakness of the evidence against him, even questioning the literacy and accuracy of his indictment. The case went to trial, but Parry, always given to feelings of betrayal by others, believed that it was a fix: 'It will be proved that the recorder [i.e. the most senior judge in London] spake with the jury. And that the foreman did drink.' Whatever the truth of his allegations, Parry was found guilty of burglary and attempted murder.

The Elizabethan punishment for a felony was hanging. But Parry, pardoned by the queen, was saved from the gallows: after all, in Lord Burghley he had a powerful patron. Yet he was nevertheless still deeply, painfully in debt. The sum of £610 he had borrowed from Hare had risen 'by usury and recompence' (to use Parry's words) to £1,000. To add to the money he owed to Hare was the fantastic sum of £2,000 in a bond of surety.

But Parry was a survivor, even if there was something reckless in the way he tried to raise money. He became in effect a confidence trickster, working to ingratiate himself with a young heir called Edward Hoby. Parry, clever and plausible, was facing financial ruin: Hoby, who was twenty-one years old, was young, rich and inexperienced. He was also Lord Burghley's nephew, and in November 1581 Hoby's mother, Lady Russell, wrote to her powerful brother-in-law 'in my extremity of grief for a matter of no small importance to my heart'. She had heard of Parry's 'ill dealing' used towards her son 'in compassing bargains at his hands' concerning some of Hoby's properties. Parry had given his oath to Lady Russell. He had broken it, and she was desperate: 'if this be not prevented the boy is undone. I beseech your lordship most humbly off my knees, good lord commit Parry to some prison'. It seems that Burghley did exactly that, for by the middle of December Parry was in the Poultry Counter in London, a filthy prison between Old Jewry and the Royal Exchange, not far from Cheapside. There he reflected upon the debts he owed to Hugh Hare, with no prospect of a handsome fee from Edward Hoby.

To Parry it was obvious that he was the wronged party. He wrote to the Privy Council, 'driven by this extraordinary mean' to petition for redress of the grievances done to him by Hare. He craved their lordships' favour and desired justice. He was very angry: 'God knoweth and my conscience beareth me witness that I have deserved better of my prince and country than to be thus tormented in prison and credit by a known cunning and shameless usurer.' These were strong words to use for a man in Parry's position.

Twelve men had stood surety for Parry, together raising the necessary bond for good behaviour of £2,000. It was clear he had influential and rich friends. One of the guarantors was Edward Stafford, soon to be Elizabeth's resident ambassador at the French court; on one level at least Parry must have been a persuasive man. Yet his difficulties continued. In late January 1582 Parry wrote again to Burghley. Those 'best friends' of his who had been willing to be bound to Hugh Hare for £600 were, he said, 'by the practise of my adversaries drawn from me'. Parry could rely only upon Burghley to 'stand my good lord'. If Burghley did nothing, Parry was 'like to lie here a good while' in what he called his 'bad lodging' in prison. So Parry, the traveller and intelligencer, made a suggestion to Burghley: 'If my absence at Paris for three years may do any service to your lordship (thereby also to avoid the offence of all men here) I will gladly undertake it.' His 'singular devotion' to Burghley and resolution to honour and serve him made Parry 'thus bold'. He wanted, in other words, once again to spy for Burghley: it was the price he offered to pay for his release from prison.

Burghley seems to have accepted Parry's offer. Freed from the Poultry Counter, in early August 1582 he prepared to set out for Paris. He stayed in the city for just over a month, leaving for Lyons on 25 September. By January 1583 he was in Venice. He appeared now supremely untroubled by any obligation to Burghley: the urgency of the Poultry Counter was soon swept away by the pleasures of travelling through France and northern Italy. He had clear ideas already about what he did and did not want to do for Elizabeth's lord treasurer. After all, he was no ordinary informant; he knew he had special talents. 'I find it a matter very unpleasant to be troubled or tied to the advertisement of ordinary occurents,' he wrote. If anything happened that he thought was of importance, Parry said, he would not fail to inform Burghley.

And yet for all Parry's spectacular wilfulness, he does seem to have begun fairly vigorously to gather news and information from Venice, a city which had for a long time been a European hub for intelligence from the Mediterranean and the Iberian peninsula. Much of it was gossip, though some of it was useful. In a letter to Burghley in late February 1583 Parry sent news from Flanders, Naples, Spain and Portugal. He wrote, too, of a new book that had been printed in Rome called *De Persecutione Anglicana*, known in an English edition as

An epistle of the persecution of Catholickes in Englande. It was the work of Robert Persons, Edmund Campion's fellow Jesuit in England, and had been first printed in Rouen in 1582.

Parry had never before shown very much interest in religion; he was drawn more to fine dinners in grand company. But here, for the first time, Parry hinted at his private view on what in Persons's argument was the persecution of Catholics in England. Parry took the book very seriously. He told Burghley that it gave 'a barbarous opinion of our [i.e. English] cruelty', especially in the hanging, drawing and quartering of traitors: 'I could wish that in those cases it might please Her Majesty to pardon the dismembering and quartering.' Parry continued on this theme six days later when he wrote once again to Burghley: 'I pray you tell Master Secretary [Sir Francis Walsingham] that here is so great speech of his persecution and cruelty that your lordship (sometime in the same predicament) is almost forgotten.' Walsingham, the Earl of Huntingdon and the Earl of Leicester were 'the men most wondered at' in the great persecution. For a man who never wore faith on his sleeve, William Parry's views on Robert Persons's *Persecution* were surprisingly vigorous.

Any study of William Parry must point to his inflated self-regard, his snobbery, his peculiarly distorted sense of reality, his naive faith in Lord Burghley's patronage and good fortune, his gambler's instinct for taking wild chances, his stratagems and schemes. Parry was variable and vain, possessed of self-confidence over ability. In the spring of 1583 it would have been harder to find a more contrastingly different man to Parry than Thomas Phelippes, servant to Sir Francis Walsingham, who was engaged in secret work in France.

Phelippes was deliberate, able and self-reliant: a thoughtful, careful and compact man. He set out his letters with care; he wasted few words. He wrote in an italic hand, the mark of an educated man. His script was minute, perhaps showing something of the technical precision of a mathematician, which as one of the most gifted breakers of secret code and cipher in Europe Phelippes certainly was. Born in about 1556, he was the eldest son of William Phelippes, a London cloth merchant. He was a student, probably, of Trinity College in Cambridge. Beyond this, it is hard to be sure of the facts of Phelippes's early life: he is one of the most secret and secretive characters in this book.

Phelippes was in France in July 1582, though it is not clear for what purpose. In Bourges he replied to a letter from Walsingham. His master had sent a letter in cipher for Phelippes to make sense of. For Walsingham this was a risk; the danger of having packets intercepted was real – indeed the letter Phelippes applied himself to was itself intercepted by Elizabeth's government. It may have been one of William Allen's letters, which were either stolen or bought from the European couriers fairly regularly in the early 1580s; or perhaps it was a packet sent to the Queen of Scots's ambassador in Paris, the Archbishop of Glasgow. In 1580 the archbishop had complained to William Parry about a number of his letters that had been intercepted.

Whatever the letter was, to send it all the way to Phelippes in France was a measure of his unique skills in Elizabethan cryptanalysis. Phelippes told Walsingham that he had 'travailed to the uttermost in the cipher'. He had had, he wrote, some success, 'if not so good as was wished, sufficient yet I hope as to satisfy Her Majesty'. He gave a technician's appreciation of the difficulty of the task, 'won as it were out of the hard rock'. The problem was the writer's terrible Latin: 'whether it were of ignorance or policy the writer hath made so many faults as well in the Latin as the orthography that I was fain [compelled] to supply it almost everywhere by conjecture to make sense'.

Phelippes left Bourges in August and went on to Sancerre, between Nevers and Briare on the main post road out of Lyons. There he kept himself to himself: 'I kept myself close in places of small bruits [rumours].' He wanted to get to Paris, but his path was blocked by plague and sickness and the filthy winter weather of early 1583. He arrived in the city on or near to 13 March, for he was keen to report immediately to his master: 'Being here now at the last arrived at Paris,' he wrote to Walsingham, 'the first thing I think it my part to do, is to remember my most humble duty unto your honour.' In the letter he gave away little of his mission, though it seems to have been somewhere off the beaten track of Anglo-French diplomacy. In July Sir Henry Cobham, Elizabeth's ambassador, knew that Phelippes was in Bourges and had sent his servant to visit him. Now in Paris Phelippes was sure that Walsingham would forgive the long delays of the journey. This was the confidence, not of a man like Parry, but of a trusted and discreet servant who could assure himself of Walsingham's 'gracious interpretation' of his actions with few words of excuse.

The mystery of Thomas Phelippes's mission remains its object and purpose. Phelippes had been in France for at least eight months. Perhaps he was gathering news from France or making contact with possible sources of information. Given that he spent some time hidden away on the main post road from Lyons to Paris, a route commonly used by priests travelling between the English College in Rome and William Allen's seminary in Rheims, he may have been watching for émigrés or intercepting their letters. Whatever the nature of his mission, it did not involve a long stay in Paris. He had only just reached the city when he wrote his first letter to Walsingham, and already he was preparing to leave for England, giving 'these few lines' to let his master know of his return. He offered his 'poor service' to Walsingham at home or abroad.

While William Parry was in Venice vaunting his pre-eminent abilities to disrupt the queen's enemies, the considerably more able Phelippes was engaged on a mission for Walsingham. He was a linguist and a mathematician, a talented young man in his late twenties. Above all, he was discreet and careful. In the coming years – from 1585 especially – Thomas Phelippes would prove himself to be Walsingham's most secret and trusted servant, truly a man of the shadows.

William Parry, in contrast to Phelippes, enjoyed the light of attention and praise. He was a man who bored easily. He was worried that he heard very little from England, which meant that he was not sure 'what to write or how to send' it. To Burghley, Parry was a man of marginal significance, useful enough to cultivate but safe also to ignore. In Parry's mind, however, he was his lordship's faithful servant in Queen Elizabeth's 'special services'. He wrote: 'I have presumed that your lordship hath ever esteemed me for a true man to my prince and country. So much whatsoever do come to your ears, I beseech you to promise for me and I will not fail to perform it God willing.' To the world, William Parry was a poor and heavily indebted gentleman and a pardoned felon. In his own mind, he was a secret servant of great ability. This is why, in the early spring of 1583, he offered himself, without Burghley's knowledge, as a double agent in Elizabeth's service. He decided upon a great plan: to use the Pope's ambassador to the government of Venice, the nuncio Cardinal Campeggio, to infiltrate the Church of Rome and prevent their conspiracies against Queen Elizabeth.

Parry first made contact with Cardinal Campeggio, to whom he was introduced by Jesuits in the city. Parry was certainly conferring with one Jesuit, Benedetto Palmio, with whom he discussed Robert Persons's *Persecution*. Campeggio also received a good account of Parry from an English doctor living in Venice. He is likely to have been John Bradley, a man with a wife, children and property in the city whom Parry certainly knew.

Campeggio was Parry's route to Rome, or so Parry hoped. The nuncio wrote to the Cardinal of Como, the cardinal secretary of state, in March 1583. Campeggio enclosed with his own a letter from Parry to the cardinal. It read:

> I, William Parry, an English nobleman, after twelve years in the service
> of the Queen, was given a licence to travel abroad on secret and impor-
> tant business. Later, after pondering over the task committed to me and
> having conferred with some confidants of mine, men of judgment and
> education, I came to the conclusion that it was both dangerous to me
> and little to my honour. I have accordingly changed my mind and made
> a firm resolution to relinquish the project assigned to me and, with
> determined will, to employ all my strength and industry in the service
> of the Church and the Catholic faith.

Only Parry could have written with such style and abandon. He asked permission to come to Rome for a secret audience with the Pope.

Parry was overjoyed at the success of his secret approach to Campeggio and Como. He left Venice for Lyons, unable to stay in Italy, though whether on Burghley's or Walsingham's orders or because of money is unclear; Parry wrote of being 'overruled by the necessity of my departure'. But nothing could tarnish his great secret coup. He wrote to Burghley, flourishing his talents, feeling victorious:

> If I be not deceived I have shaken the foundation of the English seminary
> in Rheims and utterly overthrown the credit of the English pensioners

in Rome. My instruments were such as pass for great, honourable and grave. The course was extraordinary and strange, reasonably well devised, soundly followed and substantially executed without the assistance of any one of the English nation.

Parry, the master spy, was preening himself. He wrote to Burghley that he would either discover and prevent all 'Roman and Spanish practices' against England or lose his life trying. This, he said, was a testimony of his loyalty to the queen and his duty to the honourable friends who had protected him. He wrote: 'If it please your lordship to confer with Master Secretary touching my letters herewith sent, to advise and direct me, I am ready to do all I shall be able and am commanded.'

It seems very unlikely that either Walsingham or Burghley knew what Parry was up to in any precise way. In his letters he said nothing at all about his contacts with Campeggio, Como and Palmio. It could have been fatal for Parry to mention in his letters to London the approaches he had made to Rome. He never used code or cipher. As he wrote to Walsingham, 'the miscarrying of my letters to you may cost me my life'. Parry – in seeking an audience with Pope Gregory XIII or indeed in working without the direct sanction of Burghley or Walsingham – was taking the greatest risk of his uncertain life.

Parry went from Venice to Lyons with the idea of building a network of agents. He was not shy in asking Walsingham for money. Whatever he spent, he said, he thought 'well bestowed'. To recruit agents cost money: the cheapest of Parry's contacts, so he claimed, was a secretary. Not surprisingly, Parry's espionage, which reflected social rank and status, was expensive. One of his sources, a gentleman in Venice, came highly recommended: 'This man (in my opinion) is well worthy Her Majesty's entertainment in Venice where his credit and acquaintance amongst the nobility is very great. He is prepared already if it please your honour to use him.' He came with Parry's highest praise, 'a very sufficient man to be entertained in Venice', an ambassador to some of the greatest princes in Germany, and very honest.

In Lyons in the summer of 1583 Parry picked up the rumblings of a minor political scandal. Edward Unton, an English gentleman whose family connections extended to the Earl of Leicester and to Walsingham himself, had been imprisoned by the inquisition of Milan in late 1582 or early 1583. By June 1583 Unton was free and in Lyons, where Parry got to know him. 'Master Unton speaketh very great honour of your lordship,' he wrote to Burghley. He was, Parry wrote, a very proper and thankful gentleman, full of devotion to his prince and country: 'I would to Christ England bred no other.'

Edward Unton's companion in the inquisition's prison had been an English Catholic called Salamon Aldred. This Aldred was once a tailor of Birchin Lane in London but by 1579 he was living in Rome. In fact, he was the same man who knew Charles Sledd, the spy whose evidence had helped to convict Edmund Campion and other priests in 1581, and helped to lodge Sledd in Rome. Aldred, like Sledd and now Parry, played a little at espionage. In 1582 he had offered to supply the Cardinal of Como with letters stolen from English diplomats abroad. Como had refused the advance. A few months later, one of Walsingham's agents reported that 'there is also at Lyons one Aldred, who hath a pension of ten crowns a month of the Pope, and he doth advertise Rome of all Englishmen that pass'. Aldred would soon come to the notice of Walsingham. In early 1583 he visited the English seminary in Rome. Parry and Aldred were by now men of the same world, of shady contacts, suspicion, and uncertain and divided loyalties. We have to wonder whether they fully understood the consequences of so tangled a life.

In the summer months of 1583 Parry was still alert to intelligence, though with what kind of critical filter it is hard to tell, especially given his continued contact with Campeggio. On 18 August he wrote: 'I am advertised by more than an ordinary man that there is some great practice in hand in the north part of England. How true it is God knoweth.' This was a short note to Burghley in Parry's hand but without a signature. At the foot of the sheet of paper Parry wrote 'Burn'. He rarely underplayed the dramatic aspects of his work. Still in Lyons, he reported on the movements of Salamon Aldred and Edward Unton. But by now he wanted to become a scholar as well as a spy. He suggested the idea was Walsingham's: 'The liberty that

I am aduertised by more then an ordynary man that there is some great practise in hand in the North part of England. how true yt is god knoweth.

I haue heretofore written to yo'r L. my opinion of the Humbletons. I do now confirme yt and vpon my head assure you that the Qu. Ma. cannot trust theym. I dare trust hym that told me this tale. /

28 Aug. 1583

A secret report by William Parry for Lord Burghley, 1583.

I have long desired to withdraw myself to some university is at last (by Master Secretary's advice and favour) granted.' He told Burghley that he would now spend the rest of his time abroad in Orleans and Paris, to return to England with 'reasonable contentation' – 'if', he added, reflecting upon his difficult times at home, 'I be not to blame'.

And so William Parry – spy, gentleman, debtor, convicted felon, prisoner, recruiter of agents and aspiring scholar – went off to Orleans. He hoped to spend the winter there, but was driven on to Paris by the threat of plague. In the city he had the good fortune to meet his old associate Master Stafford, now Sir Edward Stafford, the queen's resident ambassador at the French court, and to make the acquaintance of Lord Burghley's grandson, seventeen-year-old William Cecil, 'whose good nature and towardness [aptitude or promise] beginneth to make a very good show already'. As ever he wished to show how grateful he was to Burghley: 'I will do my best to make it appear how much I am bound to your lordship,' he wrote. 'And for my lord ambassador if anything come to my hands worthy his knowledge I have promised him the preferment.'

For all these flattering professions of service, it is clear that Parry's contacts with Rome in autumn 1583 were just as strong as ever. Parry's secret was that he had betrayed Burghley and Walsingham. Deluded by his own cleverness, he had proposed to the Catholic authorities a plan to betray Elizabeth's government. Only the events of the coming months, when that plan matured into a plot to kill the queen, would show where his double loyalties really lay.

IO

'The enemy sleeps not'

In 1583 the Duke of Guise, cousin to Mary Queen of Scots, gave money, time and men to a plan for the invasion of England. English historians have long known it as the Throckmorton Plot, thanks to the small but significant part played in its planning by Francis Throckmorton, a young English Catholic gentleman. The cast of principal English characters is a fairly narrow one: Throckmorton himself, who worked as a courier for the Spanish ambassador in London; Charles Paget, an English émigré and one of Guise's men; his brother Thomas, Lord Paget, an English nobleman whose support for the invasion was sought by the duke; the Catholic earls of Northumberland and Arundel, both of whom had convenient strongholds near the coast where the invading army would land; and finally Lord Henry Howard, an elusive and subtle man, a Catholic and a supporter of the Queen of Scots.

The story begins in two very different places and with two quite different men: in the busy French port of Dieppe with a Sussex shipmaster, and then, some miles to the south-east, in Paris with the great Duke of Guise himself.

The man who called himself Wattes made his approach to John Halter in Dieppe on the feast day of Saint Bartholomew, 24 August, in 1583. Halter was the master and part owner of a bark, a small ship out of Arundel on the coast of Sussex. He was working for a London merchant, carrying a cargo of wooden boards to Dieppe, and in late August he was getting ready to return with nine fardels of cards and writing paper. Wattes told Halter that he lived in Rouen. He asked the shipmaster to take a gentleman over to England and then to bring him back

The shipmaster John Halter's account of Charles Paget's secret journey to England, December 1583.

to Dieppe. The price they agreed for this mysterious passenger was £7; once safely returned to France Halter would 'stand to the gentleman's reward'. A condition of the arrangement was absolute anonymity for the passenger, who, Halter later remembered, was earnest in requiring of him 'in no wise neither in England nor in France to ask his name'. Halter knew him only as 'the gentleman'. When he was later examined the shipmaster of Arundel gave no physical description of the man.

In the first week of September a favourable wind blew, and John Halter's bark set out from the harbour of Dieppe. The crossing to England took fourteen hours, and they went ashore at Arundel haven. The gentleman asked Halter to take him to the house of one William Davies at Patching, some four miles north-east of the haven, where they arrived at two o'clock in the morning of probably either Sunday, 8 September or Monday the 9th. Halter left the gentleman with Davies and returned to Patching about ten days later, where they had to wait three or four days for the wind and tide. When he was ready to sail, Halter spoke to Davies 'to call the gentleman to come on board at the haven mouth'. On 25 September, the Wednesday before Michaelmas, Halter, the gentleman and his manservant, as well as a servant to William Shelley of Michelgrove and a man Halter did not know, went down to the haven. With only the gentleman and his servant as passengers, Halter's bark landed at Dieppe on Friday, 27 September. It was a quiet crossing: the shipmaster and the gentleman did not speak on the return voyage because, as Halter later said, his passenger 'was so sick at sea'. The gentleman stayed at Dieppe for a whole day, probably to recover from the rigours of his journey, before returning to Rouen.

John Halter was practised at smuggling people across the English Channel. Usually his passengers went only one way, from England to France, either to Le Havre or Dieppe. Many of those he took to France were members of the Earl of Northumberland's household. They were Catholics or at least had Catholic connections. And they relied upon Halter's discretion. The shipmaster did not ask questions: sometimes he knew who his passengers were, sometimes he did not. But they had to have lots of money, for bribing the English port officials was an expensive business. The going rate to pay off the searcher of Arundel, whose job it was to check ships and their passengers, was £40, though for this great sum of money the searcher had let 'divers pass'. Or so said the writer of a secret report for William Allen in Rheims.

What was unusual, however, about John Halter's gentleman passenger in September 1583 was a fact Halter may have suspected from the especially secretive means of their entry into England. The mysterious man who suffered so badly with sea sickness had come to Sussex to spy out the land for an invasion of Queen Elizabeth's kingdoms by the Catholic powers of mainland Europe.

Behind it all was a meeting in Paris four months earlier, in June 1583, convened by Henry, Duke of Guise to discuss an invasion of the British Isles. Six men attended the meeting. They were Guise himself, one of the most powerful men in Europe and a passionate believer in the rescue of Elizabeth's England from heresy; the duke's spiritual confessor, Claude Matthieu; Archbishop James Beaton of Glasgow, the ambassador at the French court of the imprisoned Mary Queen of Scots; the Pope's Nuncio in Paris, Castelli; William Allen, the guide and moral compass of English Catholics in exile; and François de Roncherolles, one of the duke's men, who gave a military briefing.

Some, like Doctor Allen, favoured an assault upon England; others thought that any army should land in Scotland. By the end of June Guise had his plan. A force of 12,000 troops under the command of the Duke of Bavaria's brother – most of them Spaniards, Germans and Italians – would sail from Spain to Flanders and land eventually in Lancashire, provoking a popular uprising of English Catholics in the north of England. Duke Henry would land with a second, smaller army on the Sussex coast, where he would use the local strongholds of the Earl of Northumberland at Petworth in Sussex and the Earl of Arundel at Arundel Castle. This was at last a serious effort to decapitate Elizabeth's government once and for all: no wonder that in the spring and summer of 1583 the diplomatic connections between Spain, Rome and Paris buzzed with activity.

The Duke of Guise, cousin of Mary Queen of Scots, was thirty-three years old, tall and handsome, with a fair complexion and strawberry-blond hair. He was intelligent, athletic and charming, but also possessed the kind of arrogance and sense of high position that came of long nobility. In a country riven by religious civil war, the Guise family was immensely powerful, driven by a passionate hatred of Protestantism and the desire to revenge the murder of the second Duke of Guise by an assassin in 1563. They were not afraid to oppose even the French kings.

But the ambitions of Duke Henry went beyond the borders of France. Since the 1570s he had wanted to mount an invasion of England. His plans were often frustrated by a lack of either political and military will by King Philip of Spain or money, but Guise was always persistent in their pursuit. In 1578 he had consulted William Allen and representatives of Spain in the cause of his cousin Mary. The following year his chief agent travelled secretly throughout Europe. In December 1581 the duke had met Robert Persons, not long out of England, and William Crichton. Crichton, also a Jesuit priest, was an essential contact on Scotland, and a few months later, in spring 1582, he was involved in a project to restore Scotland to the

Catholic faith through the agency of Esmé Stuart, Duke of Lennox, then in favour at the court of young King James VI. Lennox would command an army and restore the Catholic faith; Guise, Crichton and others discussed an invasion of 8,000 men planned for September 1582. But it all came to nothing because of the collapse of Lennox's influence at James's court, the cooling of King Philip's support and the Pope's unwillingness to provide money for the expedition.

But the Duke of Guise was not a man to give up easily. The meeting in Paris in June 1583 meant that a definitive battle plan was at last agreed, and in July Henry went to Normandy to begin to prepare for the invasion. He sent a gentleman of his household to negotiate secretly at Petworth with the Earl of Northumberland and, through intermediaries, with the Spanish ambassador at Elizabeth's court, Don Bernardino de Mendoza. This gentleman's name was Charles Paget.

Of all the English Catholic families caught between faith and loyalty, few were grander than the Pagets of Beaudesert in the county of Staffordshire. Of these Pagets none was subtler than Charles. He was a younger son of a noble family. His brother Thomas, a man in his middle thirties, was the third Baron Paget, inheriting the title in 1568 on the death of an elder brother, Henry. Their father, the first baron, was William Paget, one of the most powerful English politicians of the 1540s and 1550s, an adviser to monarchs, a diplomat and something of a king-maker. He died in 1563. His wife, Charles's mother, the dowager Lady Paget, was a formidable woman who lived till 1587.

For some years before his secret visit to England Charles Paget tried to play a double game with Sir Francis Walsingham. The two men met in Paris in August 1581 when Secretary Walsingham was in the city on a special embassy. Paget's problem was that he had crossed the English Channel without the queen's licence. Paget had complained about his 'lamentable estate'. He was sick and in need of physic. He felt he might be of use to Walsingham. He proposed to change his lodgings in Paris and to live a life of secrecy: in other words, he offered himself as a spy. But Paget had not counted on the reports of Elizabeth's ambassador in Paris, Sir Henry Cobham, who made it plain to Walsingham that Paget was 'a practiser against the estate' and a known supporter of Mary Queen of Scots. Cobham had even refused to allow

Paget into his presence. Paget appealed instead to Walsingham's wisdom and humanity.

There is a clear record of what Sir Francis Walsingham thought of Charles Paget. It is a model of brilliantly compressed frankness, sharp as flint. He wrote:

> I have of late gotten some knowledge of your cunning dealing and that you meant to have used me for a stalking horse. Master Paget, a plain course is the best course. I see it very hard for men of contrary disposition to be united in good will. You love the Pope and I hate not his person but his calling. Until this impediment be removed we two shall neither agree in religion towards God nor in true and sincere devotion towards our prince and sovereign. God open your eyes and send you truly to know him.

Of a busy and inveterate plotter Walsingham, like Sir Henry Cobham, had taken full measure. Charles Paget was an exile to watch very carefully indeed.

This was the man who in September 1583 set off for the Sussex coast from the port of Dieppe. Very few people knew his real name, including John Halter the shipmaster who landed him at Arundel haven, guided him to Patching in Sussex and brought him safely back to Dieppe. The alias Paget used, when he had to, was Mope. Perhaps his choice of name – as a noun it could mean a fool and simpleton, or as a verb to wander around aimlessly or be in a daze – was in ironic counterpoint to the precision of his secret journey.

As Dame Margery Throckmorton rode in her coach from London to Lewisham on the second Wednesday in October 1583 she reflected upon the best way to leave England secretly. She was thinking about this not for herself, but for the second of her four sons, Thomas. His younger brother George had tried it already and he had failed, stopped and searched at the port. Temporarily detained, his clothes and belongings had been taken from him. Lady Throckmorton wanted Thomas to be able to pass safely with money, plate, clothes and other things 'to carry over with him for his own provision'. She wanted him to have the chance to live a new life abroad. She had heard that the safest way for Catholics to leave England was to go to the Countess of Arundel at Arundel Castle in Sussex, a few miles from where a gentleman with no name had come ashore from John Halter's bark a month before. The countess could be approached through her physician, Doctor Fryer. Very probably this was Thomas Fryer, who lived near the church of St Botolph outside the city walls of London at Aldersgate. Dame Margery had already invited Doctor Fryer to dinner at her house in Lewisham the very next day.

When Dame Margery arrived at Lewisham she wrote a letter to her eldest son, Francis, at Throckmorton House in London. She wanted Francis and his brother Thomas to act quickly. She asked Francis to be at Lewisham early the following day to meet Doctor Fryer. She sent to both of her sons God's blessing.

Francis Throckmorton received his mother's letter. He replied immediately. He did not like the idea of getting Thomas abroad with the help of the Countess of Arundel. He asked his mother to persuade – even to command – Thomas not to cross the English Channel. Francis Throckmorton was a careful man in October 1583. As a courier working secretly and treasonably for the Catholic powers of Europe, he had every reason to be.

The Tudor Throckmortons were a great sprawling and long-established family of land and some influence. Francis Throckmorton's father, Sir John, was the seventh of seven sons. One of his elder brothers, Francis's uncle Sir Nicholas Throckmorton, had served as Elizabeth's ambassador at the royal courts of Scotland and France. John Throckmorton himself was a lawyer and an important royal official. But in 1580 the family's situation was not a cheerful one. Sir John was accused of slackness and corruption in office; he spent some time in the Fleet prison in London and was burdened by the enormous fine of 1,000 marks (nearly £700), which in his will he directed Francis, as one of his executors, to pay. He had over £1,000 of debts owing to him, but himself owed more than £4,000, to gentlemen, scriveners, tailors and a vintner; he had pawned his chain and other jewels. Sir John died in May 1580, two days after making his will. He left a widow as well as four sons (Francis, Thomas, George and Edward) and two daughters (Mary and Anne), of whom all but Francis were under the age of twenty-four. Burdened by debt and the reputation of corruption, he left behind him, too, a lingering sense of family disgrace.

There seems little doubt that the Throckmorton boys were brought up as Catholics. In 1576 Dame Margery was accused of hearing mass said by a seminary priest, and it was alleged that the same priest taught her sons. As young men the two elder brothers, Francis and Thomas, travelled abroad secretly and established connections in the Low Countries with Sir Francis Englefield, long known by Elizabeth's government as a rebel and conspirator. By 1583 Francis Throckmorton was carrying letters between Mary Queen of Scots and the French ambassador in London, Michel de Castelnau, through Castelnau's secretary, Claude de Courcelles. Throckmorton was a regular visitor to Castelnau's residence at Salisbury Court, just off Fleet Street. Sir Francis Walsingham knew about this part of Francis Throckmorton's life, for, though Throckmorton did not know it, Walsingham had Salisbury Court under close and effective surveillance.

Through the French embassy, Throckmorton became acquainted with three powerful men of the English Catholic nobility. The first was Henry Percy, eighth Earl of Northumberland, whose brother Thomas, the seventh earl, had been executed for treason in 1572. The second was Lord Henry Howard, the brother of Thomas, fourth Duke of Norfolk, beheaded as a traitor also in 1572. Lord Henry was forty-three years old, an exceptionally bright man and frequently suspected of murky political dealings with Catholics at home and abroad; these suspicions always seemed to lack firm evidence. It was once written of Lord Henry that 'his spirit . . . is within no compass of quiet duty'. His subtle intelligence was peculiar among the Elizabethan nobility. The third of Francis Throckmorton's acquaintances was the weary and melancholic Lord Paget, Thomas the third Baron, whose brother was the energetic Charles Paget alias Mope. Treason, it seemed, had a habit of running in some Elizabethan families.

To the casual observer – even in fact to the reader of intercepted private letters – Thomas, Lord Paget was a loyal subject of the Tudor crown. The behaviour and reputation of his exiled brother Charles appeared to cause him some pain. In late October 1583 Lord Paget wrote from London to Charles in Rouen. The letter was short and stiffly polite. Elizabeth's government, he wrote, had not looked kindly upon Charles's stay in Paris. His move to Rouen, where he was known to be mixing with other exiles and émigrés, was similarly 'misliked'. Lord Paget advised Charles to travel further into France. He was troubled by reports – 'advertisements' – of what his brother was up to, writing: 'in some advertisements lately come, [that] you are touched as not to carry yourself so dutifully as you ought to do'. If this news was true, Lord Paget was sorry. He warned his brother to be wary, and he made his own position very clear. The plainness of his words was almost for the official record: 'if you forget what duty and loyalty you owe here, I will forget to be your brother'. He left Charles in God's keeping.

Charles Paget never received Lord Paget's stern brotherly warning: it was neatly filed away in the office of Sir Francis Walsingham and his staff. But more secret still was a fact masked by the crispness of Lord Paget's message to Charles. The letter was a smokescreen; it may even have been a coded warning for Charles to keep himself safe. In fact, in late September the brothers had met to discuss the Duke of Guise's plan to invade England.

Francis Throckmorton was arrested on the same day as Lord Henry Howard in the first week of November 1583. Throckmorton had been under surveillance for a long time, suspected 'upon secret intelligence given to the Queen's Majesty, that he was a privy [secret] conveyor and receiver of letters to and from the Scottish Queen'. By now the proof against him was fairly complete. But what may have prompted his arrest was the anxiety of Walsingham and other councillors over the strange treason of John Somerville, the Warwickshire gentleman who had set out from home to London with the intention of shooting the queen with his pistol. The government was very nervous.

On either 5 or 6 November, royal officials visited both Dame Margery Throckmorton's house in Lewisham and Throckmorton House at Paul's Wharf on the River Thames, a few streets south of St Paul's Cathedral. Francis, it seems, was almost caught in the act of treason, 'taken short at the time of his apprehension' in composing a letter in cipher to Mary Queen of Scots. He was led away and his house was searched. Officers found in Throckmorton's chamber two papers that listed the names of English Catholic noblemen and gentlemen and gave the descriptions of havens for the safe landing of foreign troops. Also found were twelve genealogical pedigrees of the ancestry of the English royal family supporting the claim of Mary Queen of Scots to Elizabeth's throne.

The searchers at Throckmorton House missed, however, one vital piece of evidence. It was a casket covered with green velvet that, thanks to the quick thinking of Francis Throckmorton's wife Anne, was spirited out of the house by their servants and taken to a friend of Throckmorton who lodged in Cheapside. The following day he handed it to one of the Spanish ambassador's servants.

Francis Throckmorton had no time to make his dispositions. His wife and servants had to cope as well as they could. Throckmorton had visited Lord Paget the evening before his arrest. Recognizing the danger he was in, Paget, from his lodgings on Fleet Street, not very far away from Paul's Wharf, began to prepare to leave England.

The day was Thursday, 7 November. Throckmorton House had been searched; so had the house of Dame Margery Throckmorton at Lewisham. Lord Paget wrote to a servant on his estates in Staffordshire: 'for that I have occasion to use money ... presently send me as much money as is any ways come to any of your hands to be here the 16 day of this month, for there I shall have occasion to use it'. He instructed his servants Twyneho and Walklate 'and such other as you shall think meet come with all, but let them keep it very secret'. There was urgency here but no rush: Lord Paget believed he had just over a week to get his affairs in order. Clearly he was beginning to sense a very serious change in his fortunes, and this only a few weeks after his stern lecture to his brother Charles about loyalty.

As Francis Throckmorton was led away to custody and his house searched, two very experienced and rather tough privy councillors, Sir Ralph Sadler and Sir Walter Mildmay, interrogated Lord Henry Howard. Howard held out for as long as he could, asking to be allowed to speak to Sir Francis Walsingham personally. Both Sadler and Mildmay knew the importance of Lord Henry's examination. Through Robert Beale, a clerk of the Privy Council, they asked to meet Walsingham on 10 November, after which they would brief the queen on their suspicions of Howard's questionable activities.

Francis Throckmorton was taken first to the house of the master of the royal posts on St Peter's Hill, one of the neighbouring streets to Paul's Wharf. Throckmorton was kept there for two or three days before going to the Tower. He was allowed to meet 'a solicitor of his law causes', who brought to him papers and books. Throckmorton used the meeting to slip a note into one of them. Denied pen and ink, he wrote on one of his lawyer's papers with a piece of coal the words 'I would fain [gladly] know whether my casket be safe'. He took a fantastic risk. And so too did his lawyer, who after leaving Throck-morton went straight to Throckmorton House – down St Peter's Hill, a right turn on to Thames Street, then the first left towards the river and Paul's Wharf – and opened up his papers. He found the note, which he gave to one of Throckmorton's household men.

On Friday, 15 November, William Herle, Lord Burghley's long-serving intelligencer, his eyes and ears in London, wrote to his master. Herle was lodged at the Bull's Head just outside the city walls at Temple Bar, close to Lord Paget's house. On the very same day Paget, if his instructions were being followed, should have been expecting the arrival within hours of the servants and money he needed to leave England secretly.

Herle was interested in conspiracy. He knew of a great international plot that involved the Duke of Guise, the Throckmorton brothers and Lord Henry Howard:

> The chief mark that is shot at, is Her Majesty's person, whom God doth and will preserve, according to her confident trust in him. The Duke of Guise is the director of the action, and the Pope is to confer the kingdom by his gift, upon such a one as is to marry with the Scottish Queen.

Rumours in London said that the elusive Lord Henry was a priest, even (more fancifully but a mark of a surprising man) that he was secretly one of the Pope's cardinals. And Herle knew all about Francis Throckmorton, for earlier that year he had told Secretary Walsingham of Throckmorton's secret meetings with the French ambassador in London, 'what long and private conferences, at seasons suspicious, and of his being at mass thereat several times'. Indeed one of Throckmorton's kinsmen had dined with the French ambassador only that Sunday, 10 November ('if I mistake not the day'). Francis Throckmorton, Herle wrote now to Burghley, was 'a party very busy and an enemy to the present state'. Herle wrote again the next day to Burghley: 'the world is full of mischief, for the enemy sleeps not'.

Under interrogation Francis Throckmorton's story was that the incriminating papers found in his chamber at Paul's Wharf were not really his. They had, he said, been the work of one 'Rogers alias Nutteby'. To support this fabrication Throckmorton 'found the means to get three cards', on the back of which he wrote secretly to his younger brother George: 'I have been examined by whom the two papers, containing the names of certain noblemen and gentlemen, and of havens, etc. were written.' He had said that they were in the handwriting of a household servant, and hoped that George would confirm the fabrication. Unfortunately for Francis, however, the cards were intercepted. On 13 November Walsingham made an entry in his notebook of the order for George Throckmorton's arrest.

Though Francis Throckmorton may have been offered a pardon for information on his serious crimes, at first he made a plain denial of any knowledge of treason. In the Tower of London, interviewed by privy councillors, he resisted examination. Thus refusing to talk, he was handed over to a number of commissioners with a warrant 'to assay [attempt, try or test] by torture to draw from him the truth of the matters'. In the official account of his examination on the rack, the phrase used was 'somewhat pinched, although not much'. The verb 'pinch' could mean a range of physical discomfort from irritation and annoyance to torture and torment.

Throckmorton was taken to the rack on 16 November. Still he refused to speak. He was given three days to recover physically, but quickly the decision was made to rack him again. On the 18th Walsingham sent the Council's torture warrant to the Tower. Pragmatic and unflinching, Walsingham was blunt: 'I suppose the grief [pain, torment] of the last torture will suffice without any extremity of racking to make him more conformable than he hath hitherto showed himself.' To one of the interrogators he offered a grim reflection, writing that he had seen men as resolute as Throckmorton stoop – to submit or yield under coercion – 'notwithstanding the great show that he hath made of a Roman resolution'.

Throckmorton spoke at last on 19 November. Walsingham, knowing the rack from experience, was correct: this time merely the threat of torture was enough to make him talk. He made a confession on 20 November, explaining how Sir Francis Englefield, in the government's view one of the queen's most dangerous enemies, had recruited him to carry letters to and from the Spanish ambassador in England. Throckmorton admitted that he had encouraged Englefield to press King Philip of Spain to invade England. He confessed, too, to having told his brother Thomas about the Duke of Guise's earlier projected invasions of Scotland. When these plans had fallen through in 1582, Guise began once again to look to England:

> if there could be a part found in England to join in the action and convenient places and means for landing, and other things necessary, there should be a supply for Guise of foreign strength. And [Throckmorton] said the Spanish ambassador in France called Juan Bautista de Tassis was acquainted with this matter.

On the day Francis Throckmorton was continuing to confess to his contacts with Sir Francis Englefield, William Herle, Lord Burghley's intelligencer, wrote to his patron of his devotion to 'public security', while Thomas, third Baron Paget left London ostensibly for his estates in Staffordshire but actually heading for the coast of Sussex.

After leaving London on the 23rd, Lord Paget and his party of servants and gentlemen were on the coast of Sussex near Ferring on 25 November. On that Monday, 'almost an hour within night', a yeoman farmer was inspecting his land. He saw eight men on horseback riding on the highway towards the sea. One man rode ahead with his sword drawn. Six of the others followed, riding two-by-two. The eighth man came behind, though the farmer could not tell whether his sword was in or out of its scabbard. They were riding 'for the most part all big horses or geldings'. He saw none of the men or their horses come back up the highway.

In this way, Thomas, Lord Paget left England secretly without the queen's licence. It was a month to the day since he had warned his brother Charles in Rouen of the duty and loyalty he owed in England, threatening to forget him as a brother. With Paget was Charles Arundel, the son of a knight and through his mother a kinsman of the noble house of Howard – another Catholic gentleman, another exile.

Elizabeth's advisers learned of Lord Paget's flight less than a week after he and his men had ridden down to Ferring. They guessed that Paget and Arundel would make for Paris. On 1 December Walsingham wrote to Sir Edward Stafford with the queen's order for her ambassador to keep a watchful eye on them. They had lately left England without leave; Stafford should seek very carefully to learn what they practised against the state.

In London there began a strenuous investigation of the facts. In the Tower Francis Throckmorton admitted that his 'plat' – his 'platform' or plan – of the harbours of Sussex was taken from maps. He had not scouted the coast for himself: that task was left to others. On 2 December he confessed to the involvement of Charles Paget in the Duke of Guise's project to land fourteen or fifteen thousand troops in Sussex. Paget 'was thereupon sent into Sussex in September 1583 to sound some noblemen and gentlemen there therein, and to view the havens'.

Although by the end of 1583 some pieces of the puzzle were still missing, it was clear that Walsingham and the Privy Council had discovered a major plot for an invasion of England. Elizabeth's government knew from at least two sources – the interrogations of Francis Throckmorton and the information of Burghley's intelligencer William Herle – that behind the plan was Henry, Duke of Guise. Both the French and Spanish ambassadors appeared to be involved. Lord Henry Howard was suspected of complicity, though the evidence against him was not yet conclusive. Lord Paget had left England without a licence in a great hurry. His brother Charles Paget was already deeply suspected of conspiracy. There was, in other words, a great tangle of suspicious activity: by Francis Throckmorton and his family and accomplices, by the Paget brothers and by Lord Henry Howard, on the streets of London and in the villages and hamlets of Sussex. In the weeks that followed, Walsingham and his men spared no effort to get to the root of one of the most pernicious conspiracies ever engineered against Queen Elizabeth and her government.

I I

'A very unadvised enterprise'

From the city of Paris Thomas, third Baron Paget, the new exile, wrote two letters. One was to Lord Burghley. The second was to his mother, the dowager Lady Paget, which contained a note for his sister Anne. To all three people, in quite different ways, Lord Paget had to explain why he had arrived so unexpectedly in Paris.

It was a week to the day since he and his party of armed men had secretly left the Sussex coast. Lord Paget, using the new calendar of Pope Gregory XIII, which gave ten days' difference between England and France, reckoned it to be the 12th. But for Paget there was no easy acclimatization to new surroundings. Without a proper complement of his servants, and above all without any warning of his flight from England even for his family, he found himself an unlicensed émigré and exile. From now on he would live a strange and disjointed sort of life, suspected by Elizabeth's government of conspiracy and treason.

Paget chose to make his explanation to Lord Burghley, firstly because Burghley was the most powerful man at Elizabeth's court, and secondly because Paget believed (though wrongly) that Burghley would give him a sympathetic hearing. Thirty years earlier Burghley had been something of a protégé of Paget's father, William, the first Baron, a tough and experienced politician very different in character and temperament to his son. In 1582 Burghley had been a mediator in Lord Paget's domestic difficulties with his wife, with whom, the baron complained, he lived 'with continual jars'. So now from Paris he set out his position in a letter that was a masterpiece of deliberate under-statement. Lord Paget quite understood that Burghley would believe he had 'taken in hand a very unadvised enterprise in coming into these parts'. Not so, he wrote: he had long wanted to travel, claiming as reasons the treatment of his gout ('with the which I am many times so miserably afflicted': Burghley was a fellow sufferer) and (a more sensitive matter) his conscience. Paget wrote that he needed the spiritual food of the Catholic sacraments.

To his mother, who was known to shelter Catholic priests, Lord Paget was more candid. Clearly he felt there was no choice for him but to leave England, where the conditions in which he found himself were intolerable. He asked the dowager Lady Paget to consider his disgrace at home, the protection he required from the 'entrapping of mine enemies', and his conscience. It had been no sudden decision, he said, but one of 'long time and deliberation'. He said nothing explicitly about the treason of Francis Throckmorton. Paget's letter had the tone of a man trying to convince himself against good evidence of the rightness of what he had done: 'Surely this journey that I have begun is by God's appointment and for his service and therefore it cannot be but for the best.' There was about it, too, a feeling of aggrieved melancholy.

Paget had told almost no one of his plan to leave England. His solicitor and secretary knew, and a few other close servants; others may have guessed. His mother had expected him at her house in Staffordshire, where he had had an appointment to see her. He apologized from Paris for not keeping their meeting. His sister, Lady Anne Lee, was entirely in the dark, though he wanted her now to make the official arrangements necessary for his servants to be sent to him. Lady Anne's husband was Sir Henry Lee, the queen's champion, and we can guess that Lord Paget had put Lady Anne in an awkward situation. The baron also left behind him in England the heir to the Paget barony, his young son William. Paget's wife had died a few months before he left England, and so near the end of the note to Lady Anne Lee her brother wrote: 'I pray you take care of Will.'

Lord Paget's letter to Burghley went directly to England with the post of Elizabeth's ambassador in Paris, Sir Edward Stafford. The packet to his mother and sister Paget sent to a London bookbinder called Williams at the sign of the Horn on Fleet Street, from where it would be carried to Staffordshire. Lady Paget may never have read her son's letter, for it survives, probably intercepted, in the papers of Walsingham's office.

Lord Paget and his friend and companion Charles Arundel visited Sir Edward Stafford at his house in Paris. This was the day before Lord Paget composed his letters to Burghley, his mother and his sister. On 1 December Stafford wrote to the queen and to Walsingham. Just as he had sealed up the packets for the courier who would take them to London, Lord Paget and Arundel called on him. They appeared silently. 'They were behind me in my dining chamber afore anybody was aware of them,' he explained to Walsingham, leaving Sir Edward 'somewhat amazed'. Paget and Arundel began to explain why they had left England, 'for their consciences, and for fear [of] having enemies that the cause being given by the traitorous Somerville [John Somerville, Elizabeth's putative assassin] to have a hard hand over all papists'. Choosing his words very carefully, Stafford replied to them that he thought 'their coming away at this time might give cause to their enemies (if they had any) to suspect their conscience not be clear'. Sir Edward promised to write to the queen to tell her what they had said. He also asked them not to visit him again till he knew Her Majesty's pleasure. To protect himself – a sensible precaution given the suspicions of Paget and Arundel in England – he wrote to Walsingham and Burghley, and enclosed with Burghley's packet Lord Paget's letter to the lord treasurer.

Francis Throckmorton was interrogated again in the Tower of London on 2 and 4 December. He confessed to a conversation he had had with King Philip's ambassador in Paris and the 'plot laid for the enterprise of the Duke of Guise'. Throckmorton had given the ambassador an account of havens along the English coast and a list of sympathetic Catholic noblemen and gentlemen. Throckmorton said that Philip had promised to fund half the cost of the expedition. Robert Persons went to Rome to solicit the Pope for the rest. Dame Margery Throckmorton, Francis's mother, admitted to the arrangements she had made in September to get her second son, Thomas, out of England. She told her interrogators about the Countess of Arundel, Doctor Fryer and the letter she had written to Francis.

The most difficult prisoner to handle was Lord Henry Howard. Hardly any piece of evidence stuck to him. The challenge of his interrogation can be seen in the long and involved questions put to him by his interrogators. The most important of these had to do with Charles Paget and the alias the government knew he had used, Mope; with the activities of the French ambassador; with any tokens or messages Lord Henry had received from the Queen of Scots or her agents; and with any of his communications with Francis Throckmorton, Charles Arundel and Lord Paget. Howard admitted to knowing about Charles Paget's letters brought to Lord Henry's house and to the Earl of Arundel's Charterhouse. Of course he had no idea of who had delivered them and could say nothing about the two or three seals that had been used to secure the packets. He remembered that one letter handed to him in St James's Park bore the seal of a St Andrew's cross. If it came from the Queen of Scots, he said, it did so only indirectly. In the subtle evasions of clever Lord Henry Howard hard facts were elusive things.

The arrival of the two important Englishmen in Paris caused a stir in official circles. 'There is no small ado here in court of my Lord Paget's and Charles Arundel's coming hither,' Sir Edward Stafford wrote in the first week of December. Sir Edward added with a dash of acid that Lord Paget was esteemed by the French king's courtiers to be 'a greater man' than ever Stafford knew him in England. The ambassador had had Paget and Arundel watched since their arrival. He knew that Charles Paget rarely left the company of Thomas Morgan, the Queen of Scots's intelligencer in the city.

It was really only a matter of time before William Parry, that everkeen advocate of exiles and émigrés, the gentleman spy with a gift for social flattery, took it upon himself to write in the cause of Lord Paget and Charles Arundel, Paget's companion in their secret departure from England. Parry was in Paris on 26 November and fed up: 'Myself do begin to despair of better fortune, my state ... being brought to £20 [of] land.' To Walsingham he pleaded poverty. 'Fiat voluntas Dei,' he wrote, ending his letter 'with my most hearty prayer for your honourable and happy life.'

But less than a fortnight later, thrown into action by the cause of the new exiles, Parry was very busy. On 7 December he understood 'the disquietness' at home caused by the departure overseas of Paget and Arundel. A day later he was thoroughly involved in the matter.

'I find them not to complain of Her Majesty's government,' Parry wrote, 'but that, oppressed by their contraries [enemies], they were either to leave their country or to abide and suffer more disgraces than they deserved or were able to bear.' He said that they spoke very honourably of Walsingham and commended him 'for as real a gentleman as liveth'. Parry wrote: 'I have had sundry conferences with them whereof I mean to make you privy upon my return.'

It was unlikely in early December 1583 that Sir Francis Walsingham would have been much affected by the flattery of either William Parry or Charles Arundel. He was more concerned by the facts of conspiracy that were being gathered and assembled. Dozens of possible witnesses – gentlemen, shipmasters, yeoman farmers, household servants – were interviewed in Sussex by justices of the peace and in London and Westminster by clerks of the Privy Council.

Edward Caryll, a Sussex gentleman who had been in London, denied hearing anything of 'the going away of the Lord Paget and Charles Arundel' other than the common rumour in London. He had last seen Lord Paget on the street near the Temple Bar in the very early days of November. 'Good morrow, Master Caryll,' Lord Paget had said, to which Caryll replied 'Good morrow, my lord.' They had had no conversation. Caryll had seen Charles Arundel once or twice in London during the Michaelmas law term but they not had spoken. The only thing Caryll admitted to was hearing a rumour in Sussex that Paget and Arundel had slept at Caryll's house in his own absence before leaving England. Knowing that suspicion might fall on him, Caryll had immediately gone to a Sussex justice to make a statement.

Gradually the pieces began to fall into place. Within a fortnight of Paget's illicit departure for France, Walsingham knew the names of the owner and the skipper of the boat who had met Paget and his men under cover of darkness on the Sussex coast. Even more significantly, he discovered from Paget's secretary that his lordship had met Francis Throckmorton and Lord Henry Howard only the day before Paget had left London to go into exile.

The conditions of Francis Throckmorton's confinement in the Tower of London were by early December proving surprisingly leaky.

He was, after all, a state prisoner under close observation, around whom was gathering a formidable body of evidence of treason and espionage. But Throckmorton had a contact on the inside. She was Sislye Hopton, the daughter of the Tower's lieutenant, who became friendly with Francis Throckmorton's brother George, sent to the Tower some time after 13 November. George 'moved her for some device to have his brother [Francis] out of the Tower'. Sislye did not agree to this: but nor did she tell her father about it.

Very probably with Sislye Hopton's help, George Throckmorton managed to get a letter from Francis to his wife Anne. It arrived at dinnertime on Friday, 13 December, brought by a little boy with long hair. Two days later, one of the Throckmortons' servants said under interrogation that the opening words of the letter were 'My good sweetheart'. He then revealed the existence of the little velvet-covered casket that had been smuggled out of Throckmorton House and given to the Spanish ambassador's servant. The Throckmorton family was questioned, as was the little boy who had carried the letter from the Tower. He was sent to Bridewell hospital to be held for further examination. Sislye Hopton, who was much too friendly with traitors in the Tower of London, found herself in a great deal of trouble.

By the middle of December Walsingham knew that Charles Paget, using the alias of Mope, had come to England secretly from Dieppe in September of that same year. His purpose had been to spy out the land for an invasion of the Sussex coast by the Duke of Guise. Essential to Guise's plan were two English Catholic noblemen who had strongholds close to the point where the duke wanted to land his troops, the Earl of Northumberland and Philip Howard, thirteenth Earl of Arundel, and Lord Henry Howard's nephew. Both men inevitably found themselves under suspicion.

On 15 December Northumberland was held under guard in his London house, accused of having secretly met Charles Paget in September. He quickly confessed to the meeting with Paget, but said that it had to do with the private affairs of Lord Paget. Walsingham thought the earl was lying. He wrote to Elizabeth's ambassador in Paris: 'Charles Paget is a most dangerous instrument, and I wish for the Earl of Northumberland's sake, he had never been born.'

In Paris ambassador Stafford himself was pursuing several lines of inquiry. He reported to Walsingham that Charles Paget and Thomas Morgan, Mary Stuart's chief spy in Paris, were inseparable. Lord Paget now had money: 4,000 French crowns sent to Paris by a London merchant; the exchange of currency had come through the city of Rouen. In London Walsingham's men began to make out Lord Paget's movements and itinerary in October and November 1583, weeks before he had left England. They learned one crucial fact. Francis Throckmorton had met Lord Paget 'the last term about Hallowtide' (1 November) 'and supped with my lord at his lodgings in Fleet Street'.

Equally, the details of Charles Paget's secret visit to England were all the time becoming clearer. Thanks to careful investigations in Sussex, Walsingham's men found and questioned the shipmaster who had brought Paget across the English Channel from Dieppe. The Earl of Northumberland was interrogated further about his dealings with Francis Throckmorton, his conversations with the Paget brothers and Lord Henry Howard. Significant was Charles Paget's great interest in places and landing sites along the coast. What is more, there was growing evidence of the part Paget had played over some years in the carrying of letters between the French and Spanish ambassadors in London and Mary Queen of Scots in captivity in Derbyshire and Staffordshire. The case against the dangerous English émigré who called himself Mope began to mount up.

The principal treason was to mount an invasion of England and it was clear as day that the Duke of Guise was behind the enterprise. Charles Paget was a major player. Francis Throckmorton was a small but significant element in the machine. The French and Spanish ambassadors in London were quite clearly hostile to Elizabeth. Senior members of some of the grandest families in the kingdom were implicated in the projected invasion: the Earl of Northumberland, Thomas, Lord Paget and surely Lord Henry Howard.

The Christmas holidays did not impede an investigation that by now had great momentum. Both the Earl of Northumberland and Lord Henry Howard were interrogated once again. So were their household servants. The Earl of Arundel was questioned further. The government intercepted suspicious packets of letters sent from

England to Charles Paget in France. In Paris Sir Edward Stafford had Lord Paget and Charles Arundel followed. The two men were quite different kinds of émigré, Paget quiet and reserved, Arundel angry and talkative. One was tongue-tied, Stafford wrote, the other had it at liberty: Paget was cold and patient, Arundel choleric and impatient.

One political consequence of the uncovering of the Duke of Guise's plan for the invasion of England was a major rupture in Anglo-Spanish diplomacy. Although Guise was responsible for the project, helped by English Catholic émigrés, Francis Throckmorton had been plain about Spanish involvement in it. So it was that Don Bernardino de Mendoza, the ambassador of the King of Spain who despised Elizabeth's Protestant government with a passion, was dismissed from her court with very little ceremony. In January 1584 he was taken from Dover to Calais on board *The Scout*, a ship manned by a crew of forty sailors and twenty gunners. At the substantial cost to Elizabeth's treasury of £46 and 5 shillings, an enemy was escorted out of England across the English Channel. An English official was sent to Spain to explain Mendoza's expulsion, but King Philip did not even grant him an audience.

Francis Throckmorton was tried and condemned for treason in the Guild Hall in London on 21 May 1584. Three weeks later a full account of Throckmorton's conspiracies appeared in print, laying out in plain English his 'intelligence' with the Queen of Scots and the plottings of the Duke of Guise, Charles Paget, the Throckmorton family, Sir Francis Englefield in the Low Countries and Thomas Morgan in Paris. The names of the Earl of Northumberland and Lord Henry Howard were carefully omitted. A Latin translation of the pamphlet was printed for foreign readers; in the case of Francis Throckmorton Elizabeth's government was sensitive to criticism throughout Europe.

But the execution of Throckmorton at Tyburn on 10 July was only a temporary end to the story of the Duke of Guise's plans for the invasion of England. In *A discoverie of the treasons practised ... by Francis Throckmorton* Elizabeth's government gave at best half an account of what had happened. What forced its hand to say something further in defence of the queen's good name was the suicide in June 1585 of Henry Percy, Earl of Northumberland, one of the

1. The 'Rainbow' portrait of Queen Elizabeth I, *c.* 1600, attributed to Marcus Gheeraerts the Younger. Elizabeth's golden cloak is decorated with the eyes and ears of her attentive subjects. The art historian Sir Roy Strong notes an early seventeenth-century verse by Henry Peacham:

> Be serv'd with eyes, and listening ears of those,
> Who can from all parts give intelligence
> To gall his foe, or timely to prevent
> At home his malice, and intendiment.

2. The union of the royal houses of Lancaster and York, bringing peace out of civil war, from an engraving of 1589 by Jodocus Hondius. The great Tudor rose is topped by the crown imperial of the Tudor monarchs.

3. Four expensively dressed men of high rank play the popular card game of primero. Not all games were conducted in grand society. One Elizabethan writer on dice play, Gilbert Walker, warned his readers against the taverns and gaming houses that would have been familiar to the spies and intelligencers of London: 'now such is the misery of our time, and such the licentious outrage of idle misgoverned persons'.

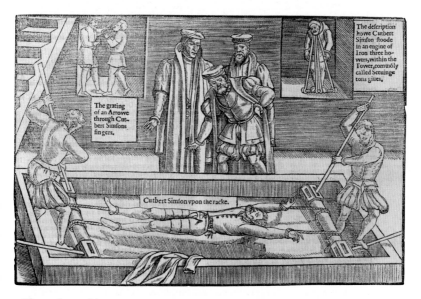

4. The rack, used here to torment a Protestant in the reign of Queen Mary I, from John Foxe's *Book of Martyrs*.

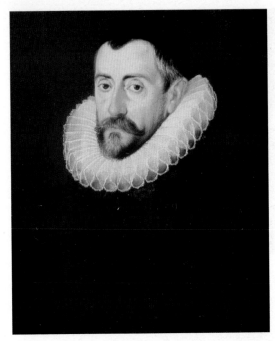

5. Sir Francis Walsingham, c. 1585, attributed to John De Critz the Elder.

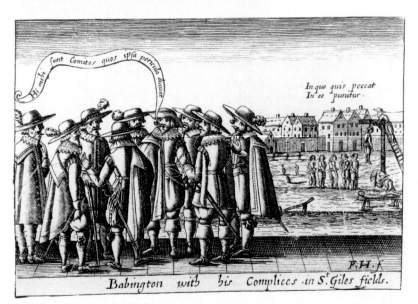

6. Anthony Babington and his gentleman accomplices, from a late seventeenth-century engraving, accompanied by the verse: 'Here Babington and all his desperate band / Ready prepar'd for royal murder stand'.

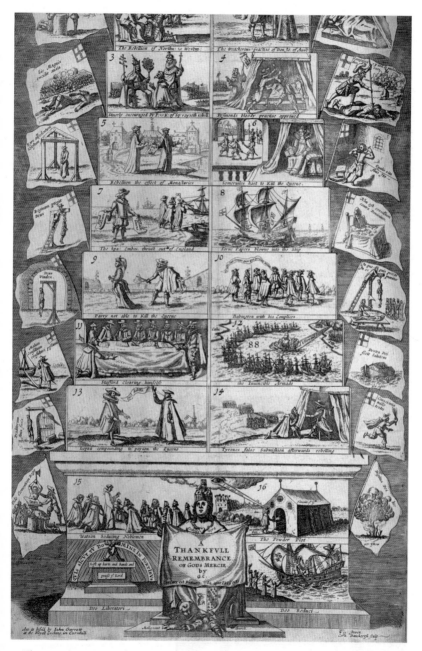

7. The reverberations of treason: Catholic conspiracies from Elizabeth I's reign to the Gunpowder Plot of 1605, from *Popish Plots and Treasons*, engraved in the late seventeenth century.

8. William Parry's attempt to kill Elizabeth I in 1584, from a later engraving. This is an imaginative fiction: Parry never drew his dagger on the queen, though according to his co-conspirator Edmund Nevylle it was his preferred weapon: '"As for a dag [pistol]", said Parry, "I care not: my dagger is enough."'

9. The Heneage Jewel, *c.* 1595, a locket of enamelled gold set with diamonds and rubies. The portrait of Elizabeth I is by Nicholas Hilliard. The locket bears the inscription 'Hei mihi quod tanto virtus perfusa decore non habet eternos inviolata dies': 'Alas, that so much virtue suffused with beauty should not last for ever inviolate'.

10. Mary Queen of Scots as a young woman, *c.* 1560, by François Clouet. Later images of Mary were heavily influenced by what Catholics saw as her martyrdom.

11. Mary Queen of Scots's prayer book and rosary, now in Arundel Castle. Objects owned (or most often believed to be owned) by the Queen of Scots have always had a special significance for those who see her as a victim of Elizabeth's tyranny.

12. A letter in cipher of 1585 or 1586 produced by Thomas Phelippes, Sir Francis Walsingham's expert on codes and ciphers, as evidence of Mary Queen of Scots's secret treasonable correspondence. Phelippes patiently gathered the papers that sent Mary to the executioner's block at Fotheringhay Castle.

13. The effigy of Elizabeth I, wearing the Tudor crown imperial even in death, from her tomb in the Lady Chapel of Westminster Abbey.

principal conspirators. There were, predictably, open rumours and suspicions of a political murder in the Tower of London, where the earl was still being held in custody eighteen months after being arrested. The government knew full well that Northumberland's death looked like the convenient disposal of a traitor. So his case – his suicide and the treasons and conspiracies that in the view of the authorities had led to it – was put to Star Chamber by the crown's lawyers on 23 June. The full story was printed and published, once again by Elizabeth's official printer, Christopher Barker.

The pamphlet related how on the evening of Sunday, 20 June one of Northumberland's gentleman servants in the Tower served supper to his master and saw him to bed at about nine o'clock. He went to an outer chamber, leaving the door to the earl's room ajar. Northumberland got up and bolted the door himself, saying that he could not sleep without the door locked shut. At midnight the servant, who was fast asleep, awoke to a very loud and sudden noise. 'My lord,' he shouted through the door to the earl's chamber, 'know you what this is?' Northumberland did not reply. He knocked on the door, calling out 'My lord, how do you?' At last he sent for the lieutenant of the Tower, Sir Owen Hopton.

On Hopton's instructions, the door to Northumberland's chamber was broken down. Hopton found Henry Percy in his bed, dead. Sir Owen realized that the earl's bedsheets were covered in blood. He quickly discovered a wound in the earl's breast, thinking at first that it had been made with a knife. It was only later, after first ordering the chamber to be locked and then writing to the Privy Council with news of the earl's death, that he went into Northumberland's room and found the pistol lying on the floor about three feet from a table. Sir Owen said that he had not noticed the pistol before because it lay in the table's shadow.

The dag had been hidden in the chimney of Northumberland's bed-chamber. On the evening of 20 June the earl had taken no chances. He charged the pistol with three bullets and a heavy amount of gunpow-der. He removed his waistcoat. Lying on his back, he had taken the dag in his left hand putting the muzzle of the pistol against his chest. The shot, which badly scorched the earl's shirt, more importantly left a large wound in his left breast. A surgeon removed the bullets from

under the earl's right shoulder blade. After entering his body they had torn his heart into pieces, shattered three of his ribs, and broken his spine into two. That, at least, was the official story.

Northumberland's treasons, said the government, explained the desperate manner of his self-destruction. In the official pamphlet the authorities gave in plain, vigorous Elizabethan prose a public summing-up and a narrative of the treasons of Charles Paget and his comrades and the plans of the Duke of Guise. At last they told the full story of the most audacious attempt yet by England's foreign enemies and Catholic fugitives to topple the government of Queen Elizabeth.

Francis Throckmorton had been recommended to Don Bernardino de Mendoza, the Spanish ambassador in London, who told Throckmorton about the invasion plans of the Duke of Guise. Throckmorton provided Mendoza with maps of suitable landing sites on the south coast of England and with the names of English noblemen and gentlemen who would be willing to help in Guise's plan.

Throckmorton said that the main purpose of the expedition was to force Elizabeth to grant toleration of religion to England's Catholics. If this toleration could not be achieved without altering the government, then it should be toppled and the queen removed from power. An important element of the project was the liberation of Mary Queen of Scots from English captivity; the Duke of Guise told his cousin about his plan to free her by military force. Throckmorton and Mendoza had together discussed how this could be achieved.

The ambassador said to Throckmorton that a man calling himself Mope had come secretly into England to talk to the Earl of Northumberland and other important men in Sussex. Mendoza later explained to Throckmorton that Mope's real name was Charles Paget, and that he had come not only to talk to Northumberland but also to spy out the land for an invasion, to view landing places and ports, and to consider provisions. Local men content to join Guise's invading army would levy troops in the name of the queen but then use them to help the invaders. Thomas, Lord Paget agreed to this proposal.

Charles Paget visited the Earl of Northumberland's house near the Sussex coast, Petworth, for a secret meeting with the earl. Late at night he was taken into the long gallery at Petworth and there spoke

to Northumberland for an hour or more. For over a week he stayed secretly in a lodge on the estate. Lord Paget came to Petworth and talked to his brother and Northumberland several times.

During his stay in England, Charles Paget said that:

> Foreign princes would seek revenge against Her Majesty of the wrongs by her done unto them, and would take such time and opportunity as might best serve them for that purpose, and said that those princes disdained to see the Scottish Queen so kept and used here as she was, and would use all their forces for her delivery: that the Duke of Guise would be a dealer therein, and that the Earl of Northumberland would be an assistant unto them . . . saying further, that the Earl of Northumberland was affected to the Scottish Queen, and would do what he could for her advancement.

> [And] That the Duke of Guise had forces in a readiness to be employed for the altering of the state of religion here in England, and to set the Scottish Queen at liberty.

The Earl of Northumberland had sought to protect himself. He was privy to the activities of Francis Throckmorton and he was a confederate of Charles Paget and his brother. It was Northumberland who, on hearing of Throckmorton's arrest and torture, decided to get Lord Paget out of England. Throckmorton had confessed to Charles Paget's visit to Petworth. Only Lord Paget could say what he, his brother and Northumberland had talked about there. Thus the safety of Northumberland rested on Paget's swift departure from the kingdom. So it was that the melancholy baron was now an exile in Paris.

At first even the arrest and interrogation of Francis Throckmorton in November 1583 did not deter the Duke of Guise from executing his invasion of England. Although King Philip of Spain dragged his heels over its funding, absorbed by the military efforts of Spain in the Low Countries, the arrival in Paris in 1584 of Philip's former ambassador to Elizabeth, Don Bernardino de Mendoza, gave Guise an important ally. The duke was confident of success as late as the spring of 1584. What diverted his attention, however, was the death in June 1584 of the Duke of Anjou, King Henry III's brother, which threw open the succession to the French throne. Important as England and the liberation of the Queen of Scots were, the vast energies of the Duke of Guise were from now on consumed by a French civil war of succession and religion that would last for thirteen years. Guise himself would die in the cause: after the duke stormed into Paris in 1588 King Henry ordered his powerful rival's assassination. Henry, Duke of Guise was stabbed to death in the chamber of the royal council in December of the same year.

The efforts of the Catholic émigrés to topple Elizabeth's government and free the Queen of Scots suffered only a temporary setback in 1584. Of all the English conspirators only Francis Throckmorton and the Earl of Northumberland were dead. The Earl of Arundel, only partly involved in the plot, was in the Tower of London, and there would remain until his death in 1595. But the Paget brothers and Thomas Throckmorton, Francis's conspiring brother, were free. In August 1585 one of Walsingham's spies reported that Charles Paget was in Rouen writing a book to answer the English government's account of Francis Throckmorton's treason. A few weeks later the same spy said that Thomas Throckmorton was about to meet Lord Paget in Genoa. Lord Henry Howard, that most extraordinary Elizabethan, remained in England, managing to profess loyalty to Elizabeth's government while at the same time maintaining contacts with Spain.

So there were traitors left to conspire, who still waited for their moment to come. Without the Duke of Guise they hoped for the support of the King of Spain and the Pope in mounting an invasion of England. One particular treason had been quashed by the Elizabethan authorities. But the busy minds of men like Charles Paget were rarely at rest.

12

Dangerous Fruits

When it came to loyalty two factors – money and flattery – directed the flow of William Parry's mercurial mind. Parry, the gentleman spy, was a snob; he enjoyed nothing more than a comfortable life mingling with important men. To Parry espionage was a means to secure for himself material comfort and influence, though he had few doubts that he was very good at it. Probably no other character in this book was as accomplished as he at self-deception. Taking an extraordinary risk, in 1583 he wrote to one of the Pope's cardinals with an offer of service for the Catholic cause. Then, just as heroically, he reported to Lord Burghley and Sir Francis Walsingham his solo work as a master spy for queen and country.

In 1583 he had enjoyed himself in Venice, Lyons and Paris. By the time Parry returned to London in the summer of 1584, he was doctor of laws of the University of Paris. Whichever side he chose ultimately to serve – Rome or England – would rest on who gave him the patronage he felt he deserved and how effectively they tickled his vanity. Within months Parry's life unravelled in an extraordinary way when, falling victim to his own deviousness, he sought and then failed to put into action a disastrous plan to kill Queen Elizabeth.

All through his career as a spy for Burghley and Walsingham, William Parry had consorted with Elizabeth's enemies, seeking to reconcile them to the queen. The communications he had opened up with Rome in spring 1583, through the Pope's nuncio in Venice, Campeggio, were on a very different scale; it was an elaborate and dangerous deception. This was probably why before his return to London he had told Sir Edward Stafford in Paris that he had intelligence for the queen's ears only.

Parry was playing, in other words, a double game, but neither Lord Burghley nor Cardinal Campeggio knew whom he really served. Parry, in fact, was on no one's side but his own. He played his double bluff so successfully that he found himself tangled up in a deception he could not control. On balance, however, he was probably Rome's spy, for when he was in Paris in September 1582 he was secretly reconciled to the Catholic Church. More extraordinary still is that in 1583, influenced by the prospect of money and fame, he made a genuine offer to murder Queen Elizabeth. On this mission he blew hot and cold all the way through 1584. Probably if Lord Burghley had given Parry the patronage he wanted so desperately, then his bizarre story may not have ended on the gallows. Parry might then have preferred to forget his solemn promises to cardinals and priests. But this never happened. The cold welcome he found in London and the fear of financial ruin only fixed in his mind a desperate mission to assassinate the queen.

When Parry was reconciled to the Catholic Church in 1582, he was advised to live quietly in Paris. Few of the English émigrés in the city trusted him; they knew that he was in contact with Lord Burghley. From Paris, Parry went to Lyons and then Milan, where he satisfied the local inquisitor that he was a Catholic. He was in Venice by February 1583 at the latest. It was there that Parry (as he himself wrote) 'conceived a possible mean to relieve the afflicted state of our Catholics, if the same might be well warranted in religion and conscience by the Pope'. At this time he read Robert Persons's account of the vicious persecution of Catholics in England, which he discussed with a Jesuit priest, Benedetto Palmio. Palmio introduced Parry to Campeggio, the Pope's nuncio to the Venetian government. Campeggio in turn wrote of Parry to the Cardinal of Como, the papal secretary of state.

Parry's primary motivations were money and the desire to impress powerful men, though as a scholar he was interested too in ideas and arguments. He read dangerous books. To Burghley, in 1583, he mentioned Robert Persons's polemic on the persecution of Catholics in England. A year later he read *A True, Sincere, and Modest Defence of English Catholicques*, William Allen's answer to *The execution of Justice*, Lord Burghley's account of the government's lawful prosecution of Catholic priests as traitors. Allen's *Modest Defence* was a particularly pernicious book to the Elizabethan authorities, strictly prohibited in England by royal proclamation. In just over two hundred pages, Allen condemned the persecution of English Catholics by Protestants under the pretence of treason charges, setting out also the authority of popes – indeed even of priests – to depose kings, calling them 'judges and executors' of the divine will. No prince, even a Catholic one, was beyond the Pope's justice. Parry found in Allen's powerfully persuasive book arguments that spoke directly to his conscience.

Parry wanted permission and papers to be able to travel from Venice to Rome, but for some weeks there was no clear idea of what kind of passport he should have. Nothing had been decided before Parry set off from Venice to Lyons. The fact that Parry had left for Lyons caused Campeggio to doubt whether Parry was sincere. Parry, however, was jubilant. It was only a fortnight later that he wrote the letter informing Burghley that he had shaken the foundation of the English seminary in Rheims and overthrown the credit of the Pope's English pensioners in Rome.

It is likely that Parry's high spirits came about from his meeting in Lyons with William Crichton, a Scottish Jesuit priest close to the Duke of Guise and involved in Guise's various plans for the invasion of Scotland and England. With Crichton, Parry discussed the lawfulness of killing a tyrant. Crichton, said that such an assassination was not legitimate, citing Saint Paul in the New Testament (Romans 3:8): 'Evil is not to be done that good may ensue.' Parry disagreed: 'it was not evil to take away so great an evil'. Yet in spite of their theological differences, Crichton became Parry's new contact with the authorities in Rome. By late May Parry had received, thanks to Cardinal Campeggio, a safe-conduct to travel through the Papal States. It was no wonder that in the middle of June, still in Lyons, Parry wrote to Walsingham: 'the miscarrying of my letters to you may cost me my life'.

Parry never went to Rome. He travelled instead from Lyons to Paris, where at some time between October and December 1583 he visited Thomas Morgan, Mary Stuart's chief gatherer of secret intelligence. Their conversation changed Parry's life and committed him to a desperate course of action. Morgan took him into a private chamber. Parry later described the meeting. Morgan, he said, 'told me that it was hoped and looked for, that I should do some service for God and his Church. I answered him I would do it, if it were to kill the greatest subject in England: whom I named, and in truth then hated.' 'No, no,' Morgan had said, 'let him live to his greater fall and ruin of his house.' Parry was talking about the assassination of his own patron, Lord Burghley. But, Parry claimed, Morgan in fact meant Queen Elizabeth. Parry's reply was that so great a mission could be accomplished, if of course the theological case for the queen's murder was clear: 'it were soon done, if it might [be] lawfully done, and warranted in the opinion of some learned divines'. Parry's theologian of choice was William Allen, whose *Modest Defence* had so influenced his thinking on the legitimacy of killing monarchs. But in fact it was a much humbler English priest, one Master Wattes, who, as William Crichton had done in Lyons, said plainly that it would be unlawful for Parry to assassinate the queen. Nevertheless Parry, persuaded by the arguments of Allen's *Modest Defence*, told Morgan that he would kill Elizabeth – so long as the Pope allowed him to do so and in turn granted full remission of Parry's sins.

Parry was able to convince Thomas Morgan and the Jesuits of his loyalty to their cause. He believed his reputation in Paris to be sound. But he still worried about secret enemies. For a night-time meeting with the Pope's nuncio, Parry was heavily wrapped in a cloak for disguise. At the end of November Parry wrote to the Cardinal of Como: 'There are never wanting jealous and spiteful people unacquainted with my actions who will seek to malign me and give information against me to His Holiness and your eminence.' He asked Como to trust only the reports of the Archbishop of Glasgow and the Bishop of Ross (both ambassadors of the Queen of Scots), William Crichton, Charles Paget and Thomas Morgan. Parry sent another letter to the cardinal a few weeks later in which he enclosed an attestation by a Jesuit priest that in Paris he had confessed and received the sacrament of holy communion.

Parry left Paris in the last few days of December 1583, arriving in England at the port of Rye in January. Thanks probably to Sir Edward Stafford's effusive praise (and probably also Burghley's influence) Parry had 'audience at large' with Elizabeth. Playing the loyal subject and *agent provocateur* he 'very privately discovered to Her Majesty' the conspiracy he had engineered to kill her. In spite of his privileged access to Elizabeth, he was unable to convince her of the substance of the plot; she 'took it doubtfully'. Parry was for the first time seriously worried that he had fatally incriminated himself. He left the queen's presence in fear.

So now Parry faced the problem of loyalty. He had convinced Morgan in Paris of his seriousness in the mission of killing Elizabeth. The Cardinal of Como believed him to be a loyal Catholic, in spite of repeated warnings of Parry's bad character. Could he be trusted? Charles Paget's sister thought not: in January 1584 she wrote to her brother to say that Parry was a spy, and that everything Charles said to Morgan, Morgan repeated to Parry. 'I pray you, good brother Charles, have great care with whom you converse.' Her letter, intercepted by Elizabeth's government, never reached him. Indeed Paget was certainly in contact with Parry. In February, from London, Parry thanked Paget for his 'friendly letters'. So long as Paget promised to burn Parry's letters, just as Parry destroyed Paget's, he would continue to write. At the foot of this letter Parry wrote 'Burn'. Paget, in Paris, never received it: the packet was intercepted by Elizabeth's government.

Up to his neck in conspiracy, Parry was, as ever, troubled by money. He desperately needed Burghley's patronage. Temporarily he appeared to turn away from treason, writing to Morgan in Paris to renounce his mission. He urged Morgan to burn their correspondence. Still hoping for better luck at court, in March he went to Greenwich Palace to petition Burghley for the vacant mastership of St Katharine's hospital for poor sisters, near the Tower of London. But while at Greenwich Parry received a letter from the Cardinal of Como. The Pope, Como wrote to Parry, commended 'the good disposition and resolution which you ... hold towards the service and benefit [of the] public: wherein His Holiness doth exhort you to persevere'. Desperate about his future, this was just the warrant Parry had been looking for. Suddenly his doubts disappeared. He later confessed that he found in Como's letter 'the enterprise commended, and allowed'. Parry believed he was absolved in the Pope's name of all his sins.

But Parry's mind never rested in one place for very long. At times he was determined never to kill the queen. 'I feared to be tempted,' he later said, adding with a familiar dramatic touch: 'and therefore always when I came near her, I left my dagger at home.' He pondered Elizabeth's excellent qualities. But then he asked himself: 'Why should I care for her? What hath she done for me? Have I not spent ten thousand marks since I knew her service, and never had penny by her?' True, she had given him his life when he had been pardoned of his conviction for the assault of Hugh Hare the moneylender. Still, he reflected, it would anyway have been tyranny to execute him.

In May, Parry was still hoping for Burghley's help in the mastership of St Katharine's, though Parry sent his great patron a letter the tone of which was peevish and resentful. He blamed his troubles on secret enemies. With no whisper of irony or self-doubt, he wrote of the strength of his loyalty in matters of religion and duty: quite a feat of psychological gymnastics for a man who in Paris had sworn to murder the queen. Parry was sure that Walsingham and Burghley could help him easily to secure the mastership of St Katharine's. He thought no other candidate was better suited: 'I would to Christ Her Majesty would command any further trial of me.' 'Remember me, my dearest lord,' he wrote, 'and think it not enough for a man of my fortune past to live by meat and drink. Justice itself willeth it should be credit and reward.' Yet Parry's letter came to nothing, and his hopes were frustrated. At the foot of his letter to Burghley he wrote the word 'Burn'. As usual, Burghley ignored him.

Two months later, in July, Parry read the signals correctly: he despaired of any success in promotion and preferment. He left Elizabeth's court, he later wrote, 'utterly rejected, discontented, and as Her Majesty might perceive by my passionate letters, careless of myself'. He went back to London from Greenwich Palace to find that a copy of William Allen's *Modest Defence* had been sent to him from France. Did Thomas Morgan send it or Charles Paget? Whoever gave Parry a copy of the *Modest Defence* knew his man, for once again the despondent spy and commissioned assassin felt the persuasive power of Doctor Allen's arguments. The *Modest Defence*, Parry said, 'redoubled my former conceits: every word in it was a warrant to a prepared mind: it taught that kings may be excommunicated, deprived, and violently handled: it proveth that all wars civil or foreign undertaken for religion, is [sic] honourable.'

By August 1584 Parry had regained some of his equanimity, though he was having to fight hard to convince Burghley of his loyalty. Burghley wondered instead whether Parry was quite the gentleman he claimed. Someone had cast doubt upon Parry's gentility, and Parry wanted to reassure Burghley, who was an obsessive genealogist with a keen nose for the lineage of gentlemen and noblemen, of his good name and reputation. From his lodgings in Fetter Lane near Holborn, Parry set out to defend himself.

Parry's short autobiography may suggest some of the reasons for his tangled and complicated life. He explained that his family had been long established in the county of Flintshire in north Wales. But where he had blood and ancestry, he lacked money. Parry set out his circumstances; their theme was a genteel and unfortunate poverty. He wrote that his father was a poor gentleman who had served in the king's guard. Parry was one of sixteen children by his mother (his father's second wife) and he had fourteen half brothers and sisters. His father had died early in Elizabeth's reign at the improbably fantastic age of 118 years, a father to thirty children with very little land of his own. Clearly William Parry had to compete against extraordinary domestic odds: probably the eager, often combative tone of his letters even to powerful men is not very surprising.

Parry had married twice for money, though not with great success. His second wife's income was £80 a year, four times his own. Unable to spend her money, he had to scratch a living from his own. He professed prudent domestic economy. Dice, cards, hawking and hunting, he said, had never cost him more than £20. He supported two of his nephews in their studies at Oxford and maintained four others, one of whom was in France, another in London, and two at a country school in Flintshire. For ten years he had helped a poor brother and his wife and their fifth son. He gave money weekly to twelve poor folks in the village in which he had been born. He also wrote pointedly of the cost of his 'trouble and travail', by which he meant his work abroad for the queen. So he admitted to his generosity and to his poor management of money. He said nothing of his enormous debts or of his conviction for the assault of Hugh Hare the moneylender three years earlier. He threw himself upon Burghley's mercy. His own life, and the lives of those of his family whom he supported, rested on

Burghley. With unhappy urgency he wrote: 'All this (my best lord) is as true as the Lord liveth. Help therefore I beseech you, or else you shall shortly see me and all these to fall at once. For truly they shall not lack while I have.' Burghley, predictably, was unmoved.

Though by late summer desperate for promotion and patronage and burdened by the strain of the mission he had undertaken on behalf of the Cardinal of Como, Parry was not a man to give up easily. For a long time he had believed that his interests lay with the powerful Cecil family. In Paris he had got to know Robert Cecil, Lord Burghley's son, and Burghley's grandson William Cecil. In August Robert, still in Paris, wrote to Parry with genuine affection. Parry grabbed his chance a month later, when Robert Cecil's cousin, Sir Edward Hoby, appointed Parry his solicitor at court. Hoby was twenty-four years old, schooled at Eton and Trinity College, Oxford – the very same young man Parry had tried to entangle in his dubious money-making scheme back in 1581, which had led to Parry's imprisonment in the Poultry Counter. Either Parry had not properly learned his lesson or, desperate for his chance to succeed, he carried on regardless. Parry now wrote of his work for Sir Edward with confident self-assurance: 'I am fully acquainted with his state and daily occupied in settling such matters for him as may most import him in profit and credit.' He felt 'most bound' to do all he could for Sir Edward. Young Hoby at least was convinced: he wrote to his uncle Burghley to extend to Master Doctor Parry the same credit he would give to his nephew. Parry was as ever the persistent petitioner. As he wrote to Burghley: 'if it please you to commend me as a fit man for a deanery, provostship or mastership of requests it is all I crave'.

Yet in spite of his remarkable (even delusional) persistence the months of 1584 were miserable ones for William Parry. Returned at long last from his foreign travels and travails, he was settled in London. 'I never liked country better, nor of all persons of quality received better usage,' Robert Cecil wrote to Parry from Paris. Doctor Parry's feelings in London were quite the opposite. He felt his was a cold homecoming. In May he perceived the sharp stab of failure; he was desperate for preferment; he was growing resentful that his great talents were being passed over; he discerned the slanders of secret enemies. Though he succeeded in earning the trust of an upcoming and talented young gentleman of good connection like Sir Edward Hoby, Parry believed that the sacrifices made in the service of the queen had brought him no reward. He was able to make powerful friends, yet the great prizes of patronage continued to elude him. To Burghley and Walsingham he professed loyalty and service to Elizabeth. The truth, however, is that after August 1584 Parry was working out the most effective way to assassinate the queen.

Parry recruited a fellow conspirator. His name was Edmund Nevylle, a gentleman of good connections in the north who shared a surname with the earls of Westmorland. Parry claimed Nevylle as his cousin, though he later said that Nevylle was a sponger who often came to his house on Fetter Lane to 'put his finger in my dish, his hand in my purse'. In the end Nevylle betrayed him. Parry noted sourly: 'the night wherein he accused me, [he] was wrapped in my gown'.

The facts of what happened between August 1584 and January 1585, the critical months of the conspiracy, have to be teased out of a thicket of self-justifying obfuscations in the later statements of Parry and Nevylle. Their conspiracy began with a discussion of William Allen's *Modest Defence*. Certainly they took some time to arrive at a firm plan. First Parry visited Nevylle at the Whitefriars, and Nevylle returned the courtesy one morning to find Parry lying in bed in his lodgings on Fetter Lane. At dinner they spoke about Parry's disappointment over St Katharine's hospital. His only way of redress, Parry said, was to kill the queen. According to Allen's *Modest Defence*, which had captured Parry's imagination in a powerful and dangerous way, Parry believed that such an act was lawful. Nevylle, it seems, preferred to free the Queen of Scots from her English captivity. But in the end he came round to Parry's proposal for assassinating Elizabeth, and the next morning Nevylle came again to Parry's lodging. He swore on the Bible 'to conceal and constantly to pursue the enterprise for the advancement of [the Catholic] religion'.

Eight days later Parry and Nevylle walked together in Lincoln's Inn Fields. Parry proposed a plan for them to execute. They would kill Elizabeth in Westminster near St James's Palace, recruiting eight or ten household servants on horseback, all armed with pistols, to surprise her coach from both sides. Nevylle found 'an excellent pistol-lier', a tall and resolute gentleman whom he introduced to Parry at young Sir Edward Hoby's house on Cannon Row, in the shadow of Westminster Palace. Parry, careful to keep the conspiracy between himself and Nevylle for the time being, declined the help of this sinister marksman.

At some point Parry and Nevylle discussed a much more fantastic plan. Doubtless influenced by the experience of his private audiences with the queen, Parry suggested the murder of Elizabeth in her private garden at Whitehall Palace. Helped by Nevylle, he would escape over the palace wall to one of the landing stairs near by, taking a boat on the River Thames. Both proposals were fraught with dangers, but only the assault on Elizabeth's coach near St James's was even remotely plausible. Still, even this ambitious scheme required the kind of premeditation and intricate planning for which William Parry and Edmund Nevylle were constitutionally unsuited.

The two conspirators did nothing. Doctor Parry's feelings of injustice and resentment continued to simmer away in his mind. From late November 1584 he sat in the House of Commons for the tiny borough of Queenborough in Kent, thanks very probably to his young patron Sir Edward Hoby. It was Parry's first time in parliament, and he certainly left his mark.

In December the Commons debated a bill for the queen's safety. It was the bill that became the Act for the Queen's Surety, the extraordinary statute that gave the force of law to the killing by private subjects of anyone who challenged either Elizabeth's life, throne or kingdom. It was a measure aimed squarely at the pernicious influence of Mary Queen of Scots and her supporters. Not surprisingly, though with a marked lack of judgement, Parry spoke angrily against the bill. On 17 December he said in open debate that it 'carried nothing with it but blood, danger, terror, despair, [and] confiscation'. Shocked at this violent outburst, the officials of the Commons hauled Parry out of the chamber. He was called before Elizabeth's Privy Council and disciplined by the speaker of the Commons. Next day Parry went down on his knees to say to the house that had spoken rashly and intemperately; he apologized. Disciplined and chastened, Doctor

Parry was readmitted to his seat in parliament. But he still intended to kill the queen.

The House of Commons was in recess from late December till the first week of February 1585. In this break from parliamentary business came the deciding moment of William Parry's treachery. Parry, who had volunteered in Rome to play the assassin and who could never resist a dramatic performance, began to live his role. But his cousin Edmund Nevylle was beginning to have doubts.

On Saturday, 6 February, at between five and six o'clock in the evening, Parry visited Nevylle at the Whitefriars. The time to make their final plan had come at last. He wanted to talk to his cousin alone, and so, presumably because they were in company, they withdrew to a window. Nevylle told Parry about his reservations. He would not go through with the conspiracy. It was the moment of crisis. Parry wanted Nevylle to leave England straight away, promising him a safe passage to Wales and so on to Brittany. Nevylle refused, saying that in conscience he had decided to 'lay open this his most traitorous and abhominable intention against Her Majesty'. At this last meeting between the hesitant conspirators, when their plot finally fell to pieces, it seems Edmund Nevylle paid the final insult to Doctor Parry by being wrapped in his cousin's gown. And so Nevylle surrendered himself to the authorities. He made his confession on Tuesday, 9 February, spoke again on the 11th, and was questioned for a third time a day later. Apprehended, William Parry made his own 'voluntary confession' on the 13th, at last telling the story of his reconciliation to the Church of Rome and his negotiations with the Cardinal of Como.

Parry the doctor of laws knew that two accuser-witnesses would be required to convict him of a treasonable act: it was Nevylle's word against his. This was probably Parry's reason for not taking Nevylle's gentleman marksman into his confidence at their meeting on Cannon Row. But it helps to explain why between them Parry and Nevylle, though convinced of the justice of murdering Elizabeth, had never quite come up with a feasible plan. As soon as Nevylle voiced his doubts, Parry had no choice but to abandon the mission.

In the end William Parry was undone by his own cleverness, self-possession, greed and arrogance. Probably he would have settled for

William Parry's letter to the queen, 14 February 1585: 'you may see ...
the dangerous fruits of a discontented mind'.

Burghley's patronage if it had been offered in 1584. Instead the
bitterness of service left unrewarded corroded any loyalty he had to
Burghley, Walsingham or the queen. Burghley in particular had
thrown Parry's service back in his face, or so Parry must have thought;
the obsequious letters to the great man, all that energy expended on
acting the eager gentleman, the lord treasurer's slights and the
silences – we can well imagine these provoked in a character as fractured as Parry's murderous ill-feeling. So the seeds of treason had long
been sown. Playing the great assassin in Paris, encouraged by men as

influential as Thomas Morgan, Charles Paget and the Cardinal of Como, was in the end irresistible to Parry. Those seeds were nourished by long months of frustration in England. Parry's plan was desperate, unfeasible, even a fantasy. But it was, in his own mind at least, real enough.

On Saint Valentine's Day in 1585, Sunday, 14 February, Doctor Parry wrote to Queen Elizabeth from the Tower of London: 'Your Majesty may see by my voluntary confession the dangerous fruits of a discontented mind, and how constantly I pursued my first conceived purpose in Venice for the relief of the afflicted Catholics, continued it in Lyons and resolved in Paris to put it in adventure for the restitution of England to the ancient obedience of the see Apostolic.' To the Earl of Leicester and to Lord Burghley, once his employer, he emphasized just how special he was: 'My case is rare and strange, and, for anything I can remember, singular: a natural subject solemnly to vow the death of his natural Queen . . . for the relief of the afflicted Catholics, and restitution of religion.'

A week later he was tried for treason in Westminster Hall. The clerk of the crown set out the facts and stated that Parry had been seduced from his true allegiance by the Devil. Yet Parry did his best to control even his own trial; he refuted as well as confessed, saying that he wanted to die; he was determined to explain his thinking, volunteering to read to the court his own confession and letters. Words he had written to Burghley and Leicester became part of the public record: 'My cause is rare, singular and unnatural.'

For William Parry the desire to play a great part both in secret and in public was a powerful and compelling one. His treason was, of course, sensational news. Even the trial of John Somerville in 1583, after which Somerville hanged himself in Newgate prison, had nothing like the performance of a star like Parry: with Parry being as self-possessed and fluent as ever, the crown's lawyers had found it difficult to keep him quiet. Lord Burghley was troubled about eager London printers getting their presses ready to tell Parry's story. They, like Parry himself, had to be controlled. Some of the most powerful men in England, councillors and law officers, met at Burghley's house on the Strand to discuss how best to publish what they called 'the truth' of Parry's treason. In other words, they decided what could and could not be told. The official account, produced by the queen's printer, was truly savage. Carefully edited copies of documents were used to prove Parry's vile treasons. The pamphlet demolished his character (especially his 'proud and arrogant humour') and the insulting pretensions at good family and gentility of such a 'vile and traitorous wretch'. Burghley hated a traitor, more so one who was also a social upstart.

This unrelenting public denunciation of the man was a mark of the depth and horror of Doctor Parry's betrayal. Public prayers celebrated the deliverance of Elizabeth from Parry's wicked plot. What gave his treason a special edge were the debates in parliament on the bill for the queen's safety. After the murder of the Prince of Orange in 1584, the Elizabethan political establishment had been terrified of the queen's assassination. Parry made that fear real and tangible. Nowhere in the propaganda was it admitted that he had spied for queen and country: the public story was that he had been simply an assassin hired by the Pope's cardinals to kill Elizabeth. Parry's long if erratic service to Lord Burghley, his secret intelligence from Paris, Lyons and Venice, his closeness to members of the powerful Cecil family: all these strands of his varied career were lost to official amnesia.

Parry was executed in Westminster Palace yard on 2 March, the only serving member of the English House of Commons ever to have been arrested for high treason. On the scaffold he maintained his innocence, denying any plan or even any thought to have murdered the queen:

> I die a true servant to Queen Elizabeth; from any evil thought that ever I had to harm her, it never came into my mind; she knoweth it and her conscience can tell her so ... I die guiltless and free in mind from ever thinking hurt to Her Majesty.

Perhaps he really believed that this lie was in fact the truth. If so, then William Parry had yet another reason to feel that his service to Elizabeth and Burghley, for so long unrewarded, had once again been abused. He died a traitor's death, hanged till he was almost dead, disembowelled, beheaded and dismembered, his head and limbs put on display throughout London to warn others of the cost of treason.

13

Alias Cornelys

In the story of Mary Queen of Scots's nineteen-year captivity in England no chapter is more extraordinary than the Babington Plot and no conspiracy more tangled. It involved a group of Catholic gentlemen plotting in London; the long labours of Mary's chief intelligencer in Paris; a courier for the Queen of Scots who was really a double agent working for Sir Francis Walsingham; the double agent's cousin; Walsingham's trusted right hand in secret affairs; and, of course, Mary herself, held in confinement deep in the English midlands. Aiding these principal characters was a supporting cast of secretaries, pursuivants, spies, informants and watchers, and even one brewer of good ale. The drama was played out over the nine months between December 1585 and August 1586. It encompassed practically every theme in this book, bringing together in one magnificently disturbing episode those old and deep suspicions of the treasonous disloyalty of Elizabethan Catholics, the pernicious influence of the Queen of Scots as pretender to Elizabeth's throne and terrible fears of the queen's murder.

The narrative of the Babington Plot can be compressed into a short paragraph. In Paris in December 1585 Thomas Morgan, the Queen of Scots's chief spy, recruited a young Catholic as a courier of his letters. The task of this courier, Gilbert Gifford, was to collect the letters from the house of the French ambassador in London and convey them secretly to Mary, who was being held under guard and surveillance in Staffordshire. Captured in England, Gifford became a double agent; and under the guiding hand of Thomas Phelippes, Walsingham's servant, he helped set up an ingenious system for intercepting and copying letters passing to and from the Queen of Scots. This postal system helped to expose a knot of Catholic conspirators in London who were planning Mary's freedom and Elizabeth's murder. Waiting and watching, and then trying their hand at forgery, Walsingham and Phelippes discovered evidence of the Queen of Scots's complicity in the conspirators' plans. The dramatic breaking up of the plot in August 1586 sent Anthony Babington and his fellow conspirators to the gallows. More significantly, the letters intercepted by Phelippes and Walsingham were persuasive enough as evidence against Mary Queen of Scots for a commission to be set up under the Act for the Queen's Surety. The commissioners tried Mary and found her guilty of treason against Elizabeth. In February 1587 she was beheaded.

But to tell it this briefly strips the story of much of its richness and complexity. Told fully, it offers a fascinating case study in just how far Elizabeth's government was prepared to go to save queen and country from destruction.

It all began with Thomas Morgan, chief intelligencer to Mary Queen of Scots in Paris. At his trial in 1585 William Parry had named Morgan as the man who had persuaded him to kill Elizabeth. The English government tried to have Morgan extradited from France as Parry's accomplice but instead had to make do with his imprisonment in the Bastille, where he found himself by October 1585.

From prison Morgan tried his best to reconstruct the secure and effective postal service that had operated between Paris and the Queen of Scots. This was an almost impossible task to which only a man passionate about his cause could have had the patience to attempt. Mary, too, was under restraint, though the conditions of her confinement were much tougher than those of Morgan in the Bastille. In late December 1585 she was moved from the bare and grim castle of Tutbury in Staffordshire to Chartley, a moated manor house in the same county, deep in the English midlands. The Queen of Scots's keeper was the firm and uncompromising Sir Amias Paulet, a stickler for security, who insisted on random searches of Mary's private chambers and even strip searches of any members of her household who had contact with the outside world. Of Paulet the Queen of Scots wrote that he was one of the most pitiless and zealous men she had ever known.

The strictness of the Queen of Scots's restraint was not the only one of Thomas Morgan's difficulties. He knew that even in the Bastille he was watched by servants of the English ambassador in Paris, Sir Edward Stafford. Morgan saw, too, as Elizabeth's government did also, that the city's English Catholics were at one another's throats, dividing themselves into factions. Charles Arundel, Lord Paget's fiery companion, had even drawn a dagger on Charles Paget, Morgan's great friend and comrade in Mary's cause. And yet in spite of all this Thomas Morgan persisted in his work. In the strange unreal world of the Catholic exiles he tried his best to provide the Queen of Scots, otherwise cut off from her allies and supporters in Europe, with the lifeline of information.

Morgan needed couriers to carry his letters and reports to Mary. These couriers had to be trusted intermediaries who could cross the English Channel from France, safely enter the ports of the English south coast and then travel on to London. Letters were delivered to the house of the French ambassador at Salisbury Court, not far from Fleet Street, where the packets could be taken on to Mary's household, kept under tight security, in Staffordshire. That at least was the theory; in practice it was immensely difficult to make this postal system – essentially conceived in two parts, each as challenging as the other – work successfully.

Not surprisingly, the recruits were few. But in October 1585 one English gentleman of about twenty-six years of age seemed especially suited for Morgan's difficult and important task. His name was Gilbert Gifford. He was a young man from a family of Staffordshire Catholics, and in fact a kinsman of Francis Throckmorton; this last fact, in the months after Francis's execution and his brother Thomas's exile abroad, seemed to carry a special cachet. Gilbert Gifford had been educated at the English College in Rome (where in 1579 Charles Sledd the spy had noticed him) and later at William Allen's seminary in Rheims, from where, in the autumn of 1585, he travelled to meet Morgan in Paris. Morgan, assured of the young man's faith and honesty, briefed him on how to be a courier and instructed him in methods of secret writing. Morgan was sure that Gilbert Gifford would solve all the problems of communicating with the Queen of Scots in England.

*

In Paris at the same time as Thomas Morgan and Gilbert Gifford was Nicholas Berden, one of Sir Francis Walsingham's most trusted and prolific secret agents. He knew of, and may have even known, Gifford. Berden's keen eyes did not miss the fact that in December 1585 Gifford had set out from Paris for England.

Berden was a modest kind of gentleman, the son of a citizen of London comfortably in business. First suggested for secret service by Sir Horatio Palavicino, a wealthy international merchant who also did intelligence work for Walsingham, Berden wrote regular 'secret advertisements'. He was in London between March and May 1585 but went over to Rouen in early August. By late August he was in Paris, where he stayed till the early months of 1586, alert to the business of the Catholic exiles. With a busy pen, Berden noted rumours of the plans of the Duke of Guise and news of the movements of William Allen, the Paget brothers and Thomas Throckmorton. He was a useful spy.

In London Berden's reports were noted and filed by Thomas Phelippes, the young man who been in Bourges and Paris in 1582 on a mission for Walsingham, a careful and discreet member of Sir Francis's household staff and a skilled breaker of codes and ciphers. By hard work, application, ingenuity and cunning, Phelippes was Walsingham's trusted right hand in all secret matters and operations.

So it was Phelippes who from one of Nicholas Berden's reports learned in late December 1585 that Gilbert Gifford had left Paris. Berden's news was that Pope Sixtus V had published a 'new excommunication' of the queen to reinforce the bull of his predecessor Pius V in 1570, denouncing Elizabeth as a bastard heretic schismatic. The rumours circulating in Paris said that this new excommunication had been smuggled into England; it was 'gone already about five weeks past, and that either Gilbert Gifford or some of the priests that went in about the same time did carry it'. Gifford, it was said in Paris, had been arrested in England. Phelippes wrote on the outside of Berden's secret report the following words: 'New proclamation to go into England. Gilbert Gifford's apprehension in England known.' Within weeks, however, the news in Paris had changed. Berden reported to Walsingham: 'Here is great joy made that Gilbert Gifford did escape your honour's hands so easily and he hath certified hither that

England is in great fear to be invaded.' Once again, Thomas Phelippes calmly noted the fact, giving the packet from Berden a special cipher mark.

The items of news and gossip Berden reported were both true and false. The first report, which said that Gilbert Gifford had been captured, was correct. He was arrested at the port of Rye trying to enter England and on about 20 December he was interviewed by Walsingham. The second report, of Gifford's freedom, was false. It was, however, essential to Walsingham's purpose, for Sir Francis had recruited Gifford as a double agent to work against Thomas Morgan and Mary Queen of Scots. The rumour in Paris of the young man's freedom was either a lucky coincidence for Walsingham or may have been planted in émigré circles and nourished for a definite purpose. Whatever the truth, one fact was startling: Walsingham and his servant Phelippes now possessed a potentially devastating weapon against the cause of the Queen of Scots. Her new trusted courier – Thomas Morgan's great hope for the service of his mistress Mary – was Walsingham's spy.

Walsingham knew from long experience exactly how to persuade Gifford to work for Elizabeth's government. Probably Gifford's motivations were, in order of necessity, freedom, continued protection and money. One point of vulnerability may have been a confused sense of loyalty and identity common in English Catholics, formed by the strange unreality of exile, the idealisms, hopes and anxieties, always strained, never achieved. Leaving behind him an émigré community in Paris divided against itself, in Walsingham and Phelippes Gifford met an absolute steadiness of purpose. Perhaps also he enjoyed the prospect of living on the dangerous edge of conspiracy.

So Gifford, Mary's supposedly loyal courier, was a gift to Walsingham. If Gifford behaved himself – and if of course Walsingham and Phelippes played a clever game – he could carry the letters Morgan wanted him to and allow Elizabeth's government access to them. For a long time letters had been piling up at the French ambassador's house at Salisbury Court; now, with a new courier in place, they could be taken to the Queen of Scots. Thomas Morgan's relief at finding so ideal a man was Walsingham's chance to penetrate Mary's correspondence. Gifford became the bridge between Thomas Morgan, the new French ambassador in London, Guillaume de l'Aubépine Baron de Châteauneuf, and Mary Queen of Scots. No wonder that under Phelippes's watchful eye Gifford was quickly put to work.

Morgan did the best he could to keep Mary informed of what was happening in Europe. With the help of other émigrés Morgan was able to get letters out of the Bastille. Each one of them was long and intricate, consisting of many folios of dense cipher; Morgan must have been a very patient man. There was no guarantee that the Queen of Scots or her secretaries would ever read Morgan's letters, and probably little chance that any reply by Mary would leave Chartley, let alone reach Paris. Morgan knew that sometimes letters were intercepted, though of course he would have been horrified to know that those reports on which he had worked for hours were now being handed by Gifford to Walsingham and Phelippes.

As well as Gilbert Gifford, Morgan had another agent in England. He was a poor English gentleman called Robert Poley. Poley's name, like Gifford's, is one to remember: he would play an important part in the Babington Plot. Also like Gifford, Poley was a volunteer for the cause of the Queen of Scots. He knew the ways from England into Scotland, and Morgan felt that this geographical knowledge made him a good man for ambassador Châteauneuf to know about.

As well as working as a courier, Poley spied for Morgan in England. Morgan placed Poley in the household of Sir Philip Sidney and his wife Lady Frances. She was Sir Francis Walsingham's daughter, and so it seemed to Morgan that Poley was in an ideal position to be able to give valuable information. But Robert Poley, like Gilbert Gifford, was Walsingham's man. Without knowing it, Thomas Morgan was helping once again to set the spring of the trap that within months would catch and hold Mary Queen of Scots fast.

In the early months of 1586 Thomas Phelippes worked tirelessly with Gilbert Gifford. He gave Gifford tasks and supervised the quality of his agent's work. Doubtless, too, he acted as his adviser and perhaps also his friend, while always keeping the kind of distance that was necessary in so delicate a professional relationship. Always a careful and discreet man, Phelippes referred in letters to Walsingham only of his work with 'the party'. This was in late February 1586, when Gifford had brought to Phelippes twenty-one packets 'great and small' from the house of ambassador Châteauneuf. Now, thanks to Gifford, coaxed and coached by Phelippes, the letters began to move again.

Phelippes and Gifford seem to have worked well together. Phelippes had the rare ability to combine the mastery of fine detail with a profound sense of the object of a task. Above all, he possessed imaginative cunning. There can be no doubt that Gifford did what he was told to do, but he had initiative and sense. The two young men were in many ways an enviable pairing.

With these foundations set down, Walsingham began to move other pieces into place. In early March Gifford's father John, a recusant Catholic who had suffered heavy fines and imprisonment, was licensed by the Privy Council to leave London to take the waters for his health. He was even allowed to visit his house in Staffordshire. All of this may have been a discreet favour for Gilbert, but it also opened up new possibilities for his journeys into the English midlands. Not surprisingly, Phelippes and Walsingham did everything they could to facilitate the easy carrying of letters between Morgan in Paris, ambassador Châteauneuf in London and the Queen of Scots at Chartley.

Like any example of the subtle art of double-cross, it was a delicate business. Certainly Gilbert Gifford's work was most secret – so secret, in fact, that any danger to Gifford came not from Morgan or the French ambassador but from zealous English officials who knew nothing of whose side he was really working for. Phelippes, protective of Gifford and his work, was worried about the informants that Richard Young, a zealous justice of Westminster with a nose for Catholic conspiracy, had positioned close to the French ambassador. He feared they would compromise Gifford as a courier of letters, something Phelippes felt would prejudice their task of trying penetrate the Queen of Scots's correspondence. Phelippes wanted Walsingham to be firm with Young: 'it may please you to limit him by some peremptory speech'.

By the spring of 1586 Walsingham had his best informants hard at work. The two most prolific were Maliverey Catilyn, long used by Walsingham to spy on Catholics in England, and Nicholas Berden, the agent who had worked for Walsingham and Phelippes in Paris in the later months of 1585.

Using his many local contacts, Catilyn wrote a long paper giving the names and descriptions of Catholic men and women throughout England. Thomas Phelippes, who read the report, called it Catilyn's 'observations touching corrupt subjects'. In early summer, Catilyn was sent off to spy on Catholics in Portsmouth with 'a pair of writing tables' (a 'table-book' was a notebook or memorandum book) hidden in the padding of his doublet.

Berden, returned from Paris to London, was busy in April scouring the streets and lodging houses of the city for dangerous Catholics. Berden informed Walsingham of the espionage of one of Thomas Morgan's spies in the royal household, a man who kept company with Catholic priests living secretly and illegally in London, and who was on familiar terms with Walsingham's servants. Berden kept a record of where many of the priests lodged in London. Among many suspicious Catholics in London, he noted the name of one 'Fortescue alias Ballard'. Berden probably as yet knew very little about him. Yet he soon would: John Ballard, another of the enterprising Thomas Morgan's agents, quickly became one of the most wanted men in England.

In spring 1586 Nicholas Berden's contacts in Paris were paying off handsomely. To his surprise, he found himself recruited as a courier for Charles Paget, Charles Arundel, William Allen, Robert Persons and other Catholic exiles. True, the terms of his employment were a little uncertain, though there was nothing so unusual in that. He had no precise idea of what he was expected to do. Berden wrote to Walsingham: 'From Charles Paget I have only received a cipher without any other directions whatsoever, except that he prayed me to promise him to receive letters hereafter when he should send them to me.' Their arrangement was that, fearing Berden's arrest, Paget would send nothing till he knew of his safe arrival in England and the hope of Berden's 'quiet continuance' as a free man.

Berden had the promise of more enemy ciphers than he knew what to do with. One was for letters to and from Charles Paget. Another would allow him to communicate with Charles Arundel. Reflecting bitter arguments among the émigrés in Paris, Arundel did not know that Berden was in contact with Paget, while Paget believed that Berden wrote only to him. Even Don Bernardino de Mendoza, the King of Spain's ambassador in Paris, had intimated to Berden that he too might use Berden's services.

This, as Berden recognized, was potentially the means to unlock the secrets of some of the most dangerous men in Europe. To have the cipher keys, or 'alphabets', of the enemy meant that their increasingly complex systems of secret communication could be easily broken. A skilled cryptographer like Thomas Phelippes could see immediately the symbols chosen for important international politicians and churchmen, and begin to make sense of the three or four cipher characters that could be used for each letter of the alphabet. He could also avoid the traps of 'nulls', symbols or characters of no significance that were inserted to mislead and confuse an enemy trying to crack the cipher. So it seemed that Berden had stumbled across a treasure trove of secret cipher: the alphabets of Charles Paget, Robert Persons, the émigré Catholic printer Stephen Brinkley, as well as the texts of Brinkley's letters to Jesuit priests. As the Elizabethan scholar and politician Francis Bacon wrote:

> This art of ciphering, hath for relative, an art of deciphering ... For suppose that ciphers were well managed, there be multitudes of them which exclude the decipherer. But in regard of the rawness and unskilfulness of the hands, through which they pass, the greatest matters, are many times carried in the weakest ciphers.

Who knew what secrets might be revealed through Berden's correspondence?

The weight of all this responsibility certainly made Nicholas Berden nervous. He knew how useful he could be; he was also worried, like Phelippes, about Richard Young. Justice Young, his eyes sharp for suspicious men, had nearly arrested him: 'if the said Master Young be not warned by your honour to be silent my travail will be but vain.' Berden asked Walsingham to assure his free movement and safety.

Nicholas Berden ended his letter with a declaration of loyalty: 'I shall be always ready ... to manifest myself a public persecutor rather than a private practiser with any traitor or their confederates.' By 'persecutor' Berden meant a pursuer. English Catholics, however, would have taken him at his word.

Thomas Morgan the intelligencer in Paris; Morgan's young couriers

Gilbert Gifford and Robert Poley in England; Thomas Phelippes, Sir Francis Walsingham's right hand in secret matters; John Ballard the Catholic in London; Nicholas Berden the spy: all of these men became key players in the Babington Plot.

Always close to Mary Queen of Scots at Chartley were her two loyal secretaries, Claude Nau, who was responsible for her French correspondence, and Gilbert Curll, who wrote for Mary in English. They worked as efficiently as they could under the harsh conditions of security imposed by zealous Sir Amias Paulet. After all, monarchs – even those not free to do as they wished – could hardly be expected to write everything for themselves.

If Gilbert Gifford wanted to establish proper contact with Mary Queen of Scots he had to be able to write to Curll or Nau. By what appeared to be Gifford's hard work and ingenuity (though in fact it was facilitated for obvious reasons by Thomas Phelippes and Sir Amias Paulet) Gifford got a letter to Curll in the last week of April 1586. He affirmed his loyalty to Mary and prayed Curll not to spare him any work. Curll, Gifford wrote, knew him as well as 'good Francis did': he meant Francis Throckmorton, that martyr to the Queen of Scots's cause. In other words, Gilbert Gifford was a man Curll and his mistress could trust.

Naturally Gifford wrote this letter under the control and direction of Thomas Phelippes, and indeed it was Phelippes who went one step further in May by setting out the main points of a report from Gifford to Thomas Morgan in Paris. Before Gifford had come over to England, he and Morgan had agreed code names. Gifford was Nicholas Cornelys; Morgan was Thomas Germin. Never a man to disregard a perfectly good arrangement, Phelippes too used Cornelys as an alias for his double agent.

The one complication to Gifford's courier system in April and May 1586 was the journey he had to make to France to meet two Catholics who were willing to work for Walsingham, one of whom was a Gifford kinsman. This meant that a temporary courier had to be found. It was a delicate job, for in the interests of security this courier had to know nothing about Gifford's work for Phelippes. But Gifford had just the man. He and Phelippes called him Roland, though his real name was Thomas Barnes and he was Gifford's cousin. Gifford recruited Barnes in about the middle of the Easter law term (between 20 April and 16 May), when they met in Barnes's chamber probably in London. Gifford called the job of carrying Mary's letters 'a piece of service'. Apparently with no reservations, Barnes agreed to take it on. He took to his new task with ease. He was set quickly to work, showing at times a worrying over-enthusiasm that must have caused Phelippes, who could work with Barnes only through intermediaries, some anxiety. Barnes, like his cousin Gifford, was not shy in professing his loyalty to the Queen of Scots – though unlike Gifford he probably meant it.

And yet somehow the system held together. More than this, in fact, it worked beautifully. At the centre of the mechanism was Phelippes. From the beginning Phelippes recognized Gifford's potential. The use of Thomas Barnes as a substitute courier was a complication, though knowing something of Thomas Phelippes's methods and personality we should imagine that he and Gifford talked about cousin Barnes and the courier system in great detail. With Barnes ignorant of the government's involvement, Phelippes would have to stay very much in the background. Not to have prepared carefully would have been an extraordinary risk. It was one both Phelippes and Walsingham could not have been willing to take. They knew how valuable this operation was in divining the true intentions of the Queen of Scots.

Gifford returned to England, though now both he and Barnes travelled with letters between London and Staffordshire. In acts of delicate and secret ventriloquism, Phelippes used Gifford to communicate with Morgan in Paris. Dictating Gifford's letters to Morgan, Phelippes wanted to have the names of servants and friends of the Queen of Scots in or about London, together with Morgan's 'opinion how far every of them hath been, is or may be used' by Gifford to deliver a message or take a letter. Phelippes wanted also to have the names of 'honest friends as we may be bold to trust' in Scotland. He wanted Morgan, in other words, to expose the whole Marian network in London and Scotland.

To get the information he needed from Morgan through Gifford, yet to sustain Morgan's belief in Gifford, it was essential for Phelippes to get the balance of force and gentleness just right. He had to push, but not too much or too hard. All the time Phelippes was getting to know Gifford and, through Gifford, Morgan himself. It was a deliberate discovery of character. Phelippes understood the importance of paper, information and detail. But he also recognized the human factor of his work; and to his intuition he brought a secret inventiveness, taking the risk of working through Barnes (though without Barnes's knowledge) for the first time. In June, perfecting his techniques, Phelippes wrote in cipher as Barnes to Gilbert Curll, penetrating to the heart of Mary Queen of Scots's household at Chartley.

The target was always Mary. To Walsingham and Phelippes, and indeed to all of Elizabeth's advisers, she was the greatest enemy to Queen Elizabeth, to England and to the Protestant religion. They believed that for many years she had been at the centre of a web of international conspiracy. It was obvious to Elizabeth's Privy Council that there were few plots against England in which Mary or her supporters were not in some way connected. The Catholic cause in England was her cause: to Catholics she was the obvious legitimate alternative to Elizabeth as queen: she was always, to a lesser or greater extent, part of the effort to bring the Tudor kingdoms back from the horrible error (as the English Catholic exiles saw it) of schism and heresy.

In 1572 Elizabeth's advisers had wanted Mary to be executed for her part in the Ridolfi Plot. Elizabeth resisted, and Mary survived and in some ways prospered. Her influence was both pervasive and pernicious. But it probably seemed to Walsingham and Phelippes in 1586 that their grip was at last tightening. With the willing assistance of Gilbert Gifford, and the unconscious efforts of Thomas Barnes, they controlled the flow of Mary's letters and dispatches. They could read the correspondence between the Queen of Scots and Paris sent through the French embassy in London. Perhaps they could, if a chance so presented itself, shape and direct that correspondence.

The only surviving physical description of Thomas Phelippes comes from the Queen of Scots herself. It was in July, the 14th, a Thursday, when Phelippes was near Chartley. Mary saw from the window of her coach a youngish man 'of low stature, slender every way, dark yellow haired on the head, and clear yellow bearded'. She must have been close enough to him to see that he was 'eaten in the face with small pocks' – scarred, in other words, by smallpox. She guessed from his appearance that he was about thirty years old.

Mary smiled at Phelippes from her coach. We can only guess whether he smiled back. He wrote to Walsingham that when he saw the Queen of Scots at Chartley he had thought of the saying:

> When someone gives you a greeting
> Take care it isn't an enemy.

But Mary's smile was genuine. She had heard about a man called Phelippes in Secretary Walsingham's service. She thought he might be working secretly for her. She had not an inkling that he was reading every word of the letters she sent or received by means of her trusted couriers.

By July 1586 Phelippes was having to perform extraordinary labours in deciphering the letters passing to and from Mary at Chartley. The courier system he had worked out with Gilbert Gifford, and through Gifford with Thomas Barnes, was a phenomenal success. There was so much material to work on that Phelippes had to leave London to travel north to Staffordshire – hence Mary's physical description on the 27th of her secret pursuer.

Mary's keeper at Chartley, the redoubtable Sir Amias Paulet, was a good and old friend of Phelippes. They had worked together in Paris when Paulet was ambassador at the French court between 1576 and 1579. Phelippes had wanted to travel to Chartley in the early days of June 1586, but he was too busy in London. At last he set out for Staffordshire on Thursday, 7 July at nine o'clock on a long summer's evening. He was working furiously on Mary's correspondence. Folio after folio of deciphers survive, all in Phelippes's tiny intricate handwriting. Even with the cipher keys to hand, it was unforgiving and laborious work.

For some weeks Paulet had been overseeing a remarkable system of interception. He had bought the services of a brewer in Burton upon Trent who supplied Mary's household at Chartley with beer. Sir Amias and Phelippes both knew the brewer as 'the honest man'. There was an irony here; the brewer was interested only in money, and he was very well paid to be honest. Gifford or Barnes delivered the letters for Mary to the brewer's house in Burton. He made sure that they were securely sealed in waterproof tubes in the casks of ale going off from Burton to Chartley, where they were retrieved by Mary's men, who used the same system to return replies to Gifford or Barnes.

For Elizabeth's government, the practical difficulties of this operation were potentially immense. It had to be coordinated with Gifford and his cousin Barnes, moving up and down the country between Staffordshire and London. Walsingham was generally at court, sometimes at his London house on Seething Lane near the Tower, but often on his estate in Surrey, Barn Elms. Phelippes was first in London and then at Chartley. Paulet was always with Mary. Gilbert Gifford was a conscious volunteer, his cousin Barnes an unconscious agent. The brewer of Burton upon Trent was a highly paid and often demanding employee. The only methods of communication were by conversation or letter. The very complexity of this system was a risk. But, once again, it worked superbly well for Walsingham and Phelippes against Mary Queen of Scots.

Everything was directed at a clear end. This could be expressed in a question, given here as Walsingham and Phelippes would have asked it in July 1586. Would the Scottish queen, after years of conspiring against her cousin Elizabeth, at last betray clear and unambiguous evidence of her plottings in the letters she wrote to her supporters? There was the tantalizing prospect at last of a prosecution of Mary Queen of Scots under the Act for the Queen's Surety and the clean judicial elimination of Queen Elizabeth's greatest rival.

Any courier who gave himself to the cause of the Queen of Scots lived a dangerous life. Even for someone who, like Gilbert Gifford, worked secretly for Sir Francis Walsingham there were few guarantees of a happy future. Utility, not compassion, guided men like Walsingham. They were pragmatic and unflinching in their work for the queen. They had no time for sentiment.

Those few couriers who found themselves recruited to Mary's service were young men in their twenties, well connected, of once wealthy Catholic families. Francis Throckmorton had been one of them. He had paid the highest price for his service. Found guilty of treason at the Guild Hall in London in 1584, he had quickly thrown himself upon the queen's mercy, asking her to forgive 'the inconsiderate rashness of unbridled youth'. Elizabeth graciously allowed him to meet his wife and mother before going to the gallows. In 1586 the name of Francis Throckmorton still meant a great deal to supporters of the Queen of Scots. Indeed it was used to clever effect by Gifford and Barnes to gain the trust of Mary's secretary, Gilbert Curll. Gifford was of the same stamp as Throckmorton, a gentleman of a good family with experience of life on the continent of Europe.

Yet another young man who volunteered to carry letters for the Queen of Scots was Anthony Babington, a gentleman of Dethwick in Derbyshire, twenty-five years old, who in summer 1586 was moving between his various lodgings in London, at Hernes rents in Lincoln's Inn Fields, at his own house near the Barbican and at the house of a tailor just outside the Temple Bar on Fleet Street. Babington had spent six months in France in 1580. At Thomas Morgan's request he carried packets to the Queen of Scots, probably in 1583 and 1584. By 1586, though married and with a daughter, he was keen to be off once again on his travels.

For Anthony Babington money was no object. His father had left him a rich man; one estimate gave Anthony an income of £1,000 a year, £400 of which he had put aside for his journey; this was an enormous fortune. He wanted, in June 1586, a licence to travel for three or five years, and he went to Elizabeth's court to get it. He came to the notice of Sir Francis Walsingham, who mistakenly thought Babington might be persuaded to work for him. A gentleman close to Walsingham became friendly with Babington. His name was Robert Poley, infiltrated into the circle of Sir Francis Walsingham by Morgan in Paris but in fact one of Walsingham's agents.

History has given young Anthony Babington the dubious honour of lending a name to a conspiracy that, thanks to the system of secret correspondence with Chartley set up by Thomas Phelippes and Gilbert Gifford, sent the Queen of Scots to the executioner's block. It was evidence offered by Babington that finally caught Mary in Walsingham's trap.

But another man was as important as Babington in what became the greatest of all Elizabethan conspiracies, and the one that in the end destroyed the Queen of Scots. What historians know as the Babington Plot could so easily have been called the Ballard Plot instead.

John Ballard had been educated in Cambridge and at William Allen's seminary in Rheims. He was a priest, ordained in Châlons in 1581. He was sent by his superiors to England in March 1581 and was certainly in London in 1582. In Paris in 1584 Ballard got to know Thomas Morgan and Charles Paget, who gave him a mission to complete in England. He was again in London in the early months of 1586 living under the false names of Thompson and Turner. Sometimes (as Walsingham's spy Nicholas Berden reported) Ballard called himself Captain Fortescue or even Black Fortescue.

At the end of May 1586 Ballard had visited Anthony Babington at his lodgings in Hernes rents. The two men knew each other; they had met some time before 1584. Ballard spoke approvingly of plans by the powers of Catholic Europe – by the Pope, the King of Spain and the Duke of Guise – to invade England. Babington objected, rightly, that these powers and princes were too busy with their own affairs to be able to mount an invasion. Babington also pointed out to Ballard the immense logistical challenge for the Catholic powers. And while the queen was alive, he said, few Englishmen would rally to the invaders. Ballard replied that the way forward was to kill Elizabeth. In fact, he told Babington, the plan had already been made. The instrument was a man named Savage who, a month or so earlier, was planning the assassination. Receiving letters of support and instruction from Thomas Morgan in Paris and other émigrés, Savage plotted at the church of St Giles-in-the-Fields in London.

In June, Babington met some of his friends to talk about the situation that they as Catholic gentlemen found themselves in. They believed they faced either a massacre of Catholics in England by Elizabeth's government or the invasion and destruction of the kingdom by foreigners. Babington wanted to avoid both horrors by leaving England.

But his mind was slowly changed. By early July, talking to his friends and once more to John Ballard, he seemed willingly to be involved in a plan to free the Queen of Scots from her captivity. That plan slowly but surely became one element in a greater and more dangerous scheme, the capture or assassination of Queen Elizabeth.

And so, in the summer months of 1586, began the extraordinary, fascinating and complicated story of Babington and Ballard's plot.

14

Sleights of Hand

Thomas Phelippes was a close and secret man who trusted few beyond his immediate circle. Even with Sir Francis Walsingham's secretary, Francis Mylles, the watchers and informants Nicholas Berden and Maliverey Catilyn, Arthur Gregory the forger, and his own manservant Thomas Cassie he exercised a testing and critical judgement. Those inside the circle could be found wanting: once Cassie fell out of his master's favour and Phelippes threatened him with the Tower of London. Those outside his circle he found it harder to trust. At times he doubted the discretion of Justice Richard Young, the harrier of priests in Westminster and Middlesex. The royal messengers – the pursuivants – were certainly beyond the pale, as Phelippes wrote bluntly to Walsingham: they were 'very knaves', a view which, given common accusations of corruption and bribery, was probably a fair one. By summer 1586 Phelippes had earned the privilege to speak as plainly as this. For at least three years he had been Sir Francis's trusted right hand in secret affairs. Phelippes, always careful and precise, practised espionage, the object of which, as he saw it, was to protect the cause of God, queen and country. Phelippes often used a phrase that has a modern ring to it: the security of the state.

As well as being an expert in the breaking of codes and ciphers, Phelippes was an intuitive and skilled handler of agents. He briefed informants like Berden and Catilyn and read the reports they wrote. No less importantly, he made sure that they had money to live on. They received no salary: espionage in the reign of Elizabeth had everything to do with patronage and favour and the financial pickings, though occasionally rich, were infrequent. It was not a trivial matter when on 6 July 1586, shortly before he set out for Chartley, Phelippes attended to the reward of Nicholas Berden and Gilbert Gifford with a handsome piece of royal patronage, which to Berden alone was worth £30.

Gifford was all the time growing in confidence and trust. On Thursday, 7 July he was near Chartley, but getting ready soon to travel south. Phelippes had sent him into Staffordshire to test 'the honest man' – the brewer of Burton upon Trent – and to find Thomas Barnes. Gifford wrote as 'Cornelys' to Phelippes in London. Gifford felt the brewer could be trusted. He was very well paid and was, Gifford wrote, 'totaliter ours'. Beyond the money, 'the honest man' sought nothing more than to impress Sir Amias Paulet. But of Thomas Barnes, his cousin and fellow courier to and from Mary Queen of Scots, he could write nothing. Worryingly, Barnes had disappeared.

The fact that Gifford had no clue of Barnes's whereabouts nagged him. The brewer told Gifford that Barnes had set out for London at least a week before without fixing an appointment with him for another meeting. Gifford thought his cousin was probably in the city and, given the length of time he had been away from Staffordshire, likely to be leaving London to travel north once again. The brewer did not know Barnes's real name, and only now did Gifford give Sir Amias Paulet the identity of their mysterious second courier: 'His name is Barnes. I know him well. But I think he hath no chamber in London. Neither were it expedient [for] you to lean harder of him for the cause I told, for that would spoil all.' He undertook, for both Paulet and Phelippes, 'to cut him clean off from this course'. Cousin Barnes could expect, in other words, a stiff dressing down for disappearing – when Gifford found him. But even on 11 July there was still no sign of him. Gifford thought Barnes might be with the French ambassador but dared not go to the ambassador's house till he had a packet of letters to deliver.

On Sunday, 10 July Gifford met John Ballard for the first time in England. He knew Ballard a little already, from Paris, but not very well. He was not surprised by Ballard's visit. Thomas Morgan played his agents close to his chest, and Gifford knew from their meeting in Paris that Morgan had a scheme in play and that he had already sent someone 'to solicit matters' in England. This was Morgan's method, small revelations when the time came, no one knowing the whole picture. Gifford quickly perceived that this unexpected meeting with a man he hardly knew was another unfolding of Thomas Morgan's plan. Ballard, on the other hand, seemed to know all about Gifford and had been searching for him for some time. When he met Gifford that Sunday, he was both relieved and angry.

Ballard's anger was directed at Morgan and Charles Paget. They had promised him regular news from Paris, but he had so far heard nothing; he said he was in half a mind to return to France. Gifford tried to calm him: the delay, he said, could be explained by the usual problems of communication. Ballard thanked God that he and Gifford could now help each other. It was obvious to Gifford that Ballard knew more of Morgan's plan than he did, for Ballard said that even if they did not hear from Morgan and Paget their mission could at least be completed by Gifford and Ballard doing their parts.

Gifford asked Ballard plainly: What was it they had to do? Ballard told Gifford that he should obtain from the Queen of Scots her hand and seal 'to allow of all that should be practised for her behalf': without such a document they laboured in vain. Gifford said that this kind of warrant had never been obtained by any man, and to do so would be very difficult. They agreed to think about the proposal; Gifford would give his answer next day. Ballard left Gifford's lodgings and travelled out of London. He left his manservant to wait upon Gifford for his answer. Gifford was left with the impression after their meeting that Ballard was working alone and that he was 'marvellous earnest' in hearing Gifford's reply. Though Gifford did not yet know the full extent of Ballard's knowledge, he was sure that Ballard would reveal everything to him in time. Certainly Ballard was very keen to keep Gifford's company. Straight away Gifford wrote to Walsingham to find out what answer he should give to Ballard.

Ballard and Gifford met again two days later, a Tuesday morning, when Ballard was in what Gifford called 'a marvellous rage', still furious that he had heard nothing from either Morgan or Paget. He was again thinking about returning to France. He spoke of the great men in England, nobility and gentry, who supported him. Gifford was reluctant to press him too hard for names. Ballard had heard that Gifford was under Walsingham's protection, but Gifford was able to persuade him that he was not. Ballard railed against Thomas

Phelippes. He knew that Phelippes was at Chartley and said that Phelippes was opening and reading packets of letters, causing Gifford to suspect that Ballard had a spy close to Walsingham. Gifford advised Sir Francis to keep special guard on his correspondence.

About six days before Gilbert Gifford's second meeting with John Ballard, Anthony Babington wrote to the Queen of Scots. By now he and his group of Catholic friends had concocted a plan to free Mary from captivity. He been approached, he wrote, by a man called Ballard, who had informed him of great preparations by the Catholic princes of Europe 'for the deliverance of our country from the extreme and miserable state wherein it hath too long remained'. England would be invaded; Mary would be freed; Queen Elizabeth, 'the usurping competitor', would be dispatched. Babington's meaning was clear. Elizabeth was to be murdered, and members of his group of conspirators would do the killing:

> [for] the dispatch of the usurper, from the obedience of whom we are by excommunication of her made free, there be six noble gentlemen all my private friends, who for the zeal they bear to the Catholic cause and your Majesty's service will undertake that tragical execution.

He told Mary that he would be at Lichfield, a few miles from Chartley, where he would expect her reply. Once he had finished his letter, Babington gave it to the boy, who was unknown to him, who came to collect the Queen of Scots's packets. The boy worked for Thomas Phelippes.

Phelippes saw and read for himself Babington's letter to Mary. Waiting patiently near Chartley for Mary to betray herself in her reply to Babington, Phelippes may have remembered some words from the Act for the Queen's Surety passed by parliament only a year earlier. A special judicial commission would try the Queen of Scots on the evidence of any plot or conspiracy 'compassed or imagined, tending to the hurt of Her Majesty's royal person by any person or with the privity of any person that shall or may pretend title to the crown of this realm'. *With the privity of any pretender to the English throne*: in other words, if the Queen of Scots gave her support to the conspiracy of Babington and his friends, she would in effect sign her own death warrant.

The Queen of Scots was too clever and experienced to fall into an easy trap. She replied to Babington's letter but took ten days to do so. She was careful to leave no evidence in her own handwriting. Any notes she may have made for the letter's composition were carefully destroyed, and she dictated the letter to her secretaries. It was Gilbert Curll, Mary's secretary for the English language, who put the plain words into cipher.

The Queen of Scots acknowledged Babington's 'zeal and entire affection' to the Catholic faith and her cause and commended his efforts to prevent 'the designments of our enemies for the extirpation of our religion out of this realm with ruin of us all'. She encouraged Babington to consider each element of his proposal and to confer with Don Bernardino de Mendoza, King Philip's ambassador in Paris. The nearest she came to acknowledging Babington's conspiracy to assassinate Elizabeth was in a question: 'By what means do the six gentlemen deliberate to proceed'? But it was enough.

Leaving Babington in God's protection, Mary instructed him to destroy the letter once he had read it: 'fail not to burn this present quickly'. On 18 July Curll posted this startling document from Chartley, where it went, of course, not straight off to Babington but first, by way of Phelippes's complicated postal system, to Phelippes himself, to be deciphered, read and analysed in careful detail.

It took Phelippes less than twenty-four hours to decipher Mary's reply to Babington and to make a copy for Walsingham. 'It may please your honour. You have now this queen's answer to Babington which I received yesterday' were the opening words of Phelippes's letter to Walsingham on Tuesday, 19 July. The copy Phelippes sent by fast despatch to his master. The original he kept, and would send on to Babington if he was in Staffordshire, as Babington had said he would be. Phelippes thought that if Babington were caught quickly enough Mary's letter would 'not be so sore defaced', even though the Scottish queen had instructed the young man to destroy it. He asked Walsingham to find out from Nicholas Berden or Thomas Cassie, Phelippes's servant, whether Babington was in London.

Phelippes was confident that in what he called the 'bloody letter'

Elizabeth's government at last possessed the evidence necessary to proceed against the Queen of Scots. He hoped that God would inspire Elizabeth 'with that heroical courage that were meet [fit, appropriate] for avenge of God's cause and the security of her self and this state'. In other words, Phelippes believed the time had come to destroy Mary for the good of Elizabeth's throne and kingdom. But at the very least, Phelippes hoped that the queen would hang Mary's two secretaries, Nau and Curll.

Receiving Phelippes's letter, Walsingham briefed the queen on what had been happening at Chartley. Sir Francis wrote to Phelippes on Friday, 22 July to say that nothing would be done about Anthony Babington till Phelippes was back in London; for the time being the young man was free. Walsingham knew that Phelippes had the original of Mary's letter with him and he instructed Phelippes to bring it to court. Already Walsingham's mind, like Phelippes's, was moving. It was clear to him that so brilliant a chance for action needed thought, planning and care. He wrote: 'I hope there will be a good course had in this cause. Otherwise we that have been instruments in the discovery shall receive little comfort for our travail.' In other words, given this opportunity, there had to be decisive and definitive action against the Queen of Scots. What now, he must have wondered, should or could be done?

On 24 July 1586 Sir Francis Walsingham was at court at Greenwich Palace, expecting Thomas Phelippes's return home. Thomas Cassie was in London, carrying messages between Walsingham and his secretary, Francis Mylles. Mylles was at his house on Tower Hill. Four men – Walsingham, Phelippes, Mylles and Sir Amias Paulet at Chartley – pulled together the strands of what was becoming a difficult and complicated operation. They had to keep watch as best they could on Mary Queen of Scots and her secretaries at Chartley. They also had to keep John Ballard the conspirator under close surveillance. And they had to find and detain Anthony Babington, who was anywhere between London and Staffordshire. Phelippes scrutinized the letters passing between Mary and Babington and the other supposed conspirators. Through the eyes of Maliverey Catilyn and Nicholas Berden in London, Mylles kept watch over Ballard and others of his group. Mylles had ready their arrest warrants. And it was Mylles who, with Phelippes away at Chartley, kept (or tried to keep) in touch with the double agent Gilbert Gifford using Phelippes's servant Thomas Cassie.

It was difficult for Mylles or Cassie to know exactly where Gifford was, for like his cousin Barnes he had a habit of disappearing. Gifford was supposed to meet Mylles at night on 22 July. Mylles waited till one o'clock the next morning; Gifford did not turn up. A few hours later, before noon on Saturday, 23 July, Cassie returned to Tower Hill to tell Mylles that he too had not seen Gifford for a few days. Cassie thought that Gifford had ridden out for a day or two in the country with Ballard. By the 24th Mylles was seriously worried. Cassie, however, was sure that he would turn up eventually.

Francis Mylles pondered how best to capture Ballard without compromising any of Walsingham's men. If either Gifford or Berden arrested him, they would be shown to be government agents. Mylles wondered whether one or the other of them should be taken with Ballard and sent to prison for a time as a way to maintain his cover. Mylles was anxious about secrecy and security. He was nervous of the help to be given by the city authorities and he even said nothing of the operation to the two pursuivants lodging in his house. The difficulties of arrest impressed themselves upon Mylles's mind. A night raid, for example, meant doors could take too long to open, giving time for escape. He hoped that Ballard might be 'trained [lured, enticed] to dine or sup in any place with half an hour's knowledge'. Mylles, by now a worried man, hoped (probably against all the evidence) for an easy, tidy and efficient arrest of a very dangerous conspirator.

Phelippes left Chartley for London late on the afternoon of Tuesday, 26 July, carrying with him the original of the Queen of Scots's reply to Anthony Babington's letter. By six o'clock Sir Amias Paulet reckoned that his friend was twelve or fourteen miles on the road south. Paulet wrote to Phelippes on the 29th: 'I trust you are safely arrived at the court, and it seemeth by Master Secretary's letters that upon your coming thither some resolution will be taken.' By this Paulet meant the critical meeting that Walsingham and Phelippes would have when Phelippes arrived in London. Then they would have to decide what to do next; the 'resolution' was their plan of action. Having had Mary's 'bloody letter' for a week, there was a need for Phelippes to post it on to Babington quickly and efficiently: time was ticking by.

Walsingham and Phelippes met probably on 28 July. They discussed how exactly the Queen of Scots's letter should be delivered to Babington. But they considered a much more significant question. Was the letter as it stood strong enough evidence against Mary? If it was so, as Phelippes had believed on 19 July, then why did Walsingham seem to hesitate? There was a note of doubt in his letter to Phelippes of the 22nd. It seems he hinted of something to Paulet. And if Mary's reply to Babington did not stand as definitive evidence against her, another question may have formed itself in Walsingham's mind: What could be done to make it so?

Walsingham and Phelippes discussed this last question, or at least some formulation of it, on Thursday, 28 July. Their answer was to doctor the original 'bloody letter'. Intimately familiar with the cipher employed by the Queen of Scots and Anthony Babington, Phelippes, probably with the assistance of Arthur Gregory in opening and resealing the packet, added to the letter a postscript. The only surviving evidence of this postscript in any original (or near original) form is a draft in Walsingham's papers of eight densely packed lines of cipher characters that run when deciphered to seventy-six words. This was an audacious and risky piece of forgery. The decision to execute it may have been Walsingham's alone, or perhaps Phelippes had brought the idea with him from Chartley. The evidence seems to point, not to long premeditation, but rather to the growing realization of a possibility. But one fact is really not in doubt. When Babington eventually deciphered and read what he took to be a letter of reply from the Queen of Scots, he held in his hands a document that was not what it was when Gilbert Curll had sealed it up.

We can imagine Walsingham and Phelippes together composing their text, testing each word, measuring meaning, master and servant working together. The postscript was then put into cipher using the same method that Curll had done days earlier. Next the passage was read with great care once again. They deleted part of a sentence. This is the document that survives, which when deciphered reads:

> I w[ould] be glad to know the names and qualities of the six gentlemen
> which are to accomplish the designment, for that it may be I shall be

able upon knowledge of the parties to give you some further advice necessary to be followed therein; and ~~even so do I wish to be made acquainted with the names of all such principal persons as also w[h]o be already as also who be a~~ as also from time to time particularly how you proceed and as soon as you may for the same purpose who be already and how far every one privy hereunto.

The object of this paragraph was to prove beyond all doubt an unbreakable connection between Mary Queen of Scots and the treasonous conspiracy of Anthony Babington and his group. That suggestion was there already in the text of Mary's letter. But what Walsingham and Phelippes probably had in the mind were the precise words of the Act for the Queen's Surety and the need to have watertight evidence of the Queen of Scots's 'privity' in a conspiracy.

They must have felt this fantastic risk was one worth taking. The smallest slip could easily disable the surveillance coordinated by Mylles and, more importantly, ruin the chance to throw the net over Mary Stuart. Phelippes's forgery had to appear like a seamless continuation of a letter that had been written first in French and then in English and finally turned into cipher. It had to reflect Gilbert Curll's habits of enciphering Mary's letters. Above all it had to look like Curll's handwriting. Only someone with Phelippes's experience and sharp eye for detail could have done it.

Certainly it was a danger for Walsingham to provoke so revealing an answer from Babington. It was also a risk to put so much evidential weight on a piece of fabrication. But this second point, which caused Walsingham and the Privy Council some anxiety in the following months, was not urgent enough to prevent Sir Francis from sanctioning the forgery. After all, as Phelippes had written ten days earlier, this was for God's cause, Queen Elizabeth's safety and the security of the state. It was self-evident that Mary Queen of Scots was guilty of a most horrible crime against her royal cousin. Now Walsingham and Phelippes had the proof, by hook or by crook.

On the evening of the same day of the meeting between Walsingham and Phelippes, Thursday, 28 July, Anthony Babington gave a great supper for his friends at the Castle tavern on Cornhill right in the heart of the city of London. The Castle occupied a large stone house;

from the tavern door there was a passageway leading out to Thread-needle Street and the Royal Exchange, one of the busiest meeting places of Elizabethan London. It would seem that Babington, a very rich young man with the money to dine his companions, chose to conspire in plain sight. That evening Nicholas Berden watched the tavern closely, making his dispositions and hoping that John Ballard would be one of Babington's guests. Berden had put one of his men in the next room to Babington and his friends, from where he was able to watch who came to supper.

Hurriedly Berden wrote a letter to Francis Mylles. Rushed across London, it arrived at Mylles's house on Tower Hill at seven o'clock. Berden asked Mylles to be at the Exchange 'somewhat disguised' at eight. Mylles should use his discretion. The tavern had two doors, but Berden assured him that the place was 'most safe'. To avoid all suspicion Berden said he would stay away from the Castle. It occurred to him that he might in fact be dining with Ballard that evening. One of their mutual acquaintances had promised to bring Ballard for supper, and within the hour Berden's friend had sent over a capon and two rabbits. This was enough food for at least three, and it seemed likely that he was bringing a guest to Berden's lodging, though Berden knew not whom. Nicholas Berden ended his letter to Francis Mylles in haste and with the observation that he had no arrest warrant.

It turned out in the end that there was no opportunity to miss. John Ballard did not go to the Castle tavern, nor did he have supper with Nicholas Berden. But at least, thanks to Berden's guests for supper, Mylles and Walsingham had an idea of where Ballard was. He was in Sussex, but would very soon return to London. Berden was promised the favour of an introduction to the man who called himself Black Fortescue. Mylles was unconvinced; he thought that Ballard was probably preparing to leave England by ship. Nevertheless, still clinging to a little hope, he asked Walsingham for a blank arrest warrant to give to Berden.

On the following day, Friday, 29 July, Babington at long last received the 'bloody letter' from Mary Queen of Scots. Babington took the packet from 'a homely serving man in a blue coat' who was unknown to him. In fact, of course, the servant worked for Thomas Phelippes;

he may have been Thomas Cassie. And so the delivery was made at last. How would Babington respond to Mary Queen of Scots's supposed request for information about the six men who had volunteered to assassinate Elizabeth? Phelippes and his men watched and waited for Babington's reply.

By now, in the closing days of July 1586, Robert Poley was Anthony Babington's close companion, playing the part of Babington's friend but in fact Walsingham's man and a government informant. Babington still wanted Walsingham's favour to travel abroad; Poley was his contact with Sir Francis. Was Babington a conspirator or merely a young man caught up in a plot? To Walsingham he was a traitor, though he made use, through Poley, of Babington's tentative offer of service. On 30 July Sir Francis instructed Poley 'to move [encourage, persuade] Babington to deal with the principal practisers in the state' – in other words, to involve himself fully with the plot to kill Elizabeth.

By now Babington trusted the friend he called Robin Poley. Poley was Babington's hope for mercy and escape, his intermediary with Walsingham, his advocate and confidant. Through Poley, Babington could alert Sir Francis to the plot against the queen's life and then, with thanks for his service, leave England to travel comfortably around Europe. That was his hope and expectation; he was a naive young man.

On Saturday, 30 July Babington admitted Poley to the secret of the conspiracy. Asking for Poley's hand and promise of good faith, Babington told his friend 'that it lay much in him and certain [of] his friends either to maintain this [Protestant] state and religion as it now stood, [or] else utterly to subvert this [state], and bring in the Catholic religion, and alter the government'. The plan, in other words, was for a Catholic *coup d'état* that would overthrow Elizabeth's government and the Church of England.

Babington was not quite truthful with Poley. He suggested that the conspirators proposed to topple the queen's government, not to kill Elizabeth. But this was the very day that Babington began to decipher the all-important letter he had received only the day before from the Queen of Scots. In Babington's letter to Mary, and in the reply he was about to decipher, he and his friends and the Queen of Scots also had compassed and imagined Elizabeth's murder. The painstaking work of making sense of Mary's letter – working cipher character by cipher character to put it into plain prose – Babington found so tedious that he asked his friend and co-conspirator Chidiocke Tycheborne to help him. The task would have been more painful to him still if he had known that the postscript to the letter was the work of Thomas Phelippes.

Poley went first thing next morning, 31 July, to Babington's lodgings. Poley left because Babington was deep in conversation with his fellow conspirators John Ballard and John Savage, but he returned in the afternoon. Walking together through London, they talked about the plot. It was, said Babington, not quite ready to be executed. Poley advised him to see Walsingham as quickly as he could: if Babington revealed the conspiracy himself, he stood the best chance possible of the queen's clemency and Sir Francis's favour. Poley said that he would see Master Secretary.

They walked and spoke together for two or three hours and had supper with some of Babington's fellow plotters, including John Savage and John Ballard, at the Rose tavern at Temple Bar. That night Poley persuaded Babington to stay at his lodgings near by. On Tuesday, 2 August, Poley went to Walsingham's country house, Barn Elms in Surrey, to make the arrangements for a meeting with Babington at which the young conspirator would reveal to Sir Francis everything he knew about the plot.

Walsingham had not even the slightest intention of meeting Babington. He wanted both Babington and Ballard to be arrested, but like Phelippes he was waiting for Babington to post a reply to the 'bloody letter', the final proof (if any were needed) of a horrible treason. Walsingham needed time, and for this reason at Barn Elms he told Poley to tell Babington that he would meet him in two days. Walsingham instructed Phelippes in the meantime to apprehend Ballard and Babington and his friends. Babington and Ballard would be kept at Walsingham's house on Seething Lane near the Tower of London. Sir Francis instructed Phelippes to plan their interrogations and Nicholas Berden, the watcher, to draw up a list of the names of the 'principal practisers' in the conspiracy.

Suddenly, at this critical juncture, Babington disappeared. On Tuesday, 2 August no one other than Poley, who after leaving Barn Elms had gone off to London, knew where he was. Phelippes was worried. He was waiting for Babington's reply to the 'bloody letter'. Babington had told the courier – Phelippes's man – that he would have it ready that very day. But there was no sign of either the letter or Babington. Phelippes wrote urgently to Walsingham to say that they had been 'cozened', or deceived.

Phelippes suspected that Babington had ridden out of London. Perhaps he had gone to Lichfield in Staffordshire, where, not bothering with the London courier, he intended to post the letter himself to Chartley. Perhaps he had panicked. Phelippes, more used to sitting for hours over complicated secret ciphers, sprang into action. Something had to be done. Probably Babington had indeed gone off to Lichfield. There, as Phelippes knew, Babington would discover that the 'bloody letter' had not been posted from the town. Surely then he would suspect a trap. Babington had to be stopped, and Phelippes prepared to ride out in pursuit. He asked Walsingham for a couple of 'lusty [vigorous, strong] geldings' and a 'lusty fellow' of Sir Francis's staff. They would set out next day at one o'clock to find Anthony Babington.

15

Framing the Labyrinth

In fact Thomas Phelippes had no need for Sir Francis Walsingham's geldings. Phelippes's heroic ride to Lichfield never happened, more is the pity. Anthony Babington had not ridden out to Staffordshire. He was in London, safely under observation, if not yet under arrest. Some time at night on Tuesday, 2 August an informant told Phelippes that if he went to Robert Poley's lodgings he could take Babington and a whole knot of his friends. Phelippes went there, finding no one. Perhaps, he thought, the informant had mistaken Babington for someone else. 'I marvel,' Phelippes wrote to Walsingham, 'what mystery there is in this matter.'

As Phelippes had suspected, Anthony Babington was troubled by Walsingham's postponement of their meeting, but Poley was able to convince him that if he went to Walsingham to make a 'discovery' of the conspiracy he could save his life and secure his freedom. Poley even hinted at a royal audience for Babington, and the naive young man, excited by the thought, saw to his wardrobe, getting ready his best clothes. He said he now knew everything about the plot. He showed Poley his deciphered copy of the 'bloody letter', the text Babington and his friend Tycheborne had laboured at together. He gave no hint to Poley that he would send a reply to Mary. Instead he wanted to tell the whole story of the plot to Walsingham. Babington had no idea that he had moved one step nearer to the hangman's rope.

A little before eight o'clock on Wednesday morning, 3 August, a messenger came from Phelippes to tell Mylles that Babington was still in the city but had taken new lodgings outside London's walls in Bishopsgate Without, on the road to the village of Shoreditch.

Information could travel only as quickly as a messenger on foot in London or a courier galloping out from the city to the court at Richmond Palace. So it was that on Wednesday morning Walsingham, at Richmond, was the last to know that Babington had not slipped the net. He was sure that Babington had panicked and run, and hoped that Poley, whom he was expecting for a meeting early that morning, would be able to offer some explanation of what was going on. Walsingham was disappointed at how events had turned out. What nagged him was the thought that the forged postscript Phelippes had added to Mary's letter had 'bred the jealousy [suspicion, mistrust]' in Babington. Still, John Ballard was quite as important as Babington.

Within hours the situation had changed. Phelippes alerted Walsingham to the facts as quickly as he could. Babington was in London; it seemed he had changed his lodgings. Now Walsingham considered a question he had not had the luxury to be able to ask a few hours earlier. Was it better to have Babington in custody or to wait a little longer in the hope of intercepting his promised reply to the 'bloody letter'? Walsingham wrote to Phelippes: 'it is a hard matter to resolve. Only this I conclude: it were better to lack the answer than to lack the man.'

By now Walsingham and Phelippes were playing an extraordinarily delicate game. Relieved that Babington was in the city and determined to have him under lock and key, Walsingham needed Robert Poley to keep Babington calm. At their meeting at Richmond that Wednesday morning, Sir Francis told Poley that once again he would have to postpone his interview. The queen had been sick in the night, he said, and the Privy Council was busy with Irish affairs; he could not leave court. Walsingham now proposed to meet Babington at Barn Elms in three days' time. In the meantime, Sir Francis wanted Babington, through Poley, to make a plain report of the conspiracy. Once again it was a ruse: the purpose of the postponement was to give Phelippes plenty of time to make Babington's arrest.

Poley, showing a surprising loyalty to Babington, spoke persuasively to Walsingham on the young conspirator's behalf. He assured Sir Francis of Babington's devotion to 'the public service'. Poley told Walsingham what Babington had told him. A man called Ballard, 'a great practiser in this realm with the Catholics', was plotting to stir a rebellion, 'set on' by the ambassador of Spain and Charles Paget. This was hardly startling news to Walsingham, but, playing along, he asked Poley to thank Babington for the information.

But could he rely upon Poley? Sir Francis reflected that his agent had not dealt with him dishonestly, yet he was loath (as he wrote to Phelippes) 'to lay myself any way open unto him'. Robert Poley was not a man to be entirely trusted. At Richmond Walsingham had told Poley only as much as was necessary to provoke what was needed from Babington. Poley's task was to keep Babington occupied with the prospect of Walsingham's favour while Mylles and Phelippes organized his arrest. Indeed Walsingham ordered that Babington's apprehension should be delayed no longer than Friday, 5 August. Francis Mylles was ready with a new arrest warrant signed by Lord Howard of Effingham. Mylles and Phelippes were determined to cover up any trace of the part Secretary Walsingham had played in breaking up such a terrible conspiracy against the queen.

Poley returned from Richmond Palace to his lodgings, where he found Babington and gave him Walsingham's message about the second postponement of their meeting. Babington was worried, but Poley was able once again to reassure him of Sir Francis's friendship and favour.

The gloom of early Wednesday morning, 3 August, quickly lifted. If Walsingham and his men could not secure Anthony Babington's answer to the Queen of Scots's letter they would at least get Babington. He was under surveillance: with Babington in his new lodgings in Bishopsgate Without, in the north-east corner of London, he was watched by Walsingham's agent Nicholas Berden, who lodged nearby in the precincts of Bethlehem hospital.

Berden followed Babington and his friends, hoping to see John Ballard. Babington and some of his co-conspirators met at the Royal Exchange at about seven o'clock in the evening, where for half an hour or so they 'had some earnest discourse'. After talking, they went to the Castle tavern (their usual haunt) for supper. After supper Berden followed each gentleman to his lodging, hoping but failing to see Ballard. It was midnight when he went off duty.

Within hours, however, John Ballard, priest and conspirator, was a

Francis Mylles reports the capture of John Ballard, 4 August 1586.

prisoner. The day was Thursday, 4 August. At Poley's lodgings in the morning Babington had spoken to John Savage. Between eleven o'clock and twelve noon Poley's chambers were raided by a party consisting of a city official and two royal pursuivants, bearing a warrant for Ballard's arrest signed by Lord Admiral Howard. Neither Francis Mylles nor Thomas Phelippes was anywhere to be seen. Ballard was promptly escorted under guard to the Counter prison in Wood Street. It was not a surprising thing to happen to one of the many Catholic priests in the lodging houses and taverns of London. There was not a hint that he was a principal conspirator in a plot to murder Elizabeth. In fact the city official was the father of Phelippes's servant Thomas Cassie, and the pursuivants had been stationed with Francis Mylles for days. The raiding party was made up by Nicholas

Berden's brother-in-law. Mylles's and Phelippes's intricate plan had worked perfectly.

Or had it? After a textbook raid, Mylles was as troubled as ever. First of all, he did not trust Walsingham's contact with Babington, Robert Poley. After searching Poley's chambers Mylles had little hesitation in writing to Walsingham that Robert Poley was 'a notable knave' and could not be trusted. Mylles suspected that Poley was playing both sides for his own advantage.

Much more worrying was the effect of the raid upon Anthony Babington's nerves. Probably it was pure chance that he was there, and even if the raiding party knew who he was they could hardly do much about him: the whole purpose of the exercise was to arrest Ballard as yet another Catholic priest living secretly and illegally in England. But on 4 August Babington broke: disconcerted by the delays in meeting Walsingham, he was unnerved by Ballard's arrest. He wrote a final and remarkable letter to Robert Poley: 'Robin . . . I am ready to endure whatsoever shall be inflicted . . . What my course hath been towards Master Secretary you can witness; what my love towards you yourself can best tell. Proceedings at my lodging have been very strange. I am the same I always pretended. I pray God you be and ever so remain towards me.' He said that the furnace was prepared to try their faith. He ended as 'Thine how far thou knowest'. And then Anthony Babington ran for his life.

Thursday, 4 August became in official circles the formal date of the discovery of the conspiracy of John Ballard and Anthony Babington, the 'principal managers and contrivers' of this latest plot against Elizabeth's life, and their seventeen 'actors and assistants'. The object of the conspiracy of Babington and Ballard was to execute three treasons. Firstly, the destruction of the queen's person. Secondly, the encouragement of a foreign invasion and a domestic rebellion of Catholics and malcontents. Thirdly, the liberation of the Queen of Scots and the advancement of her claim to Elizabeth's throne. But on 4 August only John Ballard was in custody: Anthony Babington and many of his friends were free men.

On Friday, 5 August Walsingham made a report to the queen. Till this point he had kept her well briefed on the twists and turns of the plot. She trusted his discretion in keeping everything he knew of the conspiracy to himself: in Walsingham's words, 'both the depth and the manner of the discovery of this great and weighty cause'. Elizabeth clearly understood the implications of the Babington Plot, aware like her advisers of the Act for the Queen's Surety. She did not want to have set in motion the special commission to try the Queen of Scots. She did not want the blood of an anointed monarch, even one deposed and as dangerous as Mary, on her hands.

By now John Ballard was under heavy guard in the Counter prison. If he refused to speak, Walsingham thought that the best course of action was to take him to the Tower of London to be tortured for information. But Anthony Babington and all the other members of his group of conspirators had flown, so provoking the most urgent manhunt of the whole of Elizabeth's reign. One eyewitness, a Jesuit priest living and working secretly in London, saw it at first hand: 'all ways were watched, infinite houses searched, hues and cries raised, frights bruited in the people's ears, and all men's eyes filled with a smoke, as though the whole realm had been on fire'.

The authorities were furiously busy. Lord Burghley wrote a royal proclamation that called upon all subjects to search out and apprehend Babington and Chidiocke Tycheborne. Watchmen patrolled villages and towns near London. Witnesses to the activities of Babington and his companions, including their families and household servants, were closely interrogated. Pursuivants and constables searched houses throughout London. Thomas Phelippes worked tirelessly on the questions that would be put to Babington and the other conspirators when at last they were captured.

John Savage the would-be assassin was one of the first to be taken. He was interrogated by Walsingham and the queen's trusted vice-chamberlain, Sir Christopher Hatton. Of Savage's second examination, on 11 August, Phelippes made the following significant note:

Omitted by Savage in his confession in writing of that he delivered by speech to Master Vice-chamberlain and Secretary Walsingham.

That the Queen of Scots was made acquainted with the designs as well of invasion as attempt against Her Majesty's person by the letters of Babington and that there came an answer from her touching her assent and advice but what it was the contents particularly he knew not.

That one of the guard about the said Queen of Scots being a brewer was corrupted and won to serve the Queen of Scots's turn for conveyance of letters.

That by means of Gilbert Gifford they had intelligence with the French ambassador.

It was clear as day that Babington, Savage and the others had been deceived completely. Savage confirmed that in the 'bloody letter' Mary had assented to the plot to murder Elizabeth. Savage believed, wrongly, that the brewer of Burton upon Trent worked for the Queen of Scots, whereas in fact he was paid by Sir Amias Paulet and Thomas Phelippes to do exactly what they told him to do. And finally Savage thought that Gilbert Gifford was a trusted courier who carried letters between Mary and ambassador Châteauneuf in London. Here was the early confirmation, if Walsingham and Phelippes needed it, of the staggering success of their secret operation against the Queen of Scots.

It was only a matter of time before all the members of Babington's group were rounded up. A few of them managed to get well away from London: two were caught as far as Cheshire, one in Worcestershire. Most, however, made it only a little way out of London before being captured. From Westminster, Babington and two of his companions ran to St John's Wood, north of London. Joined by some of the others, they hid in deep countryside for ten days before going on to Harrow, where, by now desperately hungry, they begged for food. They were arrested on 14 August and taken to the Tower of London the following day.

Babington in particular was interrogated with an almost obsessional intensity. We know of nine separate examinations, each one accompanied by a written statement, conducted by privy councillors and the crown's law officers between 18 August and 8 September. On 1 September Babington was presented with the cipher he had used in his correspondence with the Queen of Scots, meticulously set out by Phelippes; after all, Phelippes knew the cipher better than Babington did himself. In the presence of a notary public, Babington affirmed

Mary Queen of Scots's cipher is attested to by Anthony Babington
before the Privy Council, 1 September 1586.

that it was the alphabet 'by which only I have written unto the Queen
of Scots or received letters from her'.

Just as significantly, given Savage's confession on 11 August, Babington recalled from memory the contents of the last letter he had
received from the Queen of Scots. She ended, he wrote, 'requiring to
know the names of [the] six gentlemen: that she might give her advice
thereupon'. He was referring to the forged postscript added to the
original letter by Phelippes. Babington had not the faintest idea of
Phelippes's sleight of hand.

One young man who could have given critical help in these long summer days of interrogation was Gilbert Gifford, Walsingham's prize
double agent in penetrating the conspiracies of the Queen of Scots.
Walsingham, more anxious about Babington and Ballard, had noticed
his disappearance on 3 August. Gifford, seeing that the group of conspirators was about to be broken up, panicked. Terrified of being

implicated with John Ballard and then swept up in the arrests of Babington and the others, he left England secretly. More at home in France, Gifford went to the city he knew best in Europe, Paris.

In the middle of August Gifford revealed himself to Walsingham and Phelippes. He was very nervous: he knew full well that he had left England without the queen's licence; he was now just another émigré. Choosing his words carefully, he wrote to ask Walsingham to forgive his sudden departure and offered his continued service. To Phelippes, with whom he had worked so closely for months, he excused his flight abroad, wrote of his willingness to serve Walsingham 'as long as there is blood in my body', and asked for £10.

Walsingham and Phelippes were always quick to see an opportunity. Gifford could spy once again in Paris. After all in England he had been a devastatingly effective agent and he knew the émigré scene in Paris as well as anyone. Keen to be of use to Elizabeth's government (especially after his unlicensed journey to France) he made an offer of espionage that Walsingham accepted. Within weeks Gifford wrote with joy and relief at Sir Francis's favour and protection 'in doing that dutiful service towards my dear country whereunto by all laws I am bounden'.

So by September Gifford was spying once more, picking up packets of foreign correspondence for Phelippes. He had left his cipher for Phelippes's letters in England and was signing reports with own name. He was offered a new means of secret communication. Anything of importance was to be written by Phelippes in alum: often called alum-water, this substance was normally used in medicines and to dye cloth and leather, but here Gifford suggested its use as a secret ink. Gifford asked too for money, which Phelippes was able to get to him by means of bills of exchange through Gifford's uncle, a merchant who traded out of Rouen. He was sent Phelippes's equipment 'for the manner of secret writing' with Phelippes's instructions on how to use it.

It was obvious that Gifford's cover story in Paris would have to be maintained. The blunt fact, of course, was that Elizabeth's government had to denounce Gifford as a conspirator and a traitor. As Walsingham wrote to Phelippes: 'He must be content that we both write and speak bitterly against him.' This kind of cover was necessary, but it came with a cost.

Sure by September of Walsingham's confidence, Gifford was at last completely honest in saying why he had bolted so unexpectedly in August. He called Babington, Ballard and the other conspirators 'ambitious treacherous youthful companions'. He was terrified of being exposed to their treasons. But his greatest fear was to be called as a witness in their public trials, which, when he left England, he could clearly see were imminent. Standing before a packed court-room, he would have to acknowledge that he had not only spied on the Babington group but had also betrayed the Queen of Scots. It was a profound risk he was not willing to take. For Gifford, the familiar émigré haunts of Paris were safer than the courts of royal justice in Westminster Palace. His father had little sympathy. Hearing reports and rumours of the confessions of the Babington plotters, John Gifford understood the dangerous tangle in which Gilbert found himself. He wrote to Phelippes: 'Sir, I have written to my unfortunate son. I would God he had never been born.'

Sir Francis Walsingham, Thomas Phelippes, Gilbert Gifford, Thomas Barnes, Robert Poley, Anthony Babington, Chidiocke Tycheborne, John Savage, Sir Amias Paulet, the honest brewer of Burton upon Trent: each of these in his own way, some playing greater parts than others, had set in motion judicial proceedings against Mary Queen of Scots. That was clear as early as August 1586. By the first week of September Walsingham and Lord Burghley were directing a very serious effort to gather definitive evidence of Mary Stuart's complicity in the plot to kill Elizabeth and invade her kingdoms. Their chief expert researcher, naturally, was Phelippes.

Phelippes's analysis of the evidence shows how tantalizingly close he and his masters had come to proving Mary's guilt. Phelippes reviewed her correspondence with Charles Paget, her ambassador in Paris the Archbishop of Glasgow, the Spanish ambassador Don Bernardino de Mendoza, Lord Paget and Sir Francis Englefield. He assembled for Burghley what he called the 'Proofs of a plot'. But the Queen of Scots had been careful. There was nothing in her own hand-writing, only in the hands of her secretaries Gilbert Curll and Claude Nau. There was at best a glimmer of a chance of tying Mary defini-tively to her last critical letter to Babington.

The evidence of Nau and Curll was critical. Had the Queen of Scots composed the 'bloody letter'? Arrested and put under enormous pressure in long interrogations, Nau confessed to a preparatory 'minute', or rough draft, of it. The very same day, recognizing at once its significance, Walsingham wrote to Phelippes: 'I would to God those minutes were found.' But Nau had made too convenient a confession. The next day Walsingham realized from yet another interview with Nau that 'the minute of her answer is not extant'.

Phelippes saw and understood the problem. He knew that Mary had always been at least one step removed from the letters her secretaries sent out in her name. As a practised cryptographer, he reflected that she dispatched 'more packets ordinarily every fortnight than it was possible for one body well exercised therein to put in cipher and decipher'. She was ill and of course she was a queen who had secretaries to write for her. So not surprisingly Phelippes's view was that the 'heads' (that is, the points to be included) of what he called 'that bloody letter' sent to Babington 'touching the designment of the Queen's person [i.e. the murder of Elizabeth], is of Nau his hand likewise'.

For three days, between 5 and 7 September, Phelippes found himself pulled in two directions. On the 5th, Gilbert Curll, under detention and pressed by Elizabeth's most senior privy councillors, confessed that he had deciphered Babington's letter to the Queen of Scots and that her answer had been first written in French by Nau and then translated into English and finally put into cipher by Curll himself. On the same day, suggesting something entirely different, Nau told four senior privy councillors that Mary had written the 'bloody letter' to Babington in her own hand. Both Nau and Curll cautiously acknowledged the accuracy of the government's copies of the letter, knowing they really had little choice but to do so. They were not, so far as we can tell, ever shown the forged postscript. But this was still not quite enough for Burghley and Walsingham, which explains why on 7 September Phelippes found himself to be the recipient of a peremptory letter from the court at Windsor Castle: 'Her Majesty's pleasure is you should presently repair hither, for that upon Nau's confession it should appear we have not performed the search sufficiently. For he doth assure we shall find amongst the minutes . . . the copies of the letters wanting both in French and English.'

But like the search for the philosopher's stone, neither Phelippes nor any other official could find that final and fatal proof against Mary Queen of Scots in her own hand. Elizabeth's government would have to rely on the weight of the many documents to or from Mary or in her name that Phelippes had deciphered and gathered. Against so formidable and dangerous an enemy as the Scottish Queen, they pressed on regardless.

Anthony Babington and his fellow conspirators were tried in two groups between 13 and 15 September. The case of John Savage, accused of planning from the beginning the queen's assassination, was the first to be heard. Brought to the bar, the charge was put to him: that in April 1586 at the church of St Giles-in-the-Fields he had conspired to murder Elizabeth, to disinherit her of her kingdom, to stir up sedition in the realm and to subvert the true Christian religion. Soon after this he devised with John Ballard how to bring this about, encouraged by letters he had received from Thomas Morgan and Gilbert Gifford. (It was no wonder that Gifford had fled England at the first sign of a trial.) Savage was asked to plead guilty or not guilty to the charge. He equivocated, only to be then sharply corrected by Sir Christopher Hatton:

SAVAGE : For conspiring at St Giles's I am guilty; that I received letters whereby they did provoke me to kill Her Majesty I am guilty; that I did assent to kill Her Majesty I am not guilty.

HATTON : To say that thou art guilty to that and not to this is no plea, for thou must either confess it generally or deny it generally, wherefore delay not the time, but say either guilty or no. If thou say guilty then shalt thou hear further; if not guilty, Her Majesty's learned counsel is ready to give evidence against thee.

SAVAGE : Then, sir, I am guilty.

The law officers set out the evidence against him, much of it from his own confessions. The attorney-general felt they had done quite enough to prove the case. But Hatton once again interjected with an important question for the defendant:

I must ask thee one question. Was not all this willingly and volun-
tarily confessed by thyself without menacing, without torture, or
without offer of any torture?

Savage simply said 'yes'.

Hatton asked for an adjournment of the trial to the following day,
pointing out that if the court were then to hear the evidence against
all the prisoners it would be in session till three o'clock in the morning. Over the following two days Babington and his fellow conspirators
were tried for treason. They pleaded guilty to conspiring to free the
Queen of Scots from confinement and attempting to alter England's
religion, but not guilty to planning Elizabeth's murder. Yet the evidence was overwhelming, and the jury found them guilty on all
charges. In court Babington blamed Ballard for his destruction.

Elizabeth took a special interest in how they were to be executed.
On the day before Savage's trial, she told Lord Burghley that 'considering this manner of horrible treason' against her own person, the
form of the conspirators' executions should 'for more terror' be
referred to herself and her Council. Burghley replied that the usual
way of proceeding, by 'protracting' the pain of the traitors in the sight
of the London crowd, 'would be as terrible as any other device could
be'. Burghley was talking about hanging, drawing and quartering, a
savage and brutal death. Still, Elizabeth wanted the judge and her
privy councillors to understand her royal pleasure. She wanted vengeance, for the traitors' bodies to be torn into pieces.

And so it was that Anthony Babington and his companions were
executed on gallows specially constructed near the church of St Giles-
in-the-Fields, where Savage had first concocted his murder plot, on
20 and 21 September. The deaths of Ballard, Babington, Savage and
Chidiocke Tycheborne were quite as terrible as Queen Elizabeth,
demanding the full execution of royal justice, wanted them to be.

Where the queen insisted on savage deaths for the conspirators, she
dithered on Mary Stuart. By now there was no way to avoid the
examination of the evidence against the Queen of Scots by the
commission of privy councillors and lords of parliament. The fearsome mechanism of the Act for the Queen's Surety had been set in

motion. The Queen of Scots would answer for her conspiracies against her royal cousin. In weeks of nervous preparation, councillors and lawyers directed by Lord Burghley felt their way cautiously through the evidence. There was no precedent for what they proposed to do, trying a foreign monarch, even one deposed, by English laws for treason to Elizabeth. Acutely conscious of proper form, they were not even sure what to call Mary in the proceedings of the commission. With the imagination of Elizabethan lawyers, they settled on 'the Scottish Queen'.

The commission met at Fotheringhay Castle in Northamptonshire between 12 and 15 October 1586. In the great hall Mary was brought before ten earls, one viscount and twelve barons, who sat on long benches on either side of the chamber. The queen's privy councillors occupied chairs of their own. At a table in the centre of the hall were the crown's law officers and two public notaries. The proceedings were conducted under the great cloth of state, Elizabeth's coat of arms, the mark of royal justice.

It was a contest between old enemies. Mary, forty-three years old and too long in confinement, had been worn down and prematurely aged by prison. Both Lord Burghley and Sir Francis Walsingham had been ill, yet ferociously busy in preparing for the commission. Still, the wits of Mary, Burghley and Walsingham were as sharp as ever.

The Scottish Queen wanted nothing to do with what she thought was a travesty of a hearing. She was, after all, a monarch and accountable only to God. Human justice could not touch her – or so she maintained. She contested the commission's jurisdiction over her as a foreign prince and she mocked the evidence it brought against her. She was not allowed lawyers; nor, significantly, was she permitted to examine the documents used by the crown's law officers and by Lord Burghley (who sat as a kind of presiding officer for the commission) to prove her guilt; this was common practice in treason trials, though in Mary's case it had special significance. The evidence, so carefully and diligently prepared by Thomas Phelippes, was read out loud in the great hall of Fotheringhay.

The commission was confident in the strength of an overwhelming case against the Scottish Queen. It was not, however, sure enough of the weight of Phelippes's forged postscript of Mary's 'bloody letter' to Babington. The evidence is complicated and open to a number of readings, but it seems likely that when Babington's first confession was read to the commission his reference to Mary's request to know the identities of his six fellow conspirators was left out. Likewise, the text of the 'bloody letter' put to Mary's secretaries Nau and Curll and read out at Fotheringhay did not have the postcript appended.

Why was this the case, when Walsingham and Phelippes had taken so profound a risk to forge the postscript in the first place? First, it was because the documentary evidence produced by the commission against Mary was cumulatively strong enough to prove the crown's argument. Mary had corresponded with Elizabeth's enemies; she knew well enough of their plots and conspiracies. Secondly, the weight placed by the commission on the testimonies of Nau and Curll meant that the text of the 'bloody letter' had to be consistent with what they had seen, and they had not (so far as we can tell) seen the postscript. Thirdly, the commission was nervous of anything that could jeopardize the precision of their case. By October, with the political context now wholly altered, the view of Burghley and Walsingham must have been that the postscript added nothing materially to the evidence presented at Fotheringhay; it would be too much of a risk to use it.

Not allowed to examine the documents for herself, Mary's defence followed predictable lines. She pounced on the weakness of the commission's case. She was sharp, though at times she broke off to weep. She said she did not know Babington, had never seen him or received any letter from him. It was a poor argument, she maintained, to say that because Babington had written to her she had been a party to his conspiracy. True, she desired news and intelligence from her friends. True also, that people sent her letters, though she did not know who they were or where the letters came from. Babington's confession was read out once again. She denied that she had written any such letter to him. And then she asked the question Burghley and other members of the commission must have been expecting. She asked to see her own handwriting. With the patience of an executioner before his victim, Burghley countered by showing to the commission – but probably not to Mary – copies of Babington's letters.

The Scottish Queen knew from the documentary evidence being

used in the prosecution that her secret correspondence had been penetrated. Somehow Lord Burghley had copies of letters that had passed secretly between Anthony Babington, Claude Nau and Gilbert Curll, and her friends and allies in Europe. She suspected underhand practice. Above all, she suspected Sir Francis Walsingham, who, as one of the observers of the commission, was sitting close by in the great hall of Fotheringhay. The Scottish Queen demanded of Walsingham whether he was an honest man. He stood up from his place at the opposite end of the chamber to Mary, walked to the lawyers' and notaries' table in the centre of the hall and spoke:

Madam, I stand charged by you to have practised something against you. I call God and all the world to witness I have not done anything as a private man unworthy of an honest man; nor as a public man unworthy of my calling. I protest before God that as a man careful of my mistress's safety I have been curious [anxious, concerned, solicitous].

At this reply – a masterpiece of subtle wordplay that said everything and nothing at the same time – Mary's response was to weep. She protested that she would not make a shipwreck of her soul in conspiring against her good sister Elizabeth. But she also spoke with venom against Walsingham. Those he had set for spies over her, she said, also spied for her against him. It seems unlikely that he was disconcerted by her claim. He knew both his men and his methods. And he, quite unlike the Scottish Queen, was not on trial for his life.

Soon after this the Scottish Queen made the dramatic gesture of withdrawing herself from the great hall. She wanted nothing more to do with the commission's proceedings; she had heard enough. It made little difference. In Mary's absence the commissioners continued to hear the evidence against her. Elizabeth effectively hamstrung the proceedings by ordering Lord Burghley not to allow the commission to give a sentence on Mary's guilt. But, though at first depressed by an inconclusive end to the hearing at Fotheringhay, the commissioners were not prepared to let slip their best opportunity so far to destroy the pernicious influence of the Scottish Queen.

After an adjournment of ten days, the commission met once again, in the Star Chamber in Westminster Palace. This time Mary was not present to misdirect or mislead the commissioners in their reading of the evidence against her. Her secretaries, Nau and Curll, once again swore to the accuracy of the documents they had seen, all carefully prepared and set in order by Thomas Phelippes. Even more than this, Curll said that when he had deciphered Anthony Babington's letters and then read them to his mistress he had 'admonished her of the danger of those actions, and persuaded her not to deal therein, nor to make any answer thereto'. She had of course ignored him. Curll's sworn testimony made Mary's guilt plainer than ever.

At last the commission passed sentence upon the Queen of Scots:

> By their joint assent and consent, they do pronounce and deliver their sentence and judgement ... divers matters have been compassed and imagined within the realm of England, by Anthony Babington and others ... with the privity, of the said Mary, pretending title to the crown of this realm of England, tending to the hurt, death and destruction of the royal person of our said lady the Queen.

After this it was a long and complicated road to Mary's execution, one along which Queen Elizabeth was pushed and prodded very unwillingly by her senior advisers. Elizabeth wanted Mary to be quietly killed at Fotheringhay. She made it plain to Sir Amias Paulet, Mary's keeper, that he had subscribed to the Association for the revenge of any treason against queen and country. Why, Elizabeth asked, could he not pursue her to death as he had sworn to do? Shocked at the suggestion, Paulet refused to stain his conscience.

What Elizabeth resisted for as long as she could was the act of signing her royal cousin's death warrant: she did not want the blood of her royal kinswoman on her hands. When Elizabeth at last signed the document, in February 1587, the Privy Council dispatched it to Fotheringhay so quickly and secretly that Elizabeth had no time to change her mind to any effect. The Scottish Queen was dead long before Lord Burghley happened to tell Elizabeth that the warrant had been sent off to Fotheringhay. In a furious temper, the queen blamed everyone except herself. Her junior secretary, William Davison, who had taken the signed warrant to an inner caucus of privy councillors, went before Star Chamber and then went to prison. He was lucky: Elizabeth had wanted Davison to be hanged. Lord Burghley, for the first time in his long career, was dismissed from Her Majesty's presence. It was one of the most decisive and extraordinary moments in English history. Thanks to the clandestine and ruthless work of Walsingham and Phelippes, and the resolution of Walsingham's colleagues in the Privy Council and in parliament, the politics of Elizabeth's reign were never quite the same again.

Did the end justify the means? Were queen and country served by the employment of methods that by modern standards of justice are questionable, to say the least? Certainly a forgery, the tangle of the Babington Plot and a show trial at Fotheringhay and in Star Chamber meant that Mary Queen of Scots could be eliminated once and for all. Elizabeth Tudor was at last free of her rival. But in 1587 even the cleverest of the queen's advisers could not properly apprehend what they had done. Mary's death did not take the sting out of a contested Tudor succession. War with Spain and the Pope was now certain. But there were other intangibles, the principal of them being one that would rumble on through the centuries. In defence of queen and country, Elizabeth and her ministers had killed a monarch.

PART THREE
Politics and Money

16

An Axe and an Armada

When Bull the executioner cleaved Mary Stuart's head from her shoulders in the hall of Fotheringhay Castle in February 1587 the Elizabethan world was jolted on its axis. Bull's blow helped to sever the notion of monarchy as a sacred thing. Queen Elizabeth knew this and, as she believed that divine sanction was the best defence she had against her enemies, it filled her with revulsion. Her ministers, however, being pragmatic men, argued powerfully that Mary must die. And so it was that Elizabeth, pressed by the unanimous will of Privy Council and the Lords and Commons of parliament, signed her royal cousin's death warrant. She and her kingdom now had to take the consequences.

Sir Francis Walsingham and Thomas Phelippes led Mary Queen of Scots to the headsman's block. By secret means they had uncovered her correspondence with Anthony Babington and his fellow conspirators, unearthing with great patience the evidence they needed to prove Mary's complicity in a plot to murder Elizabeth. By today's standards the methods used by Phelippes and Walsingham look unappealing. They dabbled a little in forgery. Even at the time the word entrapment was used by their enemies to describe the way Mary had been caught and held fast. Her trial by commission was unorthodox. The Queen of Scots was refused the help of lawyers (a fixed principle of Tudor treason trials) and she was not permitted to examine the documentary evidence brought against her. But to Elizabeth's government in 1586 all of this hardly mattered. After so many years of effort they had Mary where they wanted her. The evidence was robust enough for privy councillors and lords of parliament to prove what Elizabeth's advisers had known all along: simply, that the Queen of Scots was guilty of privity in compassing treason against their queen. Of course it was a political trial whose outcome was never in doubt. But at least Mary's case had been tried in a special court of justice. It would have been so simple to have her quietly killed. That, after all, was what her cousin Elizabeth had wanted: a quiet and discreet murder from which she could have distanced herself.

Even before the blow of the axe, Elizabeth's government braced itself for the coming storm. There was outrage in Catholic Europe, though that was hardly surprising. In Paris clergy preached angry sermons of revenge against Elizabeth's murderous regime. King Philip of Spain, however, was a little more ambivalent about Mary's judicial execution, for it left open his own claim to the Tudor crown. This he began to press with great energy, notionally with the Scottish Queen's blessing. Philip believed in the existence of a will made by Mary to the effect that she granted the right of English succession to Philip; he ordered a thorough search of Europe's archives to find it. It was a phantom; no such document existed.

The outrage of Europe's Catholics was for Philip an instrument of political power. They believed that England was a heretic pariah kingdom where for nearly thirty years Elizabeth's government of atheists had engaged in a vicious persecution of English Catholics, raiding their homes, putting them in prison and making martyrs of their priests on trumped-up charges of treason. That was how exiles and émigrés like William Allen saw it: they stood squarely against evil.

Allen began to work more furiously than ever for his homeland's liberation, putting his faith in what he and others called the Enterprise of England: the invasion of Elizabeth's kingdoms by the combined forces of Spain and Rome. As this chapter will show, the line of causation is clear. Mary Queen of Scots was executed in February 1587. In the following months Doctor Allen and his fellow priest, the Jesuit Robert Persons, petitioned King Philip of Spain for action, energetically supporting his claim to the English throne. With preparations for an invading naval armada in fact already under way, there was at last a reality to the notion of toppling the Elizabethan regime by a Spanish invasion. In the spring of 1588 Allen wrote a bitter, caustic attack on Elizabeth's bastardy and tyranny; his pamphlet would be handed out to the English people by victorious invading forces. Then at last, in July, King Philip's Great Armada left the coast of Spain. Driven by weather and Elizabeth's navy the Spanish fleet was dispersed before it could do any harm. But for Philip it was a temporary defeat in what became a long war against Tudor England.

Mary Stuart's execution threw open to question one of the great certainties of thirty years. Since the beginning of Elizabeth's reign, the Queen of Scots was her cousin's obvious rival heir and successor. Whatever English succession law might say, everyone – even Elizabeth's advisers – knew that there was no other plausible candidate. But Mary had always been more than a successor waiting in the wings for her cousin to die of natural causes. When Pope Pius V had declared Elizabeth a bastard heretic schismatic in 1570, the insinuation was obvious: by the word successor, Catholics like William Allen meant rightful monarch. But after February 1587 the old assumption of deposing Elizabeth from power in favour of her cousin no longer held. So who was the best candidate? The exiles and émigrés of Paris were gripped by factional tussles over competing claimants to the kingdoms of England and Ireland. One group supported the title of King Philip of Spain. Others favoured Mary's son, twenty-one-year-old King James VI of Scotland, hoping that he might make a conversion to Catholicism. Certainly James vigorously protested to Elizabeth at the execution of the mother he never knew. Yet with a pension of £4,000 a year, Elizabeth's government bought the young king's neutrality. It was clear that the real danger to Elizabeth's throne came from Spain.

Doctor Allen and Robert Persons threw their considerable intellectual and political weight behind Philip's claim. They believed, surely correctly, that only Spain had the power to topple the murderous regime of the pretender-queen Elizabeth. The two men put together evidence from the complicated family trees of the English royal line and the old chronicle histories of England. Two of the justifications for Philip's title were his descent from the royal house of Lancaster and Elizabeth's excommunication from the Catholic Church by Pope Pius V in 1570. Persons and Allen also used the theory of just war: 'conquest in a just war and for a just cause,' they wrote, 'is usually considered to give a very valid right to a kingdom'. Besides, they believed, once a Spanish army forced Elizabeth and her government from power, England's Catholics would certainly elect Philip as their king – as he had been, of course, many years before, as the husband of Elizabeth's sister Queen Mary. If Allen had ever believed what he wrote in 1581 – 'We put not our trust in princes or practices abroad, nor in arms or forces at home' – the execution of the Scottish Queen had changed things once and for all. Now he, Persons and their compatriots threw themselves behind the liberation of their homeland by the global might of King Philip's Catholic monarchy.

So by appealing to genealogy, to history and to the urgent politics of Europe Allen and Persons sought to encourage Philip to commit himself to the great Enterprise of England. They were in fact pushing hard at an open door. Philip had already made the strategic decision to support the Enterprise. After years of having to live with the offensive heresy of Elizabethan England and English provocations in politics and diplomacy, Philip and his military advisers were indeed preparing to invade Elizabeth's kingdoms. Limited only by the complexity of Spain's military dispositions and the bureaucratic bulk of Philip's government, in 1587 the Great Armada was beginning to take shape.

Here we have to make sense of nearly thirty years of Anglo-Spanish relations. In the dying days of Queen Mary's reign, in November 1558, Philip had sent his personal emissary, the Count of Feria, to find out what was happening at the English court, and in particular to interview the queen-in-waiting, Princess Elizabeth. Through Feria, Philip had offered friendship to his sister-in-law. Politely she had acknowledged it. Brushing aside Feria's advice to be a good and obedient Catholic queen, Elizabeth felt she was beholden to no one, and she said so. The new government felt its way carefully through the tangled and fraught politics of a Europe fractured by war and religion.

It had seemed so unlikely that Elizabeth and her government would survive as they did for decades. Foreign war, rebellion, disease, time, chance, conspiracy – life in the sixteenth century was a fragile thing. With no convincing Protestant successor to follow her, England might so easily have been swallowed up once again by a Catholic dynasty. That, after all, was what English exiles and émigrés and foreign potentates wanted: Mary Stuart, daughter of the ultra-Catholic Guise, Queen of England, Scotland and Ireland, the wearer of the imperial crown of Henry VIII though loyal to God and Pope, but one monarch in a Europe dominated by the earthly powers of Spain and France.

Elizabeth and her advisers never trusted Spanish professions of friendship. Time and again they found evidence of Spanish duplicity, as Philip allied himself with the Pope and other Catholic princes. And they were right to be cautious of him. He believed passionately in the unifying authority of his Catholic monarchy, writing within months of the Count of Feria's embassy of the evil that was taking place in England – taking place precisely because Elizabeth was by then queen. By 1569 it was plain to Elizabeth's Privy Council that Spain, first of all intent on crushing Protestant resistance in the Low Countries, would sooner or later shift military operations to England, bringing across the few miles of sea between Flanders and England all the horrors of European war and the instruments of the holy inquisition. And that was before rebellion in the north of England and the proof of Spanish involvement in the Ridolfi Plot of 1569–71 on behalf of the Queen of Scots.

The reality, in fact, was that Philip of Spain was much too busy in the 1560s and 1570s to consider an invasion of Elizabeth's kingdoms. Heavily committed elsewhere, he could give neither money, ships nor troops to an English campaign. To the queen's advisers, however, the plain (if secret) intention of the European Catholic powers was to crush Elizabeth's government: everything they saw over decades, from the eager plottings of émigrés and exiles to the subversive activities of foreign ambassadors consorting with the Queen of Scots, told them that sooner or later a great contest would come. All the plots, conspiracies and plans for invasion discovered in the 1580s by Burghley and Walsingham gave cumulative weight to the feeling of dangerous emergency. And behind all of these conspiracies, in some way or fashion, were the two constants of Mary Queen of Scots and King Philip of Spain. By 1587 Mary at least had been eliminated.

So with this outlook, it is hardly surprising that relations between Tudor England and Habsburg Spain were from the beginning chilled by a rather frosty diplomatic formality. Over the years this cooled still further. Ambassadors at both royal courts were expelled. Trade embargoes and confiscations were used as political weapons. English towns and cities gave refuge to Protestants fleeing war in the Spanish Netherlands. Spain's military commanders and government officials involved themselves in plots against Elizabeth's government. It was not open war, but nor was it an obvious peace. Indeed it was much as the seventeenth-century English political theorist Thomas Hobbes wrote: 'the nature of war, consisteth not in actual fighting; but in the known disposition thereto, during all the time there is no assurance to the contrary'. Today, remembering the history of the twentieth century, we might call the troubled state that existed between England and Spain before the 1580s a cold war. But the parallel is not exact, for the two sides were disproportionately matched in their capacity to fight. Faced with the power of Spain, Elizabethan England would surely be very quickly broken.

Two critical years in the irrevocable breakdown of relations between Spain and England were those of 1584 and 1585. In October of the first year Lord Burghley wrote in a policy paper that his queen had 'many just causes to think that the King of Spain mindeth to invade her realm and to destroy her person'. It was a stark analysis based upon two facts. The first was the continued military effort of Spain in the Low Countries to destroy Protestant resistance. The second was the assassination, on King Philip's orders, of William of Nassau, Prince of Orange, the leader of Dutch resistance to Spain. Coming soon after the revelations of Spanish involvement in the Throckmorton Plot, the killing of Orange provoked the appalling fear of Elizabeth's assassination. This, too, was the most powerful reason for the visceral revulsion in parliament and the Privy Council at William Parry's murder plot. A highly significant response to Orange's assassination was the Association for the revenge of any attack upon Elizabeth or her kingdom, to be followed a few months later by the Act for the Queen's Surety.

But how could England defend itself against Spanish power? At first Elizabeth's advisers had few great ambitions. Walsingham's view in the spring of 1585 was that England's naval commanders and adventurers could harry Spanish power at sea. In a proposal 'for the annoying of the King of Spain', he suggested that English ships should engage the Spanish fleet. This was exactly the sort of thinking that lay behind official support for Sir Francis Drake's voyage to the West Indies in 1585 and 1586 to attack Spanish ports and shipping and to intercept Spain's treasure fleet. Drake and his expedition caused havoc. To King Philip Sir Francis was a licensed pirate. To Elizabeth's government, by contrast, he was a blunt but effective instrument of policy.

A more powerful statement still was military intervention in the Low Countries. In summer 1585 Queen Elizabeth signed treaties with the Dutch whereby the English royal treasury would pay for thousands of soldiers to fight the King of Spain's forces. The Earl of Leicester, for many years one of the queen's closest advisers, was appointed commander of the expeditionary force. Already furious at Drake's devastating war at sea, the provocation of these Anglo-Dutch treaties was almost the last straw for Philip and his advisers. The final and decisive shift in the king's thinking came with more news in October 1585 of Drake's campaign in the West Indies. Late in the same month Philip informed Pope Sixtus that he accepted His Holiness's invitation to conquer England. The king was a little cautious; the Enterprise, he said, would have to be delayed till 1587; he could bear only half the cost at most. But the strategic case was clear. Its clinching argument was that Elizabeth's England, in supporting rebels in the Low Countries and setting Drake loose, was the greatest threat to Spanish global interests. Though doing so might risk the campaign in the Netherlands and the security of Spanish America, it was essential to divert resources temporarily to England. At the end of December 1585 Philip asked the Prince of Parma to set out a plan for the invasion.

By July 1586 the first of a number of evolving plans was ready. In the following summer a great armada of ships would sail from Lisbon for Ireland. Two months later the fleet would enter the English Channel, at which point, and not before, 30,000 veteran troops from the Spanish army of Flanders under the Prince of Parma's command would leave the Netherlands and land on the coast of Kent. The place of landing would be near Margate. Parma's forces would march on London, quickly taking the city with the queen and her government still in it. Over the following months, this remained the central proposition of the expedition.

One man more passionate than anybody else about the great Enterprise of England was William Allen. Allen's pen was always an effective weapon against his enemies in Elizabeth's government, and it was soon busy with a pamphlet about an English commander in the Low Countries, Sir William Stanley, who in 1587 surrendered himself, his regiment of English and Irish soldiers and the town of Deventer to Spanish forces. Allen vigorously defended Stanley's actions and made a public declaration of his own support for Spain. Stanley became one of the most feared and elusive of Elizabeth's émigré enemies. By the 1590s practically every plot against the queen's life, plausible as well as implausible, involved one or more of Stanley's desperate Irish renegades.

Knowing that only Spain could secure the success of the Enterprise of England, Allen worked tirelessly in the cause of King Philip and his invasion. While Spanish diplomats in Rome pressed the Pope to make Allen a cardinal, Allen used his formidable powers of encouragement and persuasion to urge King Philip 'to crown his glorious efforts in the holy cause of Christ by punishing this woman [Elizabeth], hated of God and man, and restoring the country [England] to its ancient glory and liberty'.

In July 1587 Sixtus V and Philip came at last to a formal agreement on the Enterprise of England. The Pope promised money in two instalments, the first to be paid on the landing of the Great Armada in England, the second once the kingdom was captured. Sixtus granted Philip the right to name as Elizabeth's replacement one who would 'stabilize and preserve the Catholic religion in those regions, and who will stand acceptable to the Holy Apostolic See, and accept investiture from it'. Days after the agreement William Allen became a cardinal.

If much of the money was to come from the Pope and the ships and troops from the King of Spain, it was Cardinal Allen who, as the pre-eminent expert on England, was given the task of rebuilding the Catholic Church in his homeland. But most urgently of all in 1588 Allen put his mind to a political defence of Philip's invasion. He wanted to persuade his countrymen of how much better off they would be without Elizabeth as their queen. Till this point in his career as a pamphleteer and propagandist he had only ever denounced the queen's advisers: they were atheists and Machiavellians intent on securing power through the murder of innocent Catholics. The nearest he had come to articulating a political argument for the overthrow of Elizabeth was in his *Modest Defence* (1584), where he explained how popes and even priests could remove temporal princes from power. Now, with the Great Armada so near, he cast off all inhibitions. For the first time ever in print he attacked Elizabeth personally and directly. In *An Admonition to the nobility and people of England and Ireland* Allen held nothing back. What makes his pamphlet truly gripping is that it was printed all ready to be shipped over to England once the Armada had made a successful landing.

Writing provocatively as 'the Cardinal of England', Allen excoriated Elizabeth for her bastardy, her open rebellion against Church and Pope, her 'Luciferian pride' in setting herself up as head of her own Church, her theft of the English crown, and her slaughter of Mary Queen of Scots. Just as venomous, in a form even more concentrated than the *Admonition*, was Pope Sixtus's sentence of deposition against Elizabeth. This too was Allen's work, in which he again explained and justified Spain's great Enterprise. In deposing 'this woman' and her accomplices 'so wicked and noisome to the world', Philip of Spain was England's saviour.

After years of clever evasions, William Allen's views were now plain to read. His mask, for so long held carefully in place, had at last slipped – though what Allen revealed underneath it hardly came as a surprise to Elizabeth's advisers, who knew that he was a traitor and a staunch defender of treasons. With some forewarning, Elizabeth's government saw exactly what propaganda Spain would use in its invasion. Lord Burghley had a copy of the *Admonition* four weeks before the Armada set sail. He read Allen's 'vile book' with 'much indignation'. He sent it immediately to Walsingham, so furious at Allen's pamphlet that he ended the covering letter to Sir Francis still 'in choler'. But at least Burghley and Walsingham now had the satisfaction of knowing that their enemy, coming a little more into the light, was showing his true colours.

The Great Armada of Spain was probably the worst-kept secret in sixteenth-century Europe. Philip's government was notoriously leaky; indeed some of the king's most secret planning was known in the states of Italy, long skilled at gathering foreign intelligence, within weeks of being decided in Spain. And yet it was vital nevertheless for Elizabeth's Privy Council to have reliable information of Spain's intentions. As ever, the problem was one of finding out the truth of what was really happening from the heavy fug of rumour and report. Walsingham and his colleagues knew that the news they received was often exaggerated. Sometimes the enemy planted false information. Frequently, though genuinely believed by those who provided them, reports were just plain wrong. In January 1586, for example, some sailors arrived back in England talking of rumours of great Spanish naval preparations in Lisbon. The report, Walsingham wrote, was 'but a Spanish brag': it was simply a boast.

So how could they discover the enemy's plans? By now, after practising his technique in the Babington Plot, Thomas Phelippes was adept both before and after the Armada at using double agents to extract information from Catholic exiles in mainland Europe. One of those agents was Thomas Barnes, Gilbert Gifford's cousin, whom Phelippes used to establish a correspondence with the dangerous English exile Charles Paget. Paget believed that Barnes was his agent and sent questions for Barnes to answer in England about political and military affairs. In this way, with some skill and cunning, it was possible for Phelippes to find out what Paget and his Spanish masters knew about the state of England and its preparedness for a naval assault. Barnes's reports to Paget also allowed Phelippes to deceive and disinform the enemy. With the advice of Walsingham, Phelippes carefully answered Paget's questions. They had to do with political divisions within Elizabeth's Privy Council, the morale of her subjects, those ports and havens suitable for landing an army, numbers of English soldiers, their stores of armour and ammunition and the size of the queen's navy. All of these were important topics for Spanish war planning.

As significant as Phelippes's system of double-cross was the intelligence Walsingham gathered from merchants and diplomats working abroad. He paid for reports from men positioned on the coast of France, especially in the Bay of Biscay. The London merchant and financier Sir Horatio Palavicino, a man of enviable contacts in foreign courts and embassies, was skilled at providing Walsingham with secret intelligence. Equally, Palavicino found himself to be the object of Spanish efforts to deceive and disinform Elizabeth's government. In his work for Walsingham, a man as well connected as Palavicino negotiated a steady path through a hall of mirrors. Often he succeeded; occasionally he failed.

The most vital thing of all was patiently to assess the information that came from all these sources: diplomats, merchants, intelligencers, military experts and the agents and double agents who worked for Phelippes. With a timely combination of luck, ingenuity, chance, skill and the propensity of the Spanish government to leak information, Elizabeth's advisers knew much in advance of the Great Armada of the kingdom of Spain.

Two important names here are Anthony Standen and Stephen Powle, two English gentlemen living abroad. Standen was an adventurer, a Catholic exile who lived on a Spanish pension. But his loyalty was for sale, and throughout these years he was encouraged by Walsingham to offer for money intelligence to Elizabeth's government. Sir Francis canvassed Standen about Spain's preparations at sea in April or May 1587. From Florence, Standen duly sent his reports.

Powle was a less colourful character than Standen, a keen continental traveller who (as he wrote himself) was Lord Burghley's 'feet, eyes, or ears' in Germany. In 1587 Powle moved on to Venice, from where he sent intelligence to Walsingham, proving himself a very effective gatherer of news and information. In Powle's meticulous newsletters, the earliest indications of the Armada came in December 1587. His information two months later was that the fleet would not sail out before spring of that year. By the end of March 1588, Powle's sources told him that the Duke of Medina Sidonia would command the Armada; it was intelligence that turned out to be correct.

In June and early July 1588, with the Enterprise imminent, reports began to multiply. Walsingham and other councillors turned their minds to what could be done to resist the invasion. A month before the Armada sailed from Lisbon, Walsingham's intelligence told him that the Spanish fleet would make for Sheppey, Harwich or Yarmouth on England's east coast, carrying 30,000 men of the Prince of Parma's army. Walsingham believed that the best way to defend the English coast was to have at each of the three potential landing sites a force of 1,000 footmen and 200 cavalrymen, to remain there until the Spaniards' intentions were clear.

By now naval commanders on the English south coast were receiving and weighing news of the movements of Spanish ships. Breton sailors in Dunkirk reported seeing 150 'ships of war of the King of Spain' sailing in a company from Cape Finisterre. The information had reached Dover by means of an English merchant called Skofield. However, there were competing reports of the Armada's readiness. In early June Sir Horatio Palavicino received out of Italy intelligence that men, money, ships and ammunition for the Armada were far from plentiful. Palavicino believed the source, a Genoese commander in the Spanish fleet. His assessment, wrongly, was that King Philip would wait for more favourable conditions to launch the Enterprise.

But for all the uncertainty, as well as the energetic exchange of letters between Elizabeth's senior advisers in June and early July 1588, one fact was clear. Though England's defences were far from ready to withstand the sheer weight of a concerted assault by the King of Spain's forces, Walsingham, Burghley and their colleagues had a very clear idea of the form and scale of what was heading towards the coast of England.

While it prepared in the summer of 1588 for the Spanish invasion it had so long expected, Elizabeth's government engaged King Philip in peace negotiations. The simple truth was that England was poorly prepared both militarily and financially for the fight. Its limited resources of men and money were already heavily committed in the Low Countries. Royal coffers could not hope to pay for those troops and sailors waiting for the Duke of Parma to arrive, and for this purpose the government turned to the Merchant Adventurers of London and Sir Horatio Palavicino to raise the huge sum of £40,000. In a strange way, the kind of information Walsingham was able to gather about the forces of Parma and the Duke of Medina Sidonia over months only prolonged the agonies of expectation. Intelligence perhaps shifted the balance of probability one way or another, but it could not in the end win a battle at sea or on land. It certainly could not pay the bills or alter the weather.

When it came, after long months of anxious watching, King Philip's

Great Armada of 130 ships was defeated both by the weather and by the virtuosity and aggression of the formidable naval officers under the command of Elizabeth's lord admiral, Charles Howard, second Baron Howard of Effingham. Combat between the two fleets, which were roughly equal in size, was sporadic but fierce. The Armada was beset by accident. The weather in the English Channel was terrible, and Medina Sidonia's fleet was battered by gales. One ship had to be abandoned because of an explosion of gunpowder. Another, the *Nuestra Señora del Rosario*, one of the Armada's pay ships carrying 50,000 gold ducats, found itself in difficulty and had to limp behind the other ships. It was captured, with all its gold and guns, by *The Revenge* of Sir Francis Drake. There was a ferocious battle led by two English commanders, John Hawkins and Martin Frobisher. Heading for Calais, Medina Sidonia's navy was harried by the English fleet, whose fire ships caused chaos in the Armada, forcing Spanish captains to cut their cables. Drake, ever aggressive, engaged the enemy ships in close combat.

All of this meant that careful Spanish preparations came to nothing. The final plan for the combined forces of the two dukes was for Medina Sidonia's fleet to give protection to the hundred or so vessels lying in Dunkirk harbour and the 200 boats at Nieuport waiting to carry Parma's army of 26,000 infantry and 1,000 cavalry over to England. They never made it. Instead a broken Armada fled north around the eastern coast of Scotland, pursued as far as the Firth of Forth by an English fleet left with practically no powder and shot. As Lord Admiral Howard put it, 'we put on a brag countenance [a boastful display] and gave them chase'. The Armada, and with it the cherished Enterprise of England, hoped for and then planned for so long, failed.

It was a positively miraculous deliverance. Queen Elizabeth ascribed victory, not to the weather, but to the agency of providence. God's victory in scattering the Great Armada was celebrated in verse:

> He made the winds and waters rise
> To scatter all my enemies.

But the failure of King Philip of Spain's Great Armada masked the still dangerous reality facing Elizabeth's England. No amount of English Armada propaganda could disguise what for Spain was a temporary defeat. There were other ways and methods to carry on the fight against heresy. The Duke of Parma himself anticipated this only a few days before the Armada left port. The duke spoke to one of the English commissioners at the Anglo-Spanish conference in Flanders, saying:

> In mine opinion you have more cause to desire [peace] than we, for that
> if the king my master do lose a battle he shall be able to recover it well
> enough without harm to himself, being far enough off in Spain; and if
> the battle be lost of your side, it may be to lose the kingdom and all.

The war could be fought in other ways. It was a lesson no sensible Elizabethan politician, innoculated against his own government's anti-Spanish propaganda, could ever afford to forget. Sir Francis Walsingham, for one, felt that the breaking up of the Great Armada had done little good: 'our half doings doth breed dishonour,' he wrote, 'and leaveth the disease uncured'.

Throughout the years of the 1590s the fight against Spain consumed men and money, corroding the morale of Elizabeth's subjects. English troops, ordinary men impressed into service, fought in the Low Countries. There was fighting, too, in Ireland, a long and debilitating campaign against the rebel Earl of Tyrone. The expense of all these commitments was enormous. They were paid for by loans, much of the money borrowed from the merchant community of London. The sums are eye-watering: £575,000 on the war at sea, £1,420,000 on the campaign in the Low Countries and £1,924,000 in Ireland. The Tudor crown saddled itself with debts it could not hope to repay. More than this, mutinies of troops, failed harvests, long and murderous outbreaks of plague and influenza, rising prices and fears of social unrest all punctuated and haunted the 1590s.

If this seems a cheerless way to write of the years after 1588 – was not the Armada the glorious moment of Elizabethan ambition and prosperity? – the facts speak for themselves. Elizabeth was fifty-seven years old in 1590. She had no heir and no inclination to make a new succession law. Her successor by default was likely to be King James of Scotland. What would really happen on her death was open to the vagaries of international politics and the collective will of an English political elite now more inclined to squabbling and faction than it had been so far in Elizabeth's reign. Sheer chance would surely play its part. With the rise of young and ambitious courtiers like Robert Devereux, Earl of Essex – at twenty-five in 1590 the favourite of the queen – some of the old continuities and structures at court and in council were quickly disappearing.

In fact a whole generation of Elizabeth's first advisers was dying away, leaving new men to navigate old and difficult problems of war and foreign adventure. Sir Francis Walsingham died in 1590, and along with him went his system of espionage, which was much too expensive to maintain in times of crippling government expenditure on war. Thomas Phelippes was left without a master, having to make the best of uncertain times. For the first time ever in his life Phelippes faced professional failure, even humiliation, in his espionage work. He continued to operate his own secret agents at home and abroad. But, experienced as he was, he found employment in the young Earl of Essex's fledgling intelligence service a precarious business.

The great constant of the Elizabethan political world was Lord Burghley, who, though he said he wanted to retire, found it impossible to release the mechanisms of power and patronage. Ever the dynast, Burghley was training as an apprentice his son, Robert, a young man of immense ability and talent. In 1591 Sir Robert Cecil, together with his father, recruited a secret agent called John Cecil, alias John Snowden, a priest close to the circles of Robert Persons and William Allen. For Sir Robert it was an early chance to practise the technique he would later perfect as the queen's secretary, for by the end of Elizabeth's reign in 1603 he oversaw an intelligence system probably even more formidable than Sir Francis Walsingham's had been.

These were years of war, strain and uncertainty. More than ever before we begin to hear in the 1590s the sharp notes of paranoia and anxiety as men like the Earl of Essex, Lord Burghley and Sir Robert Cecil fought their political battles at court with their spies and agents.

17

'Good and painful long services'

The queen's pursuivants pulled Thomas Barnes out of bed late at night on Thursday, 12 March 1590. They found him in his lodgings at the Saracen's Head on Carter Lane, close to St Paul's Cathedral. They suspected that he was a Catholic priest. He was in fact one of Sir Francis Walsingham's most prolific spies.

Barnes was still at the Saracen's Head the next morning; it seems that somehow he was able to talk his way out of arrest. Having no idea of who had denounced him, he took up his pen and a sheet of folio paper to compose a letter to Thomas Phelippes. He wrote quickly and heavily, correcting his mistakes as he went along, blotting some words; he was not bothered by elegant penmanship. In fact Barnes was seriously annoyed: 'You know how prejudicial this kind of trouble may be to the pretended proceedings and therefore I beseech you with all speed seek the redress.' He was meant soon to meet his émigré contact, but if that gentleman found out about the pursuivants' raid, he told Phelippes, 'alls were in dust'. Barnes signed the letter with his full name, sealed it and addressed it to his very good friend Master Thomas Phelippes.

Barnes was by now an agent of two years' experience. Walsingham and Phelippes had formally recruited him in 1588. Before that, from the spring of 1586, he had unknowingly worked for Phelippes, carrying letters secretly to and from the Queen of Scots. He was Gilbert Gifford's cousin and Gifford's substitute courier, though he knew nothing about Phelippes's operation. So when in 1588 Walsingham and Phelippes presented to Barnes the facts of what he had done for the Scottish Queen, he found himself wrongfooted and vulnerable to a charge of dangerous espionage. His future was in the hands of

Thomas Barnes writes to Thomas Phelippes from the Saracen's Head on
Carter Lane, March 1590.

Walsingham and Phelippes. They came to an agreement Barnes felt it
prudent not to refuse. To Walsingham he offered his service to God
and queen 'by discovering or bringing to light any of the treacherous
intents towards the state' of fugitives and traitors at home and abroad.

And that is exactly what he went on to do. When Thomas Barnes
wrote without ceremony to Thomas Phelippes from the Saracen's
Head he was working as Phelippes's agent. His task was to discover
the Catholic émigrés' plans and conspiracies. His contact on the continent was Charles Paget, that most dangerous of exiles, who sent
Barnes letters and questions about conditions in England. Phelippes
was by now an artist of double-cross, drafting reports that Barnes
communicated back to Paget in his own hand using the cipher they,
Paget and Barnes, had agreed between themselves. When he was not
in London, Barnes's familiar territory was Antwerp and Brussels,
from where he wrote to Phelippes in cipher. To cover any association
with Phelippes, Barnes addressed his packets to John Wytsande, a
London merchant. A man of order and habit, Phelippes had a mark to

preserve the secrecy and anonymity of Barnes's reports. It was the Greek letter alpha with a dot placed carefully over the top.

All of this was difficult and delicate work to which Phelippes brought care, patience and his customary eye for detail. The stakes were high. In these years of heavy and expensive European war it was clear that for Spain the defeat of the Great Armada of 1588 was a temporary failure. Open warfare between the Tudor and Habsburg monarchies was a fact. The seriousness of Barnes's espionage can be measured by the fact that one of his contacts abroad was Hugh Owen, the chief émigré intelligencer to the Duke of Parma. Paget and Owen and their paymasters wanted to make sense of England's capacity to withstand the military power of Spanish forces and to prepare for another armada. Phelippes sought to play Paget and Owen at their own game, trying with Barnes's help to discover what the émigrés knew and, important also, to plant false information. Always the subtle master of deliberate calculations, Phelippes misled and disinformed Elizabeth's enemies.

Phelippes understood the human factor of his secret work. He had to keep Barnes on the straight and narrow path, all the time watching Paget and Owen, through their letters to Barnes, for any suggestion of suspicion or double-dealing. As Phelippes wrote some years later: 'the principal point in matter of intelligence, is to procure confidence with those parties that one will work upon, or for those parties a man would work by.' In other words, it was an exercise in skilled manipulation. And in the case of Phelippes and Barnes the collaboration lasted for years longer than probably either man ever expected. Over a decade later, in January 1602, Phelippes's younger brother Stephen happened to come across both men hard at work writing a secret paper.

Three weeks after the pursuivants had found Barnes at his lodgings in the Saracen's Head, Sir Francis Walsingham died at his house on Seething Lane near the Tower of London. His health had been poor for many years, and he had taken frequent long leaves of absence throughout the 1570s. He suffered with a urinary complaint; he may have had a kidney stone. One of his spies, Robert Poley, suggested it was a venereal disease. In an unguarded remark Poley said of his employer: 'Marry, he hath his old disease the which is the pox in his yard [penis] the which he got of a lady in France.' It was a scurrilous and unwise thing to say about a man as powerful as the queen's secretary.

Walsingham's health began to fail for the last time in 1589. His work as secretary was overwhelming and he was pushed to the limits of his physical ability. His office was punishing enough for a healthy man. He failed to attend meetings of the Privy Council between February and June 1589. Though rallying a little at the end of that year, he made his last will and testament on 12 December.

He died an hour before midnight on Monday, 6 April 1590. On the following day Walsingham's office staff retrieved their master's will from a secret cabinet. A few hours later, at ten o'clock that Tuesday night, he was buried in St Paul's Cathedral. Walsingham wrote in his will that he wanted his body to be buried 'without any such extraordinary ceremonies as usually appertain to a man serving in my place'. This says something of his austerity: Walsingham was a powerful man, but he had never played the flamboyant courtier; he was ever the queen's loyal servant.

His will was short and compact, a sparse record of a man's life and loyalties. In it Sir Francis was concerned only with his wife and daughter. Of the bequests to charity or gifts to household servants common in the last testaments of his colleagues there was nothing, other than £10 of plate left to each of the three overseers of the will. Thomas Phelippes was nowhere mentioned.

Walsingham was disciplined, controlled and vigilant, ever watchful for the queen's security. Lord Burghley wrote of his death as 'a great loss, both for the public use of his good and painful long services, and for the private comfort I had by his mutual friendship'. He continued in the heavy language of divine providence:

> we now that are left in this vale of earthly troubles, are to employ ourselves to remedy the loss of him hath brought, rather than for grief of the lack of him that is dead, to neglect of actions meet for us, whom God permitteth still to live.

Life and politics – and espionage – carried on without Walsingham, though in a quickly changing world.

He had always possessed a passionate sense of mission. He apprehended a war between God's people and the forces of the Devil. Walsingham had seen with his own eyes the massacre in Paris at Bartholomewtide in 1572. It was clear to him that Elizabeth's Protestant England fought for its survival against enemies at home and abroad. There was no distinction in Sir Francis's mind between the political efforts of the Queen of Scots, the Duke of Guise, the Pope and the King of Spain and the work of their agents, Charles Paget, Francis Throckmorton, Anthony Babington and many others. Catholic priests and Jesuits were traitors, for in their eyes Queen Elizabeth was a heretic and a bastard. When William Allen and other priests spoke of their pastoral mission to save England from heresy and schism, Elizabeth's advisers knew that they sought to do so by force and treason. This would have been as obvious to Walsingham as it was to Burghley when both men read Allen's violent denunciation of Elizabeth's tyranny weeks before the Great Armada set sail in 1588. Walsingham's sharp eyes would not have missed Allen's allegation of the 'Machiavellian' and godless methods used by Elizabeth's government:

> she hath by the execrable practices of some of her chief ministers, as by their own hands, letters, and instructions, and by the parties' confessions it may be proved, sent abroad exceeding great numbers of intelligencers, spies, and practisers, into most princes' courts, cities, and commonwealths in Christendom, not only to take and give secret notice of princes' intentions, but to deal with the discontented of every state for the attempting of somewhat against their lords and superiors, namely against His Holiness and the King of Spain His Majesty, whose sacred persons they have sought many ways wickedly to destroy.

He may have been grimly amused at Allen's charge of Machiavellian dealing.

Certainly Walsingham had used any instrument or method he believed was necessary to defend God, queen and country. One of these was the rack in the Tower of London. He called torture by its name: he did not hide behind euphemisms. He acted with absolute surety of purpose; he had few doubts. At her trial Mary Queen of Scots accused Walsingham to his face of working against her. Sir Francis replied: 'I protest before God that as a man careful of my mistress's safety I have been curious.' This was a masterful piece of wordcraft, for though 'curious' meant in one sense attentive and careful, it also gave a meaning of something hidden and subtle. After many years of fighting a secret war against an unforgiving enemy, Walsingham captured his profession in a single adjective.

Walsingham knew full well the cost of his service, to which there is a sharp reference in his will. When he set out his wishes for a plain and simple funeral it was 'in respect of the greatness of my debts and the mean state I shall leave my wife and heir in'. He had spent private money on public business, hoping for royal patronage to offset the burden. In Walsingham's case the size of the debt was immense. When he died he owed to the crown the extraordinary sum of about £42,000, though it was established a few years later (thanks to the tenacity of his widow) that Elizabeth's treasury owed him an even greater sum.

Walsingham committed a great amount of this money to espionage. His brother-in-law Robert Beale, with whom he worked closely in the royal secretariat, maintained that Walsingham paid over forty spies and intelligencers throughout Europe. He had agents in the households of the French ambassadors to Elizabeth's court, from whom he gathered intelligence on France and Scotland. With money, Beale wrote, Walsingham 'corrupted priests, Jesuits and traitors to betray the practices against this realm'. He ran a very efficient system of intercepting letters passing on the post roads of Europe.

Elizabeth's government never entirely suppressed the exiles; that would have been impossible. But Walsingham's efforts to disrupt and confuse them had a definite psychological effect. In February 1590 Sir Francis Englefield, one of Elizabeth's most determined enemies, wrote of the 'doubt and fear' of his missing letters: 'I have lost so many, and received so few, as the want of them disjointeth much my poor affairs'. Those letters can be read today in Walsingham's papers. He and Phelippes may have taken a professional pleasure in knowing something of the confusion and uncertainty they could cause, frustrating and confounding the enemy.

As Robert Beale well knew, the key to Walsingham's method was money. Beale used the word 'liberality', with regular demands for cash, pensions and patronage by spies, informants and merchant and diplomatic contacts abroad. Reporting directly to the queen, Walsingham kept his own secret accounts, explained by wonderfully vague phrases like 'to be employed according to her Highness's direction given him'. But the days of such liberality had, for the time being, passed.

On Walsingham's death the queen did not appoint a new secretary. Instead Lord Burghley took on Walsingham's reponsibilities, a painful burden for a man of sixty-nine years who suffered terribly with what he called gout. Yet Burghley had worked for a lifetime at the edge of his physical endurance. Powerful and grand, he had served Elizabeth once before as her secretary, occupying that office for over a decade, and by 1590 he had been Lord Treasurer of England for eighteen years. There was no area of government in which Burghley's influence was not felt. Just before his death, when he was too sick to carry out his duties (probably in early 1590), Walsingham handed to Burghley his official papers on diplomacy, with special reference to England's relations with Spain. There was also 'The book of secret intelligences'. The contents of Walsingham's secure cabinets moved to Burghley's own.

He lost no time in reviewing the system for gathering intelligence he had inherited from Walsingham. Within at most three weeks of his protégé's death Burghley looked at the work of five 'intelligencers' who had served Sir Francis in continental Europe. Burghley wrote out their names in his graceful italic handwriting. They were Chasteau-Martin, Stephen de Rorque, Edmund Palmer, Filiazzi and Alexander de la Torre. Henri Chasteau-Martin, a Frenchman whose real name was Pierre d'Or, acted on behalf of English merchants trading out of Bayonne. For reports on Spanish news he received an annual salary of 1,200 Spanish escudos (something around £300 sterling), a very handsome sum of money, paid to him quarterly by the London-based international merchant and financier Sir Horatio Palavicino. Edmund Palmer was placed in Saint-Jean-de-Luz. Stephen de Rorque worked in Lisbon. Filiazzi was close to the Duke of Florence. One Alexander de la Torre, who used the alias of Batzon, had moved from Antwerp to Rome in February 1590. This was not a large network of foreign spies and intelligencers, but it was an effective one,

Lord Burghley names his secret intelligencers in Europe, 1590.

for these five men were placed at key ports and cities in France, Portugal and Italy.

The days of generous subventions for government espionage were over. Elizabeth's exchequer was dry: there had to be cuts. As if to lead by example, Burghley only once claimed the secretary's allowance of money for secret work, in May 1590, the month following Walsingham's death. After that, Burghley either wanted to cut back on the work of Sir Francis's agents and intelligencers or, more likely, asked them to sing for their suppers more sweetly – and more cheaply – than they had done before. Spies and informants had grown used to fairly rich pickings of cash and patronage. Ahead were leaner times.

For Burghley, agents' salaries raised the matter of their reliability. It was the eternal question of value for money. With the help of the vice-chamberlain of the queen's household, Sir Thomas Heneage, Burghley conducted a review, wanting to find out if the money paid to agents actually brought about useful intelligence. Drawing up secret accounts with Heneage, Burghley noted the size of Chasteau-Martin's salary. Another agent, one sent by Sir Horatio Palavicino to Lisbon, received over £94. This agent was a great rarity: she was a married woman, the wife of one David Roures; she had received the money from Francisco Rizzio, Palavicino's business agent.

But if Chasteau-Martin and the elusive Mistress Roures were worth the expense, then Edmund Palmer of Saint-Jean-de-Luz was not. After reading Palmer's letters to Walsingham, Burghley's audit exposed the amounts of money he had 'pretended' to use 'for Her Majesty's service'. Burghley also had doubts about another merchant, Edward James in Bayonne. James produced a copy of what he said were Walsingham's instructions for two secret missions. One was to Madrid to secure information about the health of King Philip and the activities of Sir William Stanley, the rogue English military commander in the Low Countries who had defected to Spain in 1587. James's second mission was to make a reconnaissance of the coastline of the Bay of Biscay. Whether or not Burghley was in the end convinced by Edward James and his work, he must have wondered about who could be relied upon to provide useful information, what they should be paid for it and whether espionage could be carried out on a much tighter budget than it had been by Sir Francis Walsingham.

But although Lord Burghley was the advocate of efficiency, he was also the most experienced of Elizabeth's advisers, and knew probably better than anyone else the dangers to queen and country. For thirty years he had made it his business to get to know his mistress's enemies. A couple of months after his audit, Burghley drew up his own report on the Catholic exiles and émigrés, making a special note of their Spanish pensions. Two were Charles Paget and Hugh Owen, chief intelligencer to the Spanish authorities in Brussels. Now dead, Burghley noted, was Lord Paget, that unwilling and melancholy exile, party to the Duke of Guise's planned invasion of England in 1583, who had left behind him a vast fortune.

For Thomas Phelippes some of the old certainties were disappearing. Walsingham, his master, was dead. To whom now was he responsible? Already he was feeling the strain of paying the expenses of Thomas Barnes from his own purse, careful to keep the signed receipts. His family circumstances were changing, too. In 1590 William Phelippes, Thomas's father, died at his house near Leadenhall in the city of London. To Thomas he bequeathed his gold signet ring and all his books, but not yet his fortune, which went to his mother, Joan.

But, like any gentleman with servants to pay, Phelippes needed money. Given the dangers as well as the costs of his secret work, he also needed a patron at Elizabeth's court. His purse was only so deep, and he was too clever to leave himself exposed to the charge that he did freelance espionage without official sanction. He once made a tantalizing reference to the queen's knowledge of his secret life: he had always gone about his business, he wrote, 'not without the Queen's privity [private knowledge] and approbation'. At first he may have tried to catch the eye of a patron with a sharp political essay on the 'Present perils of the realm'. Here, like other clever men who wanted to show off their talents, Phelippes set out the evidence of the international Catholic conspiracy faced by Elizabeth and her kingdoms. Phelippes may indeed have looked to Burghley's support, though given the fashion for austerity he did not get very far in receiving it, at least as a permanent employee.

But in the spring of 1591 there was another likely patron at Elizabeth's court. He was twenty-five years old, aggressively ambitious, fashionable and rich. For long he had lived in the shadows of older men, especially the particularly large shadow of Lord Burghley, in whose household he was raised and educated as a royal ward after the death of his father in 1576. This young nobleman's name was Robert Devereux, second Earl of Essex, and he wanted desperately to impress the queen. He knew nothing about intelligence work, a fact that made him the perfect patron for an old hand like Thomas Phelippes. Each man could do the other a favour. Essex could give Phelippes a job; Phelippes, the skilled spy, could give in return knowledge of the queen's dangerous enemies.

The effort to recruit Phelippes to Essex's fledgling intelligence service came from one of Phelippes's obscure contacts, a man called William Sterrell, whose career (like many of Phelippes's acquaintances) had so far in Elizabeth's reign been a secret one. Sterrell wanted a job in the earl's service and he needed Phelippes's help to secure it. He threw himself at both men in the hope of preferment, attaching himself limpet-like to Essex. Phelippes, however, was a harder man to persuade. He was not really convinced either by Sterrell or for the moment by Essex. Not to be put off by Phelippes's coolness, Sterrell pushed and pressed. He even invited Phelippes to dine with the earl at home. By

May 1591 Sterrell was talking personally to Essex: 'I had some little talk with my lord about you,' he wrote to Phelippes, 'which proceeded from himself.'

The proposal that formed within Essex's circle over a few weeks was to use Sterrell to penetrate the network of English Catholic exiles in Flanders. The man who sought to negotiate the terms of this mission with Phelippes was the brilliantly polymathic Francis Bacon, thirty years old, the nephew of Lord Burghley, and a close friend of the earl's. Moving in the same political circles, Bacon and Phelippes had known each other for a long time. Bacon had once been the companion of Phelippes's younger brother Stephen. Bacon courted Phelippes, recognizing his abilities, acting as intermediary between Phelippes and Essex, proposing a meeting between them. Bacon wrote to Phelippes of their prospects for success: 'I know you are very able to make good.'

The risks of joining the Earl of Essex and his men would have been plain to Phelippes. The reality of this new world of Elizabethan politics was vicious competition between Essex and other courtiers. Ambition, power and the scramble for royal patronage stimulated political faction. But after the Great Armada of 1588, in the hard years of war against Spain in the 1590s, intelligence work became more unstable and unpredictable than it had been before. Tied up with money and political standing it mirrored the politics of the Privy Council. True, the espionage system of Walsingham and Burghley was not perfect. Political agendas lurked even at the easiest of times, though there were precious few of those in Elizabeth's reign. But at least there had been something like a clear organizing intelligence behind the government's clandestine work; it was effective by its own standards and methods; and Walsingham and Phelippes, who rarely rushed even at times of high anxiety and emergency, delivered results. Essex was different. Espionage became for Essex an instrument for his political advancement. Phelippes surely knew that ahead lay danger.

In this world where loyalties were tried and tested, made sure of or found wanting, Essex had to know where Thomas Phelippes's allegiance lay. Lord Burghley, too, put his trust in Phelippes's expertise, writing in 1593 of a letter in cipher and appealing to Phelippes's loyalty. The packet, dispatched in Dieppe, came from 'a bad affected person resorting often times to the enemy'. It was addressed to Phelippes. Burghley's test was to send it to Phelippes unopened. It was an act of faith on Burghley's part, using Phelippes's skill to decipher the letter and relying upon Phelippes's honesty to alert him to any significant piece of intelligence contained in the packet. As Burghley wrote: 'I would not open the same, being assured of your good and sound affectation to the state and Her Majesty's service, that if there be any matter therein, fit to be discovered, that you will not keep it secret.'

How would Thomas Phelippes conduct himself in treacherous times without the safety and security of his service to Sir Francis Walsingham? To this question the Sterrell case would within months suggest the answer.

18

Platforms and Passports

Lord Burghley was the most formidable politician of Queen Elizabeth's reign. Only once, in the early months of 1587, did he temporarily lose Elizabeth's trust and favour: over the execution of Mary Queen of Scots. That was a price worth paying: Burghley had for many years made it his business to destroy the political and dynastic influence of the Scottish Queen. His return to political favour was swift, and by the spring of 1590, at the age of nearly seventy, he was carrying the administrative weight of practically the whole of Elizabethan government as the queen's lord treasurer and her acting secretary. Miraculously, his fragile health bore the strain.

As a courtier and politician of forty years' experience, Burghley's political instincts were finely tuned. He knew what lurked in the shadows of Elizabethan politics. He kept papers on England's enemies, the Catholic émigrés and exiles. He read their intercepted letters and understood the very real danger they, with the formidable help of Spanish power, presented to Elizabeth's kingdoms. For many years, he had made his own digests of intelligence from abroad. After Walsingham's death he took charge of his former protégé's espionage network. He was never complacent about England's security.

Burghley longed for peace and retirement in the 1590s. He felt old, weary and sick. Possessed, however, of an obsessive need to direct and control the instruments of power and patronage, he found it impossible to let go of government business. He served Elizabeth from a profound sense of duty. As he wrote to his son Robert Cecil a few days before his death: 'Serve God by serving of the Queen, for all other service is indeed bondage to the Devil.'

Robert Cecil was very much his father's heir in the family business of Tudor government. Burghley's eldest son, Sir Thomas Cecil, was a distinguished soldier and an accomplished courtier, but he was not obviously cut out for the office of a royal secretary or privy councillor. Robert, twenty-one years younger than his half-brother, showed every inclination to follow his father's distinguished career.

Robert Cecil was schooled for high political office, educated at home by private tutors, in Cambridge and at Gray's Inn. He visited Paris at the age of twenty-one, where he went to lectures in the Sorbonne, the theological school of the city's university. He studied Latin, Greek, French, Italian and Spanish, as well as mathematics, cosmography (the study of the universe) and music. His father's palace of Theobalds in Hertfordshire was itself an education for a future royal servant. Its rooms were decorated with the genealogies of the English nobility, the pedigree of the Cecil family and portraits and busts of emperors, kings and noblemen of classical and contemporary history. In the Great Gallery of Theobalds Robert could make sense of the history of Rome, the politics of the Spanish Netherlands and England's own civil wars of the fifteenth century. This was for Burghley the expression of the authority and knowledge he had built up over years of service to the queen, and one of its purposes was to fit Robert Cecil for just such a career himself.

In May 1591, a month short of his twenty-eighth birthday, the queen knighted him. A few weeks later she appointed Sir Robert to her Privy Council. It was at exactly this time in his new political career, which showed such promise, that Cecil worked with Burghley on a highly secret case. Together, father and son recruited two men who were sent off to mainland Europe to spy on Cardinal William Allen. Their names were John Snowden and John Fixer. This was Robert Cecil's apprenticeship in espionage, one that helped to make him quite as formidable as both his father and Sir Francis Walsingham in the pursuit of his country's enemies.

John Snowden was a subtle, intelligent and self-assured man who presented himself to Lord Burghley as a volunteer in the cause of his native country against its enemies. His real name was John Cecil, though if he was a kinsman of the first political family of the kingdom it was by a very distant connection. In May 1591, when he came to

Burghley's close attention, he was about thirty-two years old and a former fellow of Trinity College, Oxford. He had a companion called John Fixer, who was his college contemporary. No physical description of Snowden survives, but we know that Fixer was a tall man with a ruddy complexion and dark features. Both men were scholars, spoke foreign languages and had travelled in Italy and Spain. Also both men were Catholic priests. Snowden, indeed, was a member of the household of Cardinal William Allen.

Snowden and Fixer were spies, sent secretly to England by Robert Persons, the forty-five-year-old Jesuit priest who with Allen was always energetic in engineering plots against Queen Elizabeth. Their mission never happened: the two priests were captured even before they landed at an English port. They had set out from Portugal for Amsterdam. On the voyage their ship, *The Adulphe*, was intercepted by *The Hope* of Elizabeth's royal navy. Taken prisoner, Snowden and Fixer found themselves confined to Lord Burghley's grand townhouse on the Strand in Westminster. There they must have contemplated their futures: any priest found to be in England was guilty of high treason.

Burghley was away from Westminster, busy with the queen's ten-day visit to his great house of Theobalds. But he saw in Snowden and Fixer at least the spark of a possibility. Thrown back at the enemy as double agents, they could prove to be valuable weapons against Cardinal Allen. Of course they had to be tested, and they might be found wanting. To be sure, Burghley began to examine them by correspondence. Snowden and Fixer wrote out statements which, once they arrived at Theobalds, Burghley read with very great care. The two priests first put pen to paper on Friday, 21 May. It happened to be the very day that Queen Elizabeth knighted the clever and ambitious Sir Robert Cecil.

The first of their statements gave Burghley hope. Fixer seemed to know a great deal about two traitors in the pay of the King of Spain, the veteran rebel and conspirator Sir Francis Englefield and the turncoat military commander in the Low Countries Sir William Stanley. Snowden was close to Cardinal Allen. Both priests knew Robert Persons and had (so they claimed) valuable information about his secret plans.

But could they be trusted? It was plain from the beginning that Fixer was very nervous, more obviously so than Snowden. Fixer's statement had about it a note of self-doubt; he was anxious that he had left out something Burghley was looking for. But he seemed keen to be of help to Elizabeth's government. 'My memory is fragile and this time is short,' he wrote:

> if there be anything that hath passed or doth pass either in France or Italy or Spain whereto my small experience of those countries can reach, I beseech your honour to enquire it in particular and I will answer what I know with all truth and sincerity.

He added a caveat and a defence, saying that he would tell the truth 'notwithstanding the cardinal [Allen] and Persons do trust such matters upon my self': in other words, he could reveal only what the two men had revealed to him of their plans and conspiracies against England, which may not have been much. Seeing all too plainly the precarious situation he found himself in, Fixer put his life and death in Burghley's hands.

Snowden wrote with greater self-confidence. His statement was certainly the work of an intelligent, experienced and subtle man: too subtle, perhaps. Snowden's cleverness may have worried Burghley just as much as did Fixer's diffidence. There was no hint of fear in what he wrote. In offering his service to Burghley, he was even plainer than Fixer had been, saying without hesitation that he would give Elizabeth's government information on plots, treasons and conspiracies. But he maintained a conscientious scruple as a Catholic. Snowden distinguished absolutely between Catholics whose loyalty to the queen held firm and those, like Robert Persons, who planned for England's invasion by the foreign power of Spain. Snowden explained to Burghley in his statement that he would betray only Elizabeth's enemies, not the Catholic faith.

If Snowden was to be believed he had intended from the time of his recruitment by Persons to make an offer of service to Burghley by sending 'informations of such poor intelligence I had'. Snowden had a very long way to go before convincing Burghley of the truth of his claim. The only condition he had expected as Burghley's agent, Snowden wrote, was liberty of conscience and the freedom to practise his

Catholic faith. And so with a surprising confidence given the circumstances of his capture, though with hope now of recommending himself as Burghley's agent, Snowden gave a full account of the nature of the mission Persons had recruited him to.

Persons wanted to infiltrate small groups of priests into England and Scotland. Snowden and Fixer were two of six. Four of the group travelled on the King of Spain's passports, leaving the port of Seville in two Scottish ships; two of the priests were bound for London, the other pair to Scotland. Snowden and Fixer, by contrast, had set out from Portugal for Amsterdam. Once in London their cover was to have been trade, and their contacts were one Tayler and one Payne in the Poultry, both of whom presumably were merchants. Persons had given Snowden and Fixer a cipher for their letters, the key word of which was DEUS.

More important than the nuts and bolts of travel and communication was the object of the mission, which was, as Snowden explained it, to make contact with English Catholics. The two priests were in effect agents of Spain, returning to their homeland to spread the message that King Philip did not want to conquer England but sought instead (to use Fixer's words) 'to reform religion'. Persons wanted the two priests to draw up a list of names of everyone who would help the Spanish liberators when the day of invasion came. And here Snowden wanted to emphasize for Burghley an important point. Persons had instructed him to inflate the numbers of Spain's supporters in England. This, said Snowden, was the bait that Cardinal Allen and Father Persons fed to the King of Spain – the promise of an enthusiastic welcome for the Spanish forces.

Burghley was gripped by Snowden's paper: he wrote all over it, noting, cross-referring, underlining. And it was no wonder. On the face of it, Snowden seemed to have excellent information on how Robert Persons was trying to open up a new channel for intelligence from England. Persons's methods were revealed. Even more than this, what Snowden had to say offered proof of the continuing efforts of Spain to launch a successful invasion of Elizabeth's kingdoms. After all, King Philip was only temporarily depressed by the failure of the Great Armada in 1588. Quickly Spain had built a new fleet whose purpose after 1589 was, in Philip's words, to 'wage war in the enemy's own house', combining both navy and army in the assault upon England. Though the years 1590 and 1591 were strategically difficult ones for Philip, thanks to Spanish involvement in religious civil war in France and the political conditions of the Low Countries, experienced advisers to Elizabeth like Burghley were well enough aware of the imperial ambitions of Philip of Spain.

Perhaps, however, Snowden's intelligence was just too convenient, possessing, for all the rich and compelling detail, a suspicious relevance. It was clear to Burghley that some pieces of the priest's story did not fit together very neatly. For Snowden, Burghley's willing volunteer spy, being taken prisoner was a lucky chance. How, Burghley wondered, would Snowden and Fixer have gone about their mission, living as Catholics in England? And for all of Snowden's first protestation of loyalty to the queen, Burghley wondered how he could reconcile that with his Catholic faith. When true allegiance to the queen meant conformity to the English Church, to profess one without the other hardly made sense.

So there were the difficulties in the priests', and particularly Snowden's, papers. There were evasions and questions as yet unanswered. But already Burghley's mind was moving to the future deployment of Snowden and Fixer as spies. He wanted them to explain, first of all, how they could aid the arrest of the other priests of Robert Persons's mission without betraying themselves.

Snowden's reply, in his second statement for Burghley, was suitably brisk and businesslike. He seemed clear in his motives. He had wanted to live peaceably in his own country with the free exercise of his religion. His plan had been to write to Burghley from Amsterdam, sending the letter, along with documents he possessed, through the governor of the town of Brille. He had also intended to write a long essay on how, by granting religious freedom to those who opposed the practices of Spain, Burghley could recruit priests for Elizabeth's service. For the time being Snowden entirely avoided Burghley's question about how the other priests could be apprehended without compromising Fixer and himself.

Snowden told a tale whose facts he cleverly selected to give a certain version of the truth; his evasions were those of a careful man playing a risky game. On 23 May he made a fresh statement, writing with a touch of self-deprecation that he would set out 'confusedly yet I assure you confidently' what he could remember of the essential points of Spanish 'practices', or plots and conspiracies, against England. He again stressed his loyalty and affection to his prince and country. But he continued to press his point about loyalty. He wrote that he wanted to show Burghley 'that it is not a matter so impossible as it is commonly taken to be a good subject and a good Catholic'. And it was from this point on in his third statement that he proposed how he might work as a spy against England's enemies, William Allen and Robert Persons.

Snowden confronted head on the policy of Elizabeth's government. He suggested that to force Catholics to act against their consciences achieved nothing. Putting men to death for their faith only pleased England's enemies, giving Allen and Persons more martyrs for religion as well as justifying political action against Elizabeth. Of martyrdom Snowden wrote: 'they [the Catholics] print it and paint it and publish it in their books and pulpits and so with pretext to move princes and the world to compassion; they work the web [that] hath been so long on the loom'. His meaning was plain: martyrdom was the inspiration as well as the sustaining fuel of the international Catholic cause against Elizabeth's England. Snowden's ambitious proposal was to bring the foreign Catholic seminaries under Burghley's control, thus neutering the powerful influence of Cardinal Allen. Volunteering himself for the task, he wanted to recruit Catholics in Burghley's cause, to use them against the true enemy. But necessary to this was 'wonderful secrecy'. Snowden wanted no betrayal from the inside to wreck his plan.

Snowden's proposal, robustly set out, went against the grain of over thirty years of Elizabethan thinking. Burghley had long viewed all the English priests trained in the seminaries of France, Italy and Spain as conspirators and traitors. And yet he took Snowden seriously, once again working through his papers and setting out even more questions for the priest to answer. In the case of Snowden Burghley sacrificed time, a precious thing for the most powerful man in England, and something he was very loath to waste.

Now Burghley began to push Snowden very hard on the facts he had stated so far. Setting his prisoner's ambitious proposal to one side,

Burghley wanted to find out whether Snowden was telling the truth. The key to this lay in the elements of his story; this he told with great confidence, but it had to be rigorously examined, the facts and circumstances tested. If each one of Snowden's claims was found to have substance, then perhaps Burghley could trust the man and his motives.

The first thing to recover was the collection of papers Snowden had had with him aboard *The Adulphe*, the ship whose Flemish skipper lived in Amsterdam. The papers, Snowden told Burghley, were sealed in three packs of cork. Here potentially was evidence of Snowden's goodwill and honesty in saying that he had intended from the start to offer his services to Burghley, for among the papers (so he said) were packets of letters addressed to the lord treasurer, all ready to be sent to England by Snowden when he reached Amsterdam, which contained notes and ciphers. Snowden had copies of sensitive documents from Paris as well as papers concerning the business and personnel of the English seminaries. Snowden kept also a note by the Jesuit Robert Southwell on the executions of priests in England, and a manuscript of a book by Persons on the persecution of English priests of the newly founded seminary of Valladolid in Spain. There was a letter from Persons to Snowden and Fixer, as well as a number of letters from a Flemish merchant to the man with whom the two priests had proposed to lodge in Amsterdam.

If Snowden was indeed telling the truth about these papers, aboard *The Adulphe* was a substantial cache of material valuable to Elizabeth's government. Of their books, Snowden explained that he and Fixer had given them to the ship's cook. Snowden told Burghley that he would recover the books and papers by writing to the ship's master. If he would not or could not help, then a member of his crew and a fellow passenger on *The Adulphe* knew where Snowden had put them. And so Snowden wrote to the master in Amsterdam, while Burghley, careful to keep and mark every piece of paper, dated and endorsed his own copy of the letter.

On 25 May, the fourth day of Snowden's questioning, Burghley set out to test every part of the story so far. He wanted facts; he was looking for corroboration, and evidence that Snowden knew what and whom he was talking about. There was nothing in Burghley's hard and pressing questions about freedom of worship for English Catholics or ambitious plans to control the seminaries. He was not bothered about grand designs. Burghley wanted the physical descriptions of all the priests of Persons's mission and of the Englishmen who served the King of Spain. He wished to know more about Snowden's journey from Spain and Portugal; indeed he wanted from Snowden a full report of where he had been and how he had lived since leaving England years before. Snowden had said that he had once written to Sir Francis Walsingham using the alias of Juan de Campo: exactly when was that? Who were Snowden's kinsmen in England? Burghley asked Snowden what name he had intended to use when he came on his mission to England and how he was able to make a cipher alphabet out of the word DEUS. What did he know of the plans and dispositions of King Philip to invade England?

Here we begin to find the real John Snowden. The truth behind the self-confidence was a young man cut off from his family in England, of whom he knew nothing: it was almost nine years since he had heard from them or they from him. His two brothers were dead, killed fighting Spanish soldiers in Flanders. He had not seen his father for twelve years. Snowden had left England for Rheims in 1582 and begun to study divinity in William Allen's seminary; he was one of the priests of Allen's mission to save England. He became close to Allen, who employed Snowden as his Latin secretary.

To Burghley's question about his cover name in England Snowden gave a prickly response. He had, he said, never had any intention of carrying out the mission. The DEUS cipher was a simple substitution, moving the alphabet along so that D gave a, e gave b and so on; it was a cipher that would have troubled Thomas Phelippes for minutes at best. The King of Spain's intention, Snowden said, was to persist in the Enterprise of England, the invasion of Elizabeth's kingdoms and the queen's deposition. He ended by speculating on how he and his companion Fixer might be able to spy for Burghley, to 'go unknown and keep our intelligence secret'. But beyond the suggestion Snowden was uncharacteristically guarded: that would have to rest upon Burghley's wisdom and experience.

Perhaps he seemed to be losing some of his self-confidence, beginning, after five days of questioning, to feel the wear and tear of close examination. But Snowden quickly bounced back. He made a new and confident statement of the conspiracies of Cardinal Allen and Father Persons and gave a sure-footed technical analysis of Spain's military capabilities. For a man whose interests may have been served by exaggerating King Philip's power, Snowden's judgement was perhaps surprising: 'His domestical forces are wonderful poor and pitiful, more than can be imagined.' He believed Spain was painfully short of naval captains, soldiers, sailors, gunners and munitions. He gave the names of Cardinal Allen's principal supporters and agents in Rouen, Paris, Madrid and Flanders. He provided a long list of those priests who quietly opposed Allen's aggressive policy. And he named those of Elizabeth's subjects who favoured the Spanish. At the head of the list was the renegade English military commander Sir William Stanley, followed by Sir Francis Englefield and the Duke of Parma's intelligencer Hugh Owen.

Burghley had wanted facts: Snowden gave them willingly. The young priest who had for days been questioned very closely by the most powerful man in Elizabeth's government, still hidden away in Burghley House in Westminster, had now only to wait to hear what use would be made of him.

Burghley decided to use Snowden and Fixer as spies. The deal was done by 31 May 1591. On that Monday night Snowden met Sir Robert Cecil, to whom Burghley now left the practical arrangements of getting Snowden and Fixer safely across the English Channel to mainland Europe. Sir Robert, Fixer and Snowden talked that evening about the gathering of intelligence from Spain and Italy.

Snowden wrote to Sir Robert the following day. He was not quite satisfied with their passports and safe conducts. He received a prompt reply from Cecil: Snowden could send his own wording for the passports, and Burghley would read and consider it. Sir Robert, though now in charge of the day-to-day handling of the priest-spies, by habit and experience deferred to his father's judgement.

So it seemed that only ten days after making their first statements to Burghley Snowden and Fixer were free at last to travel. Cecil reminded the two priests that their freedom came with an obligation not to be forgotten. They were being set free for a purpose, to gather intelligence for Lord Burghley or, in Sir Robert's elegantly grand phrasing, to 'bring forth good fruit with profitable correspondency for Her Majesty's service'. Snowden was too clever to misunderstand Cecil's meaning. He wrote to Sir Robert on 4 June acknowledging Burghley's 'most benign and bounteous offer of warrant and protection, the reserving of the knowledge of us, our case and cause to his honour only'.

Soon enough, Snowden got from Burghley the passport he wanted. Its wording suggested an important mission, and no port official who saw the lord treasurer's signature would have dared to hold the two agents: 'You shall let the bearer hereof pass without trouble or vexation, for that the knowledge and examination of his cause and person I have reserved to myself for divers occasions.' Snowden promised faithful and good service. He wondered whether the 'good' Catholics they came across would be subject to England's ferocious penal laws. Snowden, like any Catholic priest, was acutely conscious of the law he and John Fixer had been so fortunate to escape, which declared any Jesuit or seminary priest in England to be guilty of high treason. Once this point was resolved, Snowden wrote, they would do good service in Italy or Spain. He sent another letter to Sir Robert on the same day with descriptions of priests. Snowden left his letter unsigned: 'Your worship knoweth the heart and hand of the writer.'

The days passed by, but for Snowden and Fixer there was no quick dispatch across the English Channel. Their mission had suffered a false start. Burghley or Sir Robert (or both father and son together) had had second thoughts.

The excitement of the first week of June quickly passed. Confident Snowden, stuck in London, began to fret about his safety. By now trusted to leave Burghley House, he walked around the city, trying to make sense of what Catholics were saying about him and Fixer. At the busy public meeting places at St Paul's Cathedral and the Royal Exchange he heard the rumour that the two priests had been arrested but then quickly released, mistaken for soldiers returning home from the wars in the Low Countries. Snowden was terrified that Catholics would get wind of any suggestion that he was now Lord Burghley's agent. So he was very relieved to have bumped into an old school friend on 12 June who gave him no suggestion of any suspicious or malicious rumours. Snowden wrote with relief that he and Fixer 'stood free from all impediments that might arise in the opinion of Catholics by our apprehension'. But quickly a new worry came to occupy his mind. Because Catholics in London had seen him walking the streets of the city, he was known to be at liberty; it followed that sharp eyes could observe he was in correspondence with Burghley. He wondered to Sir Robert whether he should be sent into the country for the sake of secrecy and security.

Snowden, brimming with a subtle self-confidence when he had first been brought with Fixer to Burghley House in Westminster, was a nervous man. On the evening of 19 June he met Lord Burghley and Sir Robert Cecil. The meeting was not a happy one. Snowden apologized the next day for his 'sharpness' and even his 'shamefulness'. Clearly Snowden recognized that he had behaved very badly. Days of worrying about who was watching him on the streets of London and Westminster, and the feeling that his offer of service was not being taken seriously, led him to lose his temper. Burghley was provocative, probably deliberately so. He told Snowden to his face that what he had given so far, or promised from his papers in Amsterdam, amounted to 'vulgar and trivial intelligences and to no great purpose'; these may have been Burghley's exact words. Snowden robustly defended his own honesty and goodwill. And he did not back down: once again he offered to do good service for his country, whatever the perils or dangers. He wanted Sir Robert to 'perceive my forwardness and desire to do something of importance'.

If the meeting on the 19th was for Snowden a bruising encounter, it also seems to have done something to release the building pressure of anxiety. But still the weeks passed while Burghley and Sir Robert Cecil waited for Snowden's books and papers to come from *The Adulphe* of Amsterdam. Some of them had arrived in Westminster by early July, for on the 3rd Sir Robert had Snowden's copy of Josephus Acosta's history of the Jews (a rare book, said Snowden) and Robert Persons's manuscript on the new martyrs of England. Also among the papers were a letter by Persons to the rector of the seminary at Rheims and Persons's letter to Snowden and Fixer dated a few weeks before they had left the coast of Portugal.

From the beginning, Burghley had wanted to be sure of the papers from Amsterdam. At first he had doubted Snowden's story; he wanted evidence of its authenticity. There had been a false start to the priests' mission in late May and early June. After leaving the details of platforms and passports to Sir Robert, Burghley was still not as sure of the priests as he needed to be. But now, with the proof he wanted from Snowden, the lord treasurer was content for his son to send the priests to Europe as spies. With the right sort of handling, they could prove to be significant weapons against the queen's enemies.

In July Snowden and Cecil began to work out the precise details of the mission. At first these had been vague. Sir Robert saw that a more precise objective was necessary. He proposed for Snowden and Fixer a difficult mission: to cause the King of Spain to doubt sources of Spanish intelligence on England. Snowden, considering this proposition carefully, applied himself to the details of how this might be done. And he offered to Sir Robert three principles by which he proposed to operate clandestinely. Firstly, he said, he would communicate with England through one man only, who would believe that he, Snowden, worked to free Catholic prisoners. Secondly, only Burghley and Sir Robert should read his reports. And thirdly, he would work for Sir Robert alone, with whom he felt he could talk openly. Burghley, he thought, was too busy to discuss and examine every aspect of Snowden's secret work. Besides, Snowden pleaded timidity and 'insufficiency' in talking to Burghley – the bruises from their fractious meeting had not entirely healed.

By now Sir Robert and Snowden were settled upon the mechanics of the mission. They had met and talked. Snowden's contact was in Saint-Jean-de-Luz, a port town close to Spain in the Bay of Biscay; he was Cecil's man and the representative of a London merchant. There was, if necessary, a second intermediary in Calais. Sir Robert and Snowden made arrangements for Snowden's passport, a cipher and an alias he could use in his reports. And of course there would be further instructions: in Snowden's words, 'the most principal and necessary points whereof you would be advised from time to time'.

A few days or weeks later (he gave neither date nor place) Snowden wrote to Sir Robert once again. He wondered whether he might have another passport in his own name. It was just an idea: 'But in this and all other my affairs as your wisdom shall determine, whose hands

I most humbly kissed and take my leave of your worship till I write from the port.'

And so it was that John Snowden alias John Cecil, the priest-spy, and one of the first of Sir Robert Cecil's many secret agents, set out upon his career in espionage. He was a volunteer and he cost nothing other than Lord Burghley's and Sir Robert's time, patience and hospitality at Burghley House. That at least satisfied the Lord Treasurer of England's taste for economy.

Snowden pursued his new career with skill and subtlety, able to convince of his loyalty men as experienced and perceptive as Robert Persons and William Allen. He continued to work and travel with John Fixer, with whom, months after taking his leave of Sir Robert Cecil, he sought to re-enter England. As before, they were captured, though this time it was probably by prearrangement with Sir Robert. In 1592 Snowden was in Rome, and then Cardinal Allen sent him to Scotland. Already there were rumours of his duplicity, and from Scotland in October of that year he sent to Allen a passionate defence of his actions. He wrote of his interview by Lord Burghley: 'But this I know and this I professed upon my salvation, that there never passed from me anything prejudicial to my faith or function . . . I always had this firm resolution, rather to be torn into one thousand pieces than to hurt willing the least hair of the meanest Catholic head in the world.'

Snowden remained in Scotland till early 1594. He set out for Rome, but in February he was again captured at sea by the great Sir Francis Drake. As he later wrote to Sir Robert: 'I discovered myself to Sir Francis Drake and Master Edgecombe [probably Richard Edgecombe, a Cornish gentleman], charging them as you willed I should in Her Majesty's name to keep me secret and take no other notice of me than as of a Scottish man till they heard from you.' To Drake he gave letters by Robert Persons and Sir Francis Englefield.

Snowden understood that he lived a dangerous life; he had been anxious for his own safety even on the streets of London in June and July 1591 and he was a good deal more exposed in Spain or Rome. He knew that even a chance remark by Cecil in London could put his life in danger. He wrote to Sir Robert: 'For this I assure you, at my last being in Spain words were laid to my charge spoken by you of me at your table to a kinsman and confident friend that had like cost me my life.' He feared the withdrawal of Cecil's favour, thinking back to his recruitment by Sir Robert and his father, and their earliest doubts about his loyalty: 'If you reposed (when I first met you) that credit in me as I deserved, I had not passed so much trouble as I have done for the performance of my promise to you.'

By a combination of skill, luck and brazenness Snowden survived. He reported to Sir Robert on Spanish political and military thinking and the efforts of the Catholic exiles in Scotland. He forwarded letters he had intercepted, these by some of Queen Elizabeth's most formidable enemies. Catholic rumours of Snowden's disloyalty never went away. In 1597 reliable sources of news in Antwerp said that Snowden was under the protection of certain English noblemen. Two years later he was even named publicly in a pamphlet as Lord Burghley's spy; in print he defended himself robustly, appealing for the truth of his story to God in heaven. And yet he continued to be trusted in Spain and Rome, all the way through to the death of Elizabeth in 1603.

But what, apart from luck and ability, was the key to John Snowden's longevity as a spy? How was he able to cope with the strains of his secret life? The answer, most probably, lies in his conscience. What he wrote to Lord Burghley, Sir Robert Cecil and William Allen was perfectly consistent. He believed that he did not betray Catholics and their faith, only the enemies of the queen. He believed what Burghley himself found it impossible to imagine: that a Catholic, even a priest, could be a loyal subject to Elizabeth; that it was possible to separate religious faith from political allegiance in a way that challenged the very notion of Elizabethan England as a confessional state. Snowden's enemies were those of his queen, Lord Burghley and Sir Robert: 'those which are the principal agents against our estate and country'.

19

The Fall and Rise of Thomas Phelippes

In 1591 William Sterrell pestered Thomas Phelippes to recommend him for service in the household of Robert Devereux, the young and ambitious Earl of Essex. Sterrell was convincing and plausible and soon found himself in the earl's employment. Phelippes was less willing to join Essex but, left by Walsingham's death without a patron, he had few other choices open to him. After some months of courtship, Francis Bacon, Essex's great friend, at last recruited Phelippes and his vast experience of operating secret agents.

Essex wanted to dazzle the queen with a great intelligence coup against Her Majesty's enemies. He had high expectations and he wanted results. But Sterrell's mission in Flanders, which was launched by Phelippes in the spring months of 1592, failed, at a cost to Essex's purse and also his patience. It was the ruin of Sterrell. And it damaged Phelippes's reputation for skill in espionage, most importantly of all in the eyes of the queen herself. In fact, it was the greatest failure of Phelippes's long career in the shadows of Elizabethan government.

The setting for the mission was Europe: Antwerp, Brussels, Liège and London. Nothing of the whole paraphernalia of Elizabethan espionage was missing from the Sterrell case. There were aliases (Sterrell alone used at least two), plausible cover stories, secret postal addresses in three European cities, a cipher and meticulous arrangements for the exchange of money. At first one and later two couriers worked for Phelippes and Sterrell, both Yorkshiremen, Reinold Bisley and Thomas Cloudesley. Both men were believed by the Catholic exiles to be their agents, but they were deceived by Phelippes's arts of double-cross. To each and every aspect of the mission Phelippes gave time and effort. A startlingly accomplished man himself – the best breaker of code and cipher in western Europe, a Cambridge-educated mathematician, a linguist fluent in five languages, a shrewd judge of men – he was supported in Sterrell's mission by Francis Bacon, one of the most prodigious intellects in Elizabethan England. And yet for all this, so technically brilliant an operation produced no worthwhile intelligence on émigrés in the pay of the King of Spain. What should have been a wonderful success for the greater glory of the ambitious Earl of Essex became for reasons of personality, circumstance and politics a confused tangle of misunderstanding and bitter recrimination.

The proposition, which employed Phelippes's familiar method of using a double agent, looked at first so promising. William Sterrell, a veteran of espionage in the Low Countries during the time of Walsingham, would work in Brussels and Antwerp to gather intelligence on the queen's enemies in Flanders, offering himself as a likely agent for Catholic émigrés who wanted to recruit an English spy. Sterrell's reports, carried by the courier Thomas Cloudesley, would be delivered to the Swan inn on Bishopsgate, just outside the city walls of London. Phelippes, who had a network of contacts in the city, would collect them from the Swan.

So convinced was the Earl of Essex of certain success, he briefed the queen on Sterrell almost before he was launched; he wanted to lose no time in showing to Elizabeth the impressive skills of his men. Even Phelippes, by nature a cautious man, was hopeful of being able to get good intelligence on important exiles. Of the émigrés three were especially dangerous: the renegade military commander Sir William Stanley; the clever Catholic intelligencer Hugh Owen; and Henry Walpole, a Jesuit chaplain in Stanley's regiment.

Phelippes wrote a passport for Sterrell that would allow him to pass easily through ports on both sides of the English Channel. His cover was trade; he was supposed to be the agent of a London merchant. Phelippes gave him £10. Essex was at first relaxed about the sums of money he would need to provide to fund the mission, though Phelippes well knew that these were more modest than Sterrell had hoped for. The earl nevertheless felt generous. As he wrote to Phelippes: 'I would wish to have full contentment in these things with no pity of my purse.' He was making an investment, expecting a quick return on his money.

Sterrell's first reports seemed very promising. He took his cover seriously, and wrote to Phelippes as a merchant's factor might write to his master. But woven into the letters were passages of cipher. Surely it was no surprise to have confidential matters of business protected in this way. In fact, Sterrell was making his secret briefings to Phelippes. One of the first of these hidden messages concerned a plot to kill the queen. Sir William Stanley, Sterrell wrote, had sent into England 'one Bisley by [i.e. by way of] Flushing, sometime a soldier there, a little short black fellow, a red face, his father an officer in York.' This was not, however, the major revelation Sterrell may have imagined it to be. As it happened, Phelippes already knew of Master Reinold Bisley, whom he had kept under close surveillance for some little time.

Phelippes's subtle mind was thinking of Bisley and the uses to which a soldier-assassin might be put. Sterrell, however, was much more preoccupied with the hardships of his new secret life abroad. He was bothered about money, feeling that he could not live in Brussels for less than £140. For a start, he was not yet dressed in the Spanish fashions of the city's elite, which he felt hindered his gathering of intelligence.

Soon he left Brussels for Liège and then he went to Antwerp. There the factor of the merchant who had been approached by Phelippes to exchange Sterrell's money said he knew nothing about the agreement; Sterrell instead made his own arrangements with a merchant from Cologne. There were difficulties, too, of communication. Phelippes, who understood the risks of sending letters from England to mainland Europe, was going to the trouble of cutting his letters to Sterrell into two halves and sending each part separately. Sterrell, however, received only some of the packets. Knowing there was a valuable market in Antwerp for intercepted letters, Sterrell wrote to Phelippes:

> Send me word always how many letters you receive with the date, that I may know if any miscarry. Let me know what was in your letter sent to the master of posts in Antwerp for it is intercepted; there is no letter can pass under any known name but will be filched by one or other; here is such extreme emulation or envy. Write all matter of importance in cipher.

The secret report on Reinold Bisley written for Thomas Phelippes, 1592.

And yet in spite of all this trouble Sterrell told Phelippes that he was sure he could find out valuable intelligence. He wrote that he could even intercept the letters of Cardinal William Allen, that most influential of English exiles working for Spain: if only, of course, he had some more money.

Reinold Bisley, named by Sterrell as an assassin on the way to England to kill the queen, was certainly a suspicious character. In the weeks before Sterrell left for Brussels Phelippes had had him watched; perhaps even then Phelippes had imagined a use for him in Sterrell's mission. Phelippes's watcher found Bisley at his lodgings near Bedlam. It was a house owned by an Italian who kept a bowling alley, one of those haunts of bawkers, gripes and vincents – Elizabethan underworld slang for players, gamblers and dupes – that so offended the high standards of Elizabethan moralists.

Phelippes's informant spent time and effort gathering as many facts as he could about the mysterious Bisley. The watcher's information was that Master Bisley had been sent to London by Sir William Stanley and Hugh Owen. He had arrived in London in the middle of the night and in conditions of great secrecy. Moving between Antwerp and London, Bisley worked as a courier who carried the letters of Stanley and Owen 'in his buttons' – that is, strangely, without any effort to conceal them. The subject of one of these letters, so the watcher reported to Phelippes, was the murder of Queen Elizabeth.

In fact Reinold Bisley was an English spy who worked for Lord Buckhurst, one of Elizabeth's privy councillors who knew a great deal about the Low Countries. Bisley was not, in other words, a dangerous Catholic: he carried a paper signed by Buckhurst and was employed secretly in the queen's service. All of this Phelippes discovered when he interviewed Bisley in July 1592, two months after Sterrell had left for the Low Countries. Bisley told Phelippes that he was a simple courier, bringing letters from the émigrés and then delivering them in London and Southwark. Certainly he knew Sir William Stanley and Hugh Owen. They believed that Bisley was posing as a spy for Elizabeth's government: that, in other words, he was their double agent. His allegiance, however, was to Lord Buckhurst, and Owen and Stanley were convinced by the deception.

Phelippes's careful account of his interview with Bisley shows that he was wary of the dark-haired Yorkshireman. One of Phelippes's sentences is particularly pungent. He wrote of Bisley: 'He will as others have done make his profit of me at one time or other.' And yet for all the warning he gave himself, Phelippes chose to take the risk of employing him. An excellent second courier for Sterrell, one who was trusted by the very men Phelippes wanted to spy on, had fallen into his lap. It was the kind of double-cross Phelippes relished.

By late summer 1592, only a few months after he had set out for Brussels, Sterrell and his mission were in trouble. Exactly why is a mystery, but it seems he panicked. Francis Bacon wrote to Phelippes that 'Mercury' was returning home in alarm, the news was known at court, and the Earl of Essex had been informed. Bacon's allusion to classical myth and astronomy was an ironic play upon Sterrell's cover in Brussels and Antwerp as an English businessman. The planet Mercury was specially associated with feats of skill, eloquence and success in commerce, and to the Romans Mercury was both a messenger and a god of trade. Sterrell, however, was proving himself considerably more inadequate than a god of the pantheon in his abilities as Essex's master spy.

For some time now, Bacon had been working closely with Phelippes, though Bacon's references to the time they spent together have all the elegant ease of a scholar only passingly aware of the world around him. In August he invited Phelippes to call on him. 'You may stay as long and as little while as you will,' Bacon wrote. 'And indeed I would be the wiser by you in many things, for that I call to confer with a man of your fulness [prosperity, affluence].' We can be sure that there was a very definite sense of purpose to a visit by one of the most cunning men in England to probably the kingdom's most intellectually gifted.

Bacon said that Sterrell had returned so unexpectedly to England 'upon some great matter'. Probably this was fear, for from the beginning of his mission he had felt exposed in enemy territory, short of money and very worried about the interception of his letters. 'I pray you meet him if you may,' Bacon wrote to Phelippes of Sterrell in September. Bacon suggested that he and Phelippes should lay their heads together so that they could save Sterrell's reputation, satisfy the demands of the Earl of Essex and 'procure good service'.

But already the damage was done. Sterrell returned to court without official approval. Essex was furious that Lord Burghley, with eyes and ears everywhere, had known of Sterrell's homecoming two days before Phelippes. The earl was particularly embarrassed that after talking of the mission is such glowing terms to the queen he was beginning to be asked uncomfortable questions by her about his agent. Even when Sterrell had sent reports, Essex wrote bitterly to Phelippes, they had 'no satisfaction of anything of worth'. In the highly charged politics of Elizabeth's court, Sterrell's short stay in Brussels and Antwerp was beginning to have about it the quality of a heavy albatross, and this only months after its inception. But even Essex, annoyed as he was, was not without hope. He told Phelippes that he thought Hugh Owen's messenger 'carrieth some probability of good service'. Essex meant here Reinold Bisley. About a month after their first interview in July, Phelippes had successfully recruited Lord Buckhurst's spy to Sterrell's mission.

The Earl of Essex's temper did not improve over the spring and summer months of 1593. He was as dissatisfied as ever with Sterrell's lack of productivity. He wrote sharply to Phelippes of the damage being done to his standing at court: 'my reputation is engaged in it'. He feared the queen's 'unquietness' (her disturbance or restlessness) and his own disgrace. This, as Essex would not have been prepared to admit, was the swift and heavy cost of making intelligence an instrument of political advancement. It was certainly not what Essex had imagined when through Francis Bacon he had recruited Phelippes to oversee a brilliant intelligence coup whose purpose was to impress the queen.

With Sterrell now in England it was the couriers, Cloudesley and Bisley, who went abroad with letters to his émigré contacts. Phelippes grimly soldiered on in a lacklustre operation. With the plague 'hot in London' in the first week of July he wrote to Sterrell, safely out of the city, with instructions for what he should write to his enemy contacts abroad. Letters in cipher were duly dispatched to the continent, but for all of these efforts no information of any value was uncovered. It was a masterclass in the futility of technique over substance, and Phelippes knew it.

Sterrell frankly blamed Cloudesley and Bisley for his poor results. Through Cloudesley's clumsiness, Sterrell told Phelippes, secret letters had been delivered to the wrong men, which, given the factional squabbling among the émigrés, he felt put at risk the whole operation. True, he could not fault Cloudesley's standing with the men they were spying upon; they trusted him. To Phelippes Sterrell hoped their courier had not 'played the knave with us'. Sterrell had even less faith in Reinold Bisley, who he was sure had counterfeited and deceived them. Phelippes's view was different. He was moderately confident in the loyalty and ability of the two couriers.

Surprisingly it was Sterrell, not Phelippes, who was right – or at least Bisley, the humble courier, who first felt the sting of the operation's failure. By September 1593 he was a prisoner in the Gatehouse prison in Westminster, accused of duplicity in his dealings with Sterrell. At their first meeting just over a year earlier Phelippes had been very wary of Bisley: 'He will as others have done make his profit of me.' Fourteen months later, however, he petitioned the queen for Bisley's release from jail. In fact he really had little choice. The unpleasant fact was that Phelippes's reputation was now tangled up with Bisley's. Phelippes approached Elizabeth through Lord Buckhurst, whose agent Bisley had been. It was a chastening experience. Buckhurst told Phelippes plainly that the queen was annoyed with him. Buckhurst had done his best for Phelippes by giving Elizabeth 'general assertions' of his 'sufficiency, fidelity, and great care and diligence used in Her Majesty's service'. The queen was unmoved by Buckhurst's character reference.

But for Phelippes, and even for Bisley, there was hope. Briefed by Lord Buckhurst, Elizabeth knew something of Bisley's secret service. Annoyed as she was, she felt that he should be put to work, though she left the details of what kind of work this might be to Phelippes and Bisley to decide between them. This was thanks to Buckhurst, who had advised Elizabeth that Bisley could do 'good service'. But without money he had no hope of success. Buckhurst asked the queen for £20 to pay most of the bill of £21 Bisley owed to the keeper of the Gatehouse for his board and lodgings in prison. She offered £10 only, with the promise of her 'princely reward' in the future. Elizabeth left it to Phelippes to tell Bisley that, as he had dealt so badly with Her Majesty, she had no reason to give him any greater reward until he deserved it.

A fortnight later Phelippes sent his servant to the Gatehouse to pay the £10 given by the queen to cover just under half of Reinold Bisley's prison bill. Phelippes, for reasons we may guess at, showed no great willingness to cover from his own purse the £11 outstanding.

To the Earl of Essex the failure of Phelippes's work with Sterrell meant political embarrassment. In a few months Sterrell had produced nothing of any significance, and the earl was not prepared to sit patiently by for success to come. Quickly he held Phelippes to account. Essex felt he had wasted money, time and effort. He had wanted speedy results: good intelligence he could take to the queen, for which at the beginning he was willing to pay generously – though not so generously as Sterrell may have wished. What he got instead from his investment was damage to his reputation at Elizabeth's court. All there was to show for Sterrell's work by 1593 was a hefty pile of inconclusive letters and reports. The experience and cunning of Thomas Phelippes had not given the earl the dazzling success he wanted. With the impatience often characteristic of powerful men, Essex redirected his interests from the Low Countries to espionage in France.

It was Sterrell who felt above all the sharpness of Essex's displeasure. Without results there was no money. He wrote plaintively to Phelippes that he was cast out of the earl's service; he was now only a 'voluntary follower' of Essex with neither wages nor security. The earl had promised him that he should have his horsemeat for free, but he was having to pay for it himself. He was no longer even able to afford properly to pay his manservant. So much for the life he had expected in Brussels, that of a gentleman spy dressed in the latest Spanish fashions. He had nothing. But, he wrote to Phelippes, he bore these indignities. He was miserably resigned: 'I am out of heart more than you think for.'

No one knew better than Thomas Phelippes that William Sterrell had failed to gather any useful information on the queen's enemies abroad, those fugitives in the pay of the King of Spain who plotted against England and sought Elizabeth's destruction. The operation, as Phelippes and probably also Francis Bacon conceived it, was in principle simple enough: to send a man to Flanders to spy on the émigrés under the cover of trade. Everything had been worked out with such care, from the aliases Sterrell and Phelippes would use and the courier system they would employ to the means of getting money abroad. But Sterrell, though he knew something of the Low Countries, was quickly out of his depth; he bolted, worried for his safety. The mistakes and possible duplicities of the couriers Cloudesley and Bisley compounded Sterrell's failings. The enormous political force being applied to Phelippes made it practically impossible to take his time in working with Sterrell, Cloudesley and Bisley. Phelippes was used to working over years, not six months. But in the end the plain fact is that Sterrell, who had been exceptionally able in convincing Essex of his merits, could not cope with the strains of the mission. Probably Phelippes had known this all along, just as he was suspicious at first of Reinold Bisley. But Phelippes showed great loyalty to his agents, however flawed they were.

And yet his failure with Sterrell rankled, and even as late as 1596, four years after the operation began, he could not quite let it go. He wrote to Essex with a review of what had gone wrong. Though polite by the formulae of Elizabethan correspondence, the letter has a sharp edge to it, and for a very good reason: Phelippes suffered the humiliation of seeing the reputation for efficient and effective service that he had built up over many years so quickly drain away. He was plain with the earl. For the queen's service, he wrote, he had opened up intelligence between Sterrell and English fugitives in the Low Countries. As he was unable to support the mission out of his own pocket, the operation was lost through the failures of the men Essex had used to manage it. Phelippes believed that the fault lay in what he called the want of good handling. What pained him most was that the queen, who disliked both Sterrell and his mission, believed that it was Phelippes who made errors of judgement. Phelippes, in other words, found himself in an extraordinary political tangle the like of which he had never experienced before.

Phelippes was finished in Essex's service. It also seemed highly unlikely that, with his talents now tarnished by the Sterrell case, the Cecils would employ him in any regular way. True, in July 1594 he untangled for Lord Burghley a confused diplomatic cipher. A year later he deciphered, once again for Burghley, a letter intercepted from the enemy, using this opportunity to advertise his expertise: 'the comparison of other intelligence I have had of the factions and proceedings of them on the other side'. The hint (in the circumstances a fairly subtle one) did him little good.

Some time after his father's death in 1590, Phelippes had been appointed to an official position in the London customs house, the kind of office that helped to keep smoothly running the wheels of royal patronage. With no fortune of his own, Phelippes took full advantage of his highly remunerative post, though at a catastrophic cost to his good name. He accumulated a debt of nearly £12,000 from customs revenue he had collected and appropriated but which by 1596 he could not afford to pay to Elizabeth's treasury. It was an almost incomprehensible mistake for a man of Phelippes's ability to make. But he could not escape from the consequences of his recklessness. The queen's mild annoyance at his failures in the Sterrell affair was as nothing to her fury over Phelippes's mishandling of her money. For the first time in his life, at about the age of forty, Phelippes saw the walls of a cell as a prisoner, not as an interrogator. He went to jail in 1596. Though released in 1597, he was soon returned again.

He found it a long, hard road back to service. Bruised by the court politics of the 1590s and burdened by his debt to the queen, he gathered his reserves of energy in the early months of a new century. Chastened by his past failures, Phelippes hoped to win the favour of Sir Robert Cecil, by now the extraordinarily able and influential secretary to the queen. Phelippes went first of all to an intermediary, William Waad, who also ran secret agents; the two men had known each other for a long time. To Waad he made what he called his 'overture'. Phelippes wrote that in spite of his troubles of the last few years he had with the queen's knowledge stayed in touch with intelligence matters. Even in prison he had broken enemy ciphers. He felt that the time had come to put his expertise properly to use.

At first he had no reply, so in the early spring of 1600 he plucked up the courage to write to Sir Robert directly. Always a perfectionist, he spent four days getting his letter to Cecil right. We know this because two copies of it exist, each with different dates written in Phelippes's tiny, precise hand. He had tested every word and sentence, trying to find just the right tone, both contrite and persuasive. This, as Phelippes knew very well, was the hard business of political patronage and favour. At last he sent the letter to Sir Robert on Friday, 18 April 1600.

Phelippes pardoned his presumption. He knew, of course, that Sir Robert had 'so many spirits and endeavours of the whole kingdom at your commandment'; but, encouraged by others who had been lucky enough to receive Master Secretary's favour, he was bold to offer his service. Phelippes had all the necessary skills. Most important of all

Thomas Phelippes's offer of secret service to Sir Robert Cecil, April 1600.

was trust: the trust of those agents he worked with and that of the men he worked against. As Phelippes put it: 'the principal point in matter of intelligence, is to procure confidence with those parties that one will work upon, or for those parties a man would work by'.

And so he offered to Secretary Cecil his service and talents: 'I will be glad and vow unto you to employ that dexterity I may have to the utmost of my power.' He ended craving pardon of his boldness, ceasing to trouble Sir Robert further.

Cecil replied to Phelippes in his own hand, a fluent, easy response to Phelippes's formal and carefully crafted prose; it made all the difference to be a magnanimous patron rather than an anxious suitor. Sir Robert wrote:

> I thank you for your offer to employ yourself in Her Majesty's service with my privity and direction; for the means you have yourself can judge; for the mind you have I know it of old and do allow it. And where you desire my favour, if you do make your services fruitful assure yourself I will very gladly do you any pleasure I can; and when you will come to me, I would confer with you of your projects . . .

For Phelippes this was a remarkable recovery. His debt to Elizabeth's treasury still hung over him; he never repaid it. But Sir Robert, in recognizing Phelippes's talents and expertise, had doubtless done much to heal the bruises of the Sterrell affair. Phelippes set to work straight away with energy and passion, using his old contacts abroad to discover the intentions of England's fugitive enemies: 'to feel their pulse on the other side', as he put it in a lively metaphor.

And so Phelippes survived. If he was not prosperous in the years after 1600 he was certainly busy. He was in Sir Robert's favour and protection – at least for the time being.

20

Politics and Prognostications

When Sir Robert Cecil accepted Thomas Phelippes's offer of service he had in place already a formidable network for gathering foreign intelligence. Phelippes joined a system of espionage that had not been rivalled since the time of Sir Francis Walsingham, set up by Sir Robert with care, ingenuity and imagination. But Master Secretary Cecil's apparently easy dominance of the Elizabethan secret world was (as Phelippes once wrote of a difficult cipher) won out of hard rock. As Phelippes found to his cost, the 1590s were troubled and difficult years blighted by the intense political competition between Robert Devereux, Earl of Essex and the great political dynasty of the Cecils.

In 1593 Essex joined the Privy Council and he was zealous, as the Sterrell affair shows, to prove his prowess in matters of secret intelligence. Recognizing Lord Burghley's dominance of politics and patronage at Elizabeth's court, the earl recruited experienced advisers and threw money at sources of information throughout Europe. Feeling that he was the natural successor to Burghley as the queen's leading adviser, Essex wanted to build for himself an unrivalled expertise in foreign affairs. Given what appeared to be Burghley's failing health in 1593, the earl imagined that the great flowering of his career in Elizabeth's service would come very soon.

If Essex underestimated Burghley's tenacious constitution, he saw plainly the lord treasurer's ambitions for Sir Robert Cecil. With an eye upon the secretaryship, Burghley did everything in his considerable power to prepare his son for office; often from his bed or couch, besieged by government business, he was the exacting master of a gifted apprentice. Kept away from court by sickness, Burghley reminded Elizabeth of his long faithfulness. 'Even now,' he wrote to

Sir Robert in February 1594, 'I received your letter, wherein you report Her Majesty's care for my health, for the which I most humbly thank her, hoping that her good wishings shall help to return me to strength for her service, which I esteem the service of God, whose place she holdeth on earth.' The contrast with Essex could not have been greater. Burghley saw it as his duty to serve the queen, to prove his loyalty and constancy as her oldest adviser. Upon that depended his power and the future prospects for Robert Cecil. In contrast to this grave and elderly councillor, Essex had risen in Elizabeth's favour with spectacular speed, quickly finding a position at court in 1587 as Elizabeth's companion and master of the royal horse, an office which gave him regular access to the queen. The young earl needed royal favour: his family was heavily in debt. There was an urgency to his political ambitions that only grew and became more intense as the years passed. Essex, too, had something to prove. As a boy, left an orphan by his father's death in Ulster, he had been made a royal ward. He grew up for a time in Burghley's house, sharing a table and a classroom with Robert Cecil and his siblings. Who knows what challenges or grievances of childhood were being settled in the 1590s?

Against a family that felt it was born to rule – against a father and son so well entrenched at Elizabeth's court – the Earl of Essex pushed and pressed. He sought power and credibility; he wanted his moment of glory at court. Between the straining ambition of Essex and the formidable power of the Cecils something had to give. The year of crisis was 1594 and it was one of blood and betrayal. A huge price was paid for the competitive vanities of powerful and ambitious men at Elizabeth's court.

*

We men are of life short, of constitution frail, of thoughts vain, of words rash, and of knowledge unperfect, taking the shadow for substance ...

The disposition of this quarter will be indifferent, yet will there be many unkind storms with sudden lightnings, and terrible thunderclaps. Sickness this quarter will not be many, but passing dangerous, hot, and fervent agues, great distemperature of men's brains, with immoderate heat, whereby many will become frantic.

An Elizabethan almanac was a store of information: a calendar, a reference book of astronomical data and a guide to astrological forecasts – a companion in uncertain times. But whatever its other virtues, the *Almanac* for 1594 failed to predict that it would also be a year of peculiar and disturbing intensity in the history of Elizabethan royal murder plots, though the prognostications of sudden storms and fevered brains captured something of the dangerous and unpredictable political intrigues at the court of the queen. Between January and August Lord Burghley and the Earl of Essex squashed three murder plots directed against Elizabeth. It seemed that the two most powerful of the queen's councillors had a remarkable nose for treason, and surely no observer in those eight months of 1594 could fault the energy of Burghley and Essex in hunting down Her Majesty's enemies.

And yet there was much more to these plots and apparently miraculous discoveries than at first meets the eye. To begin with, we have to review the bare facts of each conspiracy and then consider the politics behind them.

The first plot to be discovered, and the most startling of them all, was that of one of the queen's physicians, Doctor Roderigo Lopez, to poison Elizabeth. It was Essex himself who in January 1594 made the charge of treason against Lopez, though he had been unpicking the evidence in Lopez's case for three months before that. It seemed at the time a wild charge to make against a respected doctor. A Portuguese Jew who had converted to Christianity, Lopez had lived in London for thirty-five years; in that time he had built an enviable medical practice at court. Yet Essex was absolutely convinced that Lopez was a traitor. In January he made a very plain statement of his accusation, writing:

> I have discovered a most dangerous and desperate treason. The point of conspiracy was Her Majesty's death. The executioner should have been Doctor Lopez. The manner by poison. This I have so followed that I will make it appear as clear as the noon day.

Essex was consumed by the interrogations of Lopez, to which the earl, showing extraordinary tenacity, gave every particle of his time and energy. By the end of February he had accumulated enough evidence against Lopez to have him tried for high treason as a Spanish agent who had agreed to murder the queen by poison for the sum of

50,000 crowns paid by the King of Spain. Doctor Lopez was found guilty. A few months later, in June, he was hanged, drawn and quartered on the gallows at Tyburn.

The second plot to be discovered, in February 1594, involved an Irish soldier in the regiment of Sir William Stanley, the turncoat English military commander who fought for the King of Spain. In October 1593 Stanley, his deputy Giacomo de Franceschia (who was known simply as Captain Jacques) and the Jesuit priest William Holt were supposed to have recruited Patrick O'Collun to murder Queen Elizabeth. We do not know when O'Collun arrived in England or how he was captured, but he was questioned in the Tower of London in early February 1594. Two witnesses testified to his mission. One of these was William Polewheele, himself a soldier of Stanley's regiment who also admitted to having been sent by Stanley to assassinate Elizabeth.

One of Patrick O'Collun's interrogators was Justice Richard Young of Westminster. On the day of O'Collun's first examination, another Irishman, called John Danyell, came to Justice Young to reveal the existence of a plot to blow up the Tower of London with its own supplies of gunpowder and brimstone as well as a conspiracy to burn ships and houses in Billingsgate and to set fire to inns and woodstacks throughout London. With Danyell was Hugh Cahill, yet another Irish soldier of Stanley's regiment. Cahill's examination at Lord Burghley's house in Westminster revealed that, like O'Collun and Polewheele, Cahill had been approached by Jesuit priests, at Stanley's behest, to assassinate Elizabeth.

Acting upon the prisoners' interrogations and examinations, Lord Burghley himself took great care in ordering the arrest of suspicious persons coming into England, with special precautions to be taken against Irishmen in London and near Elizabeth's court. He gave a particular warning against any man who had served in Sir William Stanley's rebel regiment. Burghley's orders were enforced by a royal proclamation, which said that some men had come secretly into the kingdom 'with full purpose, by procurement of the Devil and his ministers, Her Majesty's enemies, and rebels on the other side the sea, to endanger Her Majesty's noble person'.

*

The third great murder conspiracy discovered in these remarkable months of intrigue and danger involved Edmund Yorke, for three years a captain in Stanley's regiment. In late June 1594 Yorke sent a letter to the Earl of Essex. Having left England without a licence, he sought the earl's help in seeking a reconciliation with the queen. Yorke wanted to be forgiven for aiding her enemies and to prove himself her loyal subject. He wrote to Essex:

> I most humbly beseech your honour to stand my gracious lord and master in obtaining pardon for me and the gentlemen with me [including Richard Williams, his companion] the which if it may please your honour to do you shall find both me and them ready to do Her Highness service in what we know against her estate next unto your honour, as in duty we shall be bound till death.

On returning to England, Yorke gave himself up to the Privy Council and was promptly sent to the Tower. Essex, far from looking leniently upon Yorke's years away from England, helped rigorously to examine him. Also interrogated were Richard Williams, Captain Yorke's friend, and a witness to their conspiracy called Henry Young. Quickly Essex discovered a plot against the queen involving Captain Yorke and Williams.

Young said that Captain Yorke had planned with Sir William Stanley and the Jesuit William Holt to raise a rebellion in north Wales. Captain Yorke made a counter-accusation, saying that it was in fact Young who had been recruited by Father Holt to kill Queen Elizabeth. Richard Williams, Yorke said, had volunteered to do just the same thing for money for his family: 'he could find in his heart to do it so as he might have great store of money that his house might be advanced for he himself was sure to die'.

Pressed by his interrogators, Yorke changed his story. Before the lieutenant of the Tower and Essex's friend Francis Bacon, he made a full and voluntary confession. Offered 40,000 crowns by Holt, Captain Yorke had agreed to return to England to kill the queen. Three times Yorke met Stanley, Holt and Charles Paget, that most dangerous of English émigrés, to talk about the mission. They gave special attention to the weapons Yorke and Williams would use in London. Though some of the group spoke of the merits of using a small steel crossbow with poisoned arrows, Yorke agreed instead to shoot the queen with a small pistol. Williams would carry a rapier tipped with a poison concocted of bacon, garlic juice and juniper.

For another week Francis Bacon and other interrogators pressed Yorke for more information about plots laid out by Stanley and his fellow conspirators against the queen. Compelling evidence against Yorke and Williams was gathered with remarkable speed. The two men confessed to their guilt and went to the gallows some time before February 1595.

Three plots, three revelations of terrible danger to the queen, the strenuous investigations of treason led by the Earl of Essex in the cases of Lopez and Captain Yorke and by Lord Burghley in the mission of O'Collun and the conspiracies revealed by John Danyell and Hugh Cahill. Each one of these murderous projects involved conspirators and assassins motivated by a cause as well as by money; behind each was a shady network of highly dangerous and organized English émigrés and exiles, or in the case of Lopez Portuguese agents working for Spain. Each conspiracy had been close to its execution: only the swift and energetic actions of Burghley and especially Essex, who barely left the Tower of London between January and March, saved the queen from destruction.

The plots of 1594 seem at first glance very similar to the Throckmorton, Parry and Babington conspiracies of the years 1584–6. And certainly they did have features in common. Murder conspiracies had always called for urgent action, stimulating great passions and provoking ferocious official denunciations of the traitors. But what had changed over a decade was the tone of the investigations, and even to some extent their methods. Patient gathering and sifting of evidence had given way to quick confessions; other documentary evidence seemed to have a marginal significance. Only in the case of Lopez were there papers to make sense of, though the Earl of Essex, soon tiring of the slog of investigation, chose the more direct route of open accusation followed by an unforgiving routine of interrogation. In 1594 everything seemed just a little out of proportion: frenetic, urgent, panicked and strained. The political atmosphere seemed especially charged.

Each of the three plots of 1594 was in fact a game for advantage in a visceral political contest between the Earl of Essex and the Cecils. They played for the highest stakes of power and royal favour. Essex and Burghley sought conspicuously to save the queen, and so the kingdom, from destruction. An organized enemy dedicated to Elizabeth's destruction; the dispatch of assassins; the work of English Jesuits in commissioning and blessing these murderous missions; the queen poisoned or shot: these were not new terrors in Elizabeth's reign, but they were still very immediate anxieties, and in the fraught war years of the 1590s they spoke to old fears of massacre and invasion. The Elizabethan imagination was always haunted by the memory of the mass killings in Paris in 1572. The nightmare was real: at the end of 1593 Londoners could see for themselves on stage the horrors of Catholic conspiracy when Christopher Marlowe's play about the shocking events in Paris on Bartholomewtide twenty-one years earlier, *The Massacre at Paris*, was performed at the Rose playhouse in Southwark.

In January 1594, when Burghley was weak and ill, the Earl of Essex struck quickly and powerfully with his charge of treason against Lopez. Burghley and Sir Robert Cecil hardly expected it to be taken seriously, but Essex was tenacious. In his efforts to impress the queen with a sensational political revelation, the earl's remarkable gamble paid off. With no way to avoid a full investigation of the facts, Burghley found that he had to throw himself behind Essex's efforts to expose Doctor Lopez's treason. He did so reluctantly. It was purely a tactical move in the political game.

The fact was that Burghley had been aware for a long time of Doctor Lopez's Spanish contacts. He knew that Lopez was a Spanish agent who had been in communication with one of King Philip of Spain's ambassadors, Don Bernardino de Mendoza. Between Lopez and Mendoza there was an intermediary, a Portuguese (like Lopez himself) called Manuel de Andrada. In 1591 Andrada was captured in England, and Burghley had him thoroughly examined. Burghley wrote very detailed instructions on how the interrogation should be conducted: friendly at first but then ending with a blunt offer: either Andrada could cooperate and tell his interrogators everything he

knew or he could lose his life. Burghley, who was aware of the correspondence between Lopez and Andrada, sent Lopez to help with
Andrada's interview.

So by 1594, three years after Andrada's capture, Doctor Lopez's
work as a Spanish agent was old news to Burghley. More than this,
Burghley had used Lopez to penetrate Spanish efforts at spying in
England and encouraged him in his work as a double agent. In 1594,
however, thrown off balance by the intensity of Essex's assault, Burghley felt compromised by his own association with Lopez. He did
nothing to frustrate the energetic investigations of Essex and his men.
In fact quite the opposite: Burghley threw himself aggressively at the
Lopez case. With the aid of Thomas Phelippes (who helped to write a
narrative of Lopez's treasons) Burghley controlled the government
propaganda on the case, levering it away from Essex. Burghley, who
only three years before had recruited Andrada as an English spy with
Lopez's help, was ferocious in his public denunciation of Lopez and
his treasons:

> Lopez the physician who should have committed the fact by poisoning
> Her Majesty under colour of physic [medicine], confesseth that he was
> of late years allured to do service secretly to the King of Spain, which
> he did by the means of one Manuel [de] Andrada a Portingale [a Por-
> tuguese] much used in France by the King of Spain's ambassador there
> Don Bernardino, by whom Lopez received a jewel of gold of good
> value garnished with a large diamond and a large ruby.

It was all very unlikely. Lopez indeed had secret connections with
Spanish spies, though in the end with Burghley's knowledge. His plot
to murder Elizabeth, however, was improbable in the extreme. Yet the
ingredients of the case against the physician were mixed powerfully
together: Essex's nakedly political campaign, the febrile worries at
court about Spanish espionage and the fact that Doctor Lopez's father
was a Jew. The effects were toxic. Far from defending Lopez, the
Cecils threw themselves behind the campaign to expose and try him
as a traitor. Sir Robert Cecil, who by February was one of the investi-
gative team with Essex's men, was present at Lopez's trial. Justice, he
felt, was done. Of the 'vile Jew' he wrote: 'the most substantial jury
that I have seen have found him guilty in the highest degree of all

treasons'. Sir Robert, like his father, was complicit in the destruction of Roderigo Lopez in the interests of family and politics.

The panic over Irishmen in London in 1594 played on the fearsome reputation of Sir William Stanley's regiment of desperate renegades, who, recruited by their officers, bribed by great fortunes of tens of thousands of crowns and blessed by Jesuit priests, came secretly to England to murder the queen. Now it may have been that some of Stanley's men were willing to take on so desperate a mission, but if they did it was not because Sir William's regiment operated as a kind of crack unit of Catholic storm-troops. Beset in the early 1590s by dissent and internal tensions, it seems highly unlikely that in 1593 Stanley and his advisers dispatched assassins to England practically every other week, as worried courtiers believed they did. Certainly he and his men fought for the King of Spain, at least after a fashion; certainly Sir William was the queen's enemy. Perhaps men like Patrick O'Collun and William Polewheele, with an eye on a fortune, were willing to try their luck as assassins: desperate times could encourage desperate measures. But it is a considerable stretch of the imagination to believe that Stanley and his regiment were organizationally capable of mounting a sustained campaign to murder Queen Elizabeth.

The statements of O'Collun, Polewheele and others present a very confused tangle of lies, evasions, half-truths and muddle. Under close examination in the Tower of London the prisoners' stories changed daily. As instruments of a ruthless plot to kill Elizabeth these men made a very poor showing. They appear to have made no serious effort to get anywhere near the queen. Polewheele was duped out of his money before he left mainland Europe; even to make the sea crossing to England seemed at the very limit of his abilities. What seems oddly disproportionate is how these shambolic hired assassins caused such a panic in government in February 1594. Their examinations and confessions had the crown's law officers scurrying to and from the Tower and a man as busy as Lord Burghley personally putting in place mechanisms to close Elizabeth's court to intruders.

Once again, however, there was a strong political angle to the Irish panic of February 1594, and this is at its clearest in the roles played by John Danyell (the man who went to Justice Young with the report of the plot to blow up the Tower) and Hugh Cahill (another supposed assassin). It looks very much like Danyell's emergency was planted by Lord Burghley himself. Cahill's mission to kill the queen was long known to Burghley: Danyell had told the lord treasurer about it eighteen months before the emergency of February 1594. The chronology of Danyell's whole story shows that it was pretty stale by the time he went to see Justice Young. Cahill met Danyell in Brussels in May 1592. Though promising to Stanley, Holt the Jesuit and Hugh Owen that he would kill the queen, the young soldier had already sworn an oath to Danyell 'never to perform it, for it is a wicked deed, and abhominable before God to do it'. Cahill went off to London. In June, from Calais, Danyell wrote to Burghley saying that he had 'intelligence of causes of great importance'. Burghley sent Danyell a passport to allow him to cross the English Channel. By August Danyell was in England. In September 1592 he met Burghley and told the lord treasurer all about Cahill's supposed mission to kill the queen.

So everything to do with Cahill's plot, which the young Irish soldier confessed to in February 1594, had happened nearly two years earlier. He and Danyell were lodging in Westminster for some months before Danyell went to the authorities in February 1594 with his report of the plot to blow up the Tower of London and burn the city. So at just the moment when Burghley by his strenuous labour defended the queen from desperate Irish assassins, his old informant Danyell happened to come forward to offer evidence of an imminent and probably deadly fire attack upon London. Neither Danyell nor, more significantly, Cahill was held under lock and key in February 1594. Cahill, the commissioned assassin, was left to Danyell's care with Burghley's full knowledge. More intriguing still is the very strong suggestion that one of the men who planned to blow up the Tower of London had three years before sent intelligence to Burghley.

How providentially fortuitous was the timing of Danyell's information in February 1594 and how politically convenient for Lord Burghley. Fear became a political currency that Burghley and Essex could use to secure Elizabeth's favour. And both men had it. The earl's ambitions only grew in 1594, and in the summer progress of that year the queen visited Burghley's palace of Theobalds in Hertfordshire, the house of Sir Robert Cecil on the Strand in Westminster and the estate of Sir Robert's elder brother Sir Thomas Cecil at Wimbledon. For the time being at least, the queen was prepared to accept for her courtiers' sakes the cost of so many treasons.

The Earl of Essex leaped upon the conspiracy of Edmund Yorke even more swiftly than he had moved against Doctor Lopez. Captain Yorke was dangerous to Essex. He had asked specially for the earl's help in reconciling him to the queen and he had come into England carrying a passport signed by Essex himself. Why, a hostile observer may have asked, did Yorke expect to find in Essex so sympathetic an intermediary? But if Yorke presented a risk to the earl's reputation, his case was also an opportunity. As the campaign against Doctor Lopez had shown so brutally, there was no better way for Essex to prove his political credibility than by exposing a murderous plot against Elizabeth's life. When it came to the English émigrés and exiles the case was more straightforward still. Essex's friend and confidant Francis Bacon called it 'the breaking of these fugitive traitors and filling them full of terror, dispair, jealousy and revolt'. And so, sensing a conspiracy easy to reveal, and following on so naturally from the panic over Stanley's assassins only a few months before, Essex and particularly Bacon moved in for the kill. Both men were present for the most important of Yorke's and Williams's confessions.

Burghley, though he had nothing to do with the investigation of Captain Yorke's treason, had a specific reason to be interested by it. There was evidence that his own life had been in danger. The queen's attorney-general witnessed and signed a short statement made by Captain Yorke saying that Henry Young, the man who had denounced Yorke as a traitor, had written to Father Holt with an offer to kill the lord treasurer. Burghley, keen no doubt to see what Essex was up to, had his own summary of the case compiled from the evidence of the traitors' confessions.

At no point in the interrogations, however, was Captain Yorke's connection with Burghley mentioned. In the lord treasurer's archives there were two letters by Yorke, one Burghley had received in 1591, the second, of 1594, from Yorke to a close friend in military service: 'Sweet Will, thy absence is more grief unto me than you can imagine.' The first letter was an offer by Yorke of military intelligence to Burghley on the taking of Rouen. The second was simply endorsed by Burghley 'Young Edmund Yorke's letter'.

The letters may suggest a certain closeness between Captain Yorke and Lord Burghley which could never be guessed from Yorke's service with Sir William Stanley's rebel regiment. There is just the possibility that, in destroying Edmund Yorke, the Earl of Essex destroyed also Burghley's once or future agent. It was, however, a matter upon which Burghley seems to have kept his counsel. After nearly half a century of Tudor politics, the old lord treasurer knew when it was necessary to make sacrifices.

When Sir Robert Cecil was appointed secretary to the queen in 1596 he found a system of espionage put under extraordinary strain by the factional ambitions of the Earl of Essex and the power games of his own family. The habit of infighting and intrigue, shown so brutally in the first eight months of 1594, encouraged everyone involved in the struggle to look inwards instead of outwards. Vicious court politics corrupted any pretence at measuring foreign intelligence accurately and intelligently. Certainly Essex recruited many foreign experts and sources, though more for ornament and self-aggrandizement than for anything else. In the end, the easy task of exposing half-baked assassination plots was a poor substitute for a serious effort to understand the enemy's political outlook and military dispositions. In the field of foreign intelligence work the Cecils had for some time lagged behind Essex.

Quickly the Cecils recovered their political initiative at court. Driven on by rumours in 1595 of Spanish preparations for another armada, Essex had pressed successfully for the joint command with Lord Admiral Howard of a naval expedition against the coast of Spain. The earl's plan, which he concealed from the queen, was to seize a Spanish port and to hold it against the enemy. The fleet sailed in June 1596. The focus of the assault was the port of Cadiz, where Essex, going ashore in the first boat, led English troops through the streets. The action in Cadiz was followed by a raid on Faro; there the plunder was considerable, including nearly two hundred books looted from the bishop's palace, which Essex later donated to Thomas Bodley's library in Oxford University. But the earl was not welcomed back at Elizabeth's court as a hero. Quite the opposite in fact: Burghley and Robert Cecil began an official investigation of Essex's plunder, and Elizabeth was furious that Essex had subverted her authority by attempting to ignore her orders. He, in turn, was mystified by the queen's lack of gratitude for his heroism.

In October 1596 King Philip of Spain did indeed launch a new naval armada against England. It was as great in size as that of 1588. To Elizabeth's government – and especially to Sir Robert Cecil – it was a timely warning of their very serious failure properly to understand the intentions of Spain. Broken by a storm off Finisterre, what remained of the fleet limped into port ten days before reports of the armada's departure from Lisbon arrived in London. Intelligence was hopelessly late. Sir Robert's agent in Bayonne, the brother of an English merchant, sent a very accurate account of the Spanish fleet but could not at first find a ship preparing to return to England skippered by a trustworthy man. Weeks after the armada's failure English coastal forces were still mobilized. The lesson to be learned was that even excellent and necessary intelligence was useless if it could not be dispatched to Sir Robert in time.

No wonder, then, that Cecil set to work with energy. Dead wood was cut away. Henri Chasteau-Martin in Bayonne, long used as a source by the Cecils (and before them by Walsingham), was found in 1596 to be in the pay of Spain. Lord Burghley had for six years doubted Chasteau-Martin's usefulness. It was the governor of Bayonne, finding a Spanish spy in his town, who had him executed. (It is hard to know whether the governor knew that Chasteau-Martin had spied for England too.) So it was obvious that Sir Robert had to start from scratch. Using the contacts of the merchant and international financier Sir Horatio Palavicino and the assistance of one of the clerks of the royal secretariat, William Waad, that is exactly what Secretary Cecil did. By about 1597 he had agents in Lisbon, Brussels, Calais and Seville, and throughout Spain more generally, Flanders and Scotland.

Sir Robert's agents did serious work, something that is clear from the meticulous accounts of expenses prepared by one of his intelligencers in Spain and France. He was the merchant Thomas Honiman, who claimed for the voyages he had made between Dover and Plymouth, the messengers he had dispatched to reconnoitre a Spanish

Sir Robert Cecil's intelligence network, 1597.

fort in Brittany, and at least three agents sent into Spain. It was Thomas Honiman's brother, Philip, who reported on the Spanish armada of 1596.

Thomas Phelippes was right to say in 1600 that Secretary Cecil commanded so many 'spirits and endeavours'. So expertly trained by his father in every aspect of government business, Sir Robert was a practical man as well as theorist: he decided what information he needed to know and the best ways he could devise to discover it. He had at his fingertips all the resources of his father's libraries: books and papers sent out of continental Europe over many years, the best maps and atlases available. As a young scholar in France in 1584 Cecil himself had compiled a survey of the kingdom's provinces and a list of the most important nobility and officials. He possessed above all a shrewd intelligence and an eye for political information.

With all of this experience and ability, it is no wonder that by January 1598 Sir Robert had put in place a formidable network of agents. He set it all out on paper in a remarkable document that exists simply because Cecil was going on an embassy to France and a trusted official needed to know how to pay the agents and receive their reports. Fascinating today, in 1598 the document would have been priceless to England's enemies.

Some of Sir Robert's agents were residents while others, he explained, 'go and come'. All were paid, though with a close eye for their importance; the highest paid worked for Sir Robert in Lisbon and Seville. Some wrote personally to Cecil, though reports from a single city often went to England through different ports, a prudent protection against accident or interception. Agents working in the same locality probably knew nothing of each other's work. Of the two agents in Seville the best paid, Massentio Verdiani, one of Sir Horatio Palavicino's men, got his letters to Sir Robert by way of the city of Rouen. The second agent in Seville posted reports to London through a merchant in Waterford in Ireland. Discreet merchants in London acted as a postal service for secret reports from Lisbon and Bayonne; they also sent money out to Sir Robert's agents. Trade was a perfect cover for secret service. It was fairly easy for an intelligencer to pass himself off as a merchant's representative. Real merchants like Thomas Honiman worked as Sir Robert's agents: what a serious businessman needed to know by sending out his servants was always useful intelligence for a busy secretary in London.

Employing a method that had been used by Walsingham, Sir Robert gave instructions for the fitting out of a ship whose purpose was to visit the ports of Spain to discover intelligence. Thomas Honiman and Cecil each bore half of the total cost of a thousand ducats. One of the sailors on the boat had 'all languages, is of good wit and discretion'. He was paid sixty ducats for his expertise and for sending reports to Sir Robert.

Enemy Europe was covered: Bayonne and the Bay of Biscay, Lisbon, Seville, the coasts of Spain, and Rome. But Sir Robert also had spies 'in such states as are friends to us', from Scotland to Holland and Zeeland, Germany, Denmark and Sweden. Like Walsingham, Cecil maintained important contacts in England. He used 'spies and false brethren [likeliest] to know of any practice against Her Majesty's person'. One of these 'false brethren', a man who pretended to be a Catholic, performed two tasks for Sir Robert. Firstly, he kept up a correspondence with the important émigré intelligencer Hugh Owen. Secondly, on his travels to Normandy he collected émigré Catholics' letters and brought them back to England, showing them to Cecil before posting them on. Other informants brought news to Sir Robert.

In London an Irishman called James Patrick 'remaineth daily where Irish do resort' and he went every day to the River Thames to report on passengers arriving at the private quays of the city.

So comprehensive a service as this was not cheap to run. Sir Robert, like his father in so many ways, did not in matters of intelligence share Lord Burghley's taste for austerity. The secret budget from Elizabeth's treasury was revived, though Sir Robert was cannier with money than Walsingham had been. The salaries of his agents came to well over 4,500 ducats or (very roughly) nearly £13,000 a year in Elizabethan money. There were other expenses on top of this: extra payments, inducements and rewards, and at least once the heavy cost of fitting out a ship to spy on Spanish ports. But for regular and sound information he knew and trusted it was a price worth paying. When armies and navies could so easily run up huge debts for Elizabeth's government it was in fact a modest investment of money and energy.

And there were results. Intelligence on the Spanish armada of 1596, though too late to be of use in England, was of high quality. Reports from Lisbon on the weaknesses of Spanish forces in 1598 were likewise accurate. True, the secret information Sir Robert received was no guarantee of success, especially in military expeditions. Raw reports were only pieces in a jigsaw whose composite picture was always changing. The secretary's skill, as Sir Francis Walsingham and Lord Burghley had known, was to sift the plausible from the implausible, the probable from the unlikely, and the plain facts from the suppositions. As Robert Beale, an official of government close to Walsingham, wrote: 'Be not too credulous lest you be deceived; hear all reports but trust not all; weigh them with time and deliberation and be not too liberal with trifles; observe them that deal on both hands lest you be deceived.' This was the instinctive talent of a man like Sir Robert Cecil.

We can be sure that behind the formal structures of Sir Robert Cecil's intelligence system – the postal systems, the money and the arrangements with London merchants – was the human factor of espionage. In the years after 1600 Thomas Phelippes brought to Cecil's service his understanding of the characters and motivations of spies as well as his formidable attention to detail. We can well imagine that Phelippes saw in Sir Robert what he had once found in Walsingham's service: a centralizing and processing intelligence at work in secret matters, seasoned with cunning and imagination. Sir Robert was ambitious, not for obvious private or political gain, but for the service of the queen and the security of the state. As a Cecil long trained for politics and service he saw neither difference nor distinction between his family's good and Elizabeth's best interests; they were identical.

By the time Thomas Phelippes was in Secretary Cecil's service, there were new recruits abroad. The few surviving records of their work give only the smallest hint of what they saw and did for God, queen and country. Together George Kendall and George Weekes spied for Sir Robert in Brussels and Dunkirk. They had generous allowances of money. When Kendall visited England in May 1601 he was given armour worth over £5. Master Douglas, a gentleman of Scotland, worked for Cecil at the Spanish court and in Lisbon for a quarterly allowance of 100 crowns. Master Fox, an Englishman, served in Venice for a yearly salary of £40. Grander still was Thomas Bradshaw, 'employed in the court of Spain' and paid £100 a year for his information. At least two agents were discharged from service, one, Robert Luff, taken prisoner in Spain, the other, Francis Lambert, in Bayonne. When they returned to London both men were pensioned off.

Perhaps one day the stories of these spies will be told. Certainly they deserve to be. In 1600 the prognostications suggested that in a new century espials and intelligencers would be kept as busy as fellow members of their profession had been for forty years.

21

Ends and Beginnings

The reign of Queen Elizabeth, which had begun early on a Thursday morning in November 1558, ended with her death at Richmond Palace on another Thursday, 24 March 1603. She was sixty-nine years old. In the course of nearly half a century so many characters had walked on to the stage of Elizabethan politics, played their parts both great and small and then moved to the wings either to make no further appearance or to wait for a future part in the drama of a new reign. Elizabeth's successor was King James VI of Scotland. His accession went remarkably smoothly. But what seemed from the outside to be an effortless transition of power rested upon the skills of men long trained in the secret arts. It is a story to be told later in this chapter.

Elizabeth outlived many of her most eminent and powerful courtiers. Two were Sir Francis Walsingham, who died in 1590, and Lord Burghley, who died eight years later. Even the dazzling Earl of Essex was dead before the queen, though not by natural causes. Essex's head was taken off by the executioner's axe in 1601 when his frustrated ambitions had boiled over into a sorry attempt at a rebellion on the streets of London. Feeling that he had never received the full recognition he deserved from the queen, at thirty-five the brightest star of Elizabeth's last decade burned himself out. Sir Robert Cecil, in the sharpest possible contrast to Essex, prospered and became as essential to the efficient running of royal government as his father had been before him.

Of the spies in government service, many disappeared into obscurity. Walsingham's informants were always shadowy men, and so it is not surprising to find that Robert Wood or Woodward and Maliverey

Catilyn, both of whom spied on Catholic families, vanish from the archives. Charles Sledd, the spy in Rome whose secret dossier helped to send so many priests to the gallows, likewise disappears. With Nicholas Berden, Walsingham's spy in Paris in the middle 1580s and one of the players in the Babington Plot, we have better luck. In 1588 he wrote to Walsingham to say that he wanted to follow 'a more public course of life' and, with Sir Francis's help, he seems to have secured a position at Elizabeth's court as the purveyor of poultry. Berden's father was a London poulter, and so after a career in espionage Berden himself set out in the family business. He swapped the uncertain life of a spy for a secure living and a regular income.

Much less fortunate was Gilbert Gifford, the double agent who worked with Walsingham and Thomas Phelippes to break the Babington Plot. He spied in Paris till his arrest in one of the city's brothels in 1587. His father wanted to have nothing to do with him, and only by Phelippes's efforts was he able to pay his prison bills. But Gilbert Gifford was never set free. Having lived with all the intensity of a man who led a secret life, he was dead at the age of thirty in 1591, mourned only by his brother Gerard, who went once to Paris to secure his freedom.

Two of the spies in this book went on to have literary connections, one distinguished, the other probably criminal. Anthony Munday, the young Londoner who went to Rome in 1579 and came back with a spy's tales of the conspiracies and treasons hatched at the English seminary there, became a popular author. He wrote prose and verse, translated from French, Italian and Spanish and by 1589 was distinguished enough a writer of plays to appear in a list of playwrights that included the name of William Shakespeare. The compiler of the list called him 'our best plotter', which, given Munday's life as a young spy, has a rather wonderful ring to it. Munday was one of the group of talented dramatists associated with the theatrical impressario Philip Henslowe at the Rose theatre in Southwark. The only surviving manuscript of his play *The Book of Sir Thomas More*, from about 1593, has kept Shakespearean scholars busy for nearly a century, for it seems to contain one of the very few samples of Shakespeare's handwriting. The manuscript shows that Munday, Shakespeare and other actor-playwrights worked together to perform the play.

There was a considerably darker association between Robert Poley and Christopher Marlowe, Shakespeare's brilliant contemporary in the playhouses of Southwark. Poley, who played Anthony Babington's special friend in 1586, went on to work secretly for Elizabeth's government throughout the years of the 1590s. To some scholars of English literature, this has given a special meaning to the fact that Poley was one of only three men present at the killing of Marlowe in Deptford, some miles outside London on the banks of the River Thames, in 1593. In view of some very hazy suggestions that Marlowe was abroad on secret government business in the later 1580s, he has been cast as an Elizabethan poet-spy. Where in truth Marlowe was a playwright who got into an argument over a tavern bill and was stabbed in the eye for it – certainly a nasty and probably a criminal business – Poley really was a spy. Where for Marlowe the evidence of secret service is sketchy and circumstantial, for the unliterary Poley it is overwhelming. In thirteen years he went on twenty-six missions for Her Majesty's 'special affairs', to France, the Low Countries, Scotland and the northern border county of Northumberland. Poley was a courier, though one important enough to have cipher alphabets and secret postal addresses in Antwerp.

Probably the strangest feature of Poley's career is its longevity. He was not an obviously trustworthy man. In fact he was a teller of tales, something of a conman and a bully and an accomplished liar. He bragged about his secret work to his landlady, whom he seduced. He was sent to the Tower of London for a time because of his suspicious behaviour in the Babington affair. As we know, he gossiped that the cause of Walsingham's urinary illness was a disease he had contracted from a French prostitute. Poley was cunning, mercurial and dangerously persuasive. But perhaps those were precisely the skills his masters needed him to employ in their secret work. Certainly Sir Robert Cecil kept him on the secret payroll till 1601.

Thomas Phelippes, unlike Poley, floundered in the years after Walsingham's death. He was a man of considerably more ability in secret affairs than Poley, more important by far and in many ways a victim of both his own talents and the wretched political struggles of the 1590s. After 1600, in the service of Sir Robert Cecil, he still possessed the practised dexterity of his early career in Walsingham's household.

But for the great deceiver of Her Majesty's enemies the most painful deception of all was to imagine for himself a future of security and prosperity.

The second great crash came for Phelippes after Elizabeth's death in 1603. The accession of James VI of Scotland as the queen's successor was a disaster for him. He was the only man still living who had played a significant part in sending James's mother, Mary Queen of Scots, to the block. For that alone King James distrusted Phelippes. But the political scene was changing, even if Phelippes was a man of old habits. War was over: in 1604 an Anglo-Spanish peace was negotiated. And yet still (though with Robert Cecil's knowledge) Phelippes kept up a correspondence with Catholic émigrés in the Low Countries. That correspondence was Phelippes's undoing. He was arrested in January 1605 for his association with Hugh Owen, the influential émigré intelligencer, and sent to prison; his books and papers were seized. Within days he sent to Cecil a difficult cipher he had just broken and an urgent plea for help. Clearly Phelippes had angered King James. 'I humbly beseech your lordship [Cecil was now Viscount Cranborne] therefore to prevent His Majesty's further displeasure,' he wrote, 'your gracious consideration of my excuse'. He asked Cecil 'to stand my friend': 'I know the credit your lordship hath to remove vain imaginations from the King's Majesty's mind.'

Phelippes was freed from prison in April 1605, still mistrusted and suspected. Worse was to come less than a year later. Once again because of his contacts with Hugh Owen, Phelippes was caught up in the great tangle of the Gunpowder Plot, the conspiracy in November 1605 by a group of Catholic gentlemen to blow up the chamber of the House of Lords in Westminster Palace and with it King James and his eldest son, the Prince of Wales, at the opening of a parliament. James denounced Hugh Owen for his apparent involvement in the plot. Given his association with Owen, Phelippes was once again sent to prison, this time to the Tower of London. By February 1606 he was desperate, writing to Robert Cecil:

> God and His ministers confound me body and soul if I be to be touched with the least miselling drop of guilt in that foul project and do not detest both the religion and policy which giveth scope to any such devilish and impious actions.

A few months later, still a prisoner, he offered as his defence the tangled unrealities of his secret life: 'The truth is that there never was any real or direct correspondence held with Owen but by a mere stratagem and sleight in the late Queen's time.' Owen's correspondent in England, he said, was an imaginary person.

Phelippes survived the Tower and the Gunpowder treason of 1605. After that, we find only fragments of his life. In 1618 he was involved in a lawsuit over his debt to the crown. Four years later he was once again in prison. The government was still using him to decipher sensitive letters as late as 1625, when he was accused of revealing the contents of one of them for the offer of money. Phelippes wrote to the king's secretary. He was alone in the King's Bench prison. Deprived once again of his papers, he was, he said, exposed to his enemies; he was miserable and without hope. And yet there is still in the letter a spark of anger and a note of bitter resentment for a government which had forgotten his services. He wrote that he could not stand the indignity of prison. He found himself 'without good ground [good reason] thus confined to a doghole without comfort or means to relieve myself and those that depend upon me'. By March 1626 he was dead. In his old age the most prolific spy of Elizabeth's reign was a forgotten and sorry figure who had been left alone with his memories of the real and imaginary characters of his past.

Was the fight worth it? The cost of defending Elizabeth's kingdom was profound. To Protestant Elizabethans their country was a model for Christendom to follow. To their Catholic enemies it was a poisonous pariah state. So many words were used to both defend and excoriate the queen's government, so much energy and effort expended on the keeping and breaking of secrets, so many lives lost in war and on the gallows. For forty years there was religious schism and an apparently endless struggle. For either side the consequence of failure was destruction: the destruction of queen, country and what Protestants called the 'true religion', or for Catholics the triumph of pernicious heresy over the faith, traditions and authority of the Church.

Looked at from the view of Elizabeth's government, probably the balance as it stood in 1603 indicates a profit. It was at least a breaking even. All the instruments of the state, from the use of the rack in the

Tower of London to the sustained deployment of propaganda, allowed Queen Elizabeth to die in her bed at Richmond Palace. It is impossible, of course, to guess what might have happened if Walsingham and Burghley and others had not fought the enemy in the way that they did. The variables of counterfactual history – history as it might have been – are just too many. But at the very beginning of this book I imagined the very scenario that held Elizabeth's advisers in a grip of anxiety. Had the queen been killed by an assassin's bullet, an emergency interregnum government would have done all it could to suppress domestic rebellion and prepare for a Spanish invasion. Surely it could not have survived for long. The queen, determined never to encourage any potential focus for opposition to her rule, had always refused to name her royal successor; there were few plausible candidates for the Privy Council, recast as a Council of State, to choose from. Equally, the Great Armada of 1588 might have succeeded. If the Duke of Parma's troops had been able to land, then with good supply lines and perhaps with the help of defecting militias they could have taken London or at least caused enough of a panic for Elizabeth and her government to leave the city. What would have been the terms of surrender? Would the queen, no queen in the eyes of the Pope, have been put on trial by Catholic Europe? Would the English people have acquiesced in the toppling of an unpopular regime and the formal installation of King Philip of Spain, heir of the house of Lancaster, as King of England?

Of course, none of these things happened. The scenarios are entertainments – exercises of the historical imagination – not facts. We know that no murder plot against Queen Elizabeth was successful and that foreign efforts to invade England failed. But the Elizabethan story was not written in the stars, as Elizabeth's advisers well knew. The narrative might have been so very different. This is why the queen's councillors treated any conspiracy with deadly seriousness. From everything they saw of the world and the operations of divine providence they expected the worst. They felt they knew their enemy, just as they understood the righteous anger of God. Though convinced of the rightness of their cause, they knew that where Spain was strong England was weak.

The plain truth is that Elizabeth Tudor lived to see the seventeenth century, and her country escaped the horrors of religious civil war and invasion against fantastic odds. The price to be paid for this was vigilance and suspicion and the determined suppression of any resistance to Elizabethan rule. It was the politics of raw survival, and it came, for all its achievements, with profound costs. In eliminating Mary Queen of Scots a blow was struck at monarchy; the reverberations would be felt into the seventeenth century. Many perfectly loyal English Catholics were sent to prison or fined, their political allegiance measured by religious faith: the consequences were felt well into the nineteenth century, with a lingering sense of persecution. Some twentieth-century Catholic scholars of Elizabethan England likened the queen's government to a police state. Almost certainly it was not, for it lacked the most modern instruments of coercion. But these were developing. Any state that justifies and defends the use of torture claims for itself special rights over any other consideration.

Many of those men who viewed Elizabeth as a bastard heretic excommunicate, and who sought actively to resist or end her rule, died before she did: Cardinal William Allen in Rome in 1594, Sir Francis Englefield at Valladolid in Spain two years later, Elizabeth's brother monarch King Philip of Spain in 1598. Others survived Elizabeth. Robert Persons's passionate faith in a Catholic restoration for his homeland came to nothing. He died in 1610 in the English College in Rome, where bright young Anthony Munday had met him thirty-one years before. Thomas Morgan, Mary Queen of Scots's busy intelligencer in Paris, had hoped for favour from her son King James. He never received it and died around 1611. However, Morgan's colleague and friend Charles Paget, held to be one of the most dangerous exiles conspiring against Elizabeth's government in the 1580s and 1590s, found in Jacobean England a home, a pardon and royal preferment.

Probably the greatest success of all for Queen Elizabeth's ministers was their tenacity in preserving the continuity of rule and the Protestant religion. Elizabeth's refusal to name her successor or to allow one of her parliaments to make a succession law caused her advisers enormous anxiety, and this only became more pronounced as the 1590s wore on. If James VI of Scotland was to Elizabeth's government the best (or the least worst) of the plausible successors, the queen's enemies had their own candidates. In 1594 Robert Persons published, anonymously, a book called *A Conference about the next succession to the Crown of England*. Persons examined all the possible claims to the English throne. Over that of James VI of Scotland Persons favoured (not surprisingly) the claim of the Infanta Isabella of Castile, daughter of King Philip of Spain. The Infanta was, Persons showed, descended from William the Conqueror, the daughters of Henry II and Henry III of England and John of Gaunt, Duke of Lancaster, the son of Edward III. This was not fanciful speculation by Persons; indeed Elizabeth's government took his work very seriously. Sir Robert Cecil got copies of *A Conference* from Antwerp, Lord Burghley read it in close detail, and the book was heavily suppressed in England.

It was impossible to escape the blunt fact that in Elizabeth the Tudor dynasty had reached its end. For Protestants, there were few places for her succession to go other than to James VI of Scotland. After decades of fighting with all the political and legal means available to deny the claim to the English throne of James's mother, Mary Queen of Scots, Elizabeth allowed James to understand that his succession would not be blocked. In 1601, briefing his ambassadors at Elizabeth's court, the king referred to 'her old promise ... that nothing shall be done by her, in her time, in prejudice of my future right'. In letters to the queen he played the part of her protégé. As early as August 1588 he promised Elizabeth to behave himself 'not as a stranger [foreigner] and foreign prince, but as your natural son and compatriot of your country in all respects'. A Protestant king and an English pensioner, James was always the most likely successor to Elizabeth; yet, as he himself recognized, his accession could never be taken for granted. His mostly smooth climb to the English throne was not without its hitches.

James's most worrying experience was in 1598 when he was accused of involvement in a plot to murder Elizabeth. It was a wild and fantastic claim by an Englishman called Valentine Thomas, who said that James had commissioned him to assassinate the queen. What worried James most was that Elizabeth did not move quickly enough to quash Thomas's allegation. The king was furious; he was also very worried that Thomas's bizarre charge would damage his claim to the English throne. Sir Robert Cecil knew this from George Nicholson, his principal intelligencer and spy in Scotland, whose secret reports made it clear that the Thomas case had reopened for James the old wound of his mother's execution by Elizabeth. The king believed that similar allegations of complicity would be made against him. James was concerned above all with the Act for the Queen's Surety, the statute that, in putting in place a mechanism for the prosecution of anyone who could be proved to have conspired against Elizabeth in favour of a royal successor, had seen his mother go to the block at Fotheringhay Castle. Through his ambassador in England, James was desperate to know that his chances of becoming King of England and Ireland had not been wrecked. He urgently requested an accurate copy of the Act.

In spite of Valentine Thomas, the Stuarts of Scotland had their dynastic victory. Mary Queen of Scots died for her blood claim to Elizabeth's throne. But the fact that King James VI of Scotland was through his mother the great-great-grandson of the first Tudor monarch, Henry VII, meant that he came peaceably to the crown of England. In 1603 the facts were that Queen Elizabeth had failed to produce a legitimate heir to the throne or to make an explicit choice of her successor. Trumped by dynastic happenstance, the long struggle for political survival seemed suddenly to count for nothing.

Yet what was most extraordinary about James's accession to the throne of England and Ireland was that every detail of it was arranged before Elizabeth's death and done so without her knowledge. Old habits of secrecy and dissimulation were hard ones to break. It was Sir Robert Cecil, so accomplished in secret matters, who from 1601 onwards negotiated the succession at the English and Scottish courts. Remarkably, only five men knew who was certain to succeed Elizabeth. One of them was Lord Henry Howard, the subtle and elusive Catholic nobleman who by a miracle had managed to get through the plots of the 1580s without being charged for treason. Of Lord Henry it was once written by one of Lord Burghley's spies: 'his spirit . . . is within no compass of quiet duty'. Sir Robert Cecil recognized in Howard, who became a trusted intermediary with James, a fellow mercurial talent for politics.

So the servants of the Elizabethan state, trained by long experience to govern whatever the crisis or emergency, guarded the continuity of monarchical rule, upon which, significantly, their own power rested. What is more, these extraordinary political negotiations of 1601 were made necessary by the methods and old habits of a controlling and authoritarian royal dynasty. Like her father, Henry VIII, Queen Elizabeth refused to her dying moment to relinquish power. It is a wonderful Tudor paradox: the more tightly monarchs tried to have their own way, the more inventive their advisers became at setting to one side royal whims and prejudices in the interests of continuous, secure government. This, after all, was the birth of the modern state.

There was no more adept a servant of the state than Sir Robert Cecil, of whom Lord Henry Howard wrote: 'upon the multiplicity of doubts his mind would never have been at rest, nor he would have eaten or slept quietly; for nothing makes him confident, but experience of secret trust, and security of intelligence'. This was a habit of mind, a mode of thinking, an essential way of governing: there could be no other means in dangerous times. Or so Sir Robert Cecil – or Lord Burghley or Sir Francis Walsingham – might have said. Secretary Cecil, following the same path as other ministers and royal officials before him, found the safest way to be a secret one.

As well as in the Council chamber, the private apartments of royal palaces, the grand houses of important courtiers and the residences of foreign ambassadors, secrets were kept and lost in taverns and inns, bowling alleys and gardens. Many otherwise unimportant Elizabethans were caught up in matters beyond the common experience. Characters of a skewed brilliance and cunning found in the shadows merchants, tailors, household servants and yeomen – curious meetings of the ordinary and the extraordinary, the innocent and dangerous. They did not play games in an age of carefree romance. Such adventures did not suit the tastes of Elizabeth's advisers, the rectors of seminaries who sent priests to their deaths, or the commissioners who put prisoners on the rack. All around the Tower of London and the gallows at Tyburn everyday life carried on. As the poet W. H. Auden wrote for a modern age of horror:

... even the dreadful martyrdom must run its course
Anyhow in a corner, some untidy spot
Where the dogs go on with their doggy life and the torturer's horse
Scratches its innocent behind on a tree.

What may seem to us terrible about life in the later sixteenth century could be justified at the time, for God, queen, Pope, country or Church. Many of the Elizabethans upon whom we can turn for a time the bright light of investigation quickly enough disappear into the shadows. In going about their business they left small but valuable marks on the historical record. For all the grand aims and objectives of the politicians espionage was, like so much else, transitory. Life carries on; pain passes away; memories eventually heal.

Spying even in the sixteenth century had the glamour of secrecy and technique. Thomas Phelippes wrote of his methods to Sir Robert Cecil. To Phelippes espionage involved manipulating both allies and enemies to pursue the object of deception. Phelippes's friend Francis Bacon wrote: 'The best composition and temperature [temperament] is to have openness in fame and opinion; secrecy in habit; dissimulation in seasonable use; and a power to feign, if there be no remedy.' He might have been describing the perfect spy. Sir Francis Walsingham, Sir Robert Cecil and Phelippes himself (at least when he was at the height of his powers) came near to Bacon's ideal. Few others did. But there again Francis Bacon was ever the theorist, offering perfection in the neatness of an aphorism, with all the unforgiving cleverness and narrow imagination of the Cambridge scholar. There was nothing in Bacon's words of the untidiness of life, the temptations, weaknesses and compromises; he saw little of the unremarkable and the ordinary, of those passing trials in the shaded borderland between loyalty and treachery.

Chronology

1558	(Nov) The Count of Feria's embassy to Queen Mary's court; Feria meets Princess Elizabeth
	(17 Nov) Accession of Elizabeth as Queen of England and Ireland
1559	(Jan–May) Parliament passes Act of Supremacy, making Elizabeth supreme governor of the Church of England, and Act of Uniformity, putting into law a Protestant prayer book
1568	(May) Mary Queen of Scots seeks asylum in England
	(Oct–Dec) Tribunal at York and Westminster examines the Casket Letters
1569	(Dec) The Northern Rising of the earls of Northumberland and Westmorland
1570	(Feb) Pope Pius V excommunicates Queen Elizabeth
1571	(Apr–Aug) The Ridolfi Plot
	Parliament's Treasons Act
1572	(June) Duke of Norfolk executed for treason
	(Aug) Saint Bartholomew's Day massacre in Paris
1579	(Feb) Anthony Munday arrives in Rome
	(July) Charles Sledd arrives in Rome
1580	(May) Sledd arrives in London
	(June) Edmund Campion and Robert Persons enter England
1581	(July) Campion captured
	(Nov) Campion tried
	(Dec) Campion executed
1583	(June) Duke of Guise plans the invasion of England
	(Sept) Charles Paget, alias Mope, arrives secretly in England

(Oct) John Somerville sets out to kill Elizabeth

(Nov) Francis Throckmorton arrested; Lord Paget leaves England secretly

1584   *A True, Sincere, and Modest Defence of English Catholicques*, by William Allen, printed in Rouen

(July) Francis Throckmorton executed for treason; William of Nassau, Prince of Orange assassinated

(Oct) Privy Council subscribes to the Instrument of Association

1585   (Feb) William Parry tried for treason

(Mar) Parry executed; Act for the Queen's Surety

(Dec) Gilbert Gifford leaves Paris for England

1586   (June–Aug) Babington Plot

(July) Mary Queen of Scots composes the 'bloody letter'

(Aug) Gilbert Gifford leaves England secretly for Paris

(Sept) Anthony Babington and his group tried and executed

(Oct) Commission under Act for the Queen's Surety (1585) tries Mary Queen of Scots

1587   (Feb) Queen Elizabeth signs Mary Queen of Scots's death warrant; Mary executed

(July) King Philip of Spain and Pope Sixtus V agree on the Enterprise of England

1588   (July) Philip launches his Great Armada against England

1590   (Apr) Sir Francis Walsingham dies

(May) Lord Burghley conducts an audit of Walsingham's espionage network

1591   (May) John Snowden and John Fixer recruited to spy on William Allen; Thomas Phelippes courted by the Earl of Essex and Francis Bacon

1592   (May) William Sterrell's mission begins

1594   (Jan–Feb) The Lopez Plot; Patrick O'Collun's conspiracy discovered

(June) Roderigo Lopez hanged

(Aug) Edmund Yorke's plot discovered

1596   (early) Thomas Phelippes goes to prison

1600   (Apr) Phelippes makes an offer of service to Sir Robert Cecil

1601   (summer) Cecil begins a secret correspondence with James VI of Scotland concerning the English succession

1603   (24 Mar) Queen Elizabeth dies at Richmond Palace; James VI of Scotland succeeds her as King of England and Ireland

References and Abbreviations

Two excellent guides to manuscript and printed sources for the sixteenth century are Peter Beal, *A Dictionary of English Manuscript Terminology 1450–2000* (Oxford: Oxford University Press, 2008) and Ronald B. McKerrow, *An Introduction to Bibliography for Literary Students*, with an introduction by David McKitterick (Winchester: St Paul's Bibliographies, 1994).

Manuscripts are cited by the call numbers in the relevant archive, record office or library. In citing manuscripts or printed books, the following abbreviations are used in the Notes and the Select Bibliography.

APC	*Acts of the Privy Council of England*, ed. J. R. Dasent et al., new series, 46 vols. (London: Her Majesty's Stationery Office, 1890–1964)
BL	British Library, London
Bodleian	Bodleian Library, Oxford
CP	Cecil Papers, Hatfield House, Hertfordshire
CS	Camden Society, London
CUL	Cambridge University Library
f./ff.	folio/s
MS/S	Manuscript/s
NS	New Style (the Gregorian calendar)
ODNB	*Oxford Dictionary of National Biography*, ed. H. C. G. Matthew and Brian Harrison, 60 vols. (Oxford: Oxford University Press, 2004)
OED	*Oxford English Dictionary*
OS	Old Style (the Julian calendar)
PCC	Prerogative Court of Canterbury
PCRS	Publications of the Catholic Record Society, London

sig./sigs.	signature/s
State Trials	*A Complete Collection of State Trials and Proceedings for High Treason*, ed. William Cobbett, T. B. Howell et al., 42 vols. (London: R. Bagshaw et al., 1816–98)
Statutes	*Statutes of the Realm*, ed. A. Luders, T. E. Tomlins, J. Raithby et al., 11 vols. (London: George Eyre and Andrew Strahan, 1810–28)
STC	*A Short-Title Catalogue of Books ... 1475–1640*, ed. W. A. Jackson, F. S. Ferguson and Katharine F. Pantzer, 3 vols. (London: Bibliographical Society, 1986–91)

Manuscripts preserved in the United Kingdom's National Archives at Kew in London are quoted by the call number there in use. The descriptions of the classes referred to are as follows:

PROB 11	Prerogative Court of Canterbury, Registered Copy Wills
SP 12	State Papers, Domestic, Elizabeth I
SP 14	State Papers, Domestic, James I
SP 15	State Papers, Domestic, Addenda
SP 46	State Papers, Supplementary
SP 52	State Papers, Scotland, Elizabeth I
SP 53	State Papers, Mary Queen of Scots (1568–87)
SP 59	State Papers, Border Papers
SP 63	State Papers, Ireland
SP 70	State Papers, Foreign, Elizabeth I (1558–77)
SP 77	State Papers, Foreign, Flanders (from 1585)
SP 78	State Papers, Foreign, France (from 1577)
SP 81	State Papers, Foreign, Germany (States) (from 1577)
SP 83	State Papers, Foreign, Holland and Flanders (1577–84)
SP 84	State Papers, Foreign, Holland (from 1585)
SP 89	State Papers, Foreign, Portugal (from 1577)
SP 94	State Papers, Foreign, Spain (from 1577)
SP 97	State Papers, Foreign, Turkey (from 1577)
SP 98	State Papers, Foreign, Tuscany (from 1582)
SP 101	State Papers, Foreign, News Letters (from 1565)
SP 106	State Papers, Foreign, Ciphers

Notes

DATES AND CALENDARS

The best guide to dates and calendars is *The Handbook of Dates*, eds. C. R. Cheney and Michael Jones (Cambridge: Royal Historical Society, 2000). The paper corrected by Lord Burghley on John Dee's investigation of the Gregorian calendar and the text of 'The opinion of some godly learned mathematicians' on whether New Style dating should be adopted in England are both from Bodleian, MS Don. c.52. See also a memorandum by Burghley, BL Lansdowne MS 39 f. 28r–v. Thomas, Lord Paget's letter to his mother, 2/12 Dec 1583, is SP 12/164/5.

A SECRET HISTORY

Queen Elizabeth's words to parliament on 19 Dec 1601 are from Hartley (1981–95), 281. For descriptions of the 'Ditchley' portrait (NPG 2561) and the 'Armada' portrait see Strong (1969), 1:104–7, 111, and Doran (2003), 230–32. On emergency plans for Elizabeth's government see Collinson (1994a), Collinson (1994b) and Alford (1998), 109–17, app. 2. John Florio's definition of a spy and his work are from Florio (1598), 389. The Geneva Bible of 1560 is *STC* 2093, where Numbers 13:1–2 can be found on f. 67r–v. 'God is English' is from [Aylmer] (1559), sig. P4v. On John Foxe and the account of Princess Elizabeth in Mary's reign see Freeman (2003). On the work of the queen's secretary see Robert Beale's paper from 1592, BL Additional MS 48149 ff. 3v–9v, printed in Read (1925), 1:423–43. The reference to 'The book of secret intelligences', 1590, is from a paper by Sir Francis Walsingham, SP 12/231/56. On code and cipher in the sixteenth century see Richards (1974) and Higenbottam (1975), esp. ch. 10. On couriers and postal systems in Europe see Allen (1972). The best analysis of Beale's papers is, apart from the British Library's catalogue of the Yelverton Manuscripts

(London, 1994), Taviner (2000). On Beale and his career see Basing (1994), Taviner (2000) and Collinson (2011).

CHAPTER 1: TEN DAYS IN NOVEMBER

The Count of Feria's embassy to Queen Mary's court is from Rodríguez-Salgado and Adams (1984). The Act of Succession of 1544 (35 Henry VIII, c. 1) is printed in full in *Statutes*, 3:955–8. See also Levine (1973) and Ives (2008). Mary's position on the royal succession is discussed by Loades (1989). Princess Elizabeth was at Brocket Hall on 28 Oct 1558, when she wrote to an unknown correspondent as 'Your very loving friend Elizabeth' (BL Cotton MS Vespasian F.3 f. 27r). On Elizabeth's stay at Brocket Hall see Rodríguez-Salgado and Adams (1984), 338 note 7. Sir William Cecil's papers from the first hours and days of Elizabeth's accession are SP 12/1/2 (17 Nov 1558); SP 12/1/3 (18 Nov 1558); and BL Cotton MS Caligula E.5 f. 56r. Cecil's meeting with Princess Elizabeth at Somerset House in late Feb or early Mar 1558 is discussed by Alford (2008), 80–81. Elizabeth's first royal proclamation (*STC* 7887) is printed in Hughes and Larkin (1964–9), 2:99–100. Cecil's draft of the Privy Council oath is SP 12/1/2. Elizabeth's words to Cecil and to her nobility are from SP 12/1/7, printed in Marcus, Mueller and Rose (2000), 51–2. The suggestion of Elizabeth's assassination in Mary's reign is from Gardiner (1975), 33, 35, but should be read in the light of Freeman (2003). Elizabeth's speech on finding 'treason in trust', 12 Nov 1586, is [Cecil] (1586), 15. See also Hartley (1981–95), 2:248–60. Elizabeth's poems, the first probably from 1554–5 and the second from about 1565, are printed in Marcus, Mueller and Rose (2000), 46, 132.

CHAPTER 2: THE LION'S MOUTH

The Act of Supremacy (1 Elizabeth I, c. 1) and Act of Uniformity (1 Elizabeth I, c. 2) are printed in *Statutes*, 4:350–58. On the parliament of 1559 see Cross (1969) and Hartley (1981–95), 1:1–51. The paper on fugitives in Louvain, 1571, is SP 15/20/44. The spy who prepared the catalogue of the English Catholic émigré community in France and Italy in 1579 was Charles Sledd: see ch. 4 below. Deteriorating Anglo-Spanish relations in the 1560s are discussed by Parker (1998), ch. 5. On Sir William Cecil's policy paper of 1569 see Alford (1998), 182–5. On Pope Pius V's bull *Regnans in excelsis* (1570) see Pollen (1920), ch. 5, Meyer (1967), ch. 5, and Miola (2007), 486–8. The Treasons Act, 1571 (13 Elizabeth I, c. 1) is printed in *Statutes*, 4:526–8.

See also Bellamy (1979), 62–72. The Act for Surety of the Queen's Person, 1585 (27 Elizabeth I, c. 1) is printed in *Statutes*, 4:704–5. Charles Bailly's inscription and its translation are from Edwards (1968), 29, and Harrison (2004). *A fourme of common prayer*, 27 Oct 1572, is Jugge (1572). On the massacre in Paris see Carroll (2009), ch. 8, and on the city and its people Diefendorf (1991), ch. 1. The letters by Lord Burghley and the Earl of Leicester, both of them to Francis Walsingham, 11 Sep 1572, are BL Cotton MS Vespasian F.6 ff. 148r–v, 149r. Timothy Bright's account of Walsingham's sheltering of Protestants during the massacre is from Foxe (1589). See also Read (1925), 1:219–30, and Digges (1655), 235–40. Walsingham's portrait of *c.* 1585, attributed to John de Critz the Elder, is in the National Portrait Gallery, London (NPG 1807): see Strong (1969), 1:320–32. Walsingham wrote that 'there is less danger in fearing too much than too little' in a letter to Sir William Cecil, 20 Dec 1568, SP12/48/61. 'A prayer to be delivered from our enemies' is from Jugge (1572), sig. B1v. The most recent study of Walsingham is Cooper (2011).

CHAPTER 3: ENGLISH ROMAN LIVES

Anthony Munday described his journey to France and Italy in his dedicatory letter to Munday (1579), [Munday] (1582a), sigs. C7v–D1v, and Munday (1980), 5–17. On the identity used by Anthony Munday at the English College see Kenny (1961–2) and Munday (1980), 20. The best introductions to Elizabethan London and Westminster are by Norden (1593), Stow (1908), Prockter and Taylor (1979), Lobel and Johns (1989), Orlin (2000), Saunders and Schofield (2001) and Schofield (2003). On Paul's Churchyard see Blayney (1990) and Blayney (2000). On Munday's early life see Turner (1928), Thompson (1941), Wright (1959), the introduction to Munday (1980), Hamilton (2005) and *ODNB*. Munday's description of Rome as 'Hell itself' is from Munday (1980), 21. His arrival at the English College is in Munday (1980), 22–31. Robert Persons wrote of Munday and Nowell, though without using their names, in a letter to William Goode, printed in Munday (1980), 108. Munday recounted his conversation with the priest in the garden of the college in Munday (1980), 23–5. The story of Jezebel is from the Old Testament, 2 Kings 9:30–7. Persons's treasonous talk is from [Munday] (1582a), sigs. D3v–D4r, and that of Munday's fellow students, sigs. D2r–v, D5r–v. Munday described his friendship with Luke Kirby in [Munday] (1582c), sig. C1v. The physical description of Kirby is from Talbot (1961), 209. See also [Allen] (1582), sig. B2v. The routine of life in the English College, including its punishments, is from Munday (1980), 35–44. The Elizabethan account of the Spanish inquisition is González de Montes (1569).

The account of the Roman Carnival is from Munday (1980), 95–9. Munday described the churches of Rome in Munday (1980), 45–59. On the politics of the Hospital and English College see Munday (1980), 79–94, Kenny (1961–2), Schofield (2002) and Kenny (2005). Munday's account of the scholars' audience with Pope Gregory XIII is Munday (1980), 91–3. William Allen's defence of the English colleges in Rome and Rheims is [Allen] (1581), quotations at f. 14 and f. 110. Munday's verses on Rome, 1581, are from [Munday] [1581a].

CHAPTER 4: 'JUDAS HIS PARTS'

For Anthony Munday's journey from Rome to England see Kenny (1961–2). Kenny noticed the significance of Knox (1878), 154, which records the arrival at Rheims of a priest, Askew, with one 'Antonius', who left for England a few days later. See Munday (1980), xxi–xxii, and the introductory dedication of Munday (1579). According to 'A general discourse of the Pope's Holiness' devices' by Charles Sledd, Sledd arrived in Rome on 5 July 1579. Sledd's 'Discourse' is BL Additional MS 48029 ff. 122r–142r, Talbot (1961), 193–245. BL Additional MS 48029 is either the original manuscript or close to it. Written on a quire of French paper probably of the 1570s, it may be in Sledd's handwriting, though there is no reliable sample of his hand to compare the manuscript to. Robert Beale, a clerk of the Privy Council from 1572 to 1601, gave Sledd's 'Discourse' the title 'Priests and seminaries beyond the seas'. There is a fair copy of it in Beale's papers, BL Additional MS 48023 ff. 94r–109v. Sledd's narrative for 5 July 1579 to 4 Apr 1580, upon which much of this chapter is based, is BL Additional MS 48029 ff. 132r–140r, Talbot (1961), 214–41. William Allen's reference to 'these Judas his parts' is from [Allen] (1582), sigs. b1v–b2r. Robert Barret was himself a well-travelled spy who in Jan 1581 wrote for Sir Henry Radcliffe an account of his years abroad, SP 12/147/38, SP 12/147/39, SP 12/147/40, and SP 12/147/41. In about 1571, probably at the age of eighteen, he was apprenticed to Henry Smith, a merchant adventurer, who lived in the parish of St Mary le Bow in London. Smith died some time before May 1573, when probate was granted on his will. Barret was taken on by Smith's cousin Philip Smith, a haberdasher, but his apprenticeship was claimed by the Girdlers' Company, and he was placed instead with one Richard Cobbe, whom he later served in Hamburg, Lübeck and Flanders. If Sledd and Barret knew each other in London, it may suggest that Sledd too was a merchant's apprentice. See the will of Henry Smith, PROB 11/55 PCC Peter, and SP 12/147/41. On William Allen, the English College, the mission to England and the Jesuits see Knox (1882),

Ryan (1911), Meyer (1967), ch. 2, Carrafiello (1994), McCoog (1996), chs. 3, 4, Duffy (2002) and Kenny (2005). On Sledd's supposed 'invention' of the conspiracy at Nicholas Morton's house see [Allen] (1582), sig. b1r–v. Sledd's physical descriptions of Gabriel Allen, Thomas Cottam, Humphrey Ely, Robert Johnson, Henry Orton and John Pascall are from BL Additional MS 48029 ff. 127r–128r, Talbot (1961), 207–9. On the journey from Rome to France see Bossy (1964) and more generally Bates (1987). Sledd's narrative of his time in Paris and Rheims, Apr and May 1580, is BL Additional MS 48029 ff. 140r–141v, Talbot (1961), 241–5.

CHAPTER 5: PARIS AND LONDON

William Parry's letter to Lord Burghley, 23 May 1577, is BL Lansdowne MS 25 ff. 125r–126r. On Parry's life and career see Hicks (1948). Parry's letter to Burghley, 7 Apr 1580, is BL Lansdowne MS 31 ff. 2r–v, 3v, and his letter to Lord Burghley from Paris, 1 May 1580, is BL Lansdowne MS 31 ff. 6r–7v. Sledd's activities in London, 16–26 May 1580, are from BL Additional MS 48029 f. 141v, Talbot (1961), 244–5. For Parry's intelligence of June 1580 see his letters to Burghley of 4 June 1580 (SP15/27B/17), 15 June 1580 (BL Additional MS 34079 f. 15r) and 30 June 1580 (CP 161/150). For two reports on the fate of Sir James Fitzmaurice's soldiers see the report to Sir Francis Walsingham, [11] Nov 1580, SP 63/78/27, and Lord Grey's letter to the queen, 12 Nov 1580, SP 63/78/29. Sir Henry Radcliffe's report of activities on the coast of Spain, 10 July 1580, is SP 12/140/10. The key letter from Nicholas Sander to William Allen was that of 6 Nov 1577, of which there are two official copies, SP 12/118/13, and (in the papers of Robert Beale) BL Additional MS 48029 f. 50r. For the context of the letter see Pollen (1891), Veech (1935), ch. 5, and *ODNB*. Lord Burghley's draft proclamation suppressing rumours of invasion, 15 July 1580, is SP 12/140/18, Hughes and Larkin (1964–9), 2:469–71. On the mission to England of Edmund Campion and Robert Persons see Simpson (1896), Pollen (1906), Hicks (1942), McCoog (1996), ch. 4, and McCoog (2007).

CHAPTER 6: HUNTING EDMUND CAMPION

The Marshalsea prison is described in Harrison (2000), 118. On John Hart see Anstruther (1969), 153–5, and Harrison (2000), 193–4. On the movements of Campion and Persons and the objectives of their mission see Pollen (1906), Pollen (1920), ch. 9, Hicks (1942), Meyer (1967), ch. 2, Clanchy (1988), Carrafiello (1994), McCoog (1996), McCoog (2001) and Bossy

(2007). Campion's letter to the Privy Council is printed in Miola (2007), 64–6, Charke (1580) and Hanmer (1581). On Stephen Brinkley's secret printing press see Pollen (1906), 182, Hicks (1942), Southern (1950), 355, and Bennett (1965), 114–21. The dates of imprisonment in the Tower for Thomas Cottam, Robert Johnson, Luke Kirby, Henry Orton and Ralph Sherwin can be found in the Tower bills printed by Harrison (2000), 87–100. On the Tower of London in Elizabeth's reign see Stow (1908), 1:59, and Keay (2001), 57, 59. For the Tower inscriptions see Harrison (2004), 475–500. The answers of Ralph Sherwin to the interrogatories put to him on 12 Nov 1580 are printed in Barker (1582), sig. C1v. On Sherwin see Anstruther (1969), 311–13. John Hart's statement of 31 Dec 1580 is SP 12/144/64. For the faculties granted to Persons and Campion by the Pope see Meyer (1967), 138–43, 486–8. Hart's statement of 31 Dec 1580 was used by Lord Burghley in his defence of the government's prosecution of the priests as traitors, *The execution of Justice* (1583–4): see Kingdon (1965), 17–19. For a description of the rack and other forms of torture and punishment used in the Tower of London see Harrison (2000), 123–30. For an Elizabethan account of the Spanish inquisition see González de Montes (1569), sigs. G2r–G3r, and Kamen (1997). On Thomas Norton and torture see [Allen] (1582), sigs. b2r–b4v, c4v–c5v; Thomas Norton to Sir Francis Walsingham, 27 Mar 1582, SP12/152/72; Kingdon (1965), 44–50 (*STC* 4901); and Graves (1994), ch. 8. William Allen's account of the exchange between John Hart and Thomas Norton is from [Allen] (1582), sig. b4v. To Elizabeth's government torture was necessary in the defence of the realm. In English law torture played no part in the prosecution of crimes, as it did in many countries in Europe that used the code of Roman law. The burden of proof in a Roman law trial was very high, demanding for a conviction either the sworn evidence of two eyewitnesses or the confession of the defendant. This confession could be extracted by torture carried out according to precise and formal rules. English common law demanded nothing like this quality of evidence, and so torture was unnecessary. The torture of prisoners in the Tower of London constituted acts of state protected by the royal prerogative, those powers of a monarch blessed and ordained by God but not limited by law. If torture was thought to be necessary the instruction came from the Crown, mediated through Elizabeth's Privy Council. Elizabeth did not have a prerogative power to torture her subjects as such, but the royal prerogative did allow the queen and her Council to bypass the ordinary processes of the law. The object of threatening a prisoner with torture, or of putting him on the rack and breaking his body if he refused to talk, was simply to discover information. There was no need to force a confession from the prisoner or to make him acknowledge his wrongdoing. This was exploratory torture; the guilt of the man strapped to the rack was already assumed. The official position was that only the guilty were tortured, as Thomas Norton made clear, the innocent left unmolested. Equally, there were no rules, merely methods and conventions which grew up over time, like how a warrant for torture was phrased, who carried it to the lieutenant of the Tower and who should attend the racking chamber. See [Norton] (1583), Jardine (1837), Langbein (1977), esp. 129–30, Heath (1982), chs. 4–6, and Hansen (1991). The most powerful Catholic statement of persecution is [Allen] (1582). The allegations made against William Pittes, probably of late Feb 1581, are SP 12/147/74. On Elizabethan Catholics who were in prison for recusancy see McGrath and Rowe (1991). The quotation by Charke is from Charke (1580), sigs. A2v–A3r, and that of Hanmer is Hanmer (1581), sigs. F1v–F2r. The royal proclamation of 10 Jan 1581 is in Hughes and Larkin (1964–9), 2:481–4, quotation at 481–2 (STC 8127). The Act to Retain the Queen's Majesty's Subjects in Due Obedience (23 Elizabeth I, c. 1), which made it treason to reconcile Elizabeth's subjects to the Catholic Church, is printed in Statutes, 4:657–8. Campion's letter of 1580 to the general of the Society of Jesus, Everard Mercurian, is from [Allen] (1582), sigs. e5r–e7r (quotation at sig. e6r), printed in Miola (2007), 131–5 (quotation at 133). On Campion's Ten Reasons (Rationes decem, STC 4536.5) see Campion (1632), Campion (1914), Simpson (1896), 299–306, and Southern (1950), 356–8. For official answers to Rationes decem see Milward (1978), 57–8. Robert Persons's letter to the rector of the English College in Rome, Alphonsus Agazzari, 16 June 1581, is printed in Hicks (1942), 68–9, Edwards (1995), 50. Maliverey Catilyn's report to Walsingham, 1581, is SP 12/151/5. Stokes Bay is in the Solent near Gosport, between Lee Point and Gilkicker Point. On John Adams and the other priest brought into England, John Chapman, see Anstruther (1969), 1–2, 72–3, who notes that Cox the merchant had a sister in Gloucestershire who stored Campion's books and burned all the heretical ones. For a study of Catholic families who sheltered Catholic priests see McGrath and Rowe (1988–9). Campion's movements in July 1581 are from Simpson (1896), 311–13. The journey of David Jenkins and George Eliot to Lyford is from [Munday] (1582b), sig. B4v. On John Payne see Harrison (2000), 208–9. For George Eliot's submission to the Earl of Leicester see BL Lansdowne MS 33 ff. 145r–149r. On 5 Mar 1581 William Herle wrote to Edmund Cornwall 'that there is about Jesuits and papists at London seven books sowed of late' (SP 12/148/13, quotation at f. 54v). The story of Campion's capture at Lyford Grange was vigorously contested in 1581 and 1582. The first account was by Anthony Munday, writing simply and anonymously as A.M., in July 1581, which was followed a few months later (probably between Aug and Nov 1581) by George Eliot's narrative: [Munday] (1581b) and Eliot (1581). Most but not all of Eliot's first narrative is printed in Harrison (2000), 101–10. The account later given by Eliot and Munday together, when both men had been attacked in print by Catholic writers, is [Munday] (1582b), which seems to have been written in Mar or Apr 1582. See also Hamilton (2005), ch. 2. There are modern accounts of Campion's arrest in Simpson (1896), 307–23, and Reynolds (1980), 118–20. On the plan of Jenkins and Eliot to go to Lyford Grange see Eliot (1581), sigs. B1r–B2v. Eliot's account of Campion's sermon is from Eliot (1581), sig. B2v–B3v. The moment of Campion's discovery by Jenkins is Eliot (1581), sigs. C1r–C2r. On priest-holes generally see Fea (1901). Hodgetts (1989), 13, discusses the priest-hole at Lyford Grange. For Robert Persons's account of Campion's entry into London see Hicks (1942), 91–3. Richard Jones's licence for a pamphlet on the capture of Campion can be found in Arber (1875–94), 2:397. The reference to William Wright's shop is from [Munday] (1581c). The description of Campion's story as a 'marvellous tragedy' is from [Allen] (1582), sig. e1r. Eliot's account of what Campion said to him between Lyford Grange and the Tower is from Eliot (1581), sig. D1r. Eliot hinted at the danger to his life in Eliot (1581), sig. D1r–v. Allen's account of Campion's words to Eliot is [Allen] (1582), sig. d5v.

CHAPTER 7: OUT OF THE SHADOWS

The best accounts of the prisoners in the Tower in 1581 are Harrison (2000) and Harrison (2004). John Collerton's inscription in the Beauchamp Tower is from Harrison (2004), 480. For William Filby's dream see Eliot (1581), sig. C3r, and [Allen] (1582), sig. d5v. The only trustworthy account of Edmund Campion's examination at York House on 26 July 1581 is Colthorpe (1985). The Privy Council's instructions to Sir Owen Hopton, Doctor John Hammond, Robert Beale and Thomas Norton on how to go about questioning Campion, 30 July 1581, can be found in *APC, 1581–2*, 144–5. The texts on loyalty to Elizabeth came from Sander (1571) and Bristow (1574), the latter known popularly as 'Bristow's Motives'. On both these books see Holmes (1982) and Veech (1935). The account of Campion's examination is in Barker (1582), sig. B4r–v. A hostile critique of the Jesuits' and seminary priests' technique of answering questions about their loyalty to the queen is [Munday] (1582a), sig. E4r–v. On Campion's examination of 1 Aug 1581 see Barker (1582), sigs. B1r–B4v, and Simpson (1896). See also Sander (1571) and Bristow (1574). Campion's admissions under interrogation are set out by Simpson (1896), 342–3. A summary paper of Campion's confessions on the Catholic families who had sheltered him, annotated by Lord Burghley, is BL Lansdowne MS 30 ff. 201r–202r. See also Harrison (2000), 45. The four associates of Stephen Brinkley arrested with him and sent to the Tower were John Harris, John Hervey, John Tucker and John Compton, along with John Stonor and William Hartley: Southern (1950), 355–6, and Harrison (2004), 236–7. The Privy Council's letter to Sir Owen Hopton, Doctor John Hammond, Robert Beale and Thomas Norton, 14 Aug 1581, is *APC, 1581–2*, 171–2. See Harrison (2000), 45, for the claim by John Hart that Campion was tortured on 31 Aug 1581. The official account of the first disputation between Campion and his opponents is Nowell, Day and Field (1583), sigs. C1r–F2v. On the disputations in Sep 1581 see Nowell, Day and Field (1583), Miola (2007), 67–71, and Thomas Norton to Lord Burghley, 30 Sep 1581, BL Lansdowne MS 33 f. 150r. The best modern account of the disputations is Holleran (1999), to be read in the light of McCoog (2000). The Privy Council's letter to the commissioners in the Tower of London instructing them to torture and question Campion and other prisoners, 29 Oct 1581, as well as the record of the appearances before the Council of recusant families who had sheltered Campion, are in *APC, 1581–2*, 249. John Hart's reference to Campion's torture on 31 Oct 1581 is in Harrison (2000), 47. The account of the Star Chamber proceedings against William, Lord Vaux of Harrowden, Sir Thomas Tresham and the other habourers of Campion, 15 Nov 1581, is from Petti (1968), 5–9, quotations at 6. On Campion, Vaux and Tresham see BL Lansdowne MS 30 ff. 201r–202r. See also Hodgetts (1989), ch. 1. The priests tried with Campion were James Bosgrave, Thomas Cottam, Luke Kirby, Edward Rishton and Ralph Sherwin and the layman Henry Orton. For the indictments of Campion and other prisoners in the Tower of London see BL Lansdowne MS 33 f. 156r, [Munday] (1582a), sigs. B1r–B2r, *State Trials*, 1:1049, Simpson (1896), 393–4, and Holleran (1999), 208. William Allen's description of Campion's trial as 'The most pitiful practice' is [Allen] (1582), sig. a6v. Printed accounts of Campion's trial can be found in [Munday] (1582a), [Allen] (1582), sigs. a4v–b2r, *State Trials*, 1:1049–72, and Simpson (1896). Campion's words 'come rack, come rope', which are not recorded by Anthony Munday or William Allen, are from the account of the trial in *State Trials*, 1:1062. The claim that Thomas Norton read Sledd's dossier during the trial of Campion and the other priests is by William Allen: 'One notable trick Norton and he [Sir Owen Hopton] played together at this arraignment, [was] when Norton read the book at the bar which was pretended to be Sledd's, and Sledd sworn to the evidence.' [Allen] (1582), sigs. b1r–b2v. Anthony Munday described Sledd's 'Discourse' very accurately but he did not say whether it was read out in court: 'Charles Sledd, who sometime served Master Doctor Morton in Rome, in whose house there was many matters determined, both by Doctor Allen when he came to Rome, and divers other doctors living there in the city, as also divers of the seminary: he likewise understood of the provision for the great day, that it was generally spoken of among the Englishmen, and to be more certain, he kept a journal or book of their daily dealings, noting the day, time, place, and persons, present at their secret conferences, and very much matter hath he justified against them', [Munday] (1582a), sig. E3r. Sledd's 'Discourse' (BL Additional MS 48029) was altered in a number of ways. The name of the gentleman 'appertaining to Sir Francis Walsingham' (f. 126r) has been heavily inked out. The same is true of a name or names in the entry on Robert Persons (f. 128r). The three additions are the name of Edmund Campion (f. 128r) and the word 'paymaster' written twice next to each of the names of John Pascall and Robert Terrill. All additions to the dossier appear to be in the same handwriting. Talbot (1961), 203, 209 missed all of these alterations except for the adding of Campion's name. On the characters of George Eliot, Anthony Munday and Charles Sledd see [Allen] (1582), sigs. a4v–b2v, and [Alfield] (1582), sigs. D1v, D4v–E1v, E3v. The reference to George Eliot as 'Eliot Iscariot' is from SP 12/150/67, a letter written by an unidentified Jesuit and intercepted by Elizabeth's government. A supposedly eyewitness account of the executions of Alexander Briant, Edmund Campion and Ralph Sherwin is [Alfield] (1582), but see also [Allen] (1582). Anthony Munday offered his own narrative of the executions: [Munday] (1582b), sigs. C6r–D3r. Munday's verse is from [Munday] (1582b), sig. D8r. Alfield's verse is from [Alfield] (1582), sig. E2r. William Allen's account of Munday's presence at Tyburn on 1 Dec 1581 is [Allen] (1582), sigs. C1v–C2r. John Hart's letter to Walsingham, 1 Dec 1581, is SP 12/150/80. The case of Oliver Pluckytt is set out in Sir William Fleetwood's letter to Lord Burghley, 13 Jan 1582, BL Lansdowne MS 33 f. 153r–v. The true identity of Robert Wood (or Robert Woodward, or Robert Barnard, or simply Barnard) is very hard to be sure of. Charles Sledd wrote in his dossier of 'Robert Wood, servant to Nicholas Wendon, he is minded for to come for England shortly as himself said to me' (BL Additional MS 48029 f. 124r). In SP 12/151/23, which is a report probably from 1581, probably this same man signed himself Robert Bernard. BL Additional MS 48023 (ff. 110v–111r) is a copy of one of the reports, with a precise facsimile of Barnard's monogram. The copyist has written 'Robert Woodward' next to the monogram. Of course the copyist may have been wrong, and yet (a) the name Robert Woodward is close to Robert Wood of Charles Sledd's intelligence; (b) Sledd's Robert Wood was, like the author of the reports in question, once a servant to Nicholas Wendon; and (c) in May 1582 (SP 12/153/41) the author of the report called Sledd 'his very loving friend' (this last point is the weakest). The letter of Barnard to Walsingham of late Nov 1581, SP 12/155/96, concerns Doctor Henshaw, Jasper Heywood and William Holt. Heywood and Holt, both of whom were Jesuits, arrived at Newcastle upon Tyne in June 1581, from where they travelled to London and on to meet Robert Persons at Harrow. After this meeting the two Jesuits separated but met again in Staffordshire, as Barnard reported to Walsingham. See McCoog (1996), 160–62. The report by Barnard to Walsingham on 5 Jan 1582 is SP 12/147/2. Barnard's career is discussed (though with a few errors of detail) by Read (1925), 2:322–5, 335, 337. The proclamation declaring Jesuit and non-returning seminary priests traitors (STC 8135), 1 Apr 1582, is printed in Hughes and Larkin (1964–9), 2:488–91. Thomas Norton's letter to Walsingham about torture, 27 Mar 1582, is SP 12/152/72. His pamphlet on the torture commissions, [Norton] (1583), is printed in Kingdon (1965), 44–50. The information on books is from Richard Topclyffe's record of the interrogations of William Dean and Edward Osberne, SP 12/152/54. Barnard's report of 19 Apr 1582 is SP 12/153/14, that to Walsingham of 5 May 1582, SP 12/153/38. Barnard's letter to Charles Sledd, 10 May 1582, is SP 12/153/41. Barnard's report to Walsingham, 29 May 1582, is SP 12/153/68.

CHAPTER 8: 'SUNDRY WICKED PLOTS AND MEANS'

On the numbers of priests in England and their punishments and for Campion's 'holy rib' see Eamon Duffy's biography of William Allen in ODNB. Lord Burghley's description of the seminary priests is from Kingdon (1965), 40. Allen's words on the mission ('This is the way') are from [Allen] (1581), f. 110. The outstanding life of Mary Queen of Scots is Guy (2004). On the Ridolfi Plot and its influence on parliament see Edwards (1968), Alford (2008), chs. 12, 13, and Hartley (1981–95), 1:270–418. Two texts survive of Robert Beale's paper on the implications of the massacre in Paris, 1572: Beale's draft is BL Additional MS 48049 ff. 340r–357v; the fair copy is BL Cotton MS Titus F.3 ff. 302r–308v. On Beale's career Taviner (2000) is essential. On the Jesuit proposals for the conversion of Scotland see McCoog (1996), ch. 5. On the Duke of Guise and prospects for the liberation of Mary Queen of Scots and the invasion of England see Carroll (2009), ch. 10. On the carrying of pistols see the act of 1542 concerning crossbows and handguns (33 Henry VIII, c. 6), printed in Statutes, 3:832–5. The Elizabethan proclamations of 1559 and 1579 are in Hughes and Larkin (1964–9), 2:116, 442–5. A proclamation published in December 1594 restricted even further the carrying of dags: Hughes and Larkin (1964–9), 3:141–2. The honest traveller with the case of dags at his saddle-bow is from Harrison (1968), 238. John Doyly's examination of 'divers persons' who heard John Somerville's words spoken against the queen, [?25–26 Oct 1583] , is SP 12/163/23. The Treasons Act of 1571 (13 Elizabeth I, c. 1), the statute by which Somerville was tried, made it treason to 'compass, imagine, invent, devise or intend the death or destruction or any bodily harm tending to death, destruction, maim or wounding of the royal person' of the queen by 'speech, words or sayings'. See also Bellamy (1979), 76. Other key documents in the Somerville case are: Somerville's examination, 28 Oct 1583, SP 12/163/21, SP 12/163/22; Somerville's further examination, 31 Oct 1583, SP 12/163/26, SP 12/163/28; Somerville's confession, after 31 Oct 1583, SP 12/163/4 (misdated 6 Oct 1583); Walsingham's 'Resolution touching the prisoners', SP 12/163/49; papers drawn up for the examination of Somerville's wife, family and servants, SP12/163/47, SP12/163/48; John Popham to Walsingham, 7 Nov 1583, SP12/163/53; Thomas Wylkes to Burghley, the Earl of Leicester and Walsingham, 7 Nov 1583, SP12/163/55; Wylkes to Walsingham, 7 Nov 1583, SP12/163/54; and William Thacker's examination by Francis Mylles and Morrys Pykeryng, 21 Nov 1583, SP12/163/70. The report on the friar in Dunkirk, [?Nov 1584], is SP 12/173/104. The Instrument of an Association, 19 Oct 1584, is SP12/174/10. An exact facsimile of Mary Queen of Scots's subscription to the Association, 5 Jan 1585, in the possession of Robert Beale is BL Additional MS 48027 f. 249r. On the Association, its context and its consequences see Cressy (1982), Collinson (1994a), Collinson (1994b) and Alford (2008), 256–7. Debates on the bill on the queen's surety (or safety) are to be found in Hartley (1981–95), 2:67–193. The Act for Surety of the Queen's Person, 1585 (27 Elizabeth I, c. 1) is printed in *Statutes*, 4:704–5. Burghley's words on the queen's safety are from SP 12/176/30. See, once again, Collinson (1994a) and Collinson (1994b).

CHAPTER 9: THE SECRET LIVES OF WILLIAM PARRY

William Parry to Lord Burghley, 30 June 1580, is CP 161/150. Sir Henry Cobham to Lord Burghley, 7 July 1580, is CP 11/52. Parry to Burghley, 20 July 1580, is SP 15/27B/25. Parry to Burghley, 30 July 1580, is BL Lansdowne MS 31 ff. 18r–v, 19v. A second letter from Parry to Burghley, 30 July 1580, is SP 15/27B/27. Parry to Burghley, 11 Sep 1581, is BL Lansdowne MS 31 ff. 26r–27r. Parry's paper on the indictment against him is BL Lansdowne MS 31 f. 123r–v. The evidence against Parry in the case of Hugh Hare, with Parry's remarks upon it, is BL Lansdowne MS 43 ff. 124r–126r. Elizabeth, Lady Russell to Burghley, 8 Nov 1581, is BL Lansdowne MS 33 f. 203r. Parry's petition to Elizabeth's Privy Council, 17 Dec 1581, is SP 12/150/86. Parry to Burghley, 28 Jan 1582, is BL Lansdowne MS 34 ff. 41r–43v. On Parry's journey to Paris and Lyons see Hicks (1948), 346. Parry to Burghley, 18/28 Jan 1583, is BL Lansdowne MS 40 ff. 55r–v, 56v. On Robert Persons and *De Persecutione Anglicana* (*An epistle of the persecution*) see Milward (1978), nos. 236, 237, and Edwards (1995), 67. Parry to Burghley, 22 Feb/4 Mar 1583, is BL Lansdowne MS 37 ff. 68r–69r. Parry to Burghley, 28 Feb/10 Mar 1583, is BL Lansdowne MS 37 ff. 70r–v, 71v. Thomas Phelippes to Sir Francis Walsingham, Bourges, 19 July 1582, is SP 15/27A/99. On Phelippes's stay in Bourges, see Sir Henry Cobham to Walsingham, 16 July 1582, SP 78/7/130; and Cobham to Walsingham, 26 July 1582, SP 78/7/141. Phelippes to Walsingham, 13 Mar 1583, is SP 15/28/8. On John Bradley in Venice and his knowledge of Parry, *c*. Nov 1583, see SP 12/163/93. The text of Campeggio's letter to the Cardinal of Como, 2/12 Mar 1583, is from Hicks (1948), 347–9. Parry to Burghley, 30 Apr/10 May 1583, is BL Lansdowne MS 39 ff. 128r–129r; Parry to Walsingham, 30 Apr/10 May 1583, is SP 78/9/103. Parry's reference to the danger of his letters going astray is Parry to Walsingham, 17/27 June 1583, SP 78/9/132. The letter of the gentleman of Venice is BL Lansdowne MS 38 ff. 145r–146v, with Parry's comment at f. 146v. Parry to Burghley, 8/18 June 1583, is BL Lansdowne MS 39 f. 138r. See also Parry to Walsingham, 17/27 June 1583, SP 78/9/132. On Salamon Aldred see Hicks (1945). The reference to Aldred by Barnard, 5 May 1582, is SP 12/153/38. Parry to Burghley, 18/28 Aug 1583, is SP 78/10/31. Parry to Burghley, 8/18 Aug 1583, is SP 78/10/26. Parry to Burghley, 17/27 Aug 1583, is SP 78/10/29. Parry to Burghley, 14/24 Oct 1583, is BL Lansdowne MS 39 f. 176r–v.

CHAPTER 10: 'THE ENEMY SLEEPS NOT'

The account of Charles Paget's voyage from Dieppe to Arundel haven and then back again is from the examination of John Halter by Thomas Wylkes and Thomas Norton, 20 Dec 1583, SP 12/164/45. The description of Halter's business as shipmaster is from the examination of Christopher Haines by Robert Beale, 17 Dec 1583, SP 12/164/33. Isham of London, for whom John Halter was working, was perhaps the merchant Henry Isham: see Ramsay (1962). The secret report made for William Allen on the searcher of Arundel, *c*. Sep 1583, is SP 12/162/51. The meeting in Paris convened by the Duke of Guise in June 1583 is set out by Carroll (2009), 249–50. The most important diplomatic dispatches are Castelli to the Cardinal of Como, Paris, 22 Apr/2 May 1583, in Pollen (1922), 169 (Document A), Knox (1882), xlviii, 412–13, Kretzschmar (1892), 161–2; Juan Bautista de Tassis to Philip II, Paris, [24 Apr/4 May 1583], in Pollen (1922), 169–70 (Document B); Como to Castelli, Rome, 13/23 May 1583, in Kretzschmar (1892), 163 and Knox (1882), xlvii–xlviii, 413–14; Como to Castelli, Rome, 20/30 May 1583, in Pollen (1922), 170 (Document C), Knox (1882), 414, and Kretzschmar

(1892), 163–4; Castelli to Como, 1/11 June 1583, in Knox (1882), 415–16;
and Tassis to Philip II, Paris, [14/24 June 1583], in Pollen (1922), 170 (Document E). On Allen's part in invasion planning see Duffy (2002). The Duke of
Guise's physical attributes and character are from Carroll (2009), 185–9. The
duke's plans for the invasion of Scotland and England are discussed by Carroll (2009), ch. 10, and McCoog (1996), ch 5. The strategic position of Spain
in the early 1580s is set out in Parker (1998), 169–73. For a spirited interpretation of these plans of 1581 and 1582 and Charles Paget's part in them,
see Hicks (1964), ch. 1. Paget's letter to Sir Francis Walsingham, 8 Jan 1582,
is SP 15/27A/56. His letter to Walsingham of 6 Apr 1582 is SP 15/27A/68.
Walsingham's letter to Paget, 4 May 1582, is SP 15/27A/79. On the noun and
verb 'mope' and the adjective 'moped' (bewildered, confused, dazed) see
Crystal and Crystal (2002), 286 and *OED*. Dame Margery Throckmorton's
letter to either Francis or Thomas Throckmorton, 9 Oct 1583, is SP 12/163/8.
See also her confession of 5 Dec 1583, SP 12/164/9. Doctor Thomas Fryer of
St Botolph's parish Without Aldersgate was one of nineteen physicians
recorded in the London subsidy records for 1582: Lang (1993), 126
(no. 178). The account of the Throckmorton family is from *ODNB*, Hasler
(1981), 3:494–5, and the will of Sir John Throckmorton (20 May 1580),
PROB 11/62 PCC Arundell (proved 8 Dec 1580). On Castelnau and the
embassy at Salisbury Court see Bossy (2001), 33–4, 84–6. Thomas, Lord
Paget's letter to Charles Paget, 25 Oct 1583, is SP 12/163/18. The search of
Francis Throckmorton's house at Paul's Wharf is from Q.Z. (1584), sigs.
A1v–A2r. See also Bossy (2001), 79–81. The manuscript draft of the official
printed account of the conspiracy, corrected and revised probably by Thomas
Wylkes, is SP 12/171/86, on which see Hicks (1964), 31. In 1582 Francis
Throckmorton was assessed for tax in the parish of which Paul's Wharf was
part: Lang (1993), 274 (no. 368). The story of the casket covered in green
velvet is from the deposition of Throckmorton's servant John Throckmorton,
15 Dec 1583, SP 12/164/9, and Q.Z. (1584), sig. B2r–v. Francis Throckmorton's
friend was John Merydeth, who lodged at the King's Head in Cheapside,
on which see Stow (1908), 1:257, and Lobel and Johns (1989), 78. Lord
Paget's letter to Richard Ensor, 7 Nov 1583, is SP 12/163/52. On the outside
of the packet a member of Walsingham's staff wrote the names of Charles
Paget and Charles Arundel. Lord Paget may have been staying at his mother's
house on Fleet Street, which is referred to in a letter by 'F.V.' to Charles Paget,
20 Dec 1583, SP12/164/47. In the dowager Lady Paget's will (1 Dec 1585)
there is a reference to her 'messuage tenement [i.e. a house and outbuildings]
and garden ... lying and being in the parish of St Dunstan's in the West in
Fleet Street' and 'my messuage and house': PROB 11/72 PCC Rutland
(proved 4 May 1588). William Warde, Lord Paget's solicitor, spoke of 'the

Lord Paget's house in Fleet Street' (14 Dec 1583, SP 12/164/24). The judgement on Lord Henry Howard is by William Herle in a letter to Burghley, [23 Nov 1583], BL Cotton MS Caligula C.8 ff. 204r–206r. Robert Beale's letter to Walsingham concerning the examination of Lord Henry Howard, 9 Nov 1583, is SP 12/163/59. See also Alford (2008), 251–2. On Thomas Randolph's detention of Throckmorton see Bossy (2001), 83, and the examination of Anne Throckmorton, 18 Dec 1583, SP 12/164/41. The account of Throckmorton's meeting with the lawyer is from Q.Z. (1584), sig. B2v. If this visit did take place, then it is just possible that the lawyer was Arden Waferer of Chancery Lane. When Sheriff Spencer searched Waferer's house in Aug 1584, he found, as well as Waferer's wife, three small children and four servants, 'many letters of the Earl of Northumberland, Edward Arden [the father-in-law of John Somerville, accused of plotting to assassinate the queen], [Francis] Throckmorton and divers others'. Waferer explained to Spencer that they were 'only his clients' letters and no others'. Sheriff Spencer's search of Arden Waferer's house on 27 Aug 1584 is reported in SP 12/172/111. William Herle's letter to Lord Burghley from the Bull's Head near the Temple Bar, 15 Nov 1583, is BL Lansdowne MS 39 ff. 190v–191v. On 16 Nov 1583 he wrote to Burghley of Lord Henry Howard's book against prophesyings that was 'conceived by some of good judgment to contain sundry heresies and spices withal of treason'. This was the letter in which Herle wrote that 'the world is full of mischief, for the enemy sleeps not': Herle to Burghley, 16 Nov 1583, BL Lansdowne MS 39 f. 193r. On Herle and his career see Adams (2009). The account of Francis Throckmorton's use of three cards to write secretly to George Throckmorton is from Q.Z. (1584), sig. A2r–v. For the date of George Throckmorton's arrest see Bossy (2001), 87, and BL Harley MS 6035 f. 33r. The official account of Throckmorton's early interrogations by the Privy Council and his torture by commissioners is Q.Z. (1584), sig. A2v. See also Bossy (2001), 87–8, and Hicks (1964), 30–32. On the verb 'pinch' and the adjective 'pinched', and for a number of examples of how Shakespeare used them, see Crystal and Crystal (2002), 328. Walsingham's letter to Wylkes with instructions for Throckmorton's torture, 18 Nov 1583, is SP 12/163/65. See also Read (1925), 2:382–7. Throckmorton's second torture on the rack is described in Q.Z. (1584), sig. A3r. Throckmorton's confession of 20 Nov 1583 is SP 12/165/10. Throckmorton's other confession, probably of 23 Nov 1583, is SP 12/165/10. On the letters alleged to have passed between Sir Francis Englefield and Throckmorton, see Q.Z. (1584), sig. A3r. On Englefield and Throckmorton see Loomie (1963), 41–2. Herle's letter to Burghley, [23 Nov 1583], is BL Cotton MS Caligula C.8 ff. 204r–206r. The information about Lord Paget's departure from London comes from the examination of William Warde by Thomas Wylkes and Thomas Norton,

20 Dec 1583, SP 12/164/46. The account of the party of men at Ferring on 25 Nov 1583 is from the examination of Thomas Barnard of Sussex by William Lewkenor, 12 Dec 1583, SP 12/164/23. Lord Paget's letter to Charles Paget, 25 Oct 1583, is SP 12/163/18. Walsingham's letter to Sir Edward Stafford, 1 Dec 1583, is SP 78/10/95. Throckmorton's confession of 2 Dec 1583, and those confessions of 20 and 23 Nov and 4 Dec 1583, are in SP 12/165/10.

CHAPTER 11: 'A VERY UNADVISED ENTERPRISE'

Thomas, Lord Paget's letters from Paris of 2/12 Dec 1583 are SP 12/164/5 (to his mother and sister) and SP 12/164/6 (to Lord Burghley). Lord Paget's letter to Burghley about the 'continual jars' of living with his wife, 21 Mar 1582, is BL Lansdowne MS 34 ff. 17r, 18v. On the Pagets and Catholic recusancy, see Lord Paget to the Privy Council, 17 Nov 1580, SP 12/144/29; Lord Paget to Sir Francis Walsingham, 10 Jan 1581, SP 12/147/5; Robert Barnard's report to Walsingham on Lady Paget's support for Catholic priests, including Robert Persons, 29 May 1582, SP 12/153/68; and Barnard's intelligence that 'The old Lady Paget sent me £10 on Friday last past to give to four priests', n.d., SP 12/168/31. Stafford's copy of his letter to the queen, 1 Dec 1583, is BL Cotton MS Galba E.6 ff. 183r–186r. His letter to Walsingham, 1 Dec 1583, is SP 78/10/94, BL Cotton MS Galba E.6 ff. 187r–188v. Stafford to Burghley, 2 Dec 1583, is SP 15/28A/43. Stafford to Walsingham, 2 Dec 1583, is SP 15/28A/44. Throckmorton's examination of 4 Dec 1583 is SP 12/165/10. Dame Margery Throckmorton's confession, 5 Dec 1583, is SP 12/164/9. The interrogatories for Lord Henry Howard, n.d., are SP 12/163/39. Stafford's letter informing Walsingham of 'no small ado' caused by Lord Paget and Charles Arundel, 6 Dec 1583, is SP 78/10/98. William Parry's three letters to Walsingham in late Nov and early Dec 1583 are: 26 Nov/6 Dec 1583, SP 15/28A/45; 7/17 Dec 1583, SP 15/28A/46; and 8/18 Dec 1583, SP 15/28A/47. Thomas Lewknor's examinations of Edward Caryll, John Mychell (Caryll's servant) and Thomas Pellet, 9 Dec 1583, are set out in SP 12/164/23. The examination of William Bell, [11 Dec 1583], is SP 12/164/19. Sislye Hopton's confession, 14 Dec 1583, is SP 12/164/27. John Throckmorton's evidence, 15 Dec 1583, is SP 12/164/29. The letter from Thomas Wylkes and Thomas Norton to Walsingham, 15 Dec 1583, is SP12/164/32. The minute of Walsingham's letter to Stafford about the arrest of the Earl of Northumberland, 16 Dec 1583, is SP 78/10/107. Stafford's observations on the Pagets and the exchange of Lord Paget's money are from his letters to Walsingham, 15 Dec and c. 15 Dec 1583, SP 78/10/104 and SP 78/10/106. The examination of Christopher Haines, who talked about John Halter and

Isham of London, 17 Dec 1583, is SP 12/164/33. The interrogatories for Northumberland, 17 Dec 1583, are SP 12/164/36. Walsingham's interrogatories for George More, 18 Dec 1583, are SP 12/164/43, and More's answers to them, 20 Dec 1583, SP 12/164/44. The two intercepted letters to Charles Paget, both dated from London on 17 Dec 1583, are SP 12/164/37 and SP 12/164/47. The examinations of Anne and Mary Throckmorton, 18 Dec 1583, are SP 12/164/41. The examination of William Warde by Thomas Wylkes and Thomas Norton, 20 Dec 1583, is SP 12/164/46. The examination of George Lawe, the Earl of Arundel's servant, 20 Dec 1583, is SP 12/164/45, Pollen and MacMahon (1919), 43–5. Arundel's examination, 24 Dec 1583, is SP 12/164/53, Pollen and MacMahon (1919), 46–8. See also Arundel's letter to the Privy Council, 12 Jan 1584, SP 12/167/18, Pollen and MacMahon (1919), 48–50. Robert Beale's examination of Thomas Fells, footman to the Earl of Northumberland, 9 Jan 1584, is SP 12/167/13. On Northumberland's involvement in the Guise project more generally see Barker [1585b] and Thomas Norton's 'Chain of Treasons', BL Additional MS 48029 ff. 65v–68r. Robert Beale's examination of Lord Henry Howard, Jan 1584, is BL Cotton MS Caligula C.7 ff. 361r–362r. Two letters marked as intercepted are those of Grysseld Waldegrave to Thomas, Lord Paget, 22 Jan 1584, SP 12/167/37; and Lady Anne Lee to Charles Paget, 29 Jan 1584, SP 12/167/51. Sir Edward Stafford's description of Lord Paget and Charles Paget is from his letter to Walsingham, 27 Dec 1583, SP 78/10/53. On Mendoza's dismissal from Elizabeth's court see Jensen (1964), 59–64, and Parker (1998), 171. The estimate of the charges for *The Scout*, 17 Jan 1584, is SP 12/167/32. A copy of William Waad's instructions for his mission to Spain, 15 Jan 1584, is BL Additional MS 48027 ff. 362r–363r. The account of the trial of Francis Throckmorton in the London Guild Hall is by Q.Z. (1584), of which *STC* 24051.5 is a Latin translation. The account of the Earl of Northumberland's suicide and the narrative of the Guise plan for England's invasion are from Barker [1585b]. On Guise see Carroll (2009), chs. 10, 11. The reports on Charles Paget in Aug 1585 and Thomas Throckmorton in Sep 1585 were both by Nicholas Berden: 11–13 Aug 1585 (NS?), SP 15/29/38, SP 15/29/39, Pollen and MacMahon (1919), 79; 30 Sep 1585 (NS?), SP 15/29/45, Pollen and MacMahon (1919), 80–81.

CHAPTER 12: DANGEROUS FRUITS

Hicks (1948) is an excellent guide to the sources; see also Hicks (1964), ch. 3. Parry's account of his correspondence with Cardinal Campeggio and the Cardinal of Como and his meeting with Thomas Morgan is from [Barker]

[1585a], 11–17 (sigs. B3r–C2r). Parry's letters are: to Lord Burghley, Paris, 18/28 Jan 1583, BL Lansdowne MS 40 ff. 55r–v, 56v; to Burghley, Venice, 22 Feb/4 Mar 1583, BL Lansdowne MS 37 ff. 68r–69r; to Burghley, Venice, 28 Feb/10 Mar 1583, BL Lansdowne MS 37 ff. 70r–v, 71v; to Burghley, Lyons, 30 Apr/10 May 1583, BL Lansdowne MS 39 ff. 128r–129r; to Sir Francis Walsingham, Lyons, 30 Apr/10 May 1583, SP 78/9/103; to Walsingham, Lyons, 17/27 June 1583, SP 78/9/132; to Burghley, Lyons, 8/18 June 1583, BL Lansdowne MS 39 f. 138r; to Burghley, Lyons, 8/18 Aug 1583, SP 78/10/26; to Burghley, Lyons, 17/27 Aug 1583, SP 78/10/29; to Walsingham, Paris, 14/24 Oct 1583, SP 78/10/52; to Burghley, Paris, 14/24 Oct 1583, BL Lansdowne MS 39 f. 176r–v; to Thomas Morgan, 22 Feb 1584, SP 15/28A/61; to Burghley, May 1584, BL Lansdowne MS 43 ff. 13r, 14v; to Burghley, 2 Aug 1584, BL Lansdowne MS 43 ff. 26r, 27r–v; and to Burghley, 3 Sep 1584, BL Lansdowne MS 43 ff. 34r, 35v. Robert Cecil to Parry, 30 Aug 1584, is SP 12/172/118. Sir Edward Hoby to Burghley, 1 Oct 1584, is CP 13/61. The English translation of Robert Persons's *De Persecutione Anglicana* (*An epistle of the persecution*) is [Persons] (1582b) and Allen's *Modest Defence* is [Allen] 1584. The best modern edition of Allen's text is Kingdon (1965). Edmund Nevylle's references to Parry, his plot to kill Elizabeth, and Allen's *Modest Defence* are from his confession, 9 Feb 1585, SP 12/176/47. Parry's 'voluntary confession' of 13 Feb 1585, is from [Barker] [1585a], 11–19 (sigs. B3r–C3r). The confessions of Edmund Nevylle in manuscript are: 9 Feb 1585, SP 12/176/47; and 11 Feb 1585, SP 12/176/48. There are interrogatories for Nevylle of 12 Feb 1585, SP 12/176/52. William Crichton's answers to three interrogatories written by Walsingham, 15 Feb 1585, are from SP 12/176/54. Parry's letter to Burghley and the Earl of Leicester, 18 Feb 1585, is in [Barker] [1585a], 21–2 (sig. C4r–v). William Crichton's statement for Walsingham on his knowledge of Parry, 20 Feb 1585, is in [Barker] [1585a], 23–4 (sig. D1r–v). Parry's statement on the whereabouts of his letter from the Cardinal of Como of 20/30 Jan 1584, is [Barker] [1585a], 24 (sig. D1v), and the letter itself BL Lansdowne MS 96 f. 48r, which is printed in English translation in [Barker] [1585a], 25–6 (sig. D2r–v). William Crichton's account of Parry and his plot, from 1611, is in Pollen (1922), 165–6. Parry's letter to Charles Paget, 22 Feb 1584, is SP 12/168/23. Nevylle had lodgings in the Whitefriars, between Fleet Street and the River Thames (Nevylle's confession, 9 Feb 1585, SP 12/176/47), but Nevylle said Parry visited him a second time 'at my [Nevylle's] lodging in Hernes rents in Holborn' ([Barker] [1585a], 8 (sig. B1v)). It was here, coincidentally, that the later conspirator Anthony Babington would lodge in May 1586, 'in Hernes rents in Lincoln's Inn field' (SP 12/192/71). On Parry in the House of Commons in 1584 see Hasler (1981), 3:180–4, and Hartley (1981–95), 2:158–60.

Parry's letter to the queen of 14 Feb 1585 is BL Lansdowne MS 43 ff. 117r–118r, printed in a carefully redacted form in [Barker] [1585a], 19–20 (sig. C3r–v). Parry's letter to Burghley and Leicester, 18 Feb 1585, is from [Barker] [1585a], 21–22 (sig. C4r–v). Parry's reference in his trial to his 'rare, singular and unnatural' cause is from [Barker] [1585a], 32 (sig. E1v). Burghley's letter to Walsingham on the printing of the facts of Parry's case, 1 Mar 1585, is SP 12/177/1. See also Burghley to Walsingham, 4 Mar 1585, SP 12/177/4; and Attorney-General John Popham to Walsingham, 10 Mar 1585, SP 12/177/11. There is a copy of the warrant for Parry's execution in BL Lansdowne MS 43 f. 125r. The quotations on Parry's character and family are from [Barker] [1585a], 40 (sig. F1v). The public prayers on Parry's treason, for the diocese of Winchester, are Newberie [1585]. Parry's last words are from Hicks (1948), 357.

CHAPTER 13: ALIAS CORNELYS

On Thomas Morgan see William Parry in [Barker] [1585a], 13 (sig. B4r), and Hicks (1964). Sir Edward Stafford's letter about the Catholic exiles in Paris, 2 Jan 1586, is SP 78/15/2. On the exiles' quarrels see also [Nicholas Berden] to Sir Francis Walsingham, [6/16] Dec 1585, SP 15/29/55, and [Berden] to Walsingham, [2/12] Jan 1586, SP 15/29/85. Thomas Phelippes's decipher of Morgan's letter recommending Gilbert Gifford to Mary Queen of Scots, 5/15 Oct 1585, is SP 53/16/50. Another decipher is CP 163/121–22, Murdin (1759), 454. Charles Sledd's reference to 'Gilbarte Gifforde' as a scholar in the English College in Rome is Talbot (1961), 198. On Gifford's career in William Allen's seminary see Knox (1878). For a good introduction to Nicholas Berden's reports (though with some misreadings and inaccuracies) see Pollen and MacMahon (1919), 66–93. See also Read (1925), 2:315–16, 331–5, 415–19. Berden used the alias of Thomas Rogers: for a confusion of the two see Pollen (1922), xlii, and Read (1925), 2:415. On the intelligence work of Sir Horatio Palavicino, see Stone (1956), ch. 6. Berden wrote to Walsingham in late Apr or early May 1586 (SP 12/187/81): 'I was always persuaded by Signor Palavicino to get the credit of all the foresaid affairs [i.e. of English Catholic exiles] into my hands the better to serve your honour with their whole practices and intentions, for the gaining whereof I have used all diligence and industry, by which means I hope your honour shall be served to your full content.' Berden's report to Walsingham, [18/28] Dec 1585, is SP 15/29/62, printed (without Phelippes's abstract) in Pollen and MacMahon (1919), 83–4. Berden's report to Walsingham of [2/12] Jan 1586, is SP 15/29/85, Pollen and MacMahon (1919), 84–5. On Gilbert Gifford's capture see Pollen (1922), li and note. Phelippes's decipher of Morgan to Mary Queen Scots, 18/28 Jan 1586, the letter in which he recommended Robert Poley for service, is SP 53/17/6, of which CP 164/1–6 is a copy, printed in Murdin (1759), 470–81. On Poley see Nicholl (2002), esp. chs. 16, 17. One example of the interception of a cipher letter written by Morgan is Stafford to Walsingham, 29 Dec 1584, CP 163/66, Murdin (1759), 429. Phelippes's letter to Walsingham referring to 'the party', 25 Feb 1586, is SP 12/186/78. On 5/15 Dec 1585 Morgan referred to 'the difficulty for the reviving' of Mary's intelligence: SP 53/16/71; CP 163/126, Murdin (1759), 456. Phelippes's letter to Walsingham from London on his meeting with 'the secret party', Robert Poley and the spies of Richard Young, 19 Mar 1586, is SP 53/17/28. On Poley's service for Morgan and Charles Paget, see Phelippes's decipher of Morgan to Mary Queen of Scots, 31 Mar/10 Apr 1586, SP 53/17/33, and Phelippes's decipher of Paget to the Queen of Scots, 31 Mar/10 Apr 1586, SP 53/17/44. For copies of these letters see CP 164/30–40, Murdin (1759), 481–503. Maliverey Catilyn's paper, to which Phelippes gave the title of 'Catilyn's observations touching corrupt subjects', [May–13 June 1586], is SP 12/190/62. Catilyn wrote from Portsmouth of his 'writing tables' to Walsingham on 25 June 1586, SP 12/190/51, endorsed by Phelippes. On the meaning of 'tables' (or 'table-book') see Beal (2008), 408–9, and Crystal and Crystal (2002), 441. Berden's report on recusants and priests, 23 Apr 1586, is SP 12/188/37. His paper on Charles Paget and other exiles is from Thomas Rogers [Berden] to Walsingham, ?late Apr or early May 1586, SP 12/187/81, of which there is a short summary in Pollen and MacMahon (1919), 85–6. See also Berden's report, 15 May 1586, SP 12/189/22, Pollen and MacMahon (1919), 86–8. The quotation on cipher from Francis Bacon is from Bacon (1605), sig. Qq1r. Gilbert Curll's decipher of the letter he received from Gilbert Gifford, 24 Apr 1586, is SP 53/17/55. There appear to be references to Gilbert Gifford's arrival in France in the letter of Edward Gratley (alias John Foxley), whom Walsingham was trying to recruit as a source of information, to Walsingham, 18/28 May 1586, SP 15/29/110: 'our friend upon his arrival' and 'Master Gifford doth by the delivery of your mind herein . . .' Compare Phelippes writing to Walsingham, 8 July 1586, of the book 'that G.G. [Gilbert Gifford] brought you of Foxley's [Gratley's]': SP 53/18/38, Morris (1874), 218–19. Gratley was a friend of William Gifford, who was also approached by Walsingham in 1586. William was a kinsman of Gilbert, hence Gilbert's visit to France. On William Gifford see Butler and Pollen (1902). Thomas Barnes described his recruitment as a courier by Gilbert Gifford in a confession of Mar 1588, is SP 12/199/86, Pollen (1922), 3–5. See also his letter to Walsingham, 17 Mar 1588, SP 53/21/26. Barnes's letter to Gilbert Curll, [?28 Apr 1586], deciphered by Curll, is CP 164/55, Pollen (1922), 5–7. Curll to Barnes,

[?20 May 1586], is SP 53/17/73, Pollen (1922), 8. Barnes to Mary Queen of Scots, [9 and 10 June 1586], is SP 53/18/6, Pollen (1922), 8–10. Phelippes's draft of points for a letter from Gilbert Gifford to Morgan, 24 May [1586], is SP 12/170/89, Pollen (1922), 101–2. Phelippes's draft of a letter in the name of Barnes to Gilbert Curll, 6/16 June 1586, is SP 53/18/6, Pollen (1922), 10–11. The description of Phelippes by Mary Queen of Scots is from Phelippes's decipher of her letter to Morgan, 27 July 1586, SP 53/18/75. Phelippes noted her smile in his letter to Walsingham, 14 July 1586, SP 53/18/48. On the saying used by Phelippes see Guy (2004), 482. Sir Amias Paulet addressed Phelippes as his 'assured friend' on 29 June 1586, SP 53/18/23, Morris (1874), 214. On Paulet and Phelippes see Pollen (1922), liv. Paulet's letter to Phelippes of 3 June 1586 is SP 53/18/1, Morris (1874), 198. Paulet referred to 'a course' set down by Phelippes to Walsingham, 29 June 1586, SP 53/18/22, Morris (1874), 211–14. For Phelippes's journey to Chartley, see his letter to Walsingham from Stilton, 8 July 1586, SP 53/18/38, Morris (1874), 218–19. Gifford's letter of 7 July 1586 to Phelippes in London is SP 53/18/37, Morris (1874), 216–17, Pollen (1922), 103–5. The letters sent between Walsingham, Paulet and Phelippes in June and July 1586 in SP 53/18 are printed in Morris (1874). See also Pollen (1922), who explains the system of interception, lxi–lxiv. The official account of Francis Throckmorton's trial is Q.Z. (1584). His letter to Queen Elizabeth, with a covering letter by Sir Owen Hopton, 1 June 1584, is SP 12/171/1 and SP 12/171/1.I. Elizabeth's permission for interviews between Francis, Anne and Dame Margery Throckmorton, [June 1584], is SP 12/171/2. On Anthony Babington see Pollen (1922), civ–cvii, ODNB and Weston (1955), 99–101. The will of his father, Henry Babington, is PROB 11/55 PCC Peter (made 5 May 1571, proved 19 Feb 1573). Babington's lodgings in London are noted in Pollen (1922), 52; [?June or July] 1586, SP 12/192/71; 9 Aug 1586, SP 53/19/28; and 12 Aug 1586, SP 53/19/42. Robert Poley's account of his 'first acquaintance' with Babington, [Aug 1586], is SP 53/19/26. On John Ballard see Pollen (1922), lxvi–cix, and Anstruther (1969). The account of Babington's meeting with Ballard in May 1586 is from his confession, 18–20 Aug 1586, BL Additional MS 48027 ff. 296v–297r, Pollen (1922), 52–4.

CHAPTER 14: SLEIGHTS OF HAND

On Thomas Cassie, Thomas Phelippes's servant since probably 1583, see Cassie to Phelippes, Feb 1589, SP 12/222/93. Phelippes's letter to Sir Francis Walsingham, 6 July 1586, is SP 53/18/32. On the work of Arthur Gregory see Pollen (1922), lviii, and Gregory to Sir Robert Cecil, [?Sep] 1596,

SP 12/260/49, in which Gregory referred to a counterfeit which involved preparing new metal (presumably for a seal) and finding both the correct sort of paper and a sample of handwriting. The letter to Phelippes by Gilbert Gifford, writing as Cornelys, 7 July 1586, is SP 53/18/37, Morris (1874), 216–17, Pollen (1922), 103–5. His letter (also signed Cornelys) to Walsingham, 11 July 1586, is SP 53/18/40, Morris (1874), 220–23, Pollen (1922), 105–9. Gifford described his first meeting with John Ballard in Cornelys [Gifford] to Walsingham, 11 July 1586, SP 53/18/40, Morris (1874), 220–23, Pollen (1922), 105–9. Gifford described his second meeting with Ballard in his letter to Walsingham of 12 July 1586, BL Harley MS 286 f. 136r–v, Pollen (1922), 109–11. The official copy of Anthony Babington to Mary Queen of Scots, [6/16] July 1586, is SP 53/19/12, Pollen (1922), 18–23, Windet [1587], sigs. D1r–D2v. On the posting of the letter, see Babington's first confession, BL Additional 48027 f. 300v, Pollen (1922), 63. See also Read (1909), 28–32. The text of Mary's letter to Babington of [17/27] July 1586 is from Pollen (1922), 38–45, quotations at 38, 39, 45. On when and how Mary's letter was composed see Pollen (1922), 26, and Guy (2004), 482–4. Pollen (1922), 35–45, took great care in arranging and collating texts of the 'bloody letter'. Out of a number of texts in SP 53, the best are SP 53/19/12 and SP 53/18/53, though SP 53/18/54 was endorsed by Phelippes. See also Windet [1587], sigs. D3r–E3r, and Read (1909), 33–40. Phelippes's letter to Walsingham of 19 July 1586 is SP 53/18/61, Morris (1874), 234–6. Walsingham's letter to Phelippes, 22 July 1586, is SP 53/18/68, Morris (1874), 245. Gilbert Gifford's letter to Walsingham, 19 or 20 July 1586, is SP 53/19/5. See also Nicholas Berden to Walsingham, 21 July 1586, SP 12/191/23; Francis Mylles to Walsingham, 22 July 1586, SP 53/18/65, SP 53/18/66; Mylles to Walsingham, 23 July 1586, SP 53/18/69, SP 53/18/70; and Mylles to Walsingham, 24 July 1586, SP 53/18/71, SP 53/18/72. Paulet's letter to Walsingham, 29 July 1586, is SP 53/18/89, Morris (1874), 246–7. Paulet to Phelippes, 29 July 1586, is SP 53/18/88, Morris (1874), 246. The postscript in cipher to the 'bloody letter' is SP 53/18/55, endorsed without a date by Thomas Phelippes as 'The postscript of the Scots Queen's letter to Babington'. The postscript is deciphered using the cipher key in SP 12/193/54, Richards (1974), 54–5. See Tytler (1828–43), 8:439–51, Morris (1874), 236–43, Pollen (1922), 26–37, and Read (1925), 3:1–70. On the preparations for Ballard's arrest at the Castle tavern, see Berden to Mylles, [28 July 1586], SP 53/18/82, and Mylles to Walsingham, 29 July 1586, SP 53/18/90. Berden's watcher was 'young Paynter', who may have been Robert Paynter: see William Sterrell to Phelippes, [1594], SP 12/250/61. The Castle tavern is described in Stow (1908), 1:193. The date of Babington's receipt of the 'bloody letter' is from the official copy of Babington to Mary Queen of Scots, 3/13 Aug 1586, SP 53/19/10, Pollen

(1922), 46–7. The cipher alphabet used by Babington and Mary is SP 12/193/54, subscribed to by Babington on 1 Sep 1586 and by Gilbert Curll. A proposed new cipher between Mary and Babington is set out in BL Additional MS 48027 f. 313v. On the serving man in a blue coat see Babington's first confession, 18–20 Aug 1586, BL Additional MS 48027 f. 300v, Pollen (1922), 64. For 'homely' see *OED* and Crystal and Crystal (2002), 225. On blue as a colour for servants' livery see Cunnington and Cunnington (1970), 196. Walsingham's letter to Phelippes, 30 July 1586, is SP 53/18/92. Poley's account of his meeting with Babington on 30 July 1586 is from SP 53/19/26. Babington's recollection of what Poley had said about killing Elizabeth is from his second confession, 20 Aug 1586, BL Additional MS 48027 f. 303r, Pollen (1922), 69. On the deciphering of Mary's letters by Babington and Chidiocke Tycheborne see Babington's second confession, BL Additional MS 48027 f. 304v, Pollen (1922), 75, and Phelippes's examination of Tycheborne, 12 Aug 1586, SP 53/19/42. Poley's account of 31 July and 1 Aug 1586 is from SP 53/19/26. Walsingham's letter to Phelippes ordering the apprehension of Ballard and Babington, 2 Aug 1586, is BL Cotton MS Appendix L f. 140r–v. Phelippes's letter to Walsingham, 2 Aug 1586, is SP 53/19/3.

CHAPTER 15: FRAMING THE LABYRINTH

Thomas Phelippes's report of his near capture of Anthony Babington is from his letter to Sir Francis Walsingham, 3 Aug 1586, SP 53/19/6. Robert Poley's account of his meeting with Babington on 2 Aug 1586 is SP 53/19/26. On those conspirators who had seen Mary Queen of Scots's letter to Babington see Pollen (1922), 75. Walsingham's notes of Gilbert Gifford's disappearance are from his letters to Phelippes, 3 Aug 1586, BL Cotton MS Appendix L ff. 143r–v, 144r, Pollen (1922), 132–3, 135–6. Francis Mylles's report to Walsingham that Babington had moved his lodgings to Bishopsgate Without, 3 Aug 1586, is SP 53/19/4. Poley's conversation and meeting with Babington on the morning of 3 Aug 1586 are from SP 53/19/26. Walsingham's first surviving letter of 3 Aug 1586 is BL Cotton MS Appendix L f. 141r–v, Pollen (1922), 132–3. Phelippes's letter to Walsingham, 3 Aug 1586, is SP 53/19/6. Probably Walsingham's second letter to Phelippes of 3 Aug 1586, is BL Cotton MS Appendix L f. 141r–v, Pollen (1922), 134. Poley's account of his meeting with Walsingham on 3 Aug 1586 is from his narrative, SP 53/19/26. Walsingham's letter to Phelippes on his interview with Poley (probably his third from 3 Aug 1586) is BL Cotton MS Appendix L f. 143r–v, Pollen (1922), 135. Nicholas Berden's report to Mylles on the movements of Babington and his friends, [4 Aug 1586], is SP 53/19/13. Mylles's account of

John Ballard's capture is from his letter to Walsingham, 4 Aug 1586, SP 53/19/14. The summary of the treasons of Ballard and Babington is from the 'breviate' prepared by Edward Barker, a public notary who attended the conspirators' examinations: BL Additional MS 48027 ff. 353r–355v. Babington's letter to Poley, [4 Aug 1586], is BL Lansdowne MS 49 f. 63r. The minute of Walsingham's letter to Queen Elizabeth, [5 Aug 1586], is SP 53/19/17. Robert Southwell's characterization of the Babington Plot is from [Southwell] [1600], 39–40 (sig. C5r–v). Lord Burghley's draft proclamation for the arrest of Babington and Chidiocke Tycheborne, 2 Aug 1586, is BL Lansdowne MS 49 ff. 61r–62v, Hughes and Larkin (1964–9), 2:525–6. See also Walsingham's interrogatories for Mistress Good, 7 Aug 1586, SP 12/192/15; the examination of William Leighe, 9 Aug 1586, SP 53/19/28; the information of Swythune Welles, 9 Aug 1586, SP 12/192/18; and the information of Christopher Dunne, 10 Aug 1586, SP 12/192/21. Phelippes's note on the interrogation of John Savage on 11 Aug 1586 is SP 53/19/38. See also the copy in BL Cotton MS Caligula C.9 ff. 406r–409r. On the capture and imprisonment of Babington and his co-conspirators see Pollen (1922), clxx–clxxiii, and Harrison (2004), 248–52. The texts of Babington's confessions, 18 Aug–8 Sep 1586, are BL Additional MS 48027 ff. 296r–313r (also SP 53/19/91 for 6 Sep 1586), Pollen (1922), 49–97; those of Ballard, 16 and 18 Aug 1586, Pollen (1922), 137–9; and those of John Savage, 8 Aug 1586, SP 53/19/24 (articles), 10 and 11 Aug 1586, BL Cotton MS Caligula C.9 ff. 406r–407v, 408r–409v, SP 53/19/38, SP 53/19/39. See also the confessions of Jane Tycheborne, 10 and 11 Aug 1586, SP 53/19/35, SP 53/19/36; the examination of Peter Blake (or Blague), 11 Aug 1586, SP 53/19/39, SP 53/19/40; Phelippes's articles for Chidiocke Tycheborne, [12 Aug 1586], SP 53/19/37; the confessions of Chidiocke Tycheborne, 12 and 13 Aug 1586, SP 53/19/42, SP 12/192/33; the examination of Thomas Hewes, 13 Aug 1586, SP 12/192/34; Mylles's letter to Walsingham, 13 Aug 1586, SP 53/19/44; the confession of John Chernock, 14 Aug 1586, SP 12/192/14; and the questions put to Babington and Dunne, [?15 Aug 1586], SP 53/19/43. Gilbert Gifford's letters from Paris in Aug and Sep 1586 are: to Phelippes, 15/25 Aug 1586, SP 53/19/45; to Walsingham, 15/25 Aug 1586, SP 53/19/46; and to Walsingham, 3/13 Sep 1586, SP 53/19/82. John Gifford's letter to Phelippes, 14 Sep 1586, is SP 53/19/101. On the efforts of Burghley and Walsingham to gather evidence against the Queen of Scots see Nicasius Yetsweirt to Walsingham, 19 Aug 1586, SP 53/19/47, Morris (1874), 259–61; Yetsweirt to Walsingham, 21 Aug 1586, SP 53/19/50, Morris (1874), 261–3; the attestations by Babington and others of cipher keys, 1, 5 and 6 Sep 1586, SP 12/193/54, Pollen (1922), 139; Claude Nau to the Privy Council, 3 Sep 1586, SP 53/19/78; Walsingham to Phelippes, 4 Sep 1586, SP 53/19/83; Phelippes's notes on the evidence gathered against Mary Queen of Scots, 4 Sep 1586, SP 53/19/84; Phelippes's paper on the privity to conspiracy of Nau and Curll, 4 Sep 1586, SP 53/19/85; Burghley to Sir Christopher Hatton, 4 Sep 1586, Read (1909), 42–4; William Waad to Phelippes, 7 Sep 1586, SP 53/19/94; Walsingham to Phelippes, 9 Sep 1586, SP 53/19/95; Nau's confession, 9 Sep 1586, Pollen (1922), 141–2; Walsingham to Phelippes, 10 Sep 1586, SP 53/19/96; Nau's confession, 21 Sep 1586, Pollen (1922), 144–5; Gilbert Curll's confessions, 21 and 23 Sep 1586, Pollen (1922), 143–4, 146–7. See also three undated papers: Walsingham's note of the names of the confederates, SP 12/192/17; the plan for their arrest, SP 53/18/34; and an inventory of Babington's books, including works by Richard Bristow, Edmund Campion, Robert Persons and Nicholas Sander, BL Lansdowne MS 50 ff. 167r–168r. Elizabeth's conversation with Burghley about the punishment of Babington and his confederates is from Burghley to Hatton, 12 Sep 1586, BL Egerton MS 2124 f. 28r–v, Read (1909), 45–6. See also *State Trials*, 1:1156–8. On the executions of Babington, 20 and 21 Sep 1586, see BL Additional MS 48027 ff. 263r–271v; and BL Harley MS 290 ff. 170r–173v. On the first session of the commission at Fotheringhay Castle see Steuart (1951), Guy (2004), ch. 29, and Alford (2008), chs. 17, 18. On the commission's proceedings in Star Chamber, 25 Oct 1586, see Steuart (1951) and Guy (2004), ch. 29. The court and parliamentary politics of Mary's death warrant are discussed by Alford (2008), ch. 18. On William Davison see Wernham (1931) and *ODNB*.

CHAPTER 16: AN AXE AND AN ARMADA

On reactions in Europe to Mary Queen of Scots's execution and on her phantom will see Parker (1998), 191, and Carroll (2009), 265–6. The paper by William Allen and Robert Persons on King Philip of Spain's claim to the English throne, *c*. Mar 1587, is printed in Hicks (1942), 295–303. Allen's quotation 'We put not our trust in princes' is from [Allen] (1581), f. 110. King Philip's reference from 1559 to the evil taking place in England is from Parker (1998), 148. Sir William Cecil's policy paper of 1569, 'A short memorial', is CP 157/2–7. The quotation by Thomas Hobbes is from *Leviathan* (1651), ch. 13. On the debate over Spanish aggression in Oct 1584 see Alford (2008), 255–6. Burghley wrote other papers on 10 Oct 1584, CP 163/50–4. Walsingham's paper on Spain, *c*. Mar 1585, is SP 12/177/58, discussed by Parker (1998), 175. Spanish policy and planning with the Pope on England is from Parker (1998), 179–82. See also the important essay by Calvar (1990). King Philip's invasion plan of 1586 is from Parker (1998), 182–8. See also Jensen (1988). On William Allen's support for the 'Enterprise of England' see

Duffy (2002) and Knox (1882), lxxv–cviii. On Sir William Stanley see Loomie (1963), ch. 5, and McCoog (1996), 230–3. Allen's pamphlet on Stanley is Allen (1587). On Allen, Spain, and Rome see McCoog (1996), 239–40, and Parker (1998), 191. The memorandum on succession and invasion by Allen and Robert Persons is printed in Hicks (1942), 295–303, and Knox (1882), xcvi–c, 281–6. Rodríguez-Salgado and Adams (1991) discusses the dynastic context of England and Spain in the 1580s. On Count Olivares and Allen see Knox (1882), c–cii. Allen's briefing paper of June 1587 is printed in Hicks (1942), 303–9. On Allen's promotion see Knox (1882), cii–cv. The text of the agreement between Sixtus V and Philip II is printed in Meyer (1967), 520–3, quotation at 522. The English translation is from McCoog (1996), 245. On negotiations between Rome and Philip see also Jensen (1988). The plans of Allen and Olivares for making appointments in the English Church are from Knox (1882), cvi–cvii. Allen's attack on Elizabeth is from [Allen] [1588a] and [Allen] 1588b. On *An Admonition* see McCoog (1996), 246–51, and Duffy (2002). See also Kingdon (1965). Burghley's letter to Walsingham, 12 June 1583, is SP 12/211/15. On intelligence of the Great Armada see Parker (1998), ch. 7. Walsingham's reference to the 'Spanish brag' is from his letter to Burghley, 15 Jan 1586, BL Harley MS 6993 f. 125r–v. On Sir Horatio Palavicino see Stone (1956), ch. 6. On Anthony Standen and his career see Lea (1932) and Paul Hammer's biography in *ODNB*. The main points of a letter to be sent to Standen in Florence, probably Apr or May 1587, are SP 98/1/9. On Stephen Powle see Stern (1992), esp. chs. 4, 5. William Wynter's assessment on the likely success of a Spanish landing is from Wynter to Walsingham, 20 June 1588, SP 12/211/38. Palavicino's letter to Walsingham, 5 June 1588, is SP 12/211/6, discussed by Stone (1956), 21–2. On the actions of Sir Francis Drake, Martin Frobisher and John Hawkins see their biographies in the *ODNB* (by James Kelsey, James McDermott and Basil Morgan). The quotation by Lord Admiral Howard is from McDermott's biography of him in the *ODNB*. On the Armada and weather see Daultrey (1990). The celebratory verse on English victory over the Armada is from Doran (2003), 239. The Duke of Parma's words to Valentine Dale, 18 July 1588, are from Parker (1998), 212. On the political, economic, and social strains of the 1590s see Guy (1995), esp. introduction and chs. 1, 2, 3, 9.

CHAPTER 17: 'GOOD AND PAINFUL LONG SERVICES'

Thomas Barnes's letter to Thomas Phelippes, 12 Mar 1590, is SP 15/31/131. On the work of Barnes and Phelippes see Barnes's confession, 17 Mar 1588, SP 12/199/86, Pollen (1922), 3–5, and his letter to Sir Francis Walsingham, 17 Mar 1588, SP 53/21/26. A report of Barnes in Phelippes's hand, 31 May

1589, is SP 15/31/26. Charles Paget's questionnaire for Barnes, May 1589, is SP 15/31/27. The reply to this paper, written by Phelippes, June 1589, is also in SP 15/31/27. Phelippes's paper on Barnes's reply to Hugh Owen, 23 June 1589, is SP 15/31/32. Phelippes's reflection upon 'the principal point in matter of intelligence' is from his letter to Sir Robert Cecil, 18 Apr 1600, SP 12/274/107. Stephen Phelippes's reference to the meeting between his brother and Barnes, 31 Jan 1602, is SP 12/283/21. Robert Poley's words on Sir Francis Walsingham's disease, spoken about 1586, are from the deposition of his sometime landlord, William Yeomans, 7 Jan 1589, SP 12/222/13. Walsingham's will is PROB 11/75 PCC Drury. On his debts see Read (1925), 3:443–5, Hasler (1981), 3:574, and *ODNB*. Lord Burghley's words on Walsingham's death are from his letter to Filiazzi, 30 June 1590, BL Lansdowne MS 103 f. 194r. William Allen's allegation of the 'Machiavellian' methods practised by Elizabeth's government is from [Allen] (1588b), 23–4 (sigs. B4r–v). For the words spoken by Walsingham at the trial of the Queen of Scots see Alford (2008), 275. On the meanings of 'curious' see *OED* and Crystal and Crystal (2002), 111. Robert Beale's account of Walsingham's system of espionage is from Read (1925), 1:435–6. Phelippes's decipher of Sir Francis Englefield to Doctor Barrett, 24 Jan/3 Feb 1590, is SP 15/31/102. On Walsingham's secret budget see Read (1925), 2:371, and the paper listing warrants paid between Apr 1585 and Dec 1589, SP 12/229/49. The reference to 'The book of secret intelligences' is from Walsingham's 'A memorial of things delivered out of my custody', SP 12/231/56. Burghley's paper of the 'Names of intelligencers', Apr 1590, is SP 101/90 stamped f. 84r. The accounts of Henri Chasteau-Martin, Edmund Palmer and Edward James, as well as the references to the wife of Master Roures, June 1590, are from SP 78/21 stamped f. 243r. For the exchange rate between Spain and England see Loomie (1963), app. 3. See also Palmer to Walsingham, 31 Mar/10 Apr 1590, SP 78/21 stamped ff. 142r–143r, and Palmer to Walsingham, 13/23 Apr 1590, SP 78/21 stamped ff. 169r–171r. The 'true copy' of Walsingham's letter to Edward James, dated 28 Mar 1590 (or 18/28 Mar 1590), is SP 78/21 stamped ff. 138r–v, 139v. On Chasteau-Martin and the audit conducted by Burghley and Heneage see Hammer (1999), 154–5. Burghley's memorial on the English Catholic émigrés, 7 Aug 1590, is SP 12/233/31. On Spanish pensions paid to English Catholics see Loomie (1963), app. 3. [Barnes] to [Phelippes], 31 May/10 June 1590, is SP 15/31/145. William Phelippes's will (1 May 1590) is PROB 11/77 PCC Sainberbe (5 Feb 1591). Phelippes's reference to 'the Queen's privity' is from Phelippes to Sir Robert Cecil, 18 Apr 1600, SP 12/274/107. Phelippes's essay on 'Present perils of the realm for Master Vice-chamberlain [prob. Sir Thomas Heneage]', n.d., is SP 12/201/61. William Sterrell to Thomas Phelippes, 18 Apr 1591, is SP 12/238/125. On Sterrell, Phelippes, the Earl of Essex and 'matters of intelligence' see Hammer (1999), ch. 5. Sterrell's letter to Phelippes about a meeting with Essex, [Apr 1591], is SP 12/238/137. See also Sterrell to Phelippes, [?15 Apr 1591], SP 12/238/119. Francis Bacon to Phelippes, [?Apr 1591], is SP 12/238/138. Burghley's letter to Phelippes concerning the packet sent from Dieppe, 5 June 1593, is SP 12/245/27.

CHAPTER 18: PLATFORMS AND PASSPORTS

Lord Burghley's quotation on service to the queen is from his letter to Sir Robert Cecil, 10 July 1598, CUL MS Ee.3.56 no. 138. On John Fixer and John Cecil alias John Snowden see Anstruther (1969), 63–8, 118. The description of Fixer is from a note of seminary priests signed by Richard Young, c. 1591, SP 12/229/78. The reference to Burghley's house is from Snowden to Sir Robert Cecil, 4 June 1591, SP 12/239/12. Snowden's statement, 21 May 1591, is SP 12/238/160. Fixer's statement of the same date is SP 12/238/162. The details of Robert Persons's courier system are from Snowden's second statement, 22 May 1591, SP 12/238/167. See also Edwards (1995), ch. 9. On Spanish preparations for an invading fleet after the Armada of 1588 see Parker (1998), ch. 10. Burghley's questions for Snowden and Fixer, 22 May 1591, are SP 12/238/165. Snowden's second statement, 22 May 1591, is SP 12/238/167. Fixer's second statement, 22 May 1591, does not obviously match Burghley's questions in SP 12/238/163. Snowden's statement of 23 May 1591 is SP 12/238/168. Snowden's note of his books and papers aboard *The Adulphe*, [23] May 1591, is SP 12/238/169. On the writings of Robert Persons in the early 1590s see Houliston (2001) and *ODNB* and on those of Robert Southwell in the same period see *ODNB* and Brown (1973). Burghley's questions of [25] May 1591 are SP 12/238/178. Snowden's statement of 25 May 1591 is SP12/238/179. Snowden's letter to Burghley, 26 May 1591, is SP 12/238/180. His list of priests, [26 May] 1591, is SP 12/238/181. Sir Robert Cecil's letter to Snowden, 1 June 1591, is SP 12/239/3. See also Cecil's letter to Burghley, 2 June 1591, CP 168/25. Snowden to Cecil, 4 June 1591, is SP 12/239/12. Snowden to Cecil, 12 June 1591, is SP 12/239/26. Snowden to Cecil, 20 June 1591, is SP 12/239/46. Snowden to Cecil, 3 July 1591, is SP 12/239/78. [Persons] to Doctor Barret, 28 Oct/7 Nov 1590, is CP 167/113, noted in an undated summary of intercepted letters, SP 15/31/167. Persons to John Cecil and John Fixer, 3/13 Apr 1591, is CP 168/13. Snowden to Sir Robert Cecil, 7 July 1591, is SP 12/239/87. Snowden to Cardinal Allen, 2 Oct 1592, is SP 52/50 ff. 104v–105r, printed in Anstruther (1969). Snowden to Cecil, [?30 Dec 1595], is SP 12/155/22. See also Snowden to Cecil, n.d., SP 12/239/88. On the allegations made against Cecil alias Snowden by the Jesuit William Crichton see Anstruther (1969). On suspicions about Cecil alias Snowden in May 1597 see Petti (1959), 254–5. See also Snowden to Cecil, 14 Feb 1594, CP 169/37.

CHAPTER 19: THE FALL AND RISE OF
THOMAS PHELIPPES

The principal sources are: Sterrell to Phelippes, [?1 May] 1592, SP 12/242/3; Phelippes to the Earl of Essex, 30 May 1592, SP 12/242/33; Sterrell to Phelippes, [May] 1592, SP 12/242/37; Sterrell to Phelippes, 21 June 1592, SP 12/242/53; Sterrell to Phelippes, 26 Nov 1592, SP 12/243/66; Sterrell to Phelippes, 2 Jan [1593], SP 12/241/2; Sterrell to Phelippes, 15 Jan 1593, SP 12/244/15; Essex to Phelippes, June 1593, SP 12/245/40, on which see Hammer (1999), 156; Phelippes to Sterrell, 5 July 1593, SP 12/245/50; Sterrell to Phelippes, [?July] 1593, SP 12/246/61; Sterrell to Phelippes, [?23 July 1593], SP 12/255/52; Francis Bacon to Phelippes, 14 Aug 1592, SP 12/242/106; Lord Buckhurst to Phelippes, 8 Sep 1593, SP 12/245/92; Buckhurst to Phelippes, 10 Sep 1593, SP 12/245/93; Bacon to Phelippes, 15 Sep 1592, is SP 12/243/13. Essex's letter to Phelippes, SP 12/246/60, was endorsed by Phelippes as '93', but its context better fits Bacon's letter of 15 Sep 1592. The report on Reinold Bisley, endorsed by Thomas Phelippes, is SP 12/240/144. Phelippes's copy of the report on Bisley is SP 12/243/94. On bowling alleys in London see Salgado (1977), 38–9, and Judges (1965). The phrase 'in one's buttons', meaning very plain or easy to see, is from Crystal and Crystal (2000), 60. On Bisley as Buckhurst's agent see his letter to Buckhurst of 7 Apr 1592, SP 12/241/118. See also Richard Verstegan's report of Bisley's capture by Buckhurst, 22 Sep/2 Oct 1592, Petti (1959), 75. Phelippes's interrogatories for Bisley, c. 25 July 1592, are SP 12/243/92, and his note of Bisley's examination, 25 July 1592, is SP 12/242/88. On Thomas Cloudesley, 19 Dec 1592, see SP 12/243/91 and SP 12/243/91.I. On Hugh Owen and Sir William Stanley see Loomie (1963), chs. 3, 5, and ODNB. On William Holt see ODNB and McCoog (1996). John Sheppard's receipt for Bisley's diet and lodging in prison, 25 Sep 1593, is SP 12/245/103. On the failure of Sterrell see Phelippes to Essex, 9 Dec 1596, CP 47/6, and Hammer (1999), 162–3. Essex's letter to Phelippes, endorsed by Phelippes June 1593, is SP 12/246/60, on which see Hammer (1999), 156. Sterrell's letter to Phelippes, [1594], is SP 12/250/61. Phelippes to Sir Robert Cecil, 14 April 1600, is SP 12/274/103; and 18 April 1600, SP 12/274/107.

CHAPTER 20: POLITICS AND PROGNOSTICATIONS

On the Earl of Essex's intelligence service see Hammer (1999), ch. 5. Lord Burghley's health in the 1590s is discussed in Alford (2008), ch. 20. Burghley's letter to Sir Robert Cecil, 10 Feb 1594, is CUL MS Ee.3.56 no. 17. The prognostications for late 1593 and 1594 are from the almanacs of James Carre (*STC* 428) and Robert Westhawe (*STC* 526). On the Lopez Plot see Dimock (1894), Hammer (1999), 159–63, Green (2003), and Edgar Samuel's biography in *ODNB*. The quotation by Essex is from his letter to Anthony Bacon, 28 Jan 1594, *ODNB*. On Manuel de Andrada, who acted as intermediary between Lopez and Don Bernardino de Mendoza, see Stone (1956), 235, 244, 252–3. Two of Andrada's letters to Mendoza are [Mar] 1590, SP 94/3 stamped f. 138r, and [23 Feb/5 Mar] 1591, SP 12/238/68. Andrada's letters to Lopez are [7/17 May 1591], SP 89/2 stamped f. 130r, and 6/16 July 1591, SP 12/239/83. There is a summary in English of Andrada's letters, [July] 1591, SP 94/4 stamped ff. 25r, 33r. See also Burghley's instructions for Thomas Mylles in questioning Andrada, 3 Aug 1591, SP 12/239/123. Burghley's interrogatories for Andrada, 16 Aug 1591, are SP 12/239/142, SP 12/239/142.II, and SP 12/239/142.III. Andrada's answers to the interrogatories are SP 12/239/150 (18 Aug 1591) and SP 12/240/4 and SP 12/240/5 [4 Sep 1591]. SP 12/247/101 is a copy of Lopez's indictment, [28 Feb] 1594. 'A collection of the circumstances and particular proofs of the treasons as the same were set forth in evidence to the jury', [Feb] 1594, is SP 12/247/102. 'A true report of the detestable treasons committed by Doctor Lopez', [Feb 1594], is SP 12/247/103. William Waad's narrative of the Lopez Plot is BL Additional MS 48029 ff. 147r–184v. See also the account of Lopez's treason in the hand of Burghley's secretary Henry Maynard and corrected by Burghley and Thomas Phelippes, CP 139/41–8. On Giacomo de Franceschi, or 'Jacques', see Loomie (1963), 151–2, 155, 249. See also the confession of Henry Walpole, 13 June 1594, where he is 'Jacomo Francischi' (SP 12/249/12) and the account of the treasons of Patrick O'Collun where he is 'Jacobo de Francisco' (CP 29/74). The sources for the murder plots of O'Collun and Polewheele are: John Annyas's confession, Jan 1594, SP 12/247/33; 'Notes drawn out of the confessions of [William] Polewheele to charge John Annyas and Patrick O'Collun', 4 Feb 1594, SP 12/247/39; O'Collun's confession, 6 Feb 1594, SP 12/247/35; Annyas's confessions, SP 12/247/60 (11 Feb 1594) and SP 12/247/62 (12 Feb 1594); Burghley's order for the apprehension of suspicious persons, 17 Feb 1594, SP 12/247/66; the royal proclamation, 21 Feb 1594, *STC* 8236, Hughes and Larkin (1964–9), 3:134–6; Hugh Cahill's confession, written by Richard Topclyffe, 21 Feb 1594, SP 12/247/78; Polewheele's confession, 21 Feb 1594, SP 12/247/73; notes of O'Collun's examination, 21 Feb 1594, SP 12/247/76 and SP 12/247/77; John Danyell's statement, 21 Feb 1594, SP 12/247/79; Annyas's confession, 22 Feb 1594, SP 12/247/81; Danyell's statement, 25 Feb 1594, SP 12/247/91. On O'Collun and Annyas in the Tower see Harrison (2004), 261–2, 493. Danyell communicated with Burghley through the merchant Thomas Jefferey: [28 July/7 Aug or 7 Aug] 1592, SP 12/242/104. Danyell named Michael Modye (or Moody) as one of the men who intended to blow up the Tower of London. Modye sent letters of intelligence to Burghley in 1591 (18 May, SP 12/238/155; 27 May, SP 12/238/185), though his loyalty as an intelligencer for Elizabeth's government was called into question in Aug 1591 (SP 12/239/148). In 1592 Reinold Bisley reported, probably to Burghley, that Modye had been in England three times that year (7 Apr 1592, SP 12/241/118). Probably most significant of all, however, is Burghley's estimate of Modye in Oct 1591, in which he was minded not to reject Modye's service (Burghley to Sir Thomas Heneage, 12 Oct 1591, CP 20/44). Edmund Yorke's letters are: to William Munning, 21 Mar 1594, SP 12/248/42; to Burghley, 1 July 1591, BL Lansdowne MS 67 f. 114r; to Sir Edward Yorke, 9 June 1594, SP 12/249/8; to Essex, 23 June 1594, SP 12/249/19; and to Sir Edward Yorke, 23 June 1594, SP 12/249/18. The relevant statements and confessions are those of Richard Blundevyll, 15 Apr 1594 (SP 12/248/69) and 17 Apr 1594 (SP 12/248/74); Edmund Yorke, 12 Aug 1594 (SP 12/249/66), 15 Aug 1594 (SP 12/249/79), 20 Aug 1594 (SP 12/249/98), 21 Aug 1594 (SP 12/249/98, SP 12/249/102, SP 12/249/103), 24 Aug 1594 (SP 12/249/112), and 28 Aug 1594 (SP 12/249/125); Henry Young, 30 July 1594 (SP 12/249/41), 12 Aug 1594 (SP 12/249/64), 16 Aug 1594 (SP 12/249/92), 24 Aug 1594 (SP 12/249/114), and his letter to Lord Cobham, 13 Aug 1594 (SP 12/249/74); Richard Williams, 12 Aug 1594 (SP 12/249/68, SP 12/249/91), 15 Aug 1594 (SP 12/249/81), 20 Aug 1594 (SP 12/249/96), 21 Aug 1594 (SP 12/249/108), 27 Aug 1594 (SP 12/249/129) and 28 Aug 1594 (SP 12/249/125). See also the interrogatories put to Yorke, Young and Williams, 14 Aug 1594, SP 12/249/78; and the statement of Anthony Jenkins, 17 Aug 1594, SP 12/249/95. Burghley's summary of Yorke's case, 9 Sep 1594, is CP 28/36–8. On the plot to assassinate Burghley, see Yorke's undated statement, SP 12/249/106. Francis Bacon's quotation on 'the breaking of these fugitive traitors' is from Hammer (1999), 159. The best summary of Sir Robert Cecil's intelligence network after 1596 is Stone (1956), ch. 6 and app. 3. On the armada of 1596 see Wernham (1994), ch. 9. On Cecil's survey of France see Potter (2004). 'The names of the intelligencers', c. 1597, is SP 12/265/134. Thomas Honiman's secret accounts are SP 12/269/30 (25 Oct 1596–26 Sep 1597, 11 Nov 1597–3 Dec 1598) and SP 12/271/91 (1599). 'A memorial of intelligencers in several places' by Cecil, Jan 1598, is SP 12/265/133, printed in Stone (1956), app. 3. The advice by Robert Beale, from 1592, is BL Additional MS 48149 ff. 3v–9v, printed in Read (1925), 1:423–43, quotation at 427. The paper from 1601 on 'Intelligencers abroad' is SP 12/283/72.

CHAPTER 21: ENDS AND BEGINNINGS

Nicholas Berden's letters to Sir Francis Walsingham are: 14 Mar 1588, SP 12/209/19; and 24 Apr 1588, SP 12/209/107. On Gilbert Gifford's years in prison in Paris see Pollen (1922), 118–20. On Munday, Shakespeare and his handwriting, and 'Sir Thomas More' see Munday (1990). See also Hamilton (2005). On Robert Poley and Christopher Marlowe see Nicholl (2002). For a short but essential critique of the evidence of Marlowe's espionage see John Bossy's review of Park Honan's biography of Marlowe in *London Review of Books*, 28:24 (14 Dec 2006). Robert Poley's missions are set out in de Kalb (1933). His codes and cipher are SP 106/2 stamped ff. 73r–75r, printed in Seaton (1931). See also Boas (1928) and de Kalb (1928). The best short study of Thomas Phelippes's later years is Hasler (1981), 3:219–20 (which uses the spelling Phillips). Phelippes's letters are: to Robert Cecil, Viscount Cranborne, 29 Jan 1605 (SP 14/12/42) and 31 Jan 1605 (SP 14/12/44); to Robert Cecil, Earl of Salisbury on the Gunpowder treason, [Feb 1606] (SP 14/18/61) and 4 Feb 1606 (SP 14/18/63). On Phelippes and Hugh Owen see Loomie (1963), 83–9; and to Secretary Conway, 23 Feb 1625, SP 14/184/34. On William Allen see Duffy (2002) and on Englefield see Loomie (1963), ch. 2. On Robert Persons and the English succession see Holmes (1980), Doran (2004) and *ODNB*. On Thomas Morgan and Charles Paget after 1603 see Pollen (1922), ccvi–ccx. On Persons's *Conference about the next succession* see Holmes (1980), Doran (2004) and Lake (2004). King James VI's quotation from 1601 is from Dalrymple (1766), 6; that from 1588 in Allison (2009), 222, in which see ch. 8 more generally. The most important documents on the case of Valentine Thomas are George Nicholson's reports to Sir Robert Cecil, [June 1598], SP 52/62/39, and 1 July 1598, SP 52/62/43; Queen Elizabeth's instructions to Sir William Bowes, 1 July 1598, SP 52/62/46; negotiations between James's ambassador and Elizabeth's Privy Council, 10 Sep 1598, SP 52/63/4; and Nicholas, Master of Elphinstone to David Foulis, 26 Sep 1598, SP 52/63/17. On Thomas see Doran (2004). On the accession of James VI of Scotland to the Tudor throne see Stafford (1940), ch. 9, and Vignaux (2004). Lord Henry Howard's words about Sir Robert Cecil are from Stafford (1940), 257. W. H. Auden's poem is 'Musée des Beaux Arts' (1938). The quotation by Francis Bacon is from his essay 'Of simulation and dissimulation' in Bacon (1632), 31.

Select Bibliography

EARLY PRINTED BOOKS AND PAMPHLETS

[Alfield, Thomas.] 1582. *A true reporte of the death & martyrdome of M. Campion Jesuite and preiste, & M. Sherwin, & M. Bryan preistes, at Tiborne the first of December 1581.* STC 4537. [London: Richard Verstegan.]

[Allen, William.] 1581. *An apologie and true declaration of the Institution and endevours of the two English Colleges, the one in Rome, the other now resident in Rhemes: against certaine sinister informations given up against the same.* STC 369. [Rheims: ?John Fogny.]

—. 1582. *A Briefe Historie of the Glorious Martyrdom of XII. Reverend Priests, executed within these twelvemonethes for confession and defence of the Catholike faith. But under the false pretence of treason.* STC 369.5. [Rheims: John Fogny.]

—. 1584. *A True, Sincere, and Modest Defence of English Catholicques that suffer for their Faith both at home and abroad.* STC 373. [Rouen: Father Persons's press.]

—. 1587. *The copie of a letter written by M. Doctor Allen: concerning the yielding up, of the citie of Daventrie, unto his Catholike Majestie, by Sir William Stanley knight.* STC 370. Antwerp: Joachim Trognaesius.

—. [1588a]. *A Declaration of the Sentence and deposition of Elizabeth, the usurper and pretensed Quene of Englande.* STC 22590. [Antwerp: A. Coninncx.]

—. 1588b. *An Admonition to the nobility and people of England and Ireland concerninge the present warres made for the execution of his Holines Sentence, by the highe and mightie Kinge Catholike of Spaine.* STC 368. [Antwerp: A. Coninncx.]

[Aylmer, John.] 1559. *An harborowe for faithfull and trewe subjectes.* STC 1005. [London: John Day.]

Bacon, Francis. 1605. *The twoo bookes of Francis Bacon. Of the proficience and aduancement of learning, divine and humane.* STC 1164. London: [Thomas Purfoot and Thomas Creede for] Henrie Tomes.

—. 1632. *The Essayes or Counsels, Civill and Morall.* STC 1150. London: John Haviland.

Barker, Christopher. 1582. *A particular declaration or testimony, of the undutifull and traiterous affection borne against her Majestie by Edmond Campion Jesuite, and other condemned Priestes, witnessed by their owne confessions.* STC 4536. London: Christopher Barker.

—. [1585a]. *A True and plaine declaration of the horrible Treasons, practised by William Parry the Traitor, against the Queenes Majestie. The maner of his Arraignment, Conviction and execution, together with the copies of sundry letters of his and others, tending to divers purposes, for the proofes of his Treasons.* STC 19342. London: [Christopher Barker].

—. [1585b]. *A true and Summarie reporte of some part of the Earle of Northumberlands Treasons.* STC 19617.5. [London:] Christopher Barker.

Bristow, Richard. 1574. *A Briefe Treatise of diverse plaine and sure wayes to finde out the truthe in this doubtful and dangerous time of Heresie.* STC 3799. Antwerp: John Fowler.

Campion, Edmund. 1632. *Campion Englished, or A Translation of the Ten Reasons, in which Edmund Campian . . . insisted in his Challenge, to the Universities of Oxford and Cambridge.* STC 4535. [Rouen?]

Cecil, John. [1599.] *A discoverye of the errors committed and injuryes don to his Ma: off Scotlande and nobilitye off the same realme, and John Cecyll pryest and D. off divinitye.* STC 4894. [Paris: G. de la Noue.]

[Cecil, Robert.] 1586. *The copie of a letter to the Right Honourable the Earle of Leycester . . . with a report of certeine petitions and declarations made to the Queenes Majestie at two severall times, from all the lordes and commons lately assembled in Parliament.* STC 6052. London: Christopher Barker.

[Cecil, William, first Baron Burghley.] 1583. *The execution of Justice in England for maintenaunce of publique and Christian peace.* STC 4902. London: [Christopher Barker].

—. 1584. *The execution of Justice in England for maintenaunce of publique and Christian peace.* STC 4903. London: [Christopher Barker.]

Charke, William. 1580. *An answere to a seditious pamphlet lately cast abroad by a Jesuite, with a discoverie of that blasphemous sect.* STC 5005. London: Christopher Barker.

Digges, Dudley, ed. 1655. *The Compleat Ambassador.* London: Thomas Newcomb for Gabriel Bedell and Thomas Collins.

Eliot, George. 1581. *A very true report of the apprehension and taking of that Arche Papist Edmond Campion the Pope his right hand, with three other lewd Jesuite priests, and divers other Laie people, most seditious persons of like sort.* STC 7629. London: Thomas Dawson.

Florio, John. 1598. *A Worlde of Wordes.* STC 11098. London: Arnold Hatfield.

Foxe, John. 1589. *An abridgement of the booke of acts and monumentes of the Church: written by that Reverend Father, Maister John Fox: and now abridged by Timothe Bright, Doctour of Phisicke.* STC 11229. London: John Windet.

González de Montes, Raimundo. 1569. *A discovery and playne Declaration of sundry subtill practises of the Holy Inquisition of Spayne.* Translated by Vincent Skinner. STC 11997. London: John Day.

Hanmer, Meredith. 1581. *The great bragge and challenge of M. Champion a Jesuite, commonlye called Edmunde Campion, latelye arrived in Englande, contayninge nyne articles here severallye laide downe, directed by him to the Lordes of the Counsail.* STC 12745, STC 12745.5. London: Thomas Marsh.

Jugge, Richard. 1572. *A fourme of common prayer to be used, and so commaunded by aucthoritie of the Queenes Majestie, and necessarie for the present tyme and state. 1572. 27. Octob.* STC 16511. London: Richard Jugge.

Munday, Anthony. 1579. *The Mirrour of Mutabilitie.* STC 18276. London: John Allde.

—. [1581a.] [as A.M.] *The true reporte of the prosperous successe which God gave unto our English Souldiours against the forraine bands of our Romaine enemies, lately Arrived, (but soone inough to theyr cost) in Ireland, in the yeare .1580.* STC 17124. London: for Edward White.

—. 1581b. [as A.M.] *A Breefe discourse of the taking of Edmund Campion, the seditious Jesuit, and divers other Papistes, in Barkeshire.* STC 18264. London: for William Wright.

—. 1581c. [as M.S.] *The Araignement, and Execution, of a wilfull and obstinate Traitour, named Everalde Ducket, alias Hauns.* STC 18259.3. London: John Charlewood and Edward White.

—. 1582a. [as A.M.] *A Discoverie of Edmund Campion, and his Confederates, their most horrible and traiterous practises, against her Majesties most royall person, and the Realme.* STC 18270. London: for Edward White.

—. 1582b. [as A.M.] *A breefe Aunswer made unto two seditious Pamphlets, the one printed in French, and the other in English. Contayning a defence* of Edmund Campion and his complices, their moste horrible and unnaturall Treasons, against her Majestie and the Realme. STC 18262. London: John Charlewood.

—. 1582c. [as A.M.] A breefe and true reporte, of the Execution of certaine Traytours at Tiborne, the xxviii. and xxx. dayes of Maye. 1582. STC 18261. London: [John Charlewood] for William Wright.

—. 1582d. The English Romayne Lyfe. STC 18272. London: John Charlewood for Nicholas Ling.

Newberie, Ralfe. [1585]. An order of praier and thankes-giving, for the preservation of the Queenes Majesties life and safetie ... With a short extract of William Parries voluntarie confession, written with his owne hand. STC 16516. London: Ralfe Newberie.

Norden, John. 1593. Speculum Britanniae. The first parte. An historicall, & chorographicall discription of Middlesex. STC 18635. [London: Eliot's Court press.]

[Norton, Thomas.] 1583. A Declaration of the favourable dealing of her Majesties Commissioners appointed for the Examination of certaine Traitours, and of tortures unjustly reported to be done upon them for matters of religion. STC 4901. [London: Christopher Barker.]

Nowell, Alexander, William Day and John Field. 1583. A true report of the Disputation or rather private Conference had in the Tower of London, with Ed. Campion Jesuite. STC 18744, STC 18744.5. London: Christopher Barker.

[Persons, Robert.] 1582a. The first booke of the Christian exercise, appertayning to resolution. STC 19353. [Rouen: Father Persons's press.]

—. 1582b. An epistle of the persecution of Catholickes in Englande. Translated owt of frenche into Englishe and conferred withe the Latyne copie. by. G.T. STC 19406. [Rouen: Father Persons's press.]

Q.Z. 1584. A discoverie of the treasons practised and attempted against the Queenes Majestie and the Realme, by Francis Throckmorton. STC 24050.5. [London: Christopher Barker.] [The Latin translation of A discoverie, STC 24051.5, was printed by Christopher Barker in 1584.]

Sander, Nicholas. 1571. De Visibili Monarchia Ecclesiae. Louvain: John Fowler.

Sixtus V, Pope: see [Allen] [1588a]

[Southwell, Robert.] [1600]. An humble supplication to her majestie. STC 22949.5. n.p.

Windet, John. [1587]. A defence of the honorable sentence and execution of the Queene of Scots. STC 17566.3. London: John Windet.

MODERN PRINTED PRIMARY SOURCES
AND WORKS OF REFERENCE

Anstruther, Godfrey. 1969. *The Seminary Priests: Elizabethan 1558–1603*. Ware and Durham: St Edmund's College and Ushaw College.

Arber, Edward. 1875–94. *A Transcript of the Registers of the Company of Stationers of London, 1554–1640*. 5 vols. London: privately printed.

Beal, Peter. 2008. *A Dictionary of English Manuscript Terminology 1450–2000*. Oxford: Oxford University Press.

Brown, Nancy Pollard, ed. 1973. *Robert Southwell, S.J. Two Letters and Short Rules of a Good Life*. Charlottesville: University Press of Virginia.

Campion, Edmund. 1914. *Ten Reasons*. Translated by J. H. Pollen. London: Manresa Press.

Christie, R. C., ed. 1897. *Letters of Sir Thomas Copley*. Roxburghe Club 130. London: Chiswick Press.

Coppens, Christian, ed. 1993. *Reading in Exile: The Libraries of John Ramridge (d. 1568), Thomas Harding (d. 1572), and Henry Joliffe (d. 1573), Recusants in Louvain*. Cambridge: LP Publications.

Cross, Claire, ed. 1969. *The Royal Supremacy in the Elizabethan Church*. London: Allen and Unwin.

Crystal, David, and Ben Crystal. 2002. *Shakespeare's Words: A Glossary and Language Companion*. London: Penguin.

Dalrymple, David, ed. 1766. *The Secret Correspondence of Sir Robert Cecil with James VI*. Edinburgh: for A. Millar.

Deputy Keeper. 1843. *Fourth Report of the Deputy Keeper of the Public Records*. London: Her Majesty's Stationery Office.

Gardiner, Stephen. 1975. *A Machiavellian Treatise*. Edited and translated by Peter Samuel Donaldson. Cambridge: Cambridge University Press.

Harrison, Brian A., ed. 2000. *A Tudor Journal: The Diary of a Priest in The Tower 1580–1585*. London: St Paul's Publishing.

—, ed. 2004. *The Tower of London Prisoner Book*. Leeds: Royal Armouries.

Harrison, William. 1968. *The Description of England*. Edited by Georges Edelen. Ithaca: Cornell University Press, 1968.

Hartley, T. E., ed. 1981–95. *Proceedings in the Parliaments of Elizabeth I*. 3 vols. Leicester: Leicester University Press.

Hasler, P. W., ed. 1981. *The House of Commons*. 3 vols. History of Parliament Trust. London: Her Majesty's Stationery Office.

Hicks, Leo, ed. 1942. *Letters and Memorials of Father Robert Persons, S.J.* PCRS 39.

Hughes, P. L., and J. F. Larkin, eds. 1964–9. *Tudor Royal Proclamations*. 3 vols. New Haven and London: Yale University Press.

Judges, A. V., ed. 1965. *The Elizabethan Underworld*. London: Routledge and Kegan Paul.

Keay, Anna. 2001. *The Elizabethan Tower of London: The Haiward and Gascoyne Plan of 1597*. London: London Topographical Society.

Kingdon, Robert M., ed. 1965. *The Execution of Justice in England by William Cecil. A True, Sincere, and Modest Defense of English Catholics by William Allen*. Ithaca: Cornell University Press.

Kirk, R. E. G., and E. F. Kirk, eds. 1900–1908. *Returns of Aliens Dwelling in the City and Suburbs of London from the Reign of Henry VIII to That of James I*. 4 vols. Aberdeen: Huguenot Society.

Knox, T. F., ed. 1878. *The First and Second Diaries of the English College, Douai*. London: David Nutt.

—, ed. 1882. *The Letters and Memorials of William Cardinal Allen (1532–1594)*. London: David Nutt.

Lang, R. G., ed. 1993. *Two Tudor Subsidy Assessment Rolls for the City of London: 1541 and 1582*. London: London Record Society.

Lobel, Mary D., and W. H. Johns. 1989. *The City of London From Prehistoric Times to c. 1520*. Oxford: Oxford University Press.

Marcus, Leah S., Janel Mueller and Mary Beth Rose, eds. 2000. *Elizabeth I: Collected Works*. Chicago and London: Chicago University Press.

Milward, Peter. 1978. *Religious Controversies of the Elizabethan Age: A Survey of Printed Sources*. London: Scolar Press.

Miola, Robert S., ed. 2007. *Early Modern Catholicism: An Anthology of Primary Sources*. Oxford: Oxford University Press.

Morris John, ed. 1874. *The Letter-Books of Sir Amias Poulet, Keeper of Mary Queen of Scots*. London: Burns and Oates.

Munday, Anthony. 1980. *The English Roman Life*. Edited by Philip J. Ayres. Oxford: Clarendon Press.

—. 1990. *Sir Thomas More*. Edited by Vittorio Gabrieli and Giorgio Melchiori. Manchester: Manchester University Press.

Murdin, William. 1759. *A Collection of State Papers*. London: William Bowyer.

Petti, Anthony G., ed. 1959. *The Letters and Despatches of Richard Verstegan (c. 1550–1640)*. PCRS 52.

—, ed. 1968. *Recusant Documents from the Ellesmere Manuscripts*. PCRS 60.

Pollen, J. H., ed. 1905. 'Dr Nicholas Sander's Report to Cardinal Moroni'. PCRS *Miscellanea 1*, 1–47.

—, ed. 1906. 'The Memoirs of Father Robert Persons'. PCRS *Miscellanea* 2, 12–218.

—, ed. 1922. *Mary Queen of Scots and the Babington Plot*. Publications of the Scottish Historical Society third series 3. Edinburgh: T. and A. Constable.

—, and W. MacMahon, eds. 1919. *The Venerable Philip Howard Earl of Arundel 1557–1595*. PCRS 21.

Potter, David, ed. 2004. *Foreign Intelligence and Information in Elizabethan England: Two English Treatises on the State of France, 1580–1584*. CS fifth series 25. Cambridge: Cambridge University Press, for the Royal Historical Society.

Prockter, Adrian, and Robert Taylor. 1979. *The A to Z of Elizabethan London*. Introductory notes by John Fisher. London: London Topographical Society.

Ramsay, G. D., ed. 1962. *John Isham, Mercer and Merchant Adventurer*. Northampton: Northamptonshire Record Society.

Read, Conyers, ed. 1909. *The Bardon Papers: Documents Relating to the Imprisonment of Mary Queen of Scots*. CS third series 17. London: Camden Society.

Richards, Sheila R. 1974. *Secret Writing in the Public Records: Henry VIII–George II*. London: Her Majesty's Stationery Office.

Ryan, Patrick, ed. 1911. 'Some Correspondence of Cardinal Allen, 1579–85'. PCRS *Miscellanea* 7, 12–105.

Saunders, Ann, and John Schofield. 2001. *Tudor London: A Map and a View*. London: London Topographical Society.

Steuart, A. Francis, ed. 1951. *Trial of Mary Queen of Scots*. London, Edinburgh and Glasgow: William Hodge and Company.

Stow, John. 1908. *A Survey of London*. Edited by C. L. Kingsford. 2 vols. Oxford: Clarendon Press.

Strong, Roy. 1969. *Tudor and Jacobean Portraits*. 2 vols. London: Her Majesty's Stationery Office.

Talbot, Clare, ed. 1961. *Miscellanea: Recusant Records*. PCRS 53.

Wainewright, John B., ed. 1913. 'Two Lists of Influential Persons Apparently Prepared in the Interests of Mary Queen of Scots, 1574 and 1582'. PCRS *Miscellanea* 8, 86–142.

—, ed. 1926. 'Some Letters and Papers of Nicholas Sander, 1562–1580'. PCRS *Miscellanea* 13, 1–57.

Weston, William. 1955. *The Autobiography of an Elizabethan*. Translated by Philip Caraman. London: Longmans, Green and Co.

MODERN BOOKS, ESSAYS, ARTICLES AND DISSERTATIONS

Adams, Robyn. 2009. 'A Spy on the Payroll? William Herle and the Mid-Elizabethan Polity'. *Historical Research* 82:1–15.

Alford, Stephen. 1998. *The Early Elizabethan Polity: William Cecil and the British Succession Crisis, 1558–1569*. Cambridge: Cambridge University Press.

—. 2008. *Burghley: William Cecil at the Court of Elizabeth I*. New Haven and London: Yale University Press.

Allen, E. John B., 1972. *Post and Courier Service in the Diplomacy of Early Modern Europe*. The Hague: Martinus Nijhoff.

Allen, J., ed. 2005. *The English Hospice in Rome*. Leominster: Gracewing.

Allison, Rayne. 2009. 'A Monarchy of Letters: The Role of Royal Correspondence in English Diplomacy During the Reign of Elizabeth I'. DPhil thesis, University of Oxford.

Basing, Patricia. 1994. 'Robert Beale and the Queen of Scots'. *British Library Journal* 20:65–81.

Bate, Jonathan. 2008. *Soul of the Age: The Life, Mind and World of William Shakespeare*. London: Viking.

Bates, E. S. 1987. *Touring in 1600: A Study in the Development of Travel as a Means of Education*. Introduction by George Bull. London: Century.

Bellamy, John. 1979. *The Tudor Law of Treason: An Introduction*. London: Routledge and Kegan Paul.

Bennett, H. S. 1965. *English Books and Readers 1558 to 1603*. Cambridge: Cambridge University Press.

Blayney, Peter W. M. 1990. *Bookshops in Paul's Cross Churchyard*. London: Bibliographical Society.

—. 2000. 'John Day and the Bookshop That Never Was'. In Orlin (2000).

Boas, F. S. 1928. 'Robert Poley: An Associate of Marlowe'. *Nineteenth Century and After* 104:543–52.

Bossy, John. 1964. 'Rome and the Elizabethan Catholics: A Question of Geography'. *Historical Journal* 7:135–49.

—. 1991. *Giordano Bruno and the Embassy Affair*. New Haven and London: Yale University Press.

—. 2001. *Under the Molehill: An Elizabethan Spy Story*. New Haven and London: Yale University Press.

—. 2007. 'The Heart of Robert Persons'. In McCoog (2007).

Butler, E. C., and J. H. Pollen. 1902. 'Dr William Gifford in 1586'. *The Month* 103:243–58, 349–65.

Calvar, J. 1990. 'Summary-report on the "Nueva colección documental de las hostilidades entre España e Inglaterra (1568–1604)"'. In Gallagher and Cruickshank (1990).

Carrafiello, M. L. 1994. 'English Catholicism and the Jesuit Mission of 1580–1581'. *Historical Journal* 37:761–74.

Carroll, Stuart. 2009. *Martyrs and Murderers: The Guise Family and the Making of Europe*. Oxford: Oxford University Press.

Chambers, E. K. 1951. *The Elizabethan Stage*. 4 vols. Oxford: Clarendon Press.

Clanchy, T. H. 1988. 'The First Generation of English Jesuits 1555–1585'. *Archivum Historicum Societatis Iesu* 57:137–61.

Cleary, J. M. 1966. 'Dr Morys Clynnog's Invasion Projects of 1575–1576'. *Recusant History* 8:300–322.

Collinson, Patrick. 1994a. 'The Elizabethan Exclusion Crisis and the Elizabethan Polity'. *Proceedings of the British Academy* 84:51–92.

—. 1994b. 'The Monarchical Republic of Queen Elizabeth I'. In *Elizabethan Essays*. London and Rio Grande: Hambledon Press.

—. 2009. 'The Politics of Religion and the Religion of Politics in Elizabethan England'. *Historical Research* 82:74–92.

—. 2011. 'Servants and Citizens: Robert Beale and other Elizabethans'. In *This England: Essays on the English Nation and Commonwealth in the Sixteenth Century*. Manchester and New York: Manchester University Press.

Colthorpe, M. 1985. 'Edmund Campion's Alleged Interview with Queen Elizabeth in 1581'. *Recusant History* 17:197–200.

Cooper, John. 2011. *The Queen's Agent: Francis Walsingham at the Court of Elizabeth I*. London: Faber and Faber.

Coppens, Christian, ed. 1999. *Leuven in Books, Books in Leuven*. Louvain: Universitaire Pers Leuven.

Cressy, David. 1982. 'Binding the Nation: The Bonds of Association, 1584 and 1596'. In Guth and McKenna (1982).

Crofts, J. 1967. *Packhorse, Waggon and Post: Land Carriage and Communications under the Tudors and Stuarts*. London and Toronto: Routledge and Kegan Paul and University of Toronto Press.

Cunnington, C. Willett, and Phillis Cunnington. 1970. *Handbook of English Costume in the Sixteenth Century*. London: Faber and Faber.

Daultrey, S. 1990. 'The Weather of Northwest Europe During the Summer and Autumn of 1588'. In Gallagher and Cruickshank (1990).

de Kalb, Eugénie. 1928. 'Robert Poley: An Associate of Marlowe'. *Nineteenth Century and After* 104:715–16. [An addition to Boas (1928).]

—. 1933. 'Robert Poley's Movements as a Messenger of the Court, 1588 to 1601'. *Review of English Studies* 9:13–18.

Diefendorf, Barbara B. 1991. *Beneath the Cross: Catholics and Huguenots in Sixteenth-Century Paris*. New York and Oxford: Oxford University Press.

Dimock, Arthur. 1894. 'The Conspiracy of Dr Lopez'. *English Historical Review* 9:440–72.

Doran, Susan, ed. 2003. *Elizabeth: The Exhibition at the National Maritime Museum*. London: Chatto and Windus.

—. 2004. 'Three Late-Elizabethan Succession Tracts'. In Mayer (2004).

—, and Thomas S. Freeman, eds. 2003. *The Myth of Elizabeth*. Houndmills and New York: Palgrave Macmillan.

Duffy, Eamon. 2002. 'Cardinal William Allen'. In Schofield (2002).

Edwards, Francis. 1968. *The Marvellous Chance: Thomas Howard, Fourth Duke of Norfolk, and the Ridolphi Plot, 1570–1572*. London: Rupert Hart-Davis.

—. 1995. *Robert Persons: The Biography of an Elizabethan Jesuit 1546–1610*. St Louis: Institute of Jesuit Sources.

Fea, Allan. 1901. *Secret Chambers and Hiding-Places*. London: S.H. Bousfield and Co.

Freeman, Thomas S. 2003. 'Providence and Prescription: The Account of Elizabeth in Foxe's "Book of Martyrs"'. In Doran and Freeman (2003).

Gallagher, P., and D. W. Cruickshank, eds. 1990. *God's Obvious Design: Papers for the Spanish Armada Symposium, Sligo, 1988*. London: Tamesis Books.

Graves, Michael A. R. 1994. *Thomas Norton: The Parliament Man*. Oxford and Cambridge: Blackwell.

Green, Dominic. 2003. *The Double Life of Doctor Lopez*. London: Random House.

Griffiths, Paul. 2008. *Lost Londons: Change, Crime, and Control in the Capital City, 1550–1660*. Cambridge: Cambridge University Press.

Guth, DeLloyd J., and J. W. McKenna, eds. 1982. *Tudor Rule and Revolution*. Cambridge: Cambridge University Press.

Guy, John, ed. 1995. *The Reign of Elizabeth I: Court and Culture in the Last Decade*. Cambridge: Cambridge University Press.

—. 2004. *'My Heart is My Own': The Life of Mary Queen of Scots*. London and New York: Fourth Estate.

Hamilton, Donna B. 2005. *Anthony Munday and the Catholics, 1560–1633*. Aldershot and Burlington: Ashgate.

Hammer, Paul E. J. 1999. *The Polarisation of Elizabethan Politics: The Political Career of Robert Devereux, 2nd Earl of Essex, 1585–1597*. Cambridge: Cambridge University Press.

Hansen, Elizabeth. 1991. 'Torture and Truth in Renaissance England'. *Representations* 34:53–84.

Heath, James. 1982. *Torture and English Law: An Administrative and Legal History from the Plantagenets to the Stuarts*. Westport and London: Greenwood Press.

Hicks, Leo. 1945. 'An Elizabethan Propagandist: The Career of Solomon Aldred'. *The Month* 181:181–91.

—. 1948. 'The Strange Case of Dr William Parry: The Career of an Agent-provocateur'. *Studies* 37:343–62.

—. 1964. *An Elizabethan Problem: Some Aspects of the Careers of Two Exile Adventurers*. London: Burns and Oates.

Higenbottam, Frank. 1975. *Codes and Ciphers*. London: Hodder and Stoughton.

Hodgetts, Michael. 1989. *Secret Hiding-Places*. Dublin: Veritas Publications.

Holleran, James V. 1999. *A Jesuit Challenge: Edmund Campion's Debates at the Tower of London in 1581*. New York: Fordham University Press. [Reviewed by McCoog (2000).]

Holmes, Peter. 1980. 'The Authorship and Early Reception of *A Conference about the next succession to the crown of England*'. *Historical Journal* 23:415–29.

—. 1982. *Resistance and Compromise: The Political Thought of the Elizabethan Catholics*. Cambridge: Cambridge University Press.

Houliston, Victor. 2001. 'The Lord Treasurer and the Jesuit: Robert Persons's Satirical *Responsio* to the 1591 Proclamation'. *Sixteenth Century Journal* 32:383–401.

Ives, E. W. 2008. 'Tudor Dynastic Problems Revisited'. *Historical Research* 81:255–79.

Jardine, David. 1837. *A Reading of the Use of Torture in the Criminal Law of England Previously to the Commonwealth*. London: Baldwin and Cradock.

Jensen, D. L. 1964. *Diplomacy and Dogmatism: Bernardino de Mendoza and the French Catholic League*. Cambridge, Mass.: Harvard University Press.

—. 1988. 'The Spanish Armada: The Worst-kept Secret in Europe'. *Sixteenth Century Journal* 19:621–41.

Kamen, Henry. 1997. *The Spanish Inquisition: An Historical Revision*. London: Weidenfeld & Nicolson.

Kenny, Anthony. 1961–2. 'Anthony Munday in Rome'. *Recusant History* 6:158–62.

—. 2005. 'From Hospice to College'. In Allen (2005).

Kretzschmar, Johannes. 1892. *Die Invasionsprojekte der katholischen Mächte gegen England zur Zeit Elisabeths*. Leipzig: Verlag von Duncker & Humblot.

Lake, Peter. 2004. 'The King (the Queen) and the Jesuit: James Stuart's *True Law of Free Monarchies* in Context/s'. *Transactions of the Royal Historical Society* 14:243–60.

Langbein, John H. 1977. *Torture and the Law of Proof: Europe and England in the Ancien Régime*. Chicago: University of Chicago Press.

Lea, Kathleen M. 1932. 'Sir Anthony Standen and Some Anglo-Italian Letters'. *English Historical Review* 47:461–77.

Levine, Mortimer. 1973. *Tudor Dynastic Problems, 1460–1571*. London: George Allen and Unwin.

Loades, D. M. 1989. *Mary Tudor: A Life*. Oxford: Basil Blackwell.

Loomie, Albert J. 1963. *The Spanish Elizabethans: The English Exiles at the Court of Philip II*. London: Burns & Oates.

McCoog, Thomas M. 1996. *The Society of Jesus in Ireland, Scotland, and England 1541–1588: 'Our Way of Proceeding?'*. Leiden: E. J. Brill.

—. 2000. *Sixteenth Century Journal* 31:226–8. [A review of Holleran (1999).]

—. 2001. 'The English Jesuit Mission and the French Match, 1579–1581'. *Catholic Historical Review* 87:185–212.

—, ed. 2007. *The Reckoned Expense: Edmund Campion and the Early English Jesuits*. Rome: Institutum Historicum Societatis Iesu.

McGrath, Patrick. 1991. 'The Bloody Questions Reconsidered'. *Recusant History* 20:305–19.

— and Joy Rowe. 1988–9. 'The Elizabethan Priests: Their Harbourers and Helpers'. *Recusant History* 19:209–33.

—. 1991. 'The Imprisonment of Catholics for Religion under Elizabeth I'. *Recusant History* 20:415–35.

Mayer, Jean-Christophe, ed. 2004. *The Struggle for the Succession in Late Elizabethan England: Politics, Polemics and Cultural Representations*. Montpellier: Institut de Recherche sur la Renaissance, Université Paul-Valéry Montpellier 3.

Meyer, A. O. 1967. *England and the Catholic Church under Elizabeth*. Introduction by John Bossy. London: Routledge and Kegan Paul.

Nicholl, Charles. 2002. *The Reckoning: The Murder of Christopher Marlowe*. London: Vintage.

Orlin, Lena Cowen, ed. 2000. *Material London, ca. 1600*. Philadelphia: University of Pennsylvania Press.

Parker, Geoffrey. 1998. *The Grand Strategy of Philip II*. New Haven and London: Yale University Press.

—. 2002. 'The Place of Tudor England in the Messianic Vision of Philip II of Spain'. *Transactions of the Royal Historical Society* sixth series 12:167–221.

Pollen, J. H. 1891. 'Dr Nicholas Sander'. *English Historical Review* 6:36–47.

—. 1920. *The English Catholics in the Reign of Elizabeth*. London: Longmans, Green and Co.

Read, Conyers. 1925. *Mr Secretary Walsingham and the Policy of Queen Elizabeth*. 3 vols. Oxford: Clarendon Press.

Reynolds, E. E. 1980. *Campion and Parsons: The Jesuit Mission of 1580–1*. London: Sheed and Ward.

Rodríguez-Salgado, M. J., and Simon Adams, eds. 1984. 'The Count of Feria's

Dispatch to Philip II of 14 November 1558'. *Camden Miscellany* 28:302–44. CS fourth series 29. London: Camden Society.

—, eds. 1991. *England, Spain, and the Gran Armada, 1585–1604*. Edinburgh: John Donald.

Salgado, Gamini. 1977. *The Elizabethan Underworld*. London: Dent.

Saunders, Ann, ed. 1997. *The Royal Exchange*. London: London Topographical Society.

Schofield, John. 2003. *Medieval London Houses*. New Haven and London: Yale University Press.

Schofield, Nicholas, ed. 2002. *A Roman Miscellany: The English in Rome, 1550–2000*. Leominster: Gracewing.

Seaton, Ethel. 1931. 'Robert Poley's Ciphers'. *Review of English Studies* 7:137–50.

Simpson, Richard. 1896. *Edmund Campion: A Biography*. London: John Hodges.

Southern, A. C. 1950. *Elizabethan Recusant Prose 1559–1582*. London and Glasgow: Sands & Co.

Stafford, Helen Georgia. 1940. *James VI of Scotland and the Throne of England*. New York and London: D. Appleton-Century Company.

Stern, Virginia F. 1992. *Sir Stephen Powle of Court and Country*. London and Toronto: Associated University Presses.

Stone, Lawrence. 1956. *An Elizabethan: Sir Horatio Palavicino*. Oxford: Clarendon Press.

Taviner, Mark. 2000. 'Robert Beale and the Elizabethan Polity'. PhD dissertation, University of St Andrews.

Thompson, B. H. 1941. 'Anthony Munday's Journey to Rome'. *Durham University Journal* 24:1–14.

Turner, Celeste. 1928. *Anthony Mundy, an Elizabethan Man of Letters*. Berkeley: University of California Press. [See also Wright (1959).]

Tytler, Patrick Fraser. 1828–43. *History of Scotland*. 9 vols. Edinburgh: W. Tait.

Veech, T. M. 1935. *Dr Nicholas Sanders and the English Reformation 1530–1581*. Louvain: Bureaux du Recueil, Bibliothèque de l'Université.

Vignaux, Michèle. 2004. 'The Succession and Related Issues through the Correspondence of Elizabeth, James, and Robert Cecil'. In Mayer (2004).

Wernham, R. B. 1931. 'The Disgrace of William Davison'. *English Historical Review* 46:632–6.

—. 1994. *The Return of the Armadas: The Last Years of the Elizabethan War against Spain 1595–1603*. Oxford: Clarendon Press.

Wright, Celeste T. 1959. 'Young Anthony Mundy Again'. *Studies in Philology* 56:150–68. [See also Turner (1928).]

Acknowledgements

I first talked about the idea for this book to my old and firm friend John Cramsie in the fading autumn light of the Tudor battlefield of Flodden in the border country of Northumberland. It was a spooky place in which to discuss what turned out to be a book that tells the stories of some very shadowy Elizabethans. John and I have talked about all kinds of things (some reputable, others barely) on our many travels and adventures together; and it was through his kindness that I was able to give a public lecture at Union College in Schenectady, New York on torture in Elizabeth's reign, an important strand in *The Watchers*.

John Guy, who trained me as a historian, has been unhesitatingly and unquestioningly supportive over the years, at St Andrews and more recently in Cambridge, where our dinners at Clare College are doubly enriched by Clare's long and distinguished echoes of Tudor scholarship. I owe to John more than he perhaps realizes.

My literary agent Peter Robinson, with his sharp eyes and wise advice, helped to give a shape and purpose to the book proposal, and George Lucas saw its potential in the United States. Simon Winder at the Penguin Press and Peter Ginna at Bloomsbury USA have brought to the project their extraordinary editorial and publishing skills, as enthusiastic and patient as they have been frank; to them both I am deeply grateful. In helping me to turn a proposal into a manuscript and then a manuscript into a book they have been ably supported by Marina Kemp of Penguin in London and Pete Beatty of Bloomsbury in New York. Marina, along with Tom Penn, very kindly read the whole manuscript through. I must thank the designers at

Penguin and Bloomsbury for all their efforts, and David Watson for copy-editing the book so impeccably.

Now that I am about to say goodbye to King's as a Fellow, it seems supremely appropriate to thank my friends here for everything they have taught me about history and academic life in well over a decade, especially (though not only) Michael Bate, John Dunn, Victoria Harris, Ross Harrison, Istvan Hont, Peter Jones, Melissa Lane, Michael Sonenscher, Gareth Stedman Jones, Alice Taylor and Megan Vaughan. The King's College of Our Lady and Saint Nicholas in Cambridge has been a quite extraordinary place to teach and learn history.

Many other friends and colleagues in the Cambridge Faculty of History have over the years helped me to formulate and test my ideas. I should thank in particular Jessica Sharkey for her expertise on Rome in the sixteenth century, and Ceri Law for keeping me on my toes in our supervisions together. This has been a theme of my teaching in Cambridge. Something like four generations of undergraduate historians – especially those I was privileged to teach in my special subject on Tudor monarchy – have all helped to shape my thinking about the history of the sixteenth century. I must mention specially Ryan Day, with whom I have had some wonderful conversations about the Tudors, and who very kindly invited me to Ampleforth College to talk about Catholics and the Elizabethan state.

I have spoken about some of the characters and situations in this book in lectures and at conferences at (among other places) the University of Kent (for which I am very grateful to Robyn Adams and Rosanna Cox), the University of Warwick, and the University of Newcastle upon Tyne. Rachel Hammersley and Fred Schurink in Newcastle showed me great kindness, and I am most grateful to Luc Racaut for his help in identifying French pamphlets on Edmund Campion. I thank, too, those who hosted and attended a lecture I gave at Vauxhall Cross in London on Elizabethan spies.

The librarians and archivists of the British Library, Cambridge University Library and King's College Library and Archive Centre have been effortlessly professional. I am very proud of my membership of the Literary and Philosophical Society of Newcastle upon Tyne, which is one of the gems of British life, and where a good deal of the groundwork was done for this book. Another redoubt of intellectual engagement (though less well known nationally or even locally) is the group of deep thinkers and muses that gathers monthly in the Percy Arms Hotel in Chatton.

Without my family – my parents, Jennifer and Tony Alford; Joyce and David Scott (to whom this book is dedicated with love); Louise, Mark, Hannah and Laura Challenger; Dianne Shea; and above all Max and our darling Matilda – I should never have got very far as an historian. Only a family who lives with someone buried most of the time under paper or staring at a glowing screen knows from the inside both the fun and hard labour of writing a book. My memory of finishing *The Watchers* will always be imprinted with that of the first months Max, Matilda and I spent together. What I owe to them both for that spring and summer is beyond calculation.

Of Flash and Zorro I am reminded of the Tudor proverb: Let the cat wink and let the mouse run. Rarely do they – the mice or indeed Zorro – get very far. Flash, however, never gives second chances.

Stephen Alford
King's College, Cambridge
February 2012

Index